OXFORD WORLD'S CLASSICS

THE BELLY OF PARIS

ÉMILE ZOLA was born in Paris in 1840, the son of a Venetian engineer and his French wife. He grew up in Aix-en-Provence where he made friends with Paul Cézanne. After an undistinguished school career and a brief period of clerking in Paris, Zola joined the newly founded publishing firm which he left in 1866 to live by his pen. In 1865 he had published a novel and his first collection of short stories, and more novels and stories followed until in 1871 Zola published the first volume of his Rougon-Macquart series with the subtitle *histoire naturelle et sociale d'une famille sous le Second Empire*, in which he sets out to illustrate the influence of heredity and environment on a wide range of characters and milieus. However, it was not until 1877 that his novel *L'Assommoir*, a study of alcoholism in the working classes, brought him wealth and fame. The last of the Rougon-Macquart series appeared in 1893 and his subsequent writing was far less successful, although he achieved fame of a different sort in his vigorous and influential intervention in the Dreyfus case. His marriage in 1870 had remained childless but his extremely happy liaison in later life with Jeanne Rozerot, initially one of his domestic servants, gave him a son and a daughter. He died in 1902.

BRIAN NELSON is Professor of French Studies at Monash University, Melbourne, and editor of the *Australian Journal of French Studies*. His publications include *Zola and the Bourgeoisie* and, as editor, *The Cambridge Companion to Émile Zola*. He has translated and edited Zola's *Pot Luck* (*Pot-Bouille*), *The Ladies' Paradise* (*Au Bonheur des Dames*), and *The Kill* (*La Curée*) for Oxford World's Classics.

OXFORD WORLD'S CLASSICS

ÉMILE ZOLA

The Belly of Paris
(Le Ventre de Paris)

Translated with an Introduction and Notes by
BRIAN NELSON

OXFORD
UNIVERSITY PRESS

OXFORD

UNIVERSITY PRESS

Great Clarendon Street, Oxford ox2 6DP
Oxford University Press is a department of the University of Oxford.
It furthers the University's objective of excellence in research, scholarship,
and education by publishing worldwide in

Oxford New York

Auckland Cape Town Dar es Salaam Hong Kong Karachi
Kuala Lumpur Madrid Melbourne Mexico City Nairobi
New Delhi Shanghai Taipei Toronto

With offices in

Argentina Austria Brazil Chile Czech Republic France Greece
Guatemala Hungary Italy Japan Poland Portugal Singapore
South Korea Switzerland Thailand Turkey Ukraine Vietnam

Oxford is a registered trade mark of Oxford University Press
in the UK and in certain other countries

Published in the United States
by Oxford University Press Inc., New York

First published as an Oxford World's Classics paperback 2007

British Library Cataloguing in Publication Data

Data available

Library of Congress Cataloging in Publication Data
Zola, Émile, 1840–1902.
[Ventre de Paris. English]
The belly of Paris = Le ventre de Paris / Émile Zola; translated with an introduction and notes by
Brian Nelson.
p. cm. — (Oxford world's classics)
Includes bibliographical references.
ISBN–13: 978–0–19–280633–8 (alk. paper) 1. Paris (France)—Fiction. I. Title: Ventre de Paris.
II. Nelson, Brian. III. Title.
PQ2521.V3E5 2007
2007020620

Typeset in Ehrhardt
by Cepha Imaging Pvt. Ltd., Bangalore, India
Printed in Great Britain
on acid-free paper by
Clays Ltd., St Ives plc.

ISBN 978–0–19280633–8

1 3 5 7 9 10 8 6 4 2

CONTENTS

INTRODUCTION

*Readers who do not wish to learn details of the plot
will prefer to read the Introduction as an Afterword*

Émile Zola (1840–1902) embraced his century in a way no French
writer had done since Honoré de Balzac (1799–1850). His ambition
was to represent—as Balzac had done, but less methodically than
Zola—the whole life of his period. Zola is the quintessential novelist
of modernity, understood in terms of an overwhelming sense of
tumultuous change. The motor of change was the rapid expansion of
capitalism, with all that that entailed in terms of new forms of social
practice and economic organization, heightened political pressures,
and the altered shapes of the city. Zola was fascinated by change, and
specifically by the emergence of a new, mass society.

Zola's epic type of realism is reflected not only in the vast sweep
of his work, but also in its variety and complexity. In addition to his
thirty-one novels, he wrote five collections of short stories, a large
body of art, drama and literary criticism, several plays and libretti,
and numerous articles on political and social issues published in the
French press at various stages of his career as a journalist. He was
actively engaged in his own times. He was a major critic of literature
and painting, and a significant political commentator long before the
Dreyfus Affair, during which his campaign on behalf of Alfred
Dreyfus, the Jewish army captain falsely accused of passing military
secrets to Germany, culminated in 'J'accuse!', his famous open letter
to the President of the Republic. His main achievement, however,
was his twenty-volume novel cycle, *Les Rougon-Macquart*. In eight
months, during 1868 and 1869, Zola outlined the twenty novels he
intended to write on the theme of heredity: a family, the Rougon-
Macquarts, tainted with alcoholism and mental instability, were to
intermarry, to proliferate, and to pass on their inherited weaknesses
to subsequent generations. The fortunes of the various family members, as they spread through all levels of society, would be followed
over several decades. Through this family Zola examined systematically the social, sexual, and moral landscape of the late nineteenth

century along with its political, financial, and artistic contexts. Zola began work on the series in 1870 and devoted himself to it for the next quarter of a century.

The subtitle of the Rougon-Macquart cycle, 'A Natural and Social History of a Family under the Second Empire', suggests Zola's two interconnected aims: to use fiction to demonstrate a number of 'scientific' notions about the ways in which human behaviour is determined by heredity and environment; and to use the symbolic possibilities of a family whose heredity is tainted to represent a diseased society— the dynamic but corrupt France of Napoleon III's Second Empire (1852–70). Zola set out, in *Les Rougon-Macquart*, to tear the mask from the carnival Empire and to expose the frantic pursuit of pleasure and appetites of every kind that it unleashed. *The Belly of Paris* (*Le Ventre de Paris*, 1873) is the third novel in the Rougon-Macquart cycle, and in its social criticism it complements its immediate predecessor in the series, *The Kill* (*La Curée*, 1872). Zola wrote in his planning notes for the novel: '*The Belly of Paris* complements *The Kill*, it is the scramble for spoils of the middle classes, the sensual enjoyment of rich food and undisturbed digestion ... But it portrays the same degeneracy, the same moral and social decomposition.'[1] The novel, which is often surprisingly funny, also looks forward to the ferociously comic anti-bourgeois satire of *Pot Luck* (*Pot-Bouille*, 1882).

The Belly of Paris tells the story of Florent Quenu. He is walking through the streets, during the disturbances provoked by Louis-Napoleon's *coup d'état* on 2 December 1851, when a troop of soldiers starts firing on the crowd to disperse them. When the guns stop, he tries to get up from the ground but realizes that there is a dead young woman, wearing a pink bonnet, lying on top of his legs. She has two bullet holes above her breast from which blood trickles down onto his hands. Later that night he is arrested at a barricade and labelled dangerous, his bloody hands used as evidence of his crime. He is condemned to exile on Devil's Island. After several years he escapes, returns to Paris, and is taken in by his half-brother, Quenu, and

---

[1] See Henri Mitterand's commentary on the genesis of the novel in *Les Rougon-Macquart*, vol. i (Paris: Gallimard, 'Bibliothèque de la Pléiade', 1960), 1609–23. The novel's manuscript and Zola's accompanying planning notes are kept at the Bibliothèque nationale de France (BNF), Département des Manuscrits (MS), Nouvelles acquisitions françaises (NAF), 10335 and 10338.

Quenu's wife, Lisa. He finds the city changed beyond recognition. The Paris to which he returns is that of the Second Empire. The old Marché des Innocents has been knocked down to make way for Les Halles, the great central food markets built by the architect Victor Baltard from the beginning of the Second Empire (but still unfinished when the Empire collapsed in 1870). Their construction was the first big public works project of the regime; they were, in effect, a monument to the Empire's burgeoning market economy. It is just opposite Les Halles, in the Rue Rambuteau, that the Quenus own a prosperous new *charcuterie*.[2] Lisa tries to keep Florent's identity secret from the rest of the tradespeople, for she sees him as a troublemaker who may upset her stable petit bourgeois world. At her urging, he takes a job as inspector in the fish market. He becomes caught up, as a pawn, in the fierce rivalry between Lisa and one of the fishwives, Louise Méhudin ('La Belle Normande'). After a while, he becomes involved in Republican politics, leads an amateurish conspiracy against the regime, is denounced to the police by the people of the market, and by Lisa, and is sentenced once more to exile. Moreover, the effect of the aborted insurrection is to strengthen the Government's position, for Florent's trial becomes a propaganda coup that guarantees the passage of unpopular legislation: 'In the Corps Législatif the agitation was so great that the centre and the right forgot their differences over the law on senatorial annuities and made it up by voting in, by an overwhelming majority, an unpopular taxation bill. In the wave of panic that swept over the city, even the working-class districts went along without protest' (p. 272).

Preparatory Work

Zola's preparatory work for *The Belly of Paris* inaugurated the 'naturalist' method he used systematically in his subsequent novels. His representation of society is informed by a vast amount of first-hand observation, note-taking, and research—in the Paris slums (*L'Assommoir*), the department stores (*The Ladies' Paradise*), the theatre (*Nana*), the coal fields (*Germinal*), the railways (*La Bête humaine*), the countryside (*Earth*), and Les Halles. Zola combines the vision of a painter with the approach of a sociologist and reporter in his

---

[2] A pork butcher's shop and delicatessen.

observation of the mentality and modes of existence of particular communities and milieus. For several weeks in May and June of 1872, he explored Les Halles in all its aspects, at all hours of day and night, and in all kinds of light and weather conditions. He also explored the adjoining streets—narrow, cobbled, often insalubrious, the 'old Paris' that had escaped demolition under Haussmann. He took exhaustive notes on his impressions of the teeming life of the markets: the sights and sounds; the myriad types of food; the fantastic shapes of the pavilions; the various vendors and tradespeople; the colourful types (the market-porters with their wide-brimmed hats, the road-sweepers with their big brooms, the sellers of rat-poison, etc.). He even arranged for a security guard to show him round the cellars under the markets and to take him on a tour of the roofs. This on-the-spot observation was complemented by research in secondary sources (books about the market's history and system of organization) and by interviews with tradespeople and workers. Zola learnt how black pudding (*boudin*) was made, how butter was made, how fish auctions worked, how people lived on scraps and left-overs from the market, and so on. This preparatory material infuses the text of *The Belly of Paris*, giving it a richly documentary, even encyclopedic, quality.[3]

Zola's ambition to render the world of Les Halles in its totality corresponds to his extremely systematic treatment of his material and to the most striking feature of his novel: the dominance of description. The originality of *The Belly of Paris* has nothing to do with its plot (there is little suspense: the plot is slight, and in any case the reader of 1873 knew that there was no popular uprising in Paris in 1858). It lies, rather, in Zola's stylistic experiment with description, in his desire to test the limits of descriptive discourse. The novel's descriptions are remarkably luxuriant, with their methodically developed lists, their compendia of names and terms, their lexical borrowings from art criticism, and their elaborate synaesthetic effects (the celebrated 'symphony of cheeses' is but one of several bravura pieces).

---

[3] Zola's planning notes for his Rougon-Macquart novels represent a unique, acutely observed record of French society in the 1870s and 1880s. An edited selection is available as Émile Zola, *Carnets d'enquêtes: une ethnographie inédite de la France*, ed. Henri Mitterand (Paris: Plon, 1986). The section that concerns *The Belly of Paris* is on pp. 341–412.

Zola is famous for his descriptions, but in no other novel of his is there so much description.

The energy of Zola's fiction comes, however, not from its ethnographic richness nor from the detail of its descriptions, but from its imaginative qualities. *The Belly of Paris* is literature, not a document; it is fiction, not an inventory. The observed reality of the world is the foundation for a poetic vision. The originality of Zola's fiction lies in its movement, colour, and atmospheric intensity. *The Belly of Paris* unfolds like a series of brilliant animated tableaux reminiscent of Bosch, Brueghel, and Hogarth. Zola shows the interaction of man and milieu not as a concept but in dramatic and vivid images, making the moral conflicts palpable, visible, smellable. Documentation is used selectively to serve thematic and symbolic purposes. Zola's fiction is especially remarkable for its symbolizing effects. Emblematic features of contemporary life—the tenement building, the laundry, the mine, the apartment house, the department store, the stock exchange, the theatre, Les Halles, the city itself—are used as giant symbols of the society of his day. Zola sees allegories of the modern world everywhere. In *The Kill*, the new city under construction at the hands of Haussmann's workmen becomes a vast symbol of the corruption, as well as the dynamism, of Second Empire society. In *The Ladies' Paradise*, the department store is emblematic of the new dream world of consumer culture and of the changes in sexual attitudes and class relations taking place at the time. In *The Belly of Paris*, Les Halles are a gigantic figuration of bourgeois consumer society.

Zola's fictional naturalism becomes a kind of surnaturalism, as he infuses the material world with anthropomorphic life, magnifying reality and giving it a hyperbolic, hallucinatory quality. The play of imagery and metaphor often assumes phantasmagoric dimensions. We think, for example, of Saccard in *The Kill*, swimming in a sea of gold coins—an image that aptly evokes his growing mastery as a speculator as well as the spectacular nature of Haussmann's transformation of Paris; Nana's mansion, like a vast vagina, swallowing up men and their fortunes; the dream-like proliferation of clothing and lingerie in *The Ladies' Paradise*; the devouring pithead in *Germinal*, lit by strange fires, rising spectrally out of the darkness; and the fantastic visions of food in *The Belly of Paris*, in which the monstrous markets swallow Florent, like the whale swallowing Jonah, and spew him out eventually like a piece of waste matter.

The Fat and the Thin

The dominant symbol of *The Belly of Paris*, fundamental to Zola's conception of his novel, is Les Halles themselves:

The general idea is: the belly, the belly of Paris, Les Halles, where food floods in and piles up before flowing out to the various neighbourhoods; - the belly of humanity, and by extension the belly of the bourgeoisie ... People gorging themselves and growing fat is the philosophical and historical side of my novel. The artistic side is the modernity of Les Halles, the gigantic still lifes of the eight pavilions, the avalanches of food to be seen every morning in the centre of Paris.[4]

The markets assume multiple symbolic forms, partaking of an ambivalence characteristic of Zola—sometimes vibrant and creative, often apocalyptic and destructive.

The *charcuterie* of the Quenu-Gradelles is the central symbol of the larger symbolic world of the markets. A temple of gluttony, the shop enshrines the values of its owners. Lisa Quenu, standing behind the counter, is the shop's presiding deity, assimilated into the *charcuterie* as if she were part of its display: 'Lisa, with her thick neck, rounded hips, and swelling bosom, looked like the queen of all this dangling fat and meat' (p. 63). She embodies bourgeois conservatism, with its ideology of selfishness: 'She was a steady, sensible Macquart, reasonable and logical in her craving for well-being, having understood the truth of the proverb that as you make your bed so you lie in it. Prosperity and security were her great goals' (p. 45). She is the sister of Gervaise Macquart, the tragic working-class heroine of *L'Assommoir* (1877): 'Lisa was slightly ashamed of her sister, who had married an ordinary workman; moreover, she didn't like unsuccessful people' (p. 76). The ambitious apprentice butcher, Auguste, and his betrothed, his cousin Augustine, mirror their employers: Auguste is like a pale version of Quenu and Augustine an immature Lisa. Their name-identification reinforces their reflection of the bourgeoisie's political investment in conformity and in its own self-reproduction.

Florent's unexpected return threatens to disrupt Lisa's tranquil existence. His thinness and sickliness mark him out as suspect. The Quenus 'were all bursting with health, solidly built, sleek, in prime

[4] BNF, MS, NAF, 10338, fo. 47.

condition; they looked at him with the surprise of fat people gripped by a vague feeling of unease at the sight of someone who is thin' (p. 36). The conviction that unfortunate things only happen to the wicked lies behind the fear Florent arouses in those who live comfortably and fatly within the prescribed social order: 'A man capable of living without food for three days struck [Lisa] as a highly dangerous character. Respectable people never put themselves in that position' (p. 85). The struggle between the Fat and the Thin is the central theme of *The Belly of Paris*, developed through a pattern of hyperbolic contrasts. It gives the novel its plot and its symbolic structure. When we first see Florent, it is as a skeletal figure who has passed out from exhaustion on the road to Paris. Ever since the events of December 1851, he has been hungry. When he returns to Paris, he finds it fat and sleek, glutted with food whose proliferating abundance disturbs him. The novel turns on Florent's malaise. The story it tells is that of the French nineteenth century, with its multiple insurrections and revolutions: the bourgeois triumph repeatedly over the workers; political idealism goes nowhere. It is also the story of human history: when Claude outlines to Florent his concept of the battle between the Fat and the Thin, he takes the metaphor right back to Cain and Abel:

'Cain', he said, 'was a Fat man and Abel a Thin one. Ever since that first murder, the big eaters have sucked the lifeblood out of the small eaters. The strong constantly prey on the weak; each one swallows his neighbour and then gets swallowed up in turn' (p. 191).

The imaginative qualities of Zola's writing do not reside simply in their poetic symbolism, but also in narrative structures with strong mythical resonances. The mythical dimension of *The Belly of Paris* is particularly strong, and is underscored by Claude in his exposition to Florent:

'And you! You're an amazingly Thin man, the king of the Thin people, in fact! ... Fat people, you see, hate Thin people so much that they have to drive them out of their sight, with a bite or a kick. That's why I'd be very careful if I were you. The Quenus are Fat people, and so are the Méhudins; in fact you're surrounded by them!' (p. 191).

The story of Florent is, as Naomi Schor has aptly remarked, 'the story of Cain and Abel as retold by Darwin'.[5] Schor argues persuasively

---

[5] Naomi Schor, *Zola's Crowds* (Baltimore: Johns Hopkins University Press, 1978), 27.

that, in terms of the novel's allegorical structure, Florent functions as a human scapegoat; his eventual entrapment becomes a kind of ritual sacrifice. In political terms, the story tells how the innocent Florent and the political convictions of 1848 are sacrificed to the new, corrupted order of the Second Empire.

Florent arrives in Les Halles at night lying on a cartload of vegetables. The novel opens, in other words, with the movement from country to city—from grower to consumer. Madame François, the market gardener who picks Florent up and takes him into the city, is associated with Nature and the countryside, so strongly contrasted with the world of Les Halles, where, as the novel progresses, everything seems dead and rotting. Where the painter Claude Lantier sees Les Halles as full of life, Florent, towards the end of the novel, sees 'a huge ossuary, a place of death, littered with the remains of things that had once been alive, a charnel house reeking with foul smells and putrefaction' (p. 189). In the opening chapter Claude takes Florent on a tour of the markets. He sees in Les Halles a sublime embodiment of modernity in art, whereas Florent's reaction is one of nauseated aversion. The painter's aesthetic delight in the spectacle of the markets and their produce is juxtaposed with Florent's agony of hunger.[6] Florent feels overwhelmed, as if the foodstuffs were threatening to engulf him. The invasion of his senses ends in blind panic and a desperate desire to escape from the infernal merry-go-round of food swirling round him.

Les Halles, and their agent Lisa, seem to take possession of Florent's whole being. He is numbed by the atmosphere of comfort and well-being in the *charcuterie*. Affected by the smell of meat from the counter, he feels himself sinking into a state of torpor. The smell that affects him, however, is not just the smell of the meat, but the smell of order and sanctity exhaled by Lisa and the world she represents.

---

[6] Kate Tunstall argues that it would be mistaken to identify Claude Lantier with the narrator or too closely with Zola himself. To separate them reveals, she suggests, the presence of a Rococo aesthetic alongside Claude's quasi-Impressionist one, for Florent's perspective on Les Halles is strongly marked by *vanitas* imagery and *memento mori* in which 'nourriture' is 'pourriture'—a kind of pictorial equivalent to Zola's well-known 'entropic vision'. See Kate E. Tunstall, '"Crânement beau tout de même": Still Life and *Le Ventre de Paris*', *French Studies*, 58/2 (Apr. 2004), 177–87. For an excellent discussion of the problematical relationship between 'art' and modern life in *The Belly of Paris*, see Christopher Prendergast, *Paris and the Nineteenth Century* (Oxford: Blackwell, 1992), 66–73.

The world of the *charcuterie*, drowned in fat, weakens his will in the face of the relentless pressure Lisa exerts on him to take the job as inspector in the fish market. With the making of black pudding (pp. 78–88), the kitchen assumes a hellish appearance. It drips with grease. Florent's resistance to taking the job slowly melts along with the bacon fat in Quenu's three big pots. He begins work in Les Halles. The whole *charcuterie* is now happy.

[Florent] began to feel more relaxed, managing at last to taste the delights of the settled life he was now leading. The dining room, in pale yellow, had a bourgeois comfort and tidiness about it that disarmed him as soon as he crossed the threshold. The kind attentions of La Belle Lisa wrapped him in a fleecy warmth that softened every part of his mind and body. Mutual esteem and general harmony reigned supreme (pp. 97–8).

Florent is enveloped, however, by the Quenus' bourgeois ideology rather than being the object of their generosity. After eight months in the markets, 'his life had become so calm and regular that he hardly felt he was alive at all' (p. 119). But by degrees he becomes sickened once more by the masses of food among which he lives. The rekindling of his interest in politics is marked by one of the novel's global descriptions of Les Halles, in which the markets are seen, through Florent's feverish imagination, as a grotesque omnivorous monster. Les Halles, and the nightmare world of food they represent, are correlated with the Second Empire and with petit bourgeois greed; and bourgeois devotion to food is equated with devotion to the Government:

The giant markets, overflowing with food, had brought things to a head. They seemed like some satiated beast, embodying Paris itself, grown enormously fat, and silently supporting the Empire … Les Halles were the shopkeepers' belly, the belly of respectable petit bourgeois people, bursting with contentment and well-being, shining in the sun, and declaring that everything was for the best, since respectable people had never before grown so wonderfully fat (pp. 124–5).

Florent's presence now seems to disturb the life of the *charcuterie*. As Lisa becomes increasingly worried about Florent's political activity, the shop itself becomes gloomy and unhappy: 'the mirrors seemed pale, the marble was as white as ice, and the cooked meats on the counter stagnated in their yellow fat or in dark pools of jelly' (p. 233).

Sex and Money

Zola's evocation of a society given over to materialist values is textually embodied in various ways. Prominent features of his descriptive style are the depiction of people as extensions or appendages of their milieu, or as dehumanized, merged into their surroundings—La Sarriette and her fruit, Claire and her fish, Marjolin and the poultry, and especially, the Quenus and their *charcuterie*. Quenu's clean-shaven face, we are told, 'bore a faint resemblance to the snout of a pig, to one of the cuts of pork he handled every day' (p. 36). Furthermore, characters are reduced to body parts often denoting food and digestion. A row of fishwives at the fish auction is described as 'a display of big white aprons stretched over stomachs and enormous breasts and shoulders' (p. 94). Just before Florent's arrest, in the final chapter, 'the huge bellies and enormous breasts held their breath … Then, suddenly, there was an explosion; the breasts heaved wildly and the bellies nearly burst with malicious delight' (p. 268).

Money plays a significant role in the narrative: the inheritance from Gradelle, Florent's salary from the Government, Gavard's war profits, Lebigre's usurious loans, the frequent mention of the prices of foodstuffs. The dominance of money, and its corresponding warping of humanity, are consistently highlighted. For example, the auctioneer at the fish market is, as Sandy Petrey notes, 'a character whose linguistic performance demonstrates that numbers and units of currency are the only words needed to exhaust the full range of vocal expressiveness':[7]

[Florent's] attention was distracted by the jabbering of the auctioneer, who was just offering a magnificent turbot for sale.

'Going for thirty francs… thirty francs!… thirty francs!'

He repeated this phrase in every imaginable tone of voice, running up and down a curious scale of notes full of vocal somersaults … With blazing eyes and outstretched arms, he went on shouting:

'Thirty-one! Thirty-two! Thirty-three! Thirty-three fifty! Thirty-three fifty!'

… like a cantor coming to the final verse of a hymn, he intoned: 'Forty-two! Forty-two!… A turbot going for forty-two francs!' (p. 94).

[7] Sandy Petrey, 'Historical Reference and Stylistic Opacity in *Le Ventre de Paris*', *Kentucky Romance Quarterly*, 24/3 (1977), 325–40, at 332.

The auctioneer (who is physically deformed) is later identified as an undercover agent of the Government who both entraps Florent and extracts money from him. Food, money, and the Government are equated in the figure of a hunchback.

The novel's treatment of the theme of sexuality must be placed within the matrix that equates money, food, and power. In the kitchen of Gradelle's shop, where the young Lisa and Quenu work, their hands meet over the sausage meat: 'Sometimes she helped him, holding the sausage skins with her plump fingers while he filled them with meat and *lardons*' (p. 46). Their courtship, such as it is, is never explicitly acknowledged. When Lisa finds Gradelle's money, she invites Quenu into her bedroom for the first time, pouring the gold and silver coins out on the bed, which is left rumpled as if after some act of love. After counting the money together, they come down from the bedroom as, already, man and wife.

She and her husband carried on living as before, as the very best of friends and in perfect harmony. She still met him in the shop, their hands still met over the sausage meat, she still looked over his shoulder to see what was happening in his pans, and it was still only the big fire in the kitchen that brought a flush to their cheeks (p. 49).

Money and food function as substitutes for sexual desire. Their huge bed, with its four mattresses and four pillows, its layers of blankets and its thick eiderdown, is, we are told, 'truly a bed intended for sleep' (p. 53).

In contrast to the Quenus, the very model of bourgeois respectability, are Marjolin and Cadine. Marjolin is discovered as an infant one morning in a pile of cabbages in, significantly, the old Marché des Innocents; while Cadine is picked up one night by Mère Chantemesse, from the pavement in the Rue Saint-Denis. Marjolin, as a child, lives like a squirrel in the markets, while Cadine is a kind of sprite or imp. Together they create an idyll described as both 'innocent' and 'shameless' (p. 161), as if personifying the vitality and appetites—the Life Force—of the markets themselves:

They were on intimate terms with this giant edifice, as old friends who had seen the smallest bolt driven home. They were not afraid of the monster; they patted it and treated it like a friend; and Les Halles seemed to smile on these two urchins, who were their song, their shameless idyll (p. 161).

It is Lisa and the world she represents that threatens, and indeed damages, their idyll; in her fat roundness she fascinates Marjolin and, with her genteel caresses, arouses his lust. When she descends into the dark and secret depths of Les Halles, led by Marjolin through the labyrinthine cellars, where live birds are kept in cages, the world of animal sexuality, and of the unconscious, could not be more strongly evoked. Marjolin is indeed treated like an animal when he tries to assault Lisa. She fells him like a stockyard butcher:

She raised her arm as she had seen them do in slaughterhouses, clenched her beautiful woman's fist, and knocked Marjolin senseless with one blow between the eyes. He collapsed, smashing his head against the edge of one of the stone blocks (p. 182).

She steals away, perfectly calm, leaving him a semi-idiot. When he recovers his physical strength, we see her again, 'strok[ing] Marjolin under his satin chin with perfect impunity' (p. 234), comparing him to her husband: 'Quenu ... had rough reddish skin on the back of his neck, and his shaven chin was as rough as gnarled wood, whereas Marjolin's chin was as soft as satin' (p. 183). Lisa's sexuality remains repressed, buried under her massive 'respectability', her body forever enclosed in her huge white apron.

A similar displacement of sexuality is evident in Florent. From the moment he returns to Les Halles, he is disturbed by the materiality of food, the mud in the streets, and human flesh, especially female flesh. In the fish market, at the height of his persecution by the female stallholders, he seems lost in swirling skirts, surrounded by huge breasts and monstrous hips—'as if he were having a nightmare in which giant women, prodigiously well endowed, were closing in on him' (p. 110). He is afraid of women, with the notable exception of the maternal and masculine Madame François, and the anonymous and unthreatening dead young woman in the pink bonnet, who haunts him 'as if he had lost a loved one of his own' (p. 10). His response to the seductive wiles of La Belle Normande is eventually to tell her about the dead woman, thus incurring her jealousy.

Florent's virility is expended in dreams, as Claude's is in his painting. He becomes a republican 'as girls with broken hearts enter a convent' (p. 42). The hours he spends in Lebigre's bar are presented as a kind of substitute sexuality:

He took a sensual delight in the meetings. As he took the brass doorknob of the little room in his hand, he seemed to feel it respond to his touch, to become warm, and turn of its own accord. He could not have felt a greater thrill if he had been caressing the soft fingers of a woman (p. 137).

When Florent replaces his mother as Quenu's guardian, he becomes a surrogate father and revels in the new-found joys of immaculate paternity. Later, Quenu is replaced by Muche, La Belle Normande's little boy:

It was as if his brother Quenu had grown little again and that they were back together in the Rue Royer-Collard. His secret dream was to devote himself to someone young who would never grow up, whom he could go on teaching for ever, and through whose innocence he would be able to love all mankind (p. 117).

The child's innocence, it is suggested, protects Florent from the world's corruption, allowing him to love his fellow men and overcome his bitterness and hatred—from which he escapes into his political fantasies.

Spies

The characterization of Florent as a political fantasist, the farcical nature of the 'conspiracy' itself, and the equation—highlighted by Claude—of the artist and the revolutionary, give *The Belly of Paris* a high degree of ideological ambiguity. There is no equivocation, however, in Zola's satirical critique of the bourgeoisie and the 'high' capitalism of the Second Empire. The last words of the novel— Claude's exclamation 'Respectable people... What bastards!'— deplore the triumph of the 'Fat'. Beneath the outward 'respectability' of the bourgeoisie there is a venality and brutality that Zola portrays as monstrous. Marjolin, the young woman in the pink bonnet, and above all, Florent, are sacrificed on the altar of bourgeois greed.

The brutality of the bourgeoisie is matched, moreover, by the authoritarianism of the Government. One of the most striking features of *The Belly of Paris* is its exposé of the regime's machinery of political surveillance. It is not only a novel of spectacle—Claude Lantier and Cadine are *flâneurs* who circulate constantly in and around Les Halles, eagerly soaking up the sights of the markets, the neighbouring streets, and the shop windows—but also a novel in which the activity of surveillance assumes global proportions.

Images of windows, mirrors, watchful eyes, and attentive ears proliferate.[8] When Florent returns to Paris, he imagines the police watching at every street corner. Even Auguste and Augustine, in the photograph on the mantelpiece in his attic room, seem to watch him as he undresses. 'In times of terror,' wrote the critic Walter Benjamin, 'when everyone is something of a conspirator, everybody will be in a situation where he has to play detective.'[9] In *The Belly of Paris*, almost everyone behaves like a detective: Lisa and Louise Méhudin keep each other under intense scrutiny; Lisa is concerned to keep an eye on Florent and his activities; the Saget–Sarriette–Lecœur trio keep the Quenus and Florent under constant watch; Monsieur Lebigre and other secret police agents spy on Florent and the other conspirators in Lebigre's bar.

Mademoiselle Saget's quest to know everything about everyone in the neighbourhood is a caricatural expression of the system of global surveillance. Her panoptic[10] view of Les Halles comes to stand for the Government's use of all its subjects to police each other. Her super vision is equated with supervision, her looking is equated with overlooking—with power and control.[11]

sitting at her window, she would complete her report. The window was very high up, commanding a view of all the neighbouring houses, and

---

[8] See Naomi Schor, 'Zola: From Window to Window', *Yale French Studies*, 42 (1969), 38–51; Philip Walker, 'The Mirror, the Window, and the Eye in Zola's Fiction', *Yale French Studies*, 42 (1969), 52–67.

[9] Walter Benjamin, *Charles Baudelaire: A Lyric Poet in The Era of High Capitalism*, trans. from the German by Harry Zohn (London: Verso, 1983), 40.

[10] 'Panopticon' was the name given by Jeremy Bentham (the English philosopher, jurist, and social reformer, 1748–1832) to a proposed form of prison built radially so that a guard at a central position could at all times observe the prisoners. The Panopticon provides an extremely apposite model for political control in *The Belly of Paris*.

[11] For a fascinating and highly influential discussin of the disciplinary mode of power in Western civilization, see Michel Foucault, *Discipline and Punish: The Birth of the Prison*, trans. from the French by Alan Sheridan (New York: Vintage Books, 1995). Excellent discussions of the politics of vision in *The Belly of Paris* are: Ali Behdad, 'Visibility, Secrecy, and the Novel: Narrative Power in Brontë and Zola', *LIT: Literature Interpretation Theory*, 1/4 (1990), 253–64; and Patricia Carles and Béatrice Desgranges, '*Le Ventre de Paris* ou l'espace de la répression', *Excavatio*, 2 (1993), 34–41. Behdad and Carles and Desgranges make specific reference to Bentham's Panopticon and to Foucault. D. A. Miller, in *The Novel and the Police* (Berkeley and Los Angeles: University of California Press, 1988), argues that the novel, whose cultural hegemony coincides historically with the birth and consolidation of the police in Western Europe, acted as a vehicle of (self-)discipline throughout the nineteenth century.

it gave her endless pleasure. At all hours of the day she would install herself there, as though it were an observatory from which she kept watch on everything that went on below her. She was familiar with all the rooms opposite, both on the right and left, down to the smallest items of furniture; she could have given an account, without omitting a single detail, of the habits of the tenants, whether their households were happy or not, how they washed their faces, what they had for dinner, and even who came to call on them. She also had a view across Les Halles, which meant that there was not a woman in the neighbourhood who could walk across the Rue Rambuteau without being seen by her (pp. 237–8).

Strategically located in the centre of the neighbourhood, the old woman's attic window is emblematic of a collective obsession with panoptic vision in a society where everyone plays detective. Like a prison, the whole neighbourhood is kept under constant observation and the smallest details are recorded. Moreover, the activity of watching and the desire for knowledge have strong erotic connotations. The sexual vocabulary used to describe Mademoiselle Saget's joy when she discovers Florent's true identity is striking:

She knew at last! For nearly a year she had been dying to find out, and here she suddenly was—in full possession of the facts, and of Florent. It was unimaginably satisfying... for she really felt that Florent would have seen her to her grave had he continued to frustrate her curiosity... She uttered little sighs of delight as she entered the fruit market (p. 206).

The pleasures of voyeurism are reinforced by the use of gossip. Gossip is endemic to Les Halles, and it becomes part of the system of surveillance, a weapon used to entrap and expel someone who, like Florent, is perceived as a threat to the community. The market women's petty gossip about each other becomes directed with increasing ferocity against him; and it is orchestrated by Mademoiselle Saget, whose 'gossiping tongue was feared from the Rue Saint-Denis to the Rue Jean-Jacques Rousseau, from the Rue Saint-Honoré to the Rue Mauconseil' (p. 64). After the discovery of Florent's identity, the slander about him turns into a flood of abuse. Its fantastic nature seems to increase exponentially:

vague rumours began to circulate in the markets ... At first only a few small details were hawked about in whispers; then various versions of the story began to emerge, incidents were exaggerated, and gradually a legend grew up in which Florent played the part of a bogey man. He had killed ten gendarmes...; he had returned to France on a pirate ship whose crew massacred every living thing on the seas; and since his arrival in Paris he had been seen at night prowling about the streets with suspicious-looking characters, of whom he was obviously the leader. From that point on the imagination of the market women knew no bounds (p. 218).

As Mademoiselle Saget says, with malicious satisfaction: 'the story has got around, and it's spreading. It can't be stopped now. The truth will have to come out' (p. 236).

Although terror and fear as central constituents of the disciplinary system are always provided by the police—the effect of panopticism is to provoke the fear that there is always someone watching you—what makes the disciplinary system effective is the interiorization of the practice.[12] Having searched Florent's room, Lisa resolves to denounce him to the police, and she strengthens her resolve by recalling the advice Father Roustan had given her. Spying on others, he had implied, is an honourable act, since it is for the public good.

She was firm in her resolve, there was not a quiver in her face, only a sterner expression than usual in her eyes. As she fastened her black silk dress, stretching the material with all the strength in her fingers, she remembered what Father Roustan had said. Her conscience told her that she was about to do her duty (p. 242).

The last stage of Florent's relationship with the people of the market illustrates perfectly both the efficiency of the state machine's system of political surveillance and Florent's role in uniting the community against him. When Lisa arrives at the Palais de Justice, she learns that there already exists a bulging file on him. Virtually all the people of the market have denounced him anonymously; moreover, he has been under surveillance ever since his return to France. As Michel Foucault wrote: 'The panoptic schema, without disappearing as such or losing any of its properties, was destined to spread throughout the social body; its vocation was to become a generalized function.'[13] By diffusing its operative function, by making it the moral and social

---

[12] See Behdad, 'Visibility, Secrecy, and the Novel', 258.

[13] Foucault, *Discipline and Punish*, 207. See esp. the section of Foucault's book entitled 'Panopticism', 195–228.

responsibility of the public, the disciplinary system economizes its operation and makes itself more effective. As Lisa prepares to leave the police headquarters, and makes her way through the halls and along the corridors of the Palais de Justice, she feels 'as if she had been caught in the grip of this police world which, it now seemed to her, saw and knew everything' (p. 244).

Florent finally becomes aware of what has happened to him:

He saw again Auguste's pale face and the lowered eyes of the fishwives; he remembered the words of Mère Méhudin, La Normande's silence, the empty *charcuterie*; and he thought to himself that Les Halles had collaborated in his downfall, that it was the entire neighbourhood that was turning him in (p. 269).

The reconciliation of Lisa and Louise Méhudin becomes a kind of rite, signifying the consolidation of tribal unity following the expulsion of an outsider. Similarly, the *charcuterie* and Lisa, after Florent's sentence, are returned to a state of complete calm, as if frozen in their now impregnable complacency:

[Lisa] was a picture of absolute quietude, of perfect bliss, not only untroubled but also lifeless, as she bathed in the warm air ... And the shop window beside her seemed to display the same bliss. It too had recovered; the stuffed tongues lay red and healthy, the hams were once more showing their handsome yellow faces, and the sausages no longer had the sad look that had so upset Quenu (p. 275).

Florent's expulsion brings back peace, harmony, and above all, health: 'Once again the *charcuterie* exuded health, a kind of greasy health' (p. 275). Order has been restored, the sausages have regained their lustre, the belly is triumphant.

TRANSLATOR'S NOTE

The Belly of Paris is regarded by many as the most important novel Zola wrote before *L'Assommoir*. I am very happy to have produced the first new translation of this novel in over fifty years (the translation by David Hughes and Marie-Jacqueline Mason, under the title *Savage Paris*, was published by Elek Books in 1955). As in my previous translations of Zola, I have endeavoured to capture the structures and rhythms, the tone and texture, and the lexical choices—in sum, the particular idiom—of Zola's text, as well as to preserve the 'feel' of the social context out of which it emerged and which it represents. Engaging with Zola's extraordinary descriptions was a particular pleasure, though at times I felt I had more than an inkling of how Jonah felt inside the whale.

I wish to record my gratitude to the Camargo Foundation for granting me a residential fellowship at Cassis, France, where I completed this volume in one of the most pleasant working environments imaginable. I am also grateful to the French Ministry of Culture for a grant that enabled me to spend some time at the Centre International des Traducteurs Littéraires in Arles. My thanks, too, to Chips Sowerwine for valuable bibliographical help.

SELECT BIBLIOGRAPHY

The Belly of Paris (*Le Ventre de Paris*) was serialized in the daily newspaper *L'État* from 12 January to 17 March 1873. It was published in volume form by the Librairie Charpentier in April 1873. It is included in volume i of Henri Mitterand's superb scholarly edition of *Les Rougon-Macquart* in the 'Bibliothèque de la Pléiade', 5 vols. (Paris: Gallimard, 1960–7). Paperback editions exist in the following popular collections: Folio, ed. Henri Mitterand (Paris, 1979); Classiques de Poche, commentary and notes by Philippe Hamon and Marie-France Azéma (Paris, 1984); GF Flammarion, introduction by Robert Jouanny (Paris, 1971); Pocket, ed. Gérard Gengembre (Paris, 1999 [1991]). There is also a fine critical edition of the novel, ed. Marc Baroli (Paris: Minard, 1969).

Biographies of Zola in English

Brown, Frederick, *Zola: A Life* (New York: Farrar, Straus, Giroux, 1995; London: Macmillan, 1996).

Hemmings, F. W. J., *The Life and Times of Émile Zola* (London: Elek, 1977).

Schom, Alan, *Émile Zola: A Bourgeois Rebel* (New York: Henry Holt, 1987; London: Queen Anne Press, 1987).

Studies of Zola and Naturalism in English

Baguley, David, *Naturalist Fiction: The Entropic Vision* (Cambridge: Cambridge University Press, 1990).

——(ed.), *Critical Essays on Émile Zola* (Boston: G. K. Hall, 1986).

Bell, David F., *Models of Power: Politics and Economics in Zola's 'Rougon-Macquart'* (Lincoln, Nebr., and London: University of Nebraska Press, 1988).

Bloom, Harold (ed.), *Émile Zola* (Philadelphia: Chelsea House, 2004).

Hemmings, F. W. J., *Émile Zola*, 2nd edn. (Oxford: Clarendon Press, 1966).

Lethbridge, R., and Keefe, T. (eds.), *Zola and the Craft of Fiction* (Leicester: Leicester University Press, 1990).

Nelson, Brian (ed.), *The Cambridge Companion to Zola* (Cambridge: Cambridge University Press, 2007).

——(ed.), *Naturalism in the European Novel: New Critical Perspectives* (New York and Oxford: Berg, 1992).

——*Zola and the Bourgeoisie* (London: Macmillan; Totowa, NJ: Barnes & Noble, 1983).

Walker, Philip, *Zola* (London: Routledge & Kegan Paul, 1985).

Wilson, Angus, *Émile Zola: An Introductory Study of his Novels* (1953; London: Secker & Warburg, 1964).

Articles, Chapters of Books, and Books in English and French on 'The Belly of Paris'

Baguley, David, 'Le Supplice de Florent: à propos du *Ventre de Paris*', *Europe*, 468–9 (Apr.–May 1968), 91–7.

Behdad, Ali, 'Visibility, Secrecy, and the Novel: Narrative Power in Brontë and Zola', *LIT: Literature Interpretation Theory*, 1/4 (1990), 253–64.

Besse, Laurence, '"Le Feu aux graisses": la chair sarcastique dans *Le Ventre de Paris*', *Romantisme*, 26 (1996), 35–42.

Carles, Patricia, and Desgranges, Béatrice, *Zola: 'Le Ventre de Paris'* (Paris: Nathan, 'Balises', 1993).

——, —— '*Le Ventre de Paris* ou l'espace de la répression', *Excavatio*, 2 (1993), 34–41.

Dezalay, Auguste, '"Ceci dira cela": remarques sur les antécédents du *Ventre de Paris*', *Les Cahiers naturalistes*, 58 (1984), 33–42.

Duffy, John J., Jr., 'The Aesthetic and the Political in Zola's Writing on Art', *Australian Journal of French Studies*, 38/3 (2001), 365–78.

Gural-Migdal, Anna, 'Représentation utopique et ironie dans *Le Ventre de Paris*', *Les Cahiers naturalistes*, 74 (2000), 145–61.

Johnson, Sharon P., '"Les Halles" in Zola's *Le Ventre de Paris*: Gender, Order, and Disorder', *Excavatio*, 17/1–2 (2002), 33–54.

Jousset, Philippe, 'Une poétique de la "Nature morte": sur la pratique descriptive dans *Le Ventre de Paris*', *Les Cahiers naturalistes*, 72 (1998), 337–50.

Lavielle, Émile, *Émile Zola: 'Le Ventre de Paris'* (Paris: Bréal, 'Connaissance d'une œuvre', 1999).

Petrey, Sandy, 'Historical Reference and Stylistic Opacity in *Le Ventre de Paris*', *Kentucky Romance Quarterly*, 24/3 (1977), 325–40.

Prendergast, Christopher, *Paris and the Nineteenth Century* (Oxford: Blackwell, 1992), 66–73.

Rollins, Yvonne Bargues, '*Le Ventre de Paris* de Zola: Il y a eu un mort dans la cuisine', *Nineteenth-Century French Studies*, 30/1–2 (2001), 92–106.

Scarpa, Marie, *Le Carnaval des Halles: Une ethnocritique du* Ventre de Paris *de Zola* (Paris: CNRS Editions, 2000).

Schor, Naomi, *Zola's Crowds* (Baltimore: Johns Hopkins University Press, 1978), 21–34.

Shryock, Richard, 'Zola's Use of Embedded Narrative in *Le Ventre de Paris*: Florent's Tale', *Journal of Narrative Technique*, 22/1 (1992), 48–56.

Select Bibliography

xxvii

Sonnenfeld, Albert, 'Émile Zola: Food and Ideology', *Nineteenth-Century French Studies*, 19/4 (1991), 600–11.

Tunstall, Kate E., '"Crânement beau tout de même": Still Life and *Le Ventre de Paris*', *French Studies*, 58/2 (2004), 177–87.

Wahl Willis, Pauline, 'Comestibles et commérages dans *Le Ventre de Paris*', *Excavatio*, 14/1–2 (2001), 63–72.

Woollen, Geoff, 'Zola's Halles: A *Grande Surface* before their Time', *Romance Studies*, 18/1 (2000), 21–30.

Zarifopol-Johnston, Ilinca, *To Kill a Text: The Dialogic Fiction of Hugo, Dickens, and Zola* (Newark: University of Delaware Press, 1995) ('"Ceci tuera cela": The Cathedral in the Marketplace', 176–91).

Background and Context: The Second Empire, Haussmann, and Les Halles (works in English)

Baguley, David, *Napoleon III and His Regime: An Extravaganza* (Baton Rouge: Louisiana State University Press, 2000).

Carmona, Michel, *Haussmann: His Life and Times, and the Making of Modern Paris*, trans. Patrick Camiller (Chicago: Ivan R. Dee, 2002).

Evenson, Norma, 'The Assassination of Les Halles', *Journal of the Society of Architectural Historians*, 32/4 (1973), 308–15.

—— *Paris: A Century of Change, 1878–1978* (New Haven: Yale University Press, c. 1979), 301–09.

Harvey, David, *Consciousness and the Urban Experience: Studies in the History and Theory of Capitalist Urbanization* (Baltimore: Johns Hopkins University Press, 1985) ('Paris, 1850–1870', 63–220).

Horowitz, Roger, Pilcher, Jeffrey M., and Watts, Sydney, 'Meat for the Multitudes: Market Culture in Paris, New York City, and Mexico City over the Long Nineteenth Century', *American Historical Review*, 109/4 (2004), 1054–83.

Jordan, David, *Transforming Paris: The Life and Labors of Baron Haussmann* (New York and London: The Free Press, 1995).

Pinkney, David H., *Napoleon III and the Rebuilding of Paris* (Princeton University Press, 1958), esp. 75–9.

Plessis, Alain, *The Rise and Fall of the Second Empire, 1852–1871* (Cambridge: Cambridge University Press, 1985).

Price, Roger, *Napoleon III and the Second Empire* (London: Routledge, 1997).

Sutcliffe, Anthony, *The Autumn of Central Paris: The Defeat of Town Planning, 1850–1970* (London: Edward Arnold, 1970).

Thompson, Victoria E., 'Urban Renovation, Moral Regeneration: Domesticating the Halles in Second-Empire Paris', *French Historical Studies*, 20/1 (1997), 87–109.

Further Reading in Oxford World's Classics

Hugo, Victor, *The Essential Victor Hugo*, trans. and ed. E. H. and A. M. Blackmore.

Zola, Émile, *L'Assommoir*, trans. Margaret Mauldon, ed. Robert Lethbridge.

—— *The Attack on the Mill*, trans. Douglas Parmée.

—— *La Bête humaine*, trans. Roger Pearson.

—— *La Débâcle*, trans. Elinor Dorday, ed. Robert Lethbridge.

—— *Germinal*, trans. Peter Collier, ed. Robert Lethbridge.

—— *The Kill*, trans. Brian Nelson.

—— *The Ladies' Paradise*, trans. Brian Nelson.

—— *The Masterpiece*, trans. Thomas Walton, revised by Roger Pearson.

—— *Nana*, trans. Douglas Parmée.

—— *Pot Luck*, trans. Brian Nelson.

—— *Thérèse Raquin*, trans. Andrew Rothwell.

A CHRONOLOGY OF ÉMILE ZOLA

1840   (2 April) Born in Paris, the only child of Francesco Zola (b. 1795), an Italian engineer, and Émilie, née Aubert (b. 1819), the daughter of a glazier. The naturalist novelist was later proud that 'zolla' in Italian means 'clod of earth'

1843   Family moves to Aix-en-Provence

1847   (27 March) Death of father from pneumonia following a chill caught while supervising work on his scheme to supply Aix-en-Provence with drinking water

1852–8   Boarder at the Collège Bourbon at Aix. Friendship with Baptistin Baille and Paul Cézanne. Zola, not Cézanne, wins the school prize for drawing

1858   (February) Leaves Aix to settle in Paris with his mother (who had preceded him in December). Offered a place and bursary at the Lycée Saint-Louis. (November) Falls ill with 'brain fever' (typhoid) and convalescence is slow

1859   Fails his *baccalauréat* twice

1860   (Spring) Is found employment as a copy-clerk but abandons it after two months, preferring to eke out an existence as an impecunious writer in the Latin Quarter of Paris

1861   Cézanne follows Zola to Paris, where he meets Camille Pissarro, fails the entrance examination to the École des Beaux-Arts, and returns to Aix in September

1862   (February) Taken on by Hachette, the well-known publishing house, at first in the dispatch office and subsequently as head of the publicity department. (31 October) Naturalized as a French citizen. Cézanne returns to Paris and stays with Zola

1863   (31 January) First literary article published. (1 May) Manet's *Déjeuner sur l'herbe* exhibited at the Salon des Refusés, which Zola visits with Cézanne

1864   (October) *Tales for Ninon*

1865   *Claude's Confession*. A *succès de scandale* thanks to its bedroom scenes. Meets future wife Alexandrine-Gabrielle Meley (b. 1839), the illegitimate daughter of teenage parents who soon separated, and whose mother died in September 1849

1866   Resigns his position at Hachette (salary: 200 francs a month) and becomes a literary critic on the recently launched daily *L'Événement* (salary: 500 francs a month). Self-styled 'humble disciple' of Hippolyte Taine. Writes a series of provocative articles condemning the official Salon Selection Committee, expressing reservations about Courbet, and praising Manet and Monet. Begins to frequent the Café Guerbois in the Batignolles quarter of Paris, the meeting-place of the future Impressionists. Antoine Guillemet takes Zola to meet Manet. Summer months spent with Cézanne at Bennecourt on the Seine. (15 November) *L'Événement* suppressed by the authorities

1867   (November) *Thérèse Raquin*

1868   (April) Preface to second edition of *Thérèse Raquin*. (May) Manet's portrait of Zola exhibited at the Salon. (December) *Madeleine Férat*. Begins to plan for the Rougon-Macquart series of novels

1868–70 Working as journalist for a number of different newspapers

1870   (31 May) Marries Alexandrine in a registry office. (September) Moves temporarily to Marseilles because of the Franco-Prussian War

1871   Political reporter for *La Cloche* (in Paris) and *Le Sémaphore de Marseille*. (March) Returns to Paris. (October) Publishes *The Fortune of the Rougons*, the first of the twenty novels making up the Rougon-Macquart series

1872   *The Kill*

1873   (April) *The Belly of Paris*

1874   (May) *The Conquest of Plassans*. First independent Impressionist exhibition. (November) *Further Tales for Ninon*

1875   Begins to contribute articles to the Russian newspaper *Vestnik Evropy* (*European Herald*). (April) *The Sin of Father Mouret*

1876   (February) *His Excellency Eugène Rougon*. Second Impressionist exhibition

1877   (February) *L'Assommoir*

1878   Buys a house at Médan on the Seine, 40 kilometres west of Paris. (June) *A Page of Love*

1880   (March) *Nana*. (May) *Les Soirées de Médan* (an anthology of short stories by Zola and some of his naturalist 'disciples', including Maupassant). (8 May) Death of Flaubert. (September) First of a series of articles for *Le Figaro*. (17 October) Death of his mother. (December) *The Experimental Novel*

1882   (April) *Pot Luck* (*Pot-Bouille*). (3 September) Death of Turgenev

1883   (13 February) Death of Wagner. (March) *The Ladies' Paradise* (*Au Bonheur des Dames*). (30 April) Death of Manet

1884   (March) *La Joie de vivre*. Preface to catalogue of Manet exhibition

1885   (March) *Germinal*. (12 May) Begins writing *The Masterpiece* (*L'Œuvre*). (22 May) Death of Victor Hugo. (23 December) First instalment of *The Masterpiece* appears in *Le Gil Blas*

1886   (27 March) Final instalment of *The Masterpiece*, which is published in book form in April

1887   (18 August) Denounced as an onanistic pornographer in the *Manifesto of the Five* in *Le Figaro*. (November) *Earth*

1888   (October) *The Dream*. Jeanne Rozerot becomes his mistress

1889   (20 September) Birth of Denise, daughter of Zola and Jeanne

1890   (March) *The Beast in Man*

1891   (March) *Money*. (April) Elected President of the Société des Gens de Lettres. (25 September) Birth of Jacques, son of Zola and Jeanne

1892   (June) *La Débâcle*

1893   (July) *Doctor Pascal*, the last of the Rougon-Macquart novels. Fêted on visit to London

1894   (August) *Lourdes*, the first novel of the trilogy *Three Cities*. (22 December) Dreyfus found guilty by a court martial

1896   (May) *Rome*

1898   (13 January) 'J'accuse', his article in defence of Dreyfus, published in *L'Aurore*. (21 February) Found guilty of libelling the Minister of War and given the maximum sentence of one year's imprisonment and a fine of 3,000 francs. Appeal for retrial granted on a technicality. (March) *Paris*. (23 May) Retrial delayed. (18 July) Leaves for England instead of attending court

1899   (4 June) Returns to France. (October) *Fecundity*, the first of his *Four Gospels*

1901   (May) *Toil*, the second 'Gospel'

1902   (29 September) Dies of fumes from his bedroom fire, the chimney having been capped either by accident or anti-Dreyfusard design. Wife survives. (5 October) Public funeral

1903   (March) *Truth*, the third 'Gospel', published posthumously. *Justice* was to be the fourth

1908   (4 June) Remains transferred to the Panthéon

THE BELLY OF PARIS

CHAPTER 1

THROUGH the deep silence of the deserted avenue, the carts made their way towards Paris, the rhythmic jolting of the wheels echoing against the fronts of the sleeping houses on both sides of the road, behind the dim shapes of elms. A cart full of cabbages and another full of peas had joined up at the Pont de Neuilly with the eight carts carrying carrots and turnips from Nanterre; the horses plodded along of their own accord, their heads down as they moved forward at a steady but lazy pace, which the upward slope reduced still further. The wagoners, lying flat on their stomachs on beds of vegetables, were dozing with the reins in their hands and their greatcoats, in thin black and grey stripes, over their backs. Every now and then a gas lamp, looming out of the darkness, would illuminate the nails of a boot, the blue sleeve of a smock, or the peak of a cap, in the midst of this huge mass of vegetables—bunches of red carrots, bunches of white turnips, and the rich greenery of peas and cabbages. All along the road, and the neighbouring roads, in front and behind, the distant rumbling of carts signalled similar convoys travelling through the night, lulling the dark city with the sound of food on the move.

Madame François's horse Balthazar, a very fat animal, led the procession. He plodded on, half asleep, flicking his ears, until, reaching the Rue de Longchamp, he gave a start and came to a sudden halt. The horses behind bumped into the carts in front, and the procession stopped amid a clanking of metal and the cursing of wagoners shaken from their sleep. Madame François, sitting with her back against a plank that kept her vegetables in place, looked round, but could see nothing in the dim light shed by a small square lantern on her left, which illuminated little more than one of Balthazar's gleaming flanks.

'Come on, old girl, let's keep moving!' yelled one of the men, rising to his knees among his turnips. 'It's probably some stupid drunk.'

Madame François, however, had leaned forward and, down to her right, had seen a black shape lying across the road, almost under the horse's hooves.

'You don't want us to ride over someone, do you?' she said, jumping to the ground.

A man was lying full length on the road, spreadeagled with his face in the dust. He seemed remarkably long and as thin as a rake; it was a wonder that Balthazar had not snapped him in two with one of his hooves. Madame François thought he was dead; she crouched down, took one of his hands, and found that it was warm.

'Poor thing!' she murmured.

The wagoners were getting impatient.

'Let's get going!' said the man kneeling in his turnips, hoarsely. 'The sod's dead drunk! Push him into the gutter.'

But the man had opened his eyes. He stared at Madame François without moving. She thought he must be drunk after all.

'You can't stay here,' she said, 'or you'll get trampled on. Where were you trying to get to?'

'I don't know,' he replied in a faint voice.

Then, with an effort and an anxious look, he added:

'I was going to Paris. I fell down, that's all I can remember.'

Now she could see him better. He looked pitiful, with his black coat and trousers, so threadbare that she could almost see his scrawny arms and legs through them. His black cloth cap, pulled down over his forehead as if he was afraid of being recognized, revealed two big brown eyes, shining softly in his haggard face. Madame François thought he was far too thin to have been drinking.

'What part of Paris were you going to?' she continued.

He did not reply at once. This questioning seemed to bother him. He appeared to be thinking, and at last said hesitantly:

'Over by the markets.'

By now he had got to his feet, with great difficulty, and seemed anxious to carry on his journey. But he staggered and grabbed hold of one of the shafts of the cart.

'Are you tired?' she asked.

'Yes, very tired,' he murmured.

Then she suddenly assumed a sharp tone, as if annoyed. She gave him a push and said:

'Come on, get in the cart. We're wasting time. I'm going to the markets. I'll drop you off with my vegetables.'

As he hesitated, she pushed him up and almost threw him onto the turnips and carrots.

'Come on, don't hold us up any longer,' she cried. 'Don't get me annoyed. Didn't I say I was going to the markets? Go to sleep. I'll wake you up when we get there.'

She climbed back into the cart and sat at an angle, with her back against the plank, clutching Balthazar's reins. The horse moved forward sleepily, flicking his ears once more. The other carts followed suit, and the convoy resumed its slow progress through the darkness, while the rhythmic jolting of the wheels echoed once more against the house fronts, and the wagoners, wrapped in their greatcoats, dozed off again. The man who had called out to Madame François lay down, muttering:

'As if we'd got nothing better to do than pick up every drunk we come across! You're too kind-hearted!'

The carts rolled on, with the horses, their heads down, moving slowly forward of their own accord. The stranger was lying on his stomach, his long legs covered in the turnips that filled the back of the cart and his face buried in a pile of carrots. Exhausted, he held on to his bed of vegetables for fear of being thrown to the ground by a bump in the road, his eyes fixed on the two lines of gas lamps that stretched out ahead until they merged, in the distance, with a mass of other lights at the top of the slope. On the horizon hung a great pall of white smoke, showing where Paris slept in the luminous haze of all these flames.

'I come from Nanterre. My name's Madame François,' said the market gardener after a moment or two. 'Since my husband died I've been going to the markets every morning. It's hard! What about you?'

'My name's Florent. I come from a long way away,' replied the stranger, seeming embarrassed. 'I'm sorry, I'm so tired I can hardly talk.'

It was clear that he did not want to say any more. So Madame François fell silent, loosening the reins round Balthazar's neck as he plodded on as if he knew every cobblestone. Florent, still staring at the endless lights of Paris, was thinking about the story he had not wanted to tell. After escaping from Cayenne,* where he had been transported for his part in the resistance to Louis-Napoleon's *coup d'état*,* he had wandered about Dutch Guiana for two years, desperate to get back to France, but afraid of being caught by the police; and now he once more saw before him the great city he had missed so much. There he would hide and lead the same quiet life he had lived before. The police would be none the wiser; everyone would think he had died overseas. He recalled how he had arrived at Le Havre with just fifteen francs tied in a knot in his handkerchief. This enabled him to take the coach to Rouen, but from there he had to continue on foot, as he had only thirty sous left. At Vernon he spent his last few coins on bread. After that he could not remember anything clearly. He thought he could remember having slept for several hours in a ditch and having shown a gendarme the papers he had managed to acquire. But he had only a vague idea of what had happened. He had come all the way from Vernon without a bite to eat, overcome every now and then by despair and by such terrible pangs of hunger that he had munched leaves from the hedges as he tramped along. In pain, suffering from cramp and sickness, his stomach knotted, his eyesight blurred, his feet moving forward as if drawn, without his being aware of it, by his vision of Paris far away, so far away, summoning him from over the horizon, waiting for him to come. By the time he reached Courbevoie, the night was very dark. Paris, like a patch of starlit sky that had fallen upon the black earth, seemed to him quite forbidding, as though angered by his return. A feeling of faintness came over him and his legs almost gave way as he descended the slope. As he crossed the Pont de Neuilly, he had to hold on to the parapet; he leaned over and looked at the Seine swirling in inky waves between its huge banks. The red lamp of a buoy seemed to stare at him with a bloodshot eye. Now he had to climb the hill if he was to reach Paris. The avenue seemed incredibly long. The hundreds of miles he had already travelled were as nothing compared to this. This last stretch of road filled him with despair. He would never be able, he thought, to reach the summit, crowned with lights. The broad avenue stretched out before him, with its lines of tall trees and low houses, its wide grey footpaths stained with the shadows of branches and interspersed with gloomy hollows where roads ran off to the side; all was silence and darkness. The short yellow flames of the gas lamps, at regular intervals, were all that gave some life to this desert of death. Florent came to a standstill. The avenue seemed to grow longer and longer as Paris seemed to recede into the night. For a moment he had the impression that the gas lamps, with their single eyes, were running to left and right, carrying the road away from him; then, feeling dizzy, he stumbled and fell in a heap on the cobbles.

Now here he was, lying at ease on a bed of greenery which felt as soft as a feather bed. He raised his head a little to see the luminous haze rising above the dark roofs that could just be made out on the horizon. He was nearing his goal, he was being carried along towards it, and had nothing to do but abandon himself to the movement of the cart; and this effortless advance left him with only his gnawing hunger to contend with. It gripped him once more, causing him terrible, almost unbearable pain. Now that his limbs had fallen asleep, he could feel only his stomach, racked and twisted as by a red-hot poker. The fresh smells of the vegetables around him, especially the carrots, affected him so much that he almost fainted. He pressed as hard as he could against this deep bed of food in order to tighten his stomach and silence its groans. The nine carts behind him, with their mountains of cabbages and peas, their piles of artichokes, lettuces, celery, and leeks, seemed to be rolling over him as if to bury him beneath an avalanche of food. There was a halt, the sound of loud voices. They had reached the barrier* and the customs officials were looking into the carts. Then Florent entered Paris on a heap of carrots, his teeth clenched and in a dead faint.

'Hey! You up there!' Madame François shouted suddenly.

As he did not move, she climbed up and shook him. He sat up. He had slept and no longer felt his hunger; he was totally dazed.

'Will you help me unload?' Madame François asked, as she made him get down.

He helped her. A fat man with a walking-stick and a felt hat, and a badge* on the left lapel of his coat, was tapping on the ground with the ferrule of his stick and grumbling loudly:

'Come on, hurry up! You've got to be quicker than that! Move the cart forward a bit. How many metres' standing have you got? Four, isn't it?'

He gave Madame François a ticket and she took some large coins out of a little canvas bag. He went off to vent his anger and tap his stick a little further down the line. Madame François took hold of Balthazar's bridle and backed him so as to bring the wheels of the cart close to the footpath. Then, having let down the back of the cart and marked out her four metres with some pieces of straw, she asked Florent to pass the vegetables down to her bunch by bunch. She arranged them neatly on the ground, displaying them artistically, the tops forming a band of greenery round each pile; in no time she completed her display, which, in the pale light of early morning, looked like a symmetrically coloured tapestry. When Florent had handed her a huge bunch of parsley, which he found at the bottom of the cart, she asked him one more favour.

'It would be very nice', she said, 'if you would keep an eye on all this while I go and put the cart away. It's just round the corner in the Rue Montorgueil, at the Compas d'or.'*

Florent told her not to worry. He preferred to stay still, for his
hunger had returned since he had begun to move about. He sat down
against a pile of cabbages next to Madame François's stock. He was
all right there, he told himself, and would not make a single move,
but simply wait. He felt faint, and he had no real idea where he was.
At the beginning of September* it is quite dark in the early morning.
Around him lanterns were flitting about or were stationary in the
darkness. He was sitting on one side of a wide street which he did not
recognize; it stretched far away into the night. He could make nothing
out clearly, except the stock he was guarding; and beyond that, along
the pathways, the vague shapes of similar piles of goods. The middle
of the roadway was blocked by huge grey carts, and from one end of
the street to the other there was a sound of heavy breathing, indicating
the presence of horses in the darkness. Shouts, the sound of a piece
of wood or a metal chain falling on the cobbles, the heavy thud of
vegetables being unloaded, the rattle of a cart striking the edge of the
footpath, all these sounds filled the air with the suggestion of a mighty
awakening, which could already be felt in the throbbing darkness.
Turning round, Florent caught sight of a man snoring on the other
side of the pile of cabbages; he was wrapped up like a parcel in his
greatcoat, his head resting on some baskets of plums. Closer still, to
his left, he made out a boy of about twelve, asleep with an angelic
smile on his face between two huge piles of endives. As yet there
seemed nothing on the footpath that was truly awake except the
lanterns dancing at the end of invisible arms, flitting over the dormant
vegetables and human beings as they waited for the dawn. But what
surprised Florent most was the sight of some huge pavilions on
either side of the street, pavilions with soaring roofs that seemed to
expand and disappear from sight in shimmers of light.* In his dazed
state he thought that he was looking at a series of enormous, symmetrically built palaces, light and airy as crystal, and catching on their
façades, as though filtered through their endless shutters, a thousand
rays of light. These narrow golden bars, gleaming between slender
pillars, seemed like ladders of light ascending to the dark line of the
lower roofs, then soaring upwards to the higher ones, thus forming
an open structure of immense square halls, where a mass of grey,
dormant shapes lurked below the yellow flare of the gaslights.
Florent looked about him, frustrated at not knowing where he was
and disturbed by this huge but seemingly fragile sight. As he raised

his eyes, he caught sight of the luminous clock-face of Saint-Eustache and the grey mass of the church itself. This amazed him. He was at the Pointe Saint-Eustache.*

Madame François, in the meantime, had returned and was arguing violently with a man carrying a sack over his shoulder and who wanted to buy her carrots for a sou a bunch.

'You're mad, Lacaille!' she said. 'You'll sell them back to the Parisians at four or five sous a bunch. Admit it! You can have them for two sous a bunch, if you like.'

As the man was walking off, she added:

'Some people think things grow by themselves! Let him buy carrots for a sou a bunch somewhere else, the drunken devil! He'll be back soon enough, you'll see.'

These last remarks were addressed to Florent. She now sat down beside him.

'If you've been away from Paris for a long time, you probably don't know the new Halles. They were built five years ago at most. That market you can see just over there is for fruit and flowers. The fish and poultry markets are a bit further away, and behind them are the vegetables and butter and cheese markets. There are six markets on this side, and on the other side, opposite, there are four more: meat, tripe, poultry, and game.* The whole thing is enormous, and bitterly cold in winter. They say they're going to pull down the houses round the corn market* to build two more markets. But perhaps you know all about it?'

'No,' replied Florent. 'I've been abroad... What's that big street in front of us?'

'Oh, that's a new street. The Rue du Pont-Neuf. It runs from the Seine through here to the Rue Montmartre and the Rue Montorgueil. You'd have realized where you were if it had been daylight.'

Madame François paused and stood up, having noticed a woman looking at her turnips.

'Is that you, Mère Chantemesse?' she asked affably.

Florent, in the meantime, was staring in the direction of the Rue Montorgueil. That was where a group of *sergents de ville* had arrested him on the night of 4 December.* He had been walking along the Boulevard Montmartre at about two o'clock, making his way slowly through the crowd, smiling at the number of soldiers the Élysée* had ordered into the streets in a show of strength, when the military suddenly opened fire, shooting people at close range. It lasted a quarter of an hour. Knocked to the ground at the corner of the Rue Vivienne, he lost consciousness as the crowd, panic-stricken by the shooting, trampled over him. After a while, hearing no more noise, he tried to stand up; but across him lay a young woman in a pink bonnet, whose shawl had slipped from her shoulders to reveal a bodice sewn in tiny pleats. Above her breast, at the top of her bodice, were two bullet holes; and as he gently moved the young woman aside to free his legs, blood trickled from her wounds onto his hands. He sprang up and ran away as fast as he could, hatless, his hands wet with the blood. Out of his senses, he wandered about the streets until evening, haunted by the image of the young woman lying across his legs with her face so pale, her blue eyes wide open, her lips twisted in pain, and her look of surprise at meeting death so suddenly. He was a shy man. At the age of thirty he still hardly dared to look a woman in the face; and now he would carry this face in his heart and in his memory for the rest of his life. It was as if he had lost a loved one of his own. In the evening, without knowing how he had got there, still shaken by the terrible scenes of the afternoon, he found himself in a bar in the Rue Montorgueil, where some men were drinking and talking of throwing up barricades. He went off with them, helped them to tear up a few cobblestones, and sat on the barricade, tired out by his wanderings but ready to fight when the soldiers arrived. He did not even have a knife with him, and was still bareheaded. At about eleven o'clock he dozed off, and in his sleep he could see the two holes in the dead woman's white bodice staring at him like eyes reddened with blood and tears. When he woke up he found himself in the grip of four *sergents de ville* who were pummelling him with their fists. The men on the barricade had fled. But the *sergents* became even more violent, and almost strangled him when they saw the blood on his hands. It was the blood of the young woman.

His head full of these memories, Florent glanced up at the luminous clock of Saint-Eustache, not even noticing the position of the hands. It was nearly four o'clock. Les Halles were still asleep. Madame François was talking to Mère Chantemesse; they were haggling over the price of the turnips. Florent now remembered how they had nearly shot him against the wall of Saint-Eustache. On that spot a platoon of police had just executed five men captured at a barricade in the Rue Grenéta. The five bodies had lain across the footpath just where he thought he could now see a pile of pink radishes. He had escaped being shot only because the *sergents de ville* carried swords rather than muskets. They took him to a nearby police station and gave the officer in charge a note which bore, scribbled in pencil, the words: 'Captured with hands covered in blood. Very dangerous.' From then until the morning he had been dragged from station to station. The note accompanied him each time. He was manacled from the start and guarded as though he were a raving lunatic. At the station in the Rue de la Lingerie some drunken soldiers wanted to shoot him; they had already lighted a lantern in preparation when an order came through to take all prisoners to the depot of the Préfecture. Two days later he was in a dungeon at the fort of Bicêtre.* And ever since then he had been hungry. He had been hungry in the dungeon, and hunger had never left him. About a hundred men were squashed into the cellar-like dungeon, where, hardly able to breathe, they devoured the few mouthfuls of bread that were thrown to them like animals in a cage. When he appeared before an investigating magistrate, without any witness or defence, he was accused of belonging to a secret society; and when he swore that this was not true, the magistrate produced the note from his file: 'Captured with hands covered in blood. Very dangerous.' That was enough. He was sentenced to deportation.* Six weeks later, one night in January, a gaoler awoke him and locked him in a courtyard with more than four hundred other prisoners. An hour later this first convoy set off for the hulks* and exile, handcuffed and guarded by two files of gendarmes with loaded muskets. They crossed the Pont d'Austerlitz, followed the line of the boulevards, and arrived at the Gare du Havre. It was a carnival night. Bright lights shone from the windows of the restaurants on the boulevards. At the corner of the Rue Vivienne, at the spot where he could still picture the anonymous young woman lying dead, he saw a carriage full of masked women, with bare shoulders and laughing voices, who were complaining about being held up, and expressing their disgust at the endless procession of convicts. During the whole journey from Paris to Le Havre, the prisoners were given neither a mouthful of bread nor a drink of water. The police had forgotten to issue any rations before their departure, and it was not until thirty-six hours later, when they had been piled away in the holds of the frigate *Le Canada*, that they were at last given a bite to eat.

No, hunger had never left him. He wracked his brains, but could not recall a single moment when his stomach had felt full. He had become dry and withered; his stomach seemed to have shrunk; his skin clung to his bones. And now that he was back in Paris, he found it fat and sleek, overflowing with food. He had returned on a bed of vegetables, riding into the city on a wave of good things to eat which he had felt swarming around him, spreading everywhere and making him feel uneasy. That carnival night seemed to have lasted for seven years. Once again he saw the bright lights on the boulevards, the laughing women, the greedy city he had left on that distant January night; and it all seemed to have grown so much bigger, to match the gigantic size of Les Halles, whose heavy breathing—the result of the excesses of the day before—he could now hear.

Mère Chantemesse had decided to buy a dozen bunches of turnips. She had put them in her apron, which she held very tightly, thus making herself look even fatter; and she stayed there for a while, gossiping in her drawling voice. When she had gone, Madame François sat down again with Florent.

'Poor old Mère Chantemesse!' she said. 'She must be at least seventy-two. I can remember her buying turnips from my father when I was a little girl. She hasn't got any family, just a young good-for-nothing girl she picked up somewhere and who gives her nothing but trouble. Still, she manages somehow; she sells a bit here and there* and makes her forty sous a day. I know I could never live in this rotten city, spending the whole day in the street! If she had a family, you might understand it!'

'You've got some relations in Paris, I suppose?' she asked, seeing that Florent still seemed unwilling to talk.

He seemed not to hear. His feeling of distrust had come back. He kept thinking about the police, imagining them watching at every street corner, and getting women to sell the secrets they dragged out of poor devils like himself. Madame François was sitting close to him, but he thought she looked perfectly honest and straightforward with her wide, calm face and a black and yellow scarf tied round her head. She seemed about thirty-five, and was solidly built, with a certain hardy beauty due to her life out of doors. A pair of black eyes, which radiated kindness, softened her rather masculine features. She certainly was inquisitive, but she probably meant well.

'I've got a nephew in Paris,' she continued, without seeming at all put out by Florent's silence. 'He's turned out badly, though, and has gone into the army. It's nice to have people you can turn to, isn't it?

Your family will have a surprise when they see you. But it's always good to see each other again, isn't it?'

She kept looking at him as she spoke, no doubt feeling sorry for him because of his extreme thinness, fancying that he was a 'gentleman' beneath the dreadful black coat he was wearing, and so not daring to slip a silver coin into his hand.

At last, however, she murmured:

'In the meantime, if you need anything...'

He said immediately, however, that he had everything he needed and had a place to go to. She seemed quite pleased to hear this and, as if to reassure herself, repeated several times:

'Good, that's all right then—all you have to do is wait for it to get light.'

A heavy bell* at the corner of the fruit market, above Florent's head, began to sound. The slow, regular peals seemed gradually to dissipate the drowsiness that lingered all around. Carts were still arriving, and the shouts of the wagoners, the cracking of their whips, and the grinding of the paving stones under the iron-bound wheels and the horses' hooves made an ever-increasing din. Soon the carts could only move forward a few metres at a time, stretching out in a long line, one behind the other, until they were lost to sight in the greyness of the morning, from which a hubbub of activity arose. All the way down the Rue du Pont-Neuf carts were being unloaded, backed against the gutters, the horses standing motionless side by side as though on display at a circus. Florent's attention was caught by an enormous cart piled high with superb cabbages and which had been backed up to the footpath with the greatest difficulty. Its load towered above a lofty gas lamp, which threw its light across the cabbages' broad leaves, curled like pieces of dark green velvet, crimped and cut. A little peasant girl of about sixteen, in a blue linen blouse and bonnet, was standing in the cart up to her shoulders in cabbages, and was picking them up one by one and throwing them down to someone standing in the darkness below. Every now and then the girl would slip and vanish under an avalanche of vegetables, but her pink nose soon reappeared amidst the mass of greenery, and she would laugh as the cabbages once more flew through the air between Florent and the lamp. He counted them mechanically as they fell. When the cart was empty he felt quite disappointed.

The piles of vegetables on the footpath began to overflow onto the road. The traders had left narrow gaps between the various piles to let people pass. The wide footpath was covered from end to end with dark mounds. So far nothing could be seen, as the lanterns swung by, except the luxuriant fullness of the bundles of artichokes, the delicate green of the lettuces, the coral pink of the carrots, and the smooth ivory of the turnips. These flashes of colour appeared along the mounds of vegetables as the lanterns moved along. The footpath was now full of people: a whole crowd was now moving around among the goods on show, chattering and shouting. A loud voice in the distance cried: 'Endives! Endives!' The gates of the market where ordinary vegetables were sold had just been opened, and the retailers who had stalls there, wearing white bonnets and scarves knotted over their black calico jackets, their skirts pinned up to stop them getting dirty, were sorting out their stock for the day, depositing their purchases in huge porters' baskets spaced out on the ground. The coming and going between the roadway and the market grew more intense as people collided and cursed, while all around there was a clamour of voices growing hoarse because of prolonged wrangling over a sou or two. Florent was surprised by the calmness of the farm women with their bright headscarves and tanned faces amidst all this jabbering.

Behind him, on the footpaths of the Rue Rambuteau, fruit was being sold. Baskets of various sizes covered with canvas or straw stood in long rows, and a strong smell of overripe plums hung in the air. At last a soft, gentle voice, which he had been hearing for some time, made him turn round. He saw a charming, dark-haired little woman sitting on the ground, bargaining.

'Come on, Marcel,' she said, 'you'll take a hundred sous, won't you?'

The man to whom she was speaking was wrapped tightly in his greatcoat and did not reply; but after a silence of five minutes or more, the young woman returned to the attack.

'Come on, Marcel; a hundred sous for that basket, and four francs for the other one; that makes nine francs.'

Once again there was a pause.

'Well, tell me what you want.'

'Ten francs. You knew that; I told you... But what's happened to your fancy man, Sarriette?'

The young woman laughed as she took a handful of change out of her pocket.

'Oh,' she replied, 'he's still in bed. He says men weren't made for work.'

She paid for her two baskets and carried them into the fruit market, which had just been opened. Les Halles were still shrouded in shadows, streaked with a thousand rays of light gleaming through the shutters. People were beginning to move along the wide covered avenues intersecting the markets, but the markets in the distance were still deserted, despite the swarming activity on the footpaths. At the Pointe Saint-Eustache the bakers and wine merchants were taking down their shutters; the red-fronted shops, their gas jets flaring, stood out in the darkness. Florent noticed a baker's shop on the left-hand side of the Rue Montorgueil and fancied that he could smell the warm bread. It was now half past four.

By this time Madame François had got rid of nearly all her produce. She had only a few bunches of carrots left when Lacaille reappeared with his sack.

'Well,' he said, 'will you take one sou now?'

'I knew I'd see you again,' replied Madame François. 'You might as well take everything I've got left. There are seventeen bunches.'

'That makes seventeen sous.'

'No, thirty-four.'

They finally agreed on twenty-five. Madame François was anxious to go. When Lacaille had moved off, with the carrots in his sack, she said to Florent:

'He was watching me all the time. That's how he bargains all over the markets. He often waits until the last peal of the bell before spending four sous. Oh, these Parisians! They'll haggle for an hour over half a sou and then go and spend everything in a bar.'

Whenever Madame François talked about Paris, she spoke in a tone of ironic disdain and referred to the city as if it were some ridiculous, contemptible, faraway place, where she deigned to set foot only at night-time.

'There! I can go now,' she said, sitting down again next to Florent on some vegetables that belonged to a neighbour.

Florent lowered his head. He had just committed a theft. When Lacaille had gone off, he had noticed a carrot lying on the ground. He had picked it up and was clutching it in his right hand. Behind him some celery and bunches of parsley were giving off strong smells that struck in his throat.

'I'll be off, then!' said Madame François.

However, she was intrigued by this stranger and could see that he was suffering there on the footpath. He had not moved an inch. She repeated her offer of help, but he again refused, with an even stronger show of pride. He even stood up to show that he was feeling better. Then, as soon as she looked the other way, he popped the carrot in his mouth. But he had to hold it there for a moment, in spite of his longing to sink his teeth into it, for she turned round and, looking him full in the face, began to ask him more questions, with her honest womanly curiosity. To avoid speaking, he simply nodded or shook his head. Then, slowly, he ate the carrot.

Madame François was at last on the point of setting off when a loud voice behind her said,

'Good morning, Madame François.'

The speaker was a thin young man with big bones and a large head. He had a beard, a slender nose, and small, bright eyes. He was wearing a black felt hat, shapeless and discoloured with age, and was wrapped in a huge greatcoat, once a delicate shade of brown but which rain had streaked with long greenish stains. He stood there in his big laced boots, slightly stooped, twitching nervously in a way that was probably habitual; and his trousers, which were too short, revealed his coarse blue socks.*

'Hello, Monsieur Claude,' Madame François replied cheerfully. 'I waited for you last Monday, but since you didn't come I found a place for your canvas. I hung it on a nail in my room.'

'That's very kind, Madame François. I'll finish that painting one of these days. I couldn't come on Monday. Has that big plum tree of yours still got all its leaves?'

'Of course.'

'I was wondering, because I want to put it in a corner of the painting. It'll look good next to the hen-house. I've been thinking about it all week… What lovely vegetables there are this morning! I came very early, thinking there'd be a good sunrise effect on all these cabbages.'

He waved in the general direction of the footpath.

'Well, I must be off,' said Madame François. 'Bye for now. I'll see you soon, I hope, Monsieur Claude.'

As she turned to go, she introduced Florent to the young painter.

'This gentleman has just been on a long journey,' she said. 'He feels completely lost in this dreadful city of yours. Perhaps you can help him.'

She finally went off, pleased at having left the two men together. Claude looked at Florent with interest. This tall, thin, wavy figure struck him as something out of the ordinary. Madame François's brief introduction was enough for him, and he began to talk to Florent with the easy familiarity of a *flâneur** accustomed to all sorts of chance encounters.

'I'll come with you,' he said. 'Which way are you going?'

Florent felt ill at ease. He was not used to talking about himself. However, ever since his arrival in Les Halles, he had been dying to ask one question, and now he ventured to ask it, clearly afraid of receiving a negative reply.

'Does the Rue Pirouette* still exist?'

'Oh, yes,' answered the painter. 'It's a very quaint part of old Paris, that street. It twists and turns like a dancing-girl, and the houses bulge out like women with big bellies. I've made an etching of it that isn't too bad. You can see it when you come to my place. Is that where you're going?'

Florent, feeling relieved now that he knew the street still existed, said no, and explained that he had nowhere in particular to go. Claude's insistence, however, brought back all his distrust.

'That doesn't matter,' said Claude. 'Let's go there anyway. It has such a wonderful colour at night. Come on, it's just a few metres away.'

Florent felt that he had to go with him. They walked off, side by side, stepping over the baskets and vegetables like a couple of old friends. On the footpath in the Rue Rambuteau there were some enormous piles of cauliflowers, stacked symmetrically like cannon balls. Their soft white flesh spread out like huge roses in the midst of their thick green leaves, and they looked rather like bridal bouquets displayed on giant flower stalls. Claude stopped in his tracks, uttering little cries of admiration.

Then, turning into the Rue Pirouette, which was just opposite, he pointed out and commented on each house. A single gas lamp was burning in a corner. The houses, packed together with their peeling walls, thrust out their bay windows 'like the bellies of pregnant women', as Claude said, while their gables leaned backwards, clinging onto each other's shoulders for support. Three or four of them, set back in the darkness, seemed on the point of toppling forward. One of them was illuminated by the gas lamp, and it had a bright, fresh coat of whitewash, like a flabby, broken-down old dowager, powdered and painted in the hope of looking younger than her years. The others stretched away into the darkness, like a line of hunchbacks, cracked and green from the water dripping down from the roofs, and displaying such a variety of shapes and colours that Claude could not help laughing as he looked at them. Florent had stopped at the corner of the Rue de Mondétour, in front of the last house but one on the left. The three storeys, each with two shutterless windows, with little white curtains closely drawn, were sleeping; but, higher up, a light could be seen flitting behind the curtains of a small dormer window. But the sight of the shop beneath the bay window seemed to affect Florent deeply. It was kept by a dealer in cooked herbs and was just opening. Inside, there were some gleaming metal bowls, while on the counter stood the rounded domes and pointed steeples of tureens containing *pâtés* of spinach and endives, from which customers were served with scoops of which only the white metal handles were visible. This sight seemed to root Florent to the spot. Clearly, he had failed to recognize the place. He read the name of the shopkeeper, Godebœuf, on a red sign-board, and seemed quite disappointed. He stared at the cooked spinach with the despairing look of a man whom some terrible misfortune has befallen.

Meanwhile the dormer window had been opened, and a little old woman leaned out, looked at the sky and then towards Les Halles in the distance.

'Ah, Mademoiselle Saget's an early bird,' said Claude as he gazed up at the window. And he added, turning to his companion:

'An aunt of mine used to live in that house. It's a real hotbed of gossip!... Ah, the Méhudins are getting up. There's a light on the second floor.'

Florent was about to ask Claude something, but he found him rather forbidding in his big faded overcoat. So, without a word, he followed him. Claude went on talking about the Méhudin women. They were in the fish trade; the elder one was a magnificent creature, while the younger one, who sold freshwater fish, reminded Claude of a Murillo* virgin whenever he saw her standing with her pale face and fair hair amidst her carp and eels. From this he went on to comment sharply that Murillo painted like an ignoramus. Then all at once he stopped short in the middle of the street.

'So!' he exclaimed, 'where do you want to go?'

'Nowhere in particular,' replied Florent, feeling confused. 'Wherever you want.'

Just as they were leaving the Rue Pirouette, someone shouted to Claude from a bar on the corner. Claude went in, dragging Florent with him. The shutters had been taken down on one side only. The gas was still burning in the drowsy atmosphere; a forgotten dishcloth and some playing cards from the night before were still lying on the tables, and the draught that came in through the open door freshened the warm, wine-laden air. The landlord, Monsieur Lebigre, was serving his customers. He wore a long-sleeved waistcoat, and his fat regular features, fringed by an unkempt beard, were still pale with sleep. Groups of men with sunken eyes were drinking at the counter, coughing and spitting, trying to wake themselves up with white wine and *eau-de-vie*. Florent recognized Lacaille, whose sack was now bursting with vegetables. He had reached his third round with a friend, who was telling him a long story about the basket of potatoes he had bought. When he had emptied his glass he went to chat with Monsieur Lebigre in a little glass-partitioned room at the back, where the gas had not been lit.

'What will you have?' Claude asked Florent.

On entering he had shaken hands with the man who had called out to him. He was a strapping young man of twenty-two at most, clean-shaven except for a small moustache, with a broad-brimmed hat covered with chalk, and a woollen neck-piece with straps attached to his short blue jacket.* Claude addressed him as Alexandre, slapped him on the arm, and asked him when they were going to Charentonneau again. Then they talked about a great boating trip they had been on together on the Marne, when they had eaten a rabbit for supper.

'So, what will you have?' Claude asked again.

Florent looked at the counter, feeling very embarrassed. At one end some bowls of punch and mulled wine, circled with brass, were bubbling over the low blue and pink flames of a gas burner. At last he confessed that he would like something warm, whereupon Monsieur Lebigre served three glasses of punch. Near the bowls stood a basket of steaming-hot rolls which had only just arrived. But as neither of the others took one, Florent simply drank his punch. He felt it falling into his empty stomach like a stream of molten lead. Alexandre paid.

'He's a good bloke, Alexandre!' said Claude, when he and Florent found themselves once more on the footpath in the Rue Rambuteau.

'He's great fun to be with in the country. He likes to do strong-man acts; he's got a magnificent physique. I've seen him stripped. If I could only get him to pose for me in the nude in the open air!*... Anyway, let's take a stroll round the markets.'

Florent followed, happy to accept the bidding of his new friend. A bright glow at the end of the Rue Rambuteau announced the break of day. The noise of the markets was increasing, and every now and then the peals of a bell in one of the far pavilions cut across the growing din. They entered one of the covered avenues between the fish and poultry markets. Florent looked up at the high, vaulted roof, whose inner beams were shining amidst the black lacework of cast-iron supports. As they turned into the broad central avenue, he imagined himself in some foreign town, with its various districts, suburbs, villages, walks and streets, squares and intersections, all suddenly placed under a huge roof one rainy day by the whim of some gigantic power. The shadows, in the hollows of the roof, seemed to make the forest of pillars even bigger, and multiply to infinity the delicate ribs, fretted galleries, and transparent shutters. And high above this phantom town, stretching far away into the darkness, there appeared to be a mass of luxuriant vegetation, a monstrous jungle of metal, with spindle-shaped stems and knotted branches, covering the vast expanse as with the delicate foliage of some ancient forest.* Several sections of the markets were still asleep behind their closed iron gates. In the butter and cheese and poultry markets were rows of little trellised stalls, and long alleys, deserted beneath the lines of gas lamps. The fish market, however, had just opened, and women were moving around among the white slabs stained with the shadows of baskets and forgotten cloths. In the markets for vegetables, fruit, and flowers, the hubbub was gradually increasing. The whole town was by degrees waking up, from the populous district, where cabbages had been piled up since four o'clock in the morning, to the wealthy, lazy district which waited until eight o'clock before it started to hang pullets and pheasants outside its houses.

The great covered avenues were now teeming with life. All along the footpaths, on both sides, the market gardeners were still there, smallholders from the countryside around Paris, displaying in their baskets the harvest of the night before—bundles of vegetables and handfuls of fruit. As the crowd ebbed and flowed in all directions, carts drove in under the vaulted roof, the drivers reining in their

bell-jingling horses. Two of these carts, left at an angle, were blocking the avenue. Florent had to squeeze by one of the greyish sacks;
they were like sacks of coal, and so heavy that the axles of the carts
bent beneath them. They were quite damp and gave off a fresh smell
of seaweed; from one of them, split at one end, a stream of big, black
mussels was piling up. They had to pause at every step. The seawater
fish were arriving; one after another the drays drove up, laden with
tall wooden cages packed with hampers that had been brought by
train from the coast. To get out of the way of the fish drays, which
were arriving thick and fast, they had to dive under the wheels of the
drays loaded with butter, eggs, and cheese, huge yellow wagons
drawn by four horses and hung with coloured lanterns. The porters
were lifting down trays of eggs and baskets of cheese and butter,
which they carried into the auction enclosure, where men in caps
were making entries in ledgers by the light of the gas. Claude was in
raptures over this tumult—lost in admiration before an effect of
light, a group of figures in overalls, the unloading of a cart. At last
they freed themselves from the crowd. Continuing along the central
avenue, they soon found themselves enveloped in an exquisite perfume which seemed to be following them. They had now reached the
flower market. All over the footpaths, to right and left, women were
sitting with square baskets in front of them, full of bunches of roses,
violets, dahlias, and daisies. At times the bunches grew darker, like
bloodstains, at others they brightened into delicate silvery greys.
Near one of the baskets, a lighted candle gave the surrounding darkness a sharp note of colour, bringing out the bright cockades of the
daisies, the blood-red of the dahlias, the bluish purple of the violets, and
the warm flesh tints of the roses. Nothing could have been more gentle
or springlike than this soft breath of perfume on the footpath, after the
smells of the fish market and the stench of the butter and cheese.

Claude and Florent retraced their steps, lingering among the
flowers. They stopped to watch some women selling bunches of fern
and bundles of vine leaves, all neatly tied up in packets of twenty-five.
Then they turned into another covered avenue, which was almost
deserted, and where their footsteps echoed as though in the vault of
an empty church. Here they found a small cart, scarcely bigger than
a wheelbarrow, to which a little donkey was harnessed. He must have
felt bored, for, as soon as he saw them, he began to bray so long and
so loudly that the vast roofs of Les Halles seemed to shake. Then the

horses began to neigh in reply, there was a sound of pawing and scraping of hooves, and a great din in the distance, which grew, spread, then died away. Meanwhile, in the Rue Berger in front of them, the empty retailers' shops displayed, in the glaring light of the gas, piles of baskets and fruit, enclosed by three dirty walls covered with numbers scrawled in pencil. They were still standing there, contemplating the scene, when they caught sight of a well-dressed woman huddled in a cab stuck in a traffic jam down the street.

'There's Cinderella going home without her slippers,'* said Claude with a smile.

They were chatting now as they walked back to the central point of the markets. Claude whistled as he strolled along with his hands in his pockets, talking expansively about his love for this mountain of food which rose up every morning in the heart of Paris. He prowled about the footpaths every night, dreaming of colossal still lifes, of the most amazing paintings. He had even started on one of them, having got his friend Marjolin and that good-for-nothing Cadine to pose for him; but it was hard work to paint all those vegetables and fruits and fish and meats—they were all so beautiful! Florent, his stomach aching, listened to the artist's rapturous talk. It was obvious that Claude, at this particular moment, did not think of these beautiful objects as food to be eaten. He loved them for their colours. Suddenly, however, he fell silent and, with a characteristic gesture, tightened the big red sash he wore under his greenish coat. Then, with a sly expression, he said:

'This is where I have breakfast, with my eyes at any rate, and that's better than nothing. Sometimes, when I've forgotten to have dinner the night before, I gorge myself in the morning just by looking at all these wonderful things arriving. On mornings like that, I love my vegetables more than ever. But the frustrating thing, what's so unjust, is that those bourgeois bastards eat it all!'

He recalled a magnificent supper to which a friend had treated him at Baratte's.* They had had oysters, fish, and game. But sadly Baratte's had closed, and all the carnival life of the old Marché des Innocents* was dead and gone; instead they had those huge central markets, that iron giant, that amazing new town. Fools could say what they liked; it embodied the spirit of the times. Florent, however, could not make out whether he was condemning Baratte's picturesqueness or its fine food. Claude then began to inveigh against romanticism.* He preferred his piles of vegetables, he said, to the rags and tatters of the Middle Ages. And he ended by running down an etching he had done of the Rue Pirouette, as if it were a personal weakness. Those old slums ought to be razed to the ground and modern houses built in their place.

'Look!' he exclaimed, stopping. 'Look at the corner of the footpath over there! Isn't that a ready-made painting, far more human and alive than all their terrible sickly efforts put together?'

Along the covered avenue, women were now selling hot soup and coffee. At one corner a large circle of customers had gathered round a vendor of cabbage soup. The enamelled tin cauldron full of broth was steaming over a small brazier, through the holes of which could be seen the pale glow of the embers. The woman, armed with a ladle, took some thin slices of bread out of a basket lined with a cloth and dipped some yellow cups into the soup. She was surrounded by neatly dressed saleswomen, market gardeners in overalls, porters with jackets that bore the marks of the loads they had carried, poor ragged devils—in fact, all the hungry early-morning crowd of the markets, eating, scalding their mouths, and sticking out their chins to avoid staining their clothes as they lifted the spoons to their mouths. Claude blinked, delighted with the sight, trying to position himself so as to get the best perspective, trying to compose the scene into a satisfactory group. But the cabbage soup gave off a terrible smell. Florent turned away, put off by the sight of the full cups, which the customers emptied in silence, glancing sideways like suspicious animals. As the woman began serving a fresh customer, Claude was overwhelmed by the steam of the soup, which caught him full in the face.

He tightened his belt once more, half amused and half annoyed. Then, walking off, he remarked apropos of the punch Alexandre had bought:

'Funny, that—have you noticed that although you can always find somebody to buy you a drink, there's never anyone who will stand you something to eat?'

The day was breaking. The houses on the Boulevard de Sébastopol, at the end of the Rue de la Cossonnerie, were still in darkness; but above the sharp line of the slate roofs the arch-pieces of the covered avenue cut out a bright half-moon in the pale blue sky. Claude had been bending over some grated openings on the ground, through which he could glimpse deep cellars where gaslight glimmered, and he now glanced up at the space between the high pillars, as though scanning the dark roofs that fringed the clear sky. Again he halted, this time to stare up at one of the light iron ladders that connected the two tiers of roofing and made it possible to walk between them. Florent asked him what he could see up there.

'I'm looking for that little devil Marjolin,' said the painter. He'll be lying in some gutter, unless he spent the night in the poultry cellars. I need him for a study.'

He went on to relate how his friend Marjolin had been discovered one morning by a market woman in a pile of cabbages, and how Marjolin had grown up without a family, on the footpaths of Les Halles. When they tried to send him to school he fell sick and had to be taken back to the markets. He knew the markets like the back of his hand and loved them with filial devotion, living like a squirrel* in that forest of ironwork. They made a fine couple, he and Cadine, that good-for-nothing Mère Chantemesse had picked up one night in the old Marché des Innocents. He, a simpleton but as resplendent as a Rubens,* with a russet down on his skin that shone in the sunlight; she, slight and sly, with a comical face under a mop of black curly hair.

Claude, still talking, quickened his step. He brought his companion back to the Pointe Saint-Eustache. Florent, whose legs were giving way again, slumped down on a bench near the omnibus office. The air was growing crisper. At the far end of the Rue Rambuteau, rosy glimmers of light were streaking the milky sky, which, still higher, seemed to have been slashed by broad grey rifts. Such was the sweet balsamic scent of this dawn that for a moment Florent imagined himself in the country, high on a hill. But now Claude pointed out to him, on the other side of the bench, the market where herbs and spices were sold. All along the footpath skirting the tripe market it was as if there were fields of thyme and lavender, garlic and shallots; and round the young plane-trees on the footpath the vendors had tied long branches thick with bay leaves that shone as green as conquerors' wreaths. It was the strong smell of the bay leaves that predominated.

The luminous face of the Saint-Eustache clock was growing pale and seemed on the point of fading completely, like a night light overtaken by the morning. In the bars at the end of the neighbouring streets, the gas jets went out one by one, like stars dimming with the coming of day. Florent watched Les Halles emerge slowly from the shadows, from the dreamland in which he had seen them, stretching out like an endless series of open palaces. Greenish-grey in colour, they looked more solid now, and even more gigantic, with their amazing mast-like columns supporting the great expanse of roofs. They rose up in geometrically shaped masses; and when all the inner lights had been extinguished and the square, uniform buildings were bathed in the light of dawn, they seemed like some vast modern machine, a steam engine or a cauldron supplying the digestive needs of a whole people, a huge metal belly, bolted and riveted, constructed of wood, glass, and iron, with the elegance and power of a machine working away with fiery furnaces and wildly turning wheels.

Claude had enthusiastically jumped onto the bench. He urged his companion to admire the effect of the day dawning over the vegetables. It was like an ocean spreading between the two groups of markets from the Pointe Saint-Eustache to the Rue des Halles. In the two open spaces at either end the flood of greenery rose even higher, submerging the footpaths. Dawn came slowly, a soft grey that spread light watercolour tints everywhere. The piles of greenery were like waves, a river of green flowing along the roadway like an autumn torrent; and they assumed delicate, shadowy hues—pale violet, milky pink, and greenish yellow, all the soft, light hues that turn the sky into a canopy of shot silk as the sun rises. By degrees, as the fires of dawn rose higher and higher at the far end of the Rue Rambuteau, the mass of vegetables grew brighter and brighter, emerging more and more clearly from the bluish shadows on the ground. Lettuces, endives, chicory, open and with rich soil still clinging to their roots, exposed their swelling hearts; bunches of spinach, sorrel, and artichokes, piles of peas and beans, mounds of cos lettuces, tied up with straw, sounded every note in the scale of greens, from the lacquered green of the pods to the coarse green of the leaves; a continuous scale of rising and falling notes that died away in the mixed tones of the tufts of celery and the bundles of leeks. But the highest notes, at the very top of the scale, came from the bright carrots and snowy turnips, scattered in tremendous quantities throughout the markets, which they lit up with their medley of colours. At the intersection in the Rue des Halles, mountains of cabbages were piled up; there were enormous white ones, as hard as cannon balls, curly ones with big leaves that made them look like bronze bowls, and red ones which the dawn seemed to transform into magnificent flowers with the hue of wine-dregs, splashed with crimson and dark purple. On the other side of the markets, at the intersection near Saint-Eustache, the opening to the Rue Rambuteau was blocked by a barricade of orange pumpkins in two rows, sprawling at their ease and swelling out their bellies. Here and there gleamed the varnished golden-brown of a basket of onions, the blood-red of a heap of tomatoes, the soft yellow of a display of cucumbers, and the deep mauve of aubergines; while large black radishes, laid down in funereal carpets, formed dark patches in the brilliance of the early morning.

Claude clapped his hands at the sight. He found something extravagant, mad, sublime in all these 'amazing vegetables'! He maintained that they were not yet dead, but, having been taken from the earth the day before, were waiting now for the morning sun to rise over Les Halles and bid them farewell. He could see them moving, he declared, see their leaves stir and open as if their roots were still firmly embedded in rich soil. Even from here in the markets, he maintained, he could hear the rattle of death coming from all the allotments around Paris. Meanwhile a crowd of white caps, black jackets, and blue overalls was swarming in the narrow pathways between the various piles of produce. It was as if the countryside had come to life in the city. The big baskets on the porters' backs moved slowly along above the heads of the throng. The retail women, greengrocers, and fruiterers were all busy making their purchases. Milling around the mountains of cabbages were corporals and groups of nuns, while trainee cooks prowled about looking for bargains. The unloading continued; the carts discharged their enormous loads as if they were so many paving stones, adding their cascades to all the others, which were now flooding across the footpaths opposite. And from the far end of the Rue du Pont-Neuf fresh rows of carts continued to arrive.

'What a beautiful sight!' murmured Claude rapturously.

Florent, however, was suffering. He fancied that all this was some supernatural temptation. He wished he could no longer see; he turned towards Saint-Eustache, which he could now see at an angle from where he was standing. With its roses and its high mullioned windows, its bell tower and slate roofs, it looked as if it were painted in sepia against the blue of the sky. His eyes rested at last on the dark recesses of the Rue Montorgueil, where patches of gaudy shop signs leapt out at him, and on the corner of the Rue Montmartre, where the balconies gleamed with golden letters. When he glanced back at the intersection, his attention was caught by other shop signs, on which such inscriptions as 'Druggist and Pharmacy', 'Flour and Grain' appeared in big red and black capitals on plain backgrounds. By now the houses at the corners, with their narrow windows, were coming to life, setting amidst the airy expanse of the new Rue du Pont-Neuf a few of the ancient yellow frontages of old Paris. At the corner of the Rue Rambuteau, standing in the empty windows of the big drapery shop, smart-looking assistants in waistcoats, with crisp white cuffs and tight-fitting trousers, were preparing their displays. Further down, the Maison Guillot, looking as stern as a barracks, was carefully arranging packets of golden biscuits and jars of *petits fours* in glass showcases. All the shops were now open. Workmen in white overalls, with tools under their arms, were hurrying across the road.

Claude was still standing on the bench. He was on tiptoe so that he could see as far as he could down the streets. Suddenly, in the midst of the crowd, he caught sight of a head covered with long blond hair followed by a smaller black-haired one, with frizzy curls.

'Marjolin!' he shouted. 'Cadine!'

His voice was lost in the general uproar, and he jumped down from the bench and ran after them. Then, realizing that he had forgotten Florent, he dashed back, and said:

'I live at the end of the Impasse des Bourdonnais. My name's written in chalk on the door: Claude Lantier... Come and look at my etching of the Rue Pirouette.'

Then he vanished. He did not even know Florent's name. He left him as he had found him, by the roadside, after treating him to his views on art.

Florent was now alone, and at first this pleased him. Ever since Madame François had picked him up, exhausted, in the Avenue de Neuilly, he had been walking around in a daze, unable to take his surroundings in properly. Now at last he was free to do what he liked, and he wanted to shake himself free from the intolerable vision of teeming food that pursued him. But his head was still empty, and all he felt was a kind of vague fear. It was getting lighter, and now he could be seen quite clearly. He looked down at his shabby coat and trousers. He buttoned his coat, dusted his trousers, and tried to smarten himself up a bit, fearing that the black rags he was wearing would give away immediately the place from which he had come. He was sitting in the middle of the bench; on either side of him were some other poor devils who had settled there to wait for the sunrise. Les Halles are a favourite spot for tramps and vagrants in the small hours of the morning. Two *sergents de ville*, still in night uniform, wearing capes and *képis*, were pacing up and down the footpath side by side, their hands behind their backs; and every time they passed in front of the bench, they cast a glance at the game they scented there. Florent felt sure that they had recognized him and were deciding to make an arrest. A fresh wave of anxiety overtook him. He felt a wild desire to get up and run off. But he did not dare to do so, and had no idea how he might make his escape. The repeated glances of the *sergents de ville*, their cold, deliberate scrutiny, was more than he could bear. At last he rose from the bench, and, making a great effort not to dash away as fast as his legs would carry him, he made off step by step, his muscles tensed because of his fear of suddenly feeling the rough hands of the *sergents de ville* grabbing him by the collar.

He had but one thought and one desire, which was to get away from Les Halles. He would wait, and later, when the footpaths were clear, he would look again. The three streets that converged here— the Rue Montmartre, the Rue Montorgueil, and the Rue Turbigo— filled him with uneasiness. They were cluttered with traffic of every kind, and vegetables littered the footpaths. Florent walked straight ahead as far as the Rue Pierre-Lescot, but the cress and potato markets seemed impassable. So he turned into the Rue Rambuteau. But in the Boulevard de Sébastopol he was confronted with such a bottleneck of furniture wagons, handcarts, and traps that he turned back and proceeded along the Rue Saint-Denis. He found himself once more among the vegetables. On either side the stallholders had just set themselves up, their wooden planks placed across tall baskets; and the deluge of cabbages, carrots, and turnips began all over again. The markets were overflowing. He tried to fight his way out of the current that had swept him from the line of his escape; he tried the Rue de la Cossonnerie, the Rue Berger, the Square des Innocents, the Rue de la Ferronnerie, and the Rue des Halles.* Then he stopped, discouraged, frightened, unable to escape from the infernal merry-go-round of vegetables that seemed to be swirling round him, slowly entwining his legs with their greenery. The endless stream of horses and carts stretched as far as the Rue de Rivoli and the Place de l'Hôtel de Ville; huge wagons were carrying away supplies for all the greengrocers of an entire district; traps, their sides creaking, were setting off for the suburbs. In the Rue du Pont-Neuf he got completely lost. He stumbled upon a mass of handcarts, in which greengrocers were arranging their mobile displays of purchases. Among them he recognized Lacaille, who took off along the Rue Saint-Honoré, pushing a barrow of carrots and cauliflowers. Florent followed him, in the hope that he would guide him out of the mob. The footpath was now quite slippery, although the weather was fine; the litter of artichoke stalks, turnip tops, and leaves of all kinds made walking dangerous. He stumbled at every step. In the Rue Vauvilliers he lost sight of Lacaille. Near the corn market he again found the streets blocked with carts and wagons. This time he made no attempt to struggle; he was once more engulfed by Les Halles, the tide swept him back. Slowly retracing his steps, he found himself at the Pointe Saint-Eustache.

Now he could hear the continuous rumbling of carts as they left the markets. Paris was chewing over the daily food of its two million inhabitants. The markets were like some huge central organ pumping blood into every vein of the city. The din was as if made by colossal jaws, a mighty sound to which each phase of the provisioning contributed, from the cracking of the big buyers' whips as they started off for the district markets to the shuffling feet of the old women who hawked their lettuces in baskets from door to door.

Florent turned into a covered avenue on the left, intersecting the group of four markets whose deep, silent gloom he had noticed during the night. It was here that he hoped to take refuge, to find a place to hide. But these markets were now as busy as all the others. He walked on to the end of the avenue. Drays were arriving at a quick trot, filling the market with coops of live poultry and square baskets in which dead birds were stowed in deep layers. On the opposite pathway other drays were unloading freshly killed calves, wrapped in canvas, lying on their sides like children in big rectangular baskets, from which only the four bleeding stumps of their legs protruded. There were also whole sheep and sides and quarters of beef. Butchers in long white aprons marked the meat with a stamp, carried it off, weighed it, and hung it up on hooks in the auction enclosure. Florent, his face glued to the bars of the window, stared at the rows of suspended carcasses, at the red of beef and mutton, and the paler meat of the veal, all streaked with yellow fat and tendon, and with their bellies gaping open. Then he arrived at the counters in the tripe market and passed by the pale calves' feet and heads, the rolled tripe neatly packed in boxes, the brains delicately arranged on flat trays, the bleeding livers and purplish kidneys. He paused to look at the long two-wheeled carts, covered with tarpaulins, which brought sides of pork hung on racks on each side over a bed of straw. The open ends of the carts seemed like some candlelit mortuary chapel, suggesting the deep recesses of a tabernacle, such was the glow of all the raw meat. On the straw beds were tin cans full of blood from the pigs. Florent was in the grip of a dull fever. The stale smell of the meat, the pungent odour of the offal, overwhelmed him. He made his way out of the covered avenue, preferring to return once more to the footpath of the Rue du Pont-Neuf.

He was in agony. The cold air of early morning was too much for him; his teeth chattered, and he was afraid that he might fall down and lie on the ground unconscious. He looked round, but could see no spot on any bench; had he found one, he would have gone to sleep there, even at the risk of being woken up by the *sergents de ville*. Then, feeling giddy, he leaned against a tree, his eyes closed and his ears ringing. The raw carrot he had eaten almost without chewing was making his stomach ache, and the glass of punch he had drunk seemed to have gone to his head. He was drunk with sickness, fatigue, and hunger. Once again he felt a burning sensation in the pit of his stomach, which he clutched every now and then, as though trying to stop up a hole through which his life was oozing away. The footpath seemed to be moving beneath him; and thinking that he might feel better if he walked on, he went straight through the vegetables again, and once more got lost. He followed a narrow footpath, turned down another, retraced his steps, took a wrong turning, and found himself surrounded by greenery. Some heaps were so high that the people doing their business there seemed to be moving about between walls made of bundles and boxes, above which could be seen a procession of heads, the fleeting white or black of hats and bonnets, while the huge panniers on their backs, bobbing above the greenery, looked like little wicker boats floating on a stagnant, mossy lake. Florent kept bumping against hundreds of obstacles—porters taking up their loads, saleswomen arguing in loud voices. He slipped on the thick bed of stumps and peelings that covered the footpath and was almost suffocated by the smell. At last he halted, in a sort of confused stupor, and surrendered to the pushing and insults of the crowd; he was nothing but a piece of flotsam tossed about by the incoming tide.

He was almost past caring. He could easily have resorted to begging. He was maddened by the stupid pride he had shown the night before.

If he had accepted the charity of Madame François, if he had not been so idiotically afraid of Claude, he would not now be stranded there, at almost his last gasp among all these cabbages. He was especially angry with himself for not having asked the artist about the Rue Pirouette. Now he was alone; he might simply die there in the street like a stray dog.

He looked up one last time at Les Halles. They were blazing in the sunlight. A broad ray was shining through the covered avenue at the far end, cleaving the various markets with a portico of light, while fiery beams rained down on the roofs. The huge iron structure seemed blue and formed a dark silhouette against the background of the rising sun. High above, a pane of glass caught the fire, drops of light trickled down the broad sloping zinc sheets to the guttering. Now it had become a tumultuous city in a cloud of dancing golden dust. This great awakening had spread from the snoring of the market people, asleep beneath their greatcoats, to the louder rumbling of the food-laden drays. The whole town was opening its iron gates, the footpaths were buzzing, the markets were roaring with activity. Cries and shouts of all kinds rent the air; it was as though the phrase Florent had heard gathering force in the darkness since four o'clock had now attained its full volume. To right and left, on all sides, the yelping that accompanied the buying and selling sounded shrilly like flutes amid the deep bass tones of the crowd; and everywhere it was the same, in the fish market, in the butter and cheese market, in the poultry market, in the meat market. A pealing of bells could suddenly be heard, adding another sound to the buzz of the markets. All around him, the sun was setting the vegetables on fire. He could no longer see any of the soft watercolour tints that had predominated in the pale light of dawn. The swelling hearts of the lettuces were ablaze, the various shades of green burst wonderfully into life, the carrots glowed blood-red, the turnips became incandescent in the triumphant radiance of the sun. To the left, fresh cartloads of cabbages were being discharged. He turned and saw in the distance drays clattering their way out of the Rue Turbigo. The tide was still rising. He had felt it round his ankles, then on a level with his stomach, and now it threatened to drown him altogether. Blinded, submerged, his ears ringing, his stomach crushed by everything he had seen, feeling the presence of new, endless quantities of food, he prayed for mercy; and he began to despair completely at the thought of dying of starvation in the heart of this city glutted with food, amid this dazzling awakening of Les Halles. Big hot tears started to roll down his cheeks.

By now he had reached one of the bigger avenues. Two women, one small and old, the other tall and thin, passed quite close to him, talking as they made their way to the markets.

'So you've come to stock up, Mademoiselle Saget?' asked the tall, thin woman.

'Yes, Madame Lecœur, if you can call it that... I live on my own, you know, and I live on next to nothing... I just wanted a little cauliflower, but everything is so dear... How much is butter today?'

'Thirty-four sous. I managed to get some good butter. If you want to call in...'

'Yes, but I don't know if I want any today. I've still got some lard left.'

Making a supreme effort, Florent followed the two women. He remembered hearing Claude mention the older one's name in the Rue Pirouette; and he made up his mind to talk to her when she parted company with her friend.

'How's your niece?' asked Mademoiselle Saget.

'Oh, La Sarriette does as she likes,' Madame Lecœur replied rather sourly. 'She's decided to set up on her own. That's her affair. When her men-friends have cleaned her out, she needn't come to me for help.'

'And you were so good to her! She ought to earn some money for herself. Fruit is doing very well this year. And your brother-in-law, how's he?'

'Oh, him!'

Madame Lecœur bit her lips and seemed to want to leave it at that.

'The same as ever, I suppose?' continued Mademoiselle Saget. 'He's decent enough. But I heard that he spends his money so fast that...'

'How can people know how he spends his money?' interrupted Madame Lecœur sharply. 'He's very secretive, and an absolute miser! I'm sure he'd let me starve rather than lend me five francs! He knows very well that butter, as well as eggs and cheese, haven't done at all well this season, whereas he can sell as much poultry as he wants... But not once has he offered to help me. I'd be too proud to accept, of course; still, it would have been nice if he had offered.'

'There he is!' suddenly exclaimed Mademoiselle Saget, lowering her voice.

The two women turned and gazed at a man who was crossing the road to enter the big covered avenue.

'I'm in a hurry,' muttered Madame Lecœur. 'I left my stall unattended. Besides, I don't want to talk to him.'

Florent too had automatically turned round. Madame Lecœur's brother-in-law was a short, stocky man, with a cheery look and grey, crew-cut hair. Under each arm he was carrying a fat goose, whose heads hung down and knocked against his legs. And then, all at once, Florent threw up his hands in joy. Forgetting how tired he was, he ran after the man and, catching up, tapped him on the shoulder.

'Gavard!' he cried.

The man looked up and stared in surprise at the tall black figure in front of him. At first he did not recognize Florent. Then, overcome with amazement, he exclaimed:

'You! Is it you? Is it really you?'

He nearly dropped his geese, and seemed very excited. On catching sight, however, of his sister-in-law and Mademoiselle Saget watching from a distance, he walked on again.

'Let's not stop here,' he said. 'There are too many eyes and tongues about.'

When they were in the covered avenue they began to talk. Florent described how he had been in the Rue Pirouettte, at which Gavard seemed most amused; he laughed heartily and told Florent that his brother Quenu had moved and had reopened his *charcuterie* just a few metres away, in the Rue Rambuteau, opposite Les Halles. He was again highly amused to hear that Florent had been wandering about all morning with Claude Lantier, the oddest creature, who, as it happened, was Madame Quenu's nephew. He was on the point of taking Florent straight to the *charcuterie*, but, learning that he had returned to France with false papers, he assumed all sorts of grave and mysterious airs, and insisted on walking five paces in front of him, to avoid attracting attention. After passing through the poultry market, where he hung his geese up behind his stall, he began to cross the Rue Rambuteau, followed by Florent. There, standing in the middle of the road, he glanced meaningfully in the direction of a large, well-appointed *charcuterie*.

The sun was beginning to thread its way into the Rue Rambuteau, lighting up the fronts of the houses, in the midst of which the end of the Rue Pirouette formed a dark gap. At the other end the great mass of Saint-Eustache glittered brightly in the sunlight like some huge shrine. And right through the crowd, from the distant intersection, an army of road-sweepers was advancing in single file, their brooms swishing rhythmically, while dustmen with forks pitched the refuse into carts, which at every twenty paces or so halted with a noise like breaking crockery. But Florent's eyes were fixed on the *charcuterie*, open now and radiant in the light of the rising sun.

It was almost on the corner of the Rue Pirouette and was a joy to behold. It was bright and inviting, with touches of brilliant colour standing out amidst white marble. The signboard, on which the name QUENU-GRADELLE glittered in fat gilt letters encircled by leaves and branches painted on a soft-hued background, was protected by a sheet of glass. On the two side panels of the shop front, similarly painted and under glass, were chubby little Cupids playing in the midst of boars' heads, pork chops, and strings of sausages; and these still lifes,* adorned with scrolls and rosettes, had been designed in so pretty and tender a style that the raw meat lying there assumed the reddish tint of raspberry jam. Within this delightful frame, the window display was arranged. It was set out on a bed of fine shavings of blue paper; a few cleverly positioned fern leaves transformed some of the plates into bouquets of flowers fringed with foliage. There were vast quantities of rich, succulent things, things that melted in the mouth. Down below, quite close to the window, jars of *rillettes** were interspersed with pots of mustard. Above these were some boned hams, nicely rounded, golden with breadcrumbs, and adorned at the knuckles with green rosettes. Then came the larger dishes—stuffed Strasbourg tongues, with their red, varnished look, the colour of blood next to the pallor of the sausages and pigs' trotters; strings of black pudding coiled like harmless snakes; *andouilles** piled up in twos and bursting with health; *saucissons* in little silver copes that made them look like choristers; pies, hot from the oven, with little banner-like tickets stuck in them; big hams, and great cuts of veal and pork, whose jelly was as limpid as crystallized sugar. Towards the back were large tureens in which the meats and minces lay asleep in lakes of solidified fat. Strewn between the various plates and dishes, on the bed of blue shavings, were bottles of relish, sauce, and preserved truffles, pots of *foie gras*, and tins of sardines and tuna fish. A box of creamy cheeses and one full of snails stuffed with butter and parsley had been dropped in each corner. Finally, at the very top of the display, falling from a bar with sharp prongs, strings of sausages and saveloys hung down symmetrically like the cords and tassels of some opulent tapestry, while behind, threads of caul were stretched out like white lacework. There, on the highest tier of this temple of gluttony, amid the caul and between two bunches of purple gladioli, the altar display was crowned by a small, square fish tank with a little ornamental rockery, in which two goldfish swam in endless circles.

Florent felt a shiver of excitement run down his spine. Then he noticed a woman standing in the sun at the door of the shop. She added another note of well-being, with her air of contentment and prosperity in the midst of all these inviting things. A handsome woman, she filled the whole doorway. Though not fat, she was full in the bust with the maturity of her thirty years. She had only just got up, yet her glossy hair was already brushed smooth and arranged in little flat bands over her temples, giving her a very neat appearance. She had the fine skin and pinky-white complexion of those who spend their lives surrounded by fat and raw meat. She looked quite serious, very placid and slow, smiling with her eyes while her lips never moved. A starched linen collar encircled her neck, the white sleevelets reaching as far as her elbows, the white apron concealing the tips of her shoes, allowing only glimpses of her black cashmere dress, which clung tightly to her well-rounded shoulders and swelling bosom. The sunlight streamed over her white skin and apron. But though bathed in light, her hair bluish-black, her skin pink, her sleeves and apron blinding, she never once blinked, but enjoyed her morning bath of sunshine in blissful tranquillity, her soft eyes smiling at the teeming life of Les Halles. She looked extremely respectable.

'That's your brother's wife, your sister-in-law Lisa,' Gavard said.

He had greeted her with a slight nod. Then he darted into the alley at the side, continuing to take the most elaborate precautions, unwilling to let Florent enter through the shop, though there was no one there. He was clearly very pleased to have embarked on what he considered a dangerous adventure.

'Wait here,' he said. 'I'll go and make sure your brother is alone. Come in when I clap my hands.'

He pushed open a door at the end of the alley. But as soon as Florent heard his brother's voice, he sprang inside. Quenu, who was very attached to Florent, threw his arms round him. They embraced like children.

'God! Is it really you?' stammered the pork-butcher. 'I thought I'd never see you again. I was sure you were dead! I was saying to Lisa only yesterday, "Poor Florent!"'

He stopped short and, popping his head into the shop, called out, 'Lisa! Lisa!'

Then, turning to a little girl who had crept into a corner, he added: 'Pauline, go and fetch your mother.'

The little girl did not move. She was a lovely creature of five, with a round, chubby face very much like her mother's. She was nursing in her arms a big ginger cat, which had cheerfully surrendered to her embrace, its legs dangling; she squeezed it with her little arms, as if afraid that the shabby-looking man might steal it.

Slowly but surely Lisa made her appearance.

'It's Florent! It's my brother!' announced Quenu.

Lisa addressed him as 'Monsieur' and gave him a kindly welcome. She inspected him calmly from head to foot without seeming to be taken aback in any way. A faint pout, however, appeared for a moment on her lips. She simply stood there, finally bringing herself to smile at her husband's show of affection. Quenu began to calm down, and noticed Florent's emaciated, poverty-stricken appearance.

'You poor thing!' he exclaimed. 'Your stay away hasn't improved your looks. I've grown fat, but so what!'

He had indeed grown fat, too fat for his age. He was bursting out of his shirt and apron, out of the white linen in which he was swaddled like a huge baby. His clean-shaven face had grown longer, so that it now bore a faint resemblance to the snout of a pig, to one of the cuts of pork he handled every day. Florent could hardly recognize him. He had now sat down and was looking first at his brother, then at the beautiful Lisa, then at little Pauline. They were all bursting with health, solidly built, sleek, in prime condition; they looked at him with the surprise of fat people gripped by a vague feeling of unease at the sight of someone who is thin. Even the cat, whose skin was distended by fat, turned its round yellow eyes towards him in a glare of distrust.

'You'll stay and have something to eat, won't you?' asked Quenu. 'We eat early, at ten o'clock.'

A strong smell of cooking hung in the air. Florent thought back on the terrible night he had just spent, his arrival on a bed of vegetables, his agony in Les Halles, and the avalanches of food from which he had just escaped. Then, with a gentle smile, he murmured:

'Yes. I'm so hungry.'

CHAPTER 2

FLORENT had just begun his law studies in Paris when his mother died. She lived in Le Vigan, in Le Gard,* and had taken for her second husband a Norman called Quenu, who came originally from Yvetot* and had been transplanted to the Midi by a *sous-préfet* and then forgotten. He had stayed on at the *sous-préfecture*, for he found that part of the country delightful, the wine good, and the women very friendly. But three years after his marriage he had been carried off by a bad attack of indigestion, leaving as sole legacy to his wife a bouncing boy who looked exactly like him. The widow was already finding it very difficult to pay the school fees of her elder son, Florent, the product of her first marriage. He was a very gentle boy, devoted to his studies, and always won the top prizes at school. He met all his mother's expectations. It was on him that she lavished all her affection and based all her hopes. Perhaps, in bestowing so much love on this pale, slim youth, she was showing her preference for her first husband, an affectionate, tender-hearted Provençal, who had been totally devoted to her. Quenu, whose even temperament and good humour had at first attracted her, had perhaps become too fat and too smug, and shown too plainly that his main object of affection was himself. At all events she formed the view that her younger son—the one often sacrificed even to this day in southern families—would never make good, and she was content to send him to a school run by a neighbour, an old spinster, where all the lad learned was how to play the fool. The two brothers grew up like strangers, quite separate from each other.

When Florent arrived in Le Vigan, his mother was already buried. She had been determined to hide her illness from him until the very last moment, so as not to disrupt his studies. He found little Quenu, who was then twelve, sitting on a table in the middle of the kitchen, sobbing. A furniture dealer who lived next door told him of his mother's last hours. She had reached the end of her tether, she had killed herself with work to enable him to continue his law studies. To her modest trade in ribbons, which earned her very little, she had been obliged to add other occupations, which kept her up late into the night. Her determination to see Florent established in the town with a good position as a solicitor had made her hard, mean, and pitiless, no less with herself than with others. Little Quenu walked about with holes in his trousers and in shirts that were falling apart. He never dared to help himself at table, but waited for his mother to cut him his ration of bread. Her own she cut just as thin, and it was to the effects of this regimen that she had succumbed, in despair at having failed to accomplish her task.

This story made a deep impression on Florent. He choked back his tears, took his little stepbrother in his arms, and held him tight, kissing him as if trying to give back to him the love of which he had unwittingly deprived him. He looked at the lad's battered shoes, torn sleeves, and dirty hands, at all the signs of poverty and neglect. He repeated over and over that he would take him away and that they would live happily together. The next day, when he began to look into his mother's affairs, he began to fear that he would not even be able to muster enough money to pay for his trip back to Paris. However, he was determined to leave Le Vigan at any cost. He managed to sell the little ribbon business for quite a good price, which allowed him to pay off the money his mother owed, for despite her discipline in money matters she had run up more and more bills. Then, as there was nothing left, his mother's neighbour, the furniture dealer, offered him five hundred francs for her chattels and stock of linen. It was a good bargain for the dealer, but Florent thanked him with tears in his eyes. He fitted his brother out in a new set of clothes and took him away that same evening.

On his return to Paris he gave up all thought of continuing his studies and suspended all ambition. He arranged to give some private lessons and found a place for himself and little Quenu in the Rue Royer-Collard, at the corner of the Rue Saint-Jacques. It was just a big room, which he furnished with two iron bedsteads, a wardrobe, a table, and four chairs. Now he had a child to look after, and he greatly enjoyed this paternal role. To begin with, when he came home in the evening, he tried to give the lad some lessons, but Quenu was an unwilling pupil. He refused to learn, saying tearfully how much he missed the time when his mother had let him run wild in the streets. Florent stopped the lessons in despair, and to console the lad promised him a complete holiday. As an excuse for his weakness, he told himself that he had not brought his brother to Paris to make him unhappy. To see him grow up happy and contented became his chief desire.

He worshipped the boy, liked nothing better than to hear his merry laughter, and felt infinite joy in seeing him, carefree and healthy, by his side. Florent remained slim and lean in his shabby black coat, and his face began to turn sallow amidst all the drudgery of teaching. Quenu grew into a chubby little fellow, rather stupid, barely able to read or write, but with an unshakably even temperament, which filled the big, gloomy room in the Rue Royer-Collard with gaiety.

Several years went by. Florent, who had inherited his mother's spirit of devotion, kept Quenu at home as if he were a lazy grown-up daughter. He even spared him the most trifling duties about the house; he did all the shopping, cooking, and cleaning himself. This kept his mind off things, he said. He was given to gloominess, convinced of his own evil nature. When he returned home in the evening, spattered with mud, wearied by the trouble other people's children gave him, he was deeply touched by the embraces of the tall, sturdy lad he found spinning his top on the tiled floor of their room. Quenu laughed at his brother's clumsiness in making omelettes and at the serious expression he wore when putting stew on the fire. But once the light was out, Florent sometimes grew sad again as he lay in bed. He dreamed of resuming his studies and strove to organize his time in such a way as to be able to attend the Faculty lectures. He succeeded in doing this and, for a while, was perfectly happy. But a high temperature, which kept him in bed for a week, made such a hole in his purse and gave him such a shock that he abandoned all hope of completing his studies. The boy was now becoming quite big, and Florent took a position in a boarding school in the Rue de l'Estrapade at a salary of eighteen hundred francs a year. To him this seemed a fortune. If he saved enough money he would be able to give Quenu a start in the world. When the lad reached his eighteenth birthday, Florent still treated him as if he were a daughter for whom a dowry would have to be provided.

During his brother's brief illness, Quenu himself had been thinking about things. One morning he announced that he wanted to have a job, saying that he was now old enough to earn his own living. Florent was very touched. Just opposite, on the other side of the street, lived a watchmaker whom Quenu, through the curtainless window, could see bending over a little table, working on all sorts of delicate objects, and patiently looking at them through a magnifying glass all day long. The lad was much attracted by what he saw, and declared that

The Belly of Paris

he wanted to be a watchmaker. But after a fortnight, he became anxious and upset about it; he cried like a ten-year-old, saying that the work was much too difficult and that he would never be able to learn 'all the funny little things that go into a watch'. His next whim was to be a locksmith; but this calling he found too tiring. In a period of two years he tried more than ten different trades. Florent said he was right, that it was wrong to take up a trade one did not like. However, Quenu's difficulty in finding a trade put a serious strain on the household budget. Since he had begun flitting from one workshop to another, money had gone on new clothes, meals out, and drinks with fellow workers. Florent's eighteen hundred francs were no longer enough. He was obliged to take a couple of private pupils in the evenings. For the last eight years he had worn the same old coat.

However, the two brothers had made a friend. One side of the house in which they lived overlooked the Rue Saint-Jacques, where there was a large *rôtisserie* kept by a man called Gavard, whose wife was dying of consumption brought on by the greasy smell of poultry. When Florent came home too late to cook a piece of meat, he was in the habit of calling in at the *rôtisserie* to buy, for a dozen sous or so, a small portion of turkey or goose; these were the days of absolute feasting. After a while, Gavard grew interested in his tall, scraggy customer, learned something of his background, and coaxed Quenu down into his shop. Before long the young fellow was always there. As soon as his brother left the house, he went downstairs and installed himself at the back of the shop, enraptured with the four huge spits that turned gently round and round before the high, bright flames.

The broad copper bands of the fireplace shone brightly, the poultry steamed, the fat bubbled melodiously in the dripping-pan, and the spits seemed to talk to each other and to address kindly words to Quenu, who, with a ladle, devoutly basted the golden breasts of the fat geese and turkeys. He would stay there for hours, crimson in the dancing glow of the fire, a trifle dazed, laughing at the birds roasting before his eyes. He only woke up when the geese and turkeys were unspitted. They slid smoothly onto dishes, the spits were drawn from their carcasses smoking hot, rich gravy flowed from their bellies and from the parson's nose, filling the shop with the strong smell of roasted meat. The lad would stand there and watch the whole operation, clapping his hands, talking to the birds, telling them they were very delicious and would soon be on someone's table, and that the cats would only get their bones. He would gasp with delight whenever Gavard handed him a slice of bread, which he would put in the basting-pan so that it would soak and toast there for half an hour.

It was in Gavard's shop that Quenu's love of cookery was born. Later on, when he had tried every other trade, he returned, as if guided by fate, to the spits, the poultry, and the finger-licking gravy. At first he was afraid of annoying his brother, who was a small eater and spoke of good fare with the disdain of those who are ignorant of it; but later, seeing that Florent listened to him when he explained the preparation of some elaborate dish, he confessed his love of cookery and soon found a job in a big restaurant. From then on the two brothers' lives ran to a pattern. They continued to live in the room in the Rue Royer-Collard, to which they returned every evening, the one glowing and radiant from his hot fire, the other with the haggard look of a shabby, penniless teacher. Florent still wore his old black coat, as he sat correcting his pupils' exercises; while Quenu, to feel more at ease, donned his apron, his white jacket, and tall white hat, and moved around the stove preparing some dainty titbit in the oven. Sometimes they smiled to see themselves like that, the one all in black, the other all in white. The big room seemed half gloomy, half happy, divided between mourning and gaiety. Never, however, was there so much harmony in a household marked by such contrasts. The elder brother grew thinner and thinner, consumed by the same inner fires as his father, while the younger one grew fatter and fatter, like a true son of Normandy; and they loved each other in the brotherhood they derived from their mother—a woman of infinite devotion.

They had one relation in Paris, a brother of their mother's named Gradelle, who had a *charcuterie* in the Rue Pirouette, near the markets. He was a fat, insensitive, miserly fellow, and received his nephews as though they were paupers the first time they paid him a visit. They seldom went to see him after that. On his name day Quenu would take him a bunch of flowers and received ten sous in return. Florent, who was extremely proud, was very hurt when Gradelle eyed his shabby clothes with the suspicious look of a miser anticipating a request for a meal or the loan of a hundred sous. One day, however, Florent happened, in all artlessness, to ask his uncle if he would change a hundred-franc note for him; after this the pork-butcher was more welcoming towards the young lads, as he called them. But their dealings with each other went no further than these occasional visits.

For Florent, these years were like a long, sad dream. He tasted to the full the bitter joys of self-sacrifice. At home, life was all love and harmony; but out in the world, amid the jostling of the streets and the humiliations he suffered at the hands of his pupils, he began to have dark thoughts. His frustrated ambition embittered him. It was a long time before he could bring himself to accept his painful lot as a poor, plain, unsuccessful man. At last, wishing to avoid becoming mean-spirited, he espoused an ideal of pure virtue and sought refuge in a world of absolute truth and justice. It was then that he became a republican, entering the realm of republican ideals as girls with broken hearts enter a convent; and unable to find a republic where sufficient peace and kindness prevailed to soothe his troubled mind, he created one of his own. Books gave him no pleasure. All the scribblings amid which he lived spoke of foul-smelling classrooms, paper pellets chewed by schoolboys, and hours of drudgery. Besides, books only suggested to him a spirit of protest and rebellion, and encouraged feelings of pride, whereas it was of peace and oblivion that he felt most in need. He now spent all his leisure hours consoling himself with dreams of the ideal, imagining that he was perfectly happy and that all the world would become so too, constructing over and over again in his mind the republican society in which he would like to have lived. He no longer read any books other than those which his teaching duties obliged him to consult. Instead he would tramp along the Rue Saint-Jacques as far as the outer boulevards, occasionally going even further and returning by the Barrière d'Italie; and all along the road, gazing down at the Quartier Mouffetard spread out at his feet,* he would dream of the great moral and humanitarian reforms which would change the city from a place of suffering to a place of bliss. During the bloody upheaval of February 1848 he was very disturbed, and rushed from one club to the next demanding atonement for the blood that had been shed through 'the fraternal embrace of all republicans throughout the world'. He became one of those passionate orators who preached revolution as a new religion, built on the principles of humility and redemption.* It was not until the terrible days of December 1851, the days of the *coup d'état*, that he was weaned away from his doctrine of universal love. He let himself be taken like a lamb and treated as a wolf. He awoke from his sermons on universal brotherhood to find himself starving on the cold stone floor of a dungeon at Bicêtre.

Quenu, who was then twenty-two, was beside himself with anxiety when his brother failed to return home. The next day he went to look for his corpse in the cemetery at Montmartre, where the bodies of those shot down on the boulevards had been laid out in lines and covered with straw, from which only their ghastly heads protruded. But Quenu's courage failed him, he was blinded by tears, and had to walk twice along the lines of corpses before being certain that Florent's was not among them. At last, at the end of a terrible week, he learned at the Préfecture that his brother had been arrested. He was not allowed to see him, and when he insisted the police threatened to arrest him too. Then he ran off to his uncle Gradelle, whom he looked up to, hoping that he might be able to intervene on Florent's behalf. But Gradelle became angry, declaring that it served him right, that he ought to have known better than to have got mixed up with those awful republicans. He even added that Florent had been bound to come to a bad end, you could tell from his face. Quenu wept his heart out. His uncle, rather ashamed of himself, felt he ought to do something for the poor boy, and offered to take him in. He wanted an assistant and he knew that his nephew was a good cook. Quenu so dreaded the prospect of going back to live on his own in the room in the Rue Royer-Collard that he accepted Gradelle's offer on the spot. That night he slept in his uncle's house, in a windowless garret under the roof, where there was hardly enough room for him to lie at full length. But he was less miserable there than he would have been staring at his brother's empty bed.

After a while he succeeded in obtaining permission to see Florent. But on his return from Bicêtre, he was forced to take to his bed. For nearly three weeks he lay fever-stricken, in a stupefied, comatose state. It was his first and only illness. Gradelle kept saying that his republican nephew could go to the devil; and one morning, when he heard of Florent's departure for Cayenne, he went upstairs, woke Quenu up, and bluntly told him the news, thus provoking such a crisis in the fever that the next day the young man was up and about again. His grief wore itself out, and his soft flesh seemed to soak up his last tears. A month later he caught himself laughing, and immediately felt sad and annoyed with himself; but his natural good humour soon reasserted itself, and he began to laugh without realizing it.

He became familiar with his uncle's business, and found it even more pleasurable than cooking. Gradelle told him, however, that he should not neglect his pots and pans, because it was rare to find a *charcutier* who was also a good cook, and he had been lucky to have worked in a restaurant before coming to the shop. Gradelle made full use of his nephew's talents, asking him to cook the dinners sent out to customers, and put him in charge of all the grilling and the preparation of pork chops with gherkins. As the young man was so useful to him, he grew fond of him after his fashion and would pinch his arms when he was in a good mood. Gradelle had sold the few pieces of furniture in the Rue Royer-Collard and kept the money—forty francs or so—so that his gadabout nephew, as he said, wouldn't throw it out of the window. After a while, however, he gave him an allowance of six francs a month as pocket money.

Quenu was perfectly happy, in spite of his near-empty purse and the rough way he was sometimes treated. He accepted everything; Florent had brought him up too much like a lazy girl. Moreover, he had made a friend at his uncle's. When Gradelle lost his wife, he had been obliged to take on a girl to serve in the shop, and had taken care to choose a healthy and attractive creature, knowing that a good-looking girl would set off his display of cooked meats and help to tempt his customers. He knew a widow in the Rue Censier, near the Jardin des Plantes, whose late husband had been postmaster at Plassans,* a *sous-préfecture* in the Midi. This lady, who lived very modestly on a small annuity, had brought with her from Plassans a plump, pretty girl, whom she treated as her own daughter. Lisa, as the girl was called, was placid and somewhat serious in manner. She looked quite beautiful, however, when she smiled. Indeed, her great charm came from the delightful way in which she revealed her elusive smile. Her expression then became a caress, and her usual gravity made these sudden, seductive flashes quite priceless. The old lady often said that one day Lisa's smile would be her downfall. When an attack of asthma carried her off, she left all her savings, amounting to about ten thousand francs, to her adopted daughter. For a week Lisa lived alone in the Rue Cuvier, and it was there that Gradelle came to see her. He knew her from having often seen her with her mistress when the old lady had come to his shop in the Rue Pirouette; and at the funeral she had struck him as having grown so lovely, so handsomely built, that he had followed the hearse all the way to the cemetery. As the coffin was being lowered into the grave, he thought what a splendid sight she would be behind the counter of the *charcuterie*. He thought it over and resolved to offer her thirty francs a month, with board and lodging. When he put the offer to her, she asked for twenty-four hours to consider it. Then one morning she arrived with a little bundle of clothes and her ten thousand francs tucked in the bosom of her dress. A month later the whole house seemed to belong to her; Gradelle, Quenu, even the youngest kitchen boy, fell under her spell. Quenu would have cut off his fingers to please her. When she happened to smile, he stood rooted to the spot, laughing with delight as he gazed at her.

Lisa was the eldest daughter of the Macquarts of Plassans, and her father was still alive.* But she said that he was abroad and never wrote to him. Sometimes she mentioned in passing that her mother, who was dead, had been a hard worker and that she took after her. She worked, indeed, very hard. She sometimes added, however, that her mother had worked herself into the grave in her efforts to support her family. Then she would speak of the respective duties of husband and wife in such serious and practical terms that Quenu was enchanted. He assured her that he agreed entirely with her views. These were that everyone, man or woman, ought to work for his or her living, that everyone was responsible for his or her own happiness, that it was wicked to encourage idleness, and that if there was so much unhappiness in the world it was mainly due to sloth. These notions of hers were a sharp indictment of the legendary drinking and idleness of her father, old Macquart. But she took after her father more than she realized. She was a steady, sensible Macquart, reasonable and logical in her craving for well-being, having understood the truth of the proverb that as you make your bed so you lie in it. Prosperity and security were her great goals. Even at the age of six she had promised to stay still on her little chair all day long on condition that she would be rewarded with a cake in the evening.

In Gradelle's shop Lisa went on leading her calm, well-regulated life, illuminated by her occasional exquisite smiles. She had not accepted his offer without giving it careful thought. She reckoned on finding a benefactor in him; with the sure instinct of those who are born lucky, she foresaw perhaps that the gloomy shop in the Rue Pirouette would bring her the comfortable future she dreamed of—a life of healthy enjoyment and untiring work, each hour of which would bring its own reward. She attended to her counter with the quiet earnestness with which she had waited upon the postmaster's widow. The cleanliness of her aprons soon became proverbial in the neighbourhood.

Uncle Gradelle was so impressed with this pretty girl that sometimes, as he was stringing his sausages, he would say to Quenu:

'You know, if I wasn't sixty, I think I might take it into my head to marry her. A wife like that is worth her weight in gold to a shopkeeper, my lad.'

Quenu was growing very fond of her, though he laughed heartily one day when a neighbour accused him of being in love with Lisa. He was not in love, though they were certainly very good friends. Every evening they went up to their bedrooms together. Lisa slept in a little room next to Quenu's garret. She had made this room quite bright by hanging it with muslin curtains. The pair would stand together for a moment on the landing, holding their candles and chatting as they unlocked their doors. Then, as they closed them, they murmured in friendly tones:

'Goodnight, Mademoiselle Lisa.'

'Goodnight, Monsieur Quenu.'

As Quenu undressed he listened to Lisa making her own preparations for bed. The partition between the two rooms was so thin that he could follow every movement she made. 'She's drawing the curtains now,' he would say to himself. 'What can she be doing, I wonder, in front of her dressing table? Ah! She's sitting down now and taking off her boots. Now she's blown her candle out. Well, goodnight. Let's get to sleep.' At times, when he heard the bed creak as she got into it, he would say to himself with a smile, 'Well, Mademoiselle Lisa isn't exactly as light as a feather.' This idea seemed to amuse him, and after a while he would fall asleep, dreaming of the hams and *petit salé** he had to prepare the next morning.

This went on for a year without causing Lisa a single blush or Quenu a moment's embarrassment. When she came into the kitchen in the morning at the busiest time of day, their hands met over the sausage meat. Sometimes she helped him, holding the sausage skins with her plump fingers while he filled them with meat and *lardons.** Sometimes, too, they tasted the raw meat with the tips of their tongues, to see if it was properly seasoned. She gave excellent advice, for she knew some southern recipes with which he made some successful experiments. He often sensed her at his shoulder, looking into the pans, occasionally so close that he could feel her rounded breasts touching him. If he wanted a spoon or a dish, she would hand it to him. The heat of the fire would make their faces glow; but for nothing in

the world would he have stopped stirring the fatty *bouillies*** that thickened on the stove while she stood gravely by, discussing the amount
of boiling required. In the afternoons, when the shop was empty,
they chatted away for hours. Lisa sat behind the counter, leaning
back, knitting in a relaxed, rhythmical fashion, while Quenu sat on a
big oak chopping block, his legs dangling, tapping his heels against
the wood. The understanding between them was marvellous; they
talked about everything, but mainly cookery, and also Uncle Gradelle
and the neighbours. She told him stories as if he were a child. She knew
some very nice ones—fairy tales full of lambs and little angels, which
she told in a piping voice and wearing her most serious expression. If a
customer happened to come in, she saved herself the trouble of moving
by asking Quenu to pass her the required jar of lard or box of snails.
At eleven o'clock they went slowly up to bed as they had the previous
night. As they closed their doors, they calmly repeated the words:
   'Goodnight, Mademoiselle Lisa.'
   'Goodnight, Monsieur Quenu.'
   Suddenly one morning Uncle Gradelle was struck down by a stroke
while preparing a *galantine*.* He fell face down on the mincing table.
Lisa did not bat an eyelid. She said that the dead man should not be
left lying in the middle of the kitchen, and had the body carried into
a little back room where Gradelle used to sleep. Then, with the
kitchen boys, she worked out a story. It must be given out that the
master had died in his bed; otherwise the neighbourhood would be
disgusted and the shop would lose customers. Quenu helped to carry
the body, feeling quite confused, and surprised at being unable to shed
any tears. Later, however, he and Lisa wept together. Apart from his
brother Florent, he was the sole heir. All the old gossips in the neighbourhood believed that Gradelle had a sizeable fortune. However,
not a single piece of silver could be found anywhere. Lisa became
very restless. Quenu noticed how pensive she was, gazing around
from morning to night as though she had lost something. In the end
she decided that the shop needed a good clean, saying that people
were beginning to talk, that the story of how the old man had died
was beginning to get around and it was therefore essential to make a
great show of cleanliness. One afternoon, after she had been in the
cellar for about two hours washing the salting tubs, she came up carrying something in her apron. Quenu was mincing pig's livers. She
waited until he had finished, chatting quite casually. But there was an

unusual gleam in her eyes, and she smiled her most charming smile as she told him that she would like to have a word with him. She led the way upstairs, but not without some difficulty, for she was weighed down by what she was carrying in her apron, which was straining almost to bursting. By the time she reached the third floor she was quite out of breath and had to lean against the banisters for a moment. Quenu, intrigued, followed her into her bedroom without a word. It was the first time she had asked him in. She closed the door and let go of the corners of her apron. A stream of gold and silver coins rained gently down on the bed. She had discovered Uncle Gradelle's fortune at the bottom of a salting tub. The pile of money made a deep hollow in her soft downy bed.

Lisa and Quenu were quietly delighted. They sat on the edge of the bed, Lisa at the head and Quenu at the foot, on either side of the pile of coins, and they counted out the money on the bedspread to avoid making any noise. There were forty thousand francs in gold and three thousand francs in silver, while in a tin they found forty-two thousand francs in banknotes. It took them two hours to count it all. Quenu's hands trembled slightly, and it was Lisa who did most of the work. They stacked the gold coins on the pillow, leaving the silver in the hollow of the bedspread. When they had worked out the total amount—eighty-five thousand francs, which to them seemed a fabulous sum—they began to talk. They talked, naturally enough, about the future, and they spoke of marriage, though there had never been any mention of love between them. But the pile of money seemed to loosen their tongues. They had gradually sat further back on the bed, leaning against the wall, beneath the white muslin curtains; and as they talked, their hands, playing with the silver coins between them, met and held each other amidst the pile of five-franc pieces. They were still sitting there as dusk began to fall. Then, for the first time, Lisa blushed at finding the young man by her side. The bed had become very untidy, with the sheets hanging loosely; and the gold had made hollows on the pillow, as if their heads had rolled and twisted there while they were in the throes of passion.

They stood up, embarrassed, like two people who have made love for the first time. The untidy bed, and all that money, seemed to proclaim some illicit pleasure. It was as if they had fallen into temptation. Lisa, straightening her dress as if she had committed a sin, went to get her own ten thousand francs. Quenu wanted her to add them to his uncle's eighty-five thousand, saying with a laugh that the money must be married too. They agreed that Lisa would keep the 'loot' in her dressing table. She locked the drawers and made the bed, and they went quietly downstairs. They were now husband and wife.

They were married the following month. The neighbours regarded the match as very natural and appropriate. A vague rumour about the money had got around, and Lisa's honesty attracted endless praise. After all, said the gossips, she could have kept it all for herself and not said a word to Quenu; if she had told him about it, it was out of pure honesty, for no one had seen her find it. She certainly deserved to be married to Quenu, though he was really the lucky one, for he was far from good-looking and he had now acquired a handsome wife who had unearthed a fortune for him. Some even went so far as to whisper that Lisa had been very foolish to act as she had; but she just smiled when people vaguely suggested this. She and her husband carried on living as before, as the best of friends and in perfect harmony. She still helped him in the shop, their hands still met over the sausage meat, she still looked over his shoulder to see what was happening in his pans, and it was still only the big fire in the kitchen that brought a flush to their cheeks.

Lisa was a woman of great common sense and quickly realized how silly it would be to let their ninety-five thousand francs lie dormant in a dressing table. Quenu would have been happy to stow them away again at the bottom of the salting tub until they had earned the same amount all over again, and could retire to Suresnes, a suburb they both liked. Lisa, however, had other plans. The Rue Pirouette offended her notions of cleanliness, her need for fresh air, light, and a healthy life. The shop in which Uncle Gradelle had slowly made his fortune was dark and poky—one of those dubious-looking *charcuteries* you see in the old parts of the city, where the worn flagstones always smell of meat in spite of being constantly washed. The young woman longed for one of those bright, modern shops, decorated like a drawing room, and looking out, with big, shining windows, onto some broad street. It was not her ambition to play the fine lady behind a stylish counter, but she had realized that a modern business needed elegant surroundings. Quenu was quite alarmed when his wife suggested that they should move house and spend some of their money on fitting out a new shop. But she just shrugged her shoulders and smiled.

One evening, when night was falling and the shop lay in deep shadow, they overheard a neighbour talking to a friend outside their door.

'Definitely not! I've stopped going there,' she said. 'I wouldn't even buy a bit of black pudding from them now. They had a dead body in their kitchen, you know.'

Quenu was very upset. The story of a corpse in his kitchen was clearly getting about; and he began to blush every time he saw his customers bending down to sniff his goods. So, of his own accord, he spoke to his wife about her idea of moving. Lisa, without saying a word about it, had already been looking around and had found a new place, very well situated, just round the corner, in the Rue Rambuteau. The new markets were opening just opposite; they would treble their custom and make their shop known throughout the city. Quenu let himself be persuaded into enormous expense; he laid out over thirty thousand francs in marble, glass, and gilding. Lisa spent hours with the workmen, giving advice on the smallest details. When at last she was installed behind the counter, customers arrived in droves just to have a good look at the shop. The facing of the inside walls was done in white marble throughout. The ceiling was covered with a huge square mirror, framed by a broad gilded cornice, richly ornamented, while from the centre hung a crystal chandelier with four branches. Behind the counter, along the entire wall, on the left, and at the back of the shop, were other mirrors, fitted between the marble panels and looking like doors opening into an infinite series of brightly lit halls where all manner of meats were on display. The huge counter, on the right, was considered a fine piece of workmanship. At intervals along the front were lozenge-shaped panels of pink marble. The floor was covered with a mosaic of pink and white tiles, with a border of deep red fretting. The whole neighbourhood was proud of the shop, and there was no further mention of anyone dying in the kitchen in the Rue Pirouette. For a whole month women stood on the footpath to look at Lisa through the strings of saveloys* and caul in the window. They marvelled as much at her white and pink complexion as at the spectacle of so much marble. She seemed to be the soul, the strong and healthy goddess of the *charcuterie*; and she was baptized 'La Belle Lisa'. To the right of the shop was the dining room, neatly arranged with a sideboard, a table, and several cane-seated chairs of light oak. The matting on the floor, the light yellow wallpaper, the oil-cloth table-cover coloured to look like oak, gave the room a rather cold appearance, which was relieved only by the glitter of a brass ceiling-lamp, spreading its big shade of transparent porcelain over the table.

One of the doors from the dining room led into the huge square kitchen, at the end of which was a small paved courtyard, which was used to store lumber—tubs, barrels, pans, and all kinds of battered utensils. To the left of the water tap pots of withered flowers removed from the shop window were slowly dying, alongside the gutter which carried away the dirty water.

Business flourished. Quenu, who had been terrified by the initial outlay, now regarded his wife with something like respect and told his friends that she 'had her head screwed on the right way'. After five years, they had nearly eighty thousand francs invested in reliable concerns. Lisa always said that they were not ambitious and had no desire to make money too fast, for otherwise she would have encouraged her husband to make thousands and thousands of francs by getting into the wholesale pig trade. They were still young and had plenty of time ahead of them; besides, they didn't want to be involved in a rough, brutal business, but preferred to work at their ease and enjoy life, instead of wearing themselves out with worry.

'For instance,' Lisa would add in her more expansive moments, 'I've got a cousin in Paris, you know. I never see him, because the two families have fallen out. He changed his name to Saccard, on account of various things he wants to be forgotten. He apparently makes millions; but he gets no enjoyment out of life. He lives on his nerves and rushes about all over the place, up to his neck in all sorts of crazy projects.* Well, it's impossible, isn't it, for a man like that to sit down and eat his dinner properly? At least we can have our meals in peace. The only reason why people should care about money is that you need it to live. People like comfort, that's natural. But as for making money just for the sake of it, and giving yourself far more bother making it than you get pleasure out of it, well, I'd rather just sit quietly at home. In any case, I'd like to see all those millions he's supposed to have. I'm not sure he's got anything. I saw him the other day in a carriage. He was quite yellow and had a very sly look on his face. A man who's making money doesn't go that colour. But that's his business. We're happy to make a hundred sous at a time and be able to enjoy them.'

The family was certainly thriving. A daughter had been born to them during their first year of marriage,* and all three of them looked blooming. The business continued to prosper, without their having to work especially hard, just as Lisa preferred. She had carefully avoided any possible source of anxiety, and the days passed in an atmosphere of calm, complacent well-being. Their home was a nook of modest happiness where the food was good and where father, mother, and daughter all grew sleek and fat. Only Quenu occasionally felt sad, when he thought of his brother Florent. From time to time he received letters from him, but in 1856 they stopped coming; he read in the newspapers that three convicts had tried to escape from Devil's Island* but had drowned before reaching the coast. At the Préfecture they could give him nothing in the way of precise information; it was likely, they said, that his brother was dead. Months passed, but he did not give up hope altogether. Florent, in the meantime, was wandering about Dutch Guiana, but did not write, in the hope that one day he would be able to return to France. Quenu at last began to mourn him as one mourns those whom one has been unable to bid farewell. Lisa had never known Florent, but she was very understanding whenever she saw her husband give in to his feelings; and she listened with infinite patience when, for the hundredth time, he told her about his youth, his life in the big room in the Rue Royer-Collard, the countless trades he had tried to learn, the titbits he had cooked on the stove, dressed all in white while Florent was dressed all in black.

It was in the midst of all this happiness, ripening after such careful nurturing, that Florent arrived one September morning just as Lisa was taking her morning sunbath, and Quenu, his eyes still heavy with sleep, was lazily fingering the solidified fat left over from the evening before. His arrival caused a great stir. Gavard advised them to hide 'the outlaw', as he rather pompously referred to Florent. Lisa, paler and more serious than usual, eventually took him up to the fifth floor, where she gave him the room that belonged to the girl who helped her in the shop. Quenu cut some bread and ham, but Florent could hardly eat. He was overcome by dizziness and spasms of nausea, and went to bed, where he stayed for five days in a state of delirium, the result of an attack of meningitis which, fortunately, he was able to overcome. When he regained consciousness, he saw Lisa sitting by his bedside, silently stirring something in a cup. He tried to thank her, but she told him he must lie there and rest and that they could talk later. Three days later Florent was on his feet again. Then one morning Quenu came up to fetch him, saying that Lisa was waiting for them in her room on the first floor.

Quenu and his wife had there a little apartment of three rooms and a dressing room. An antechamber full of chairs led into a small sitting room, whose furniture, shrouded in white covers, slumbered in the gloom cast by the shutters, which were always kept closed to prevent the light blue upholstery from fading. Then came the bedroom, the only one of the three rooms that was really used. It was very comfortably furnished in mahogany. The bed, which filled the entire alcove, was most impressive, with its four mattresses and four pillows, its layers of blankets and its thick eiderdown. It was truly a bed intended for sleep. A mirrored wardrobe, a washstand with drawers, a little table with a thick lace cloth, and several chairs whose seats were protected by squares of similar lace, gave the room an appearance of solid bourgeois luxury. On the left-hand wall, on either side of the mantelpiece, on which were some landscape-painted vases on bronze stands and a gilt clock on which a figure of Gutenberg stood in an attitude of deep thought with his hand resting on a book, hung oil portraits of Quenu and Lisa, in ornate oval frames. Quenu was smiling, while Lisa wore an expression of grave respectability; both were wearing black and were depicted rather flatteringly, their features idealized, their skins wondrously smooth, their complexions soft and pink. A moquette carpet, with an elaborate pattern of roses and stars, covered the wooden floor. In front of the bed was a fluffy rug made from long strands of curly wool, the fruit of Lisa's patient labour as she sat behind her counter. But the most striking thing amongst so much new stuff was a large writing desk, set square and squat against the wall; it had been revarnished in vain, for the cracks in the marble and the scratches in the mahogany, black with age, were still visible. Lisa had wanted to keep this piece of furniture, which Uncle Gradelle had used for more than forty years. It would bring them luck, she said. Its metal fastenings were truly awesome, its lock was like that of a prison gate, and it was so heavy that it could not be moved.

When Florent and Quenu entered the room, they found Lisa sitting by the lowered flap of the desk, setting out figures in a big, round, and very legible hand. She made a sign that she was not to be interrupted, and they sat down. Florent, somewhat embarrassed, looked round the room, and especially at the two portraits, the clock, and the bed.

'There!' Lisa exclaimed at last, having carefully checked a whole page of calculations. 'What I wanted to say is that we have some accounts to settle with you, Florent.'

It was the first time she had addressed him by name. Holding the sheet of figures in her hand, she continued:

'Your Uncle Gradelle died without leaving a will, which meant that you and your brother were his only heirs. We must give you your share.'

'But I don't want anything!' exclaimed Florent. 'Nothing at all!'

Quenu had had no idea of his wife's intentions. He turned rather pale and gave her an angry look. Of course, he loved his brother dearly; but there was no reason to throw his uncle's money at him like this. They could have talked it over later.

'I know, Florent,' continued Lisa, 'that you haven't come back to claim what is rightly yours; but business is business, you know, and it's better to settle things straight away. Your uncle's savings came to eighty-five thousand francs. So I've put down forty-two thousand five hundred to your credit. Look!'

She showed him the figures on the sheet of paper.

'It isn't so easy, unfortunately, to value the shop and the business. I've only managed to put a rough figure, but I don't think I've under-estimated anything. The total amount comes to fifteen thousand three hundred and ten francs; half of that is seven thousand six hundred and fifty-five francs, so your share comes, altogether, to fifty thousand one hundred and fifty-five francs. Would you like to check it?

She had read out the figures in a clear voice, and now she handed the sheet to Florent, which he felt bound to take.

'But the old man's shop was never worth fifteen thousand francs!' cried Quenu. 'I wouldn't have given him ten thousand for it!'

His wife was beginning to annoy him, to say the least. Really, it was absurd to take honesty that far! Had Florent said a word about the business? No, in fact he had said that he didn't want anything.

'The shop was worth fifteen thousand three hundred and ten francs,' Lisa repeated calmly. 'You see, Florent, there's no need to involve a solicitor. We can divide things up ourselves. I began to think about it as soon as you arrived; and while you were ill in bed I did my best to draw up this little inventory. It covers virtually everything, as you can see. I've been through all our books and tried to remember as much as I could. Read it out. I'll explain anything you don't understand.'

Florent began to smile. He was touched by this easy and apparently spontaneous display of honesty. Placing the sheet of figures on Lisa's lap, he took her by the hand.

'I'm very glad, Lisa, that you've done so well, but I won't take your money. The inheritance belongs to you and my brother; you looked after my uncle until he died. I don't need it, and I don't want to prevent you from carrying on as usual with your business.'

Lisa insisted, and even seemed rather annoyed, while Quenu bit his nails in silence, trying to restrain himself.

'You know,' resumed Florent with a laugh, 'if Uncle Gradelle could hear you now, I think he'd come and take his money back. He never liked me much, you know.'

'That's true,' muttered Quenu, no longer able to remain silent. 'He didn't like you much.'

Lisa, however, was undeterred. She said she did not like to have money in her desk that did not belong to her; it would worry her, and she wouldn't be able to stop thinking about it. So Florent, still making light of the matter, proposed to invest his share in the shop. In any case, he said, he did not want to refuse their help, because there was little chance that he would be able to find a job straight away, and he would need a new set of clothes too, for he was hardly presentable as he was.

'Of course,' cried Quenu, 'you'll stay here, and we'll buy you what you need. That goes without saying. You know we won't leave you in the street!'

He had become quite emotional and even felt rather ashamed at his fear of having to hand over a large amount of money all at once. He began to joke and told his brother that he would take charge of fattening him up. Florent gently shook his head, while Lisa folded the sheet of figures and put it away in one of the drawers of the desk.

'You're making a mistake,' she said in conclusion. 'I've done what I had to do. Now we'll do as you wish. But I wouldn't have had a moment's peace if I hadn't made the offer. Things like that bother me.'

Then they changed the subject. Florent's presence had to be explained without arousing the suspicion of the police. He told them how he had managed to get back to France by using the papers of a poor devil who had died in his arms in Surinam* from yellow fever. By a strange coincidence this young man was also called Florent, but in his case it was his first name. Florent Laquerrière, to give him his full name, had had just one relative in Paris, a female cousin, and had been informed that she had died in America. Nothing would therefore be easier than for Quenu's stepbrother to pass himself off as the man who had died in Surinam. Lisa offered to assume the role of the cousin. They then agreed on the story they would tell: Florent had returned from abroad, where he had failed in his attempts to make a fortune, and they, the Quenu-Gradelles, as they were called in the neighbourhood, had taken him in while he looked for a job. When all this was settled, Quenu insisted on showing his brother round the whole house; not a single stool was omitted from the inspection. In the antechamber full of chairs, Lisa pushed open a door, showed Florent a small dressing room, and told him that the shop assistant would sleep there, so that he could keep the bedroom on the fifth floor.

That evening Florent was fitted out in a completely new set of clothes. He insisted on having a black coat and black trousers again, against the advice of Quenu, who found black depressing. They no longer concealed his presence in the house, and Lisa told the story they had agreed upon to everyone who cared to hear it. Florent spent almost all his time in the *charcuterie*, sitting in the kitchen or leaning against the marble pillars in the shop. At mealtimes Quenu plied him with food, and became quite annoyed when he proved such a small eater and left half of his plate untouched. Lisa had returned to her slow, benevolent ways. She tolerated her brother-in-law, even in the mornings when he got in their way. She would forget him for a while, and then, suddenly seeing his dark shape in front of her, would give a little start, but managed to find one of her beautiful smiles, lest he might feel hurt. This thin man's disinterestedness had impressed her, and she regarded him with a feeling akin to respect, mixed with vague fear. Florent, for his part, felt surrounded by feelings of affection.

When bedtime came he went upstairs, a trifle tired by the inactivity of his day, with the two young kitchen hands who slept in garrets next to Florent. Léon, the apprentice, was barely fifteen. He was a slight, gentle-looking lad, addicted to stealing stray slices of ham and bits of sausage. These he would hide under his pillow and eat at night without any bread. Several times at about one o'clock in the morning Florent almost fancied that Léon was giving a supper-party; first he heard whispering, then the sound of munching jaws and rustling paper, followed by rippling laughter like a girl's, which resembled the soft trill of a piccolo in the deep silence of the sleeping house. The other boy, Auguste Landois, came from Troyes. Fat to an unhealthy degree, he had too large a head and was already bald, although he was only twenty-eight. As he went upstairs with Florent on the first evening, he gave Florent a long, confused account of his life story. His only reason for coming to Paris had been to learn his trade properly, and to open his own shop in Troyes, where his cousin, Augustine, was waiting for him. They had the same godfather and had therefore been given the same name. However, he had grown ambitious, and now hoped to buy a shop in Paris with money left to him by his mother, which he had deposited with a solicitor before leaving Champagne. By this stage in the story they had reached the fifth floor, but Auguste went on talking, singing the praises of Madame Quenu, who had agreed to send for Augustine to replace an assistant who had turned out badly. He now knew his trade, and his cousin was learning about shop management. In a year or eighteen months they would be married, and then they would set up on their own in some populous part of Paris, at Plaisance most likely. They were in no hurry, he added, because bacon prices were quite low. He went on to tell Florent that he and his cousin had been photographed together at a fair in Saint-Ouen, and he came into the little attic room to have another look at the photograph, which Augustine had left on the mantelpiece so that the room where Madame Quenu's cousin slept would look nice. He lingered there for a moment, quite livid in the dim light of his candle, and looking round the room, which was still full of the girl's presence. Then, stepping up to the bed, he asked Florent if it was comfortable. Augustine was now sleeping downstairs, he said, and would be much better off in the winter, because the attic rooms were bitterly cold in winter. Eventually he went away, leaving Florent alone by the bed, gazing at the photograph, in which Auguste looked like a pale version of Quenu and Augustine an immature Lisa.

Florent, although on friendly terms with the kitchen hands, pampered by his brother, and accepted by Lisa, soon began to feel very bored. He had tried, but without success, to give some private lessons; moreover, he avoided the students' quarter for fear of being recognized. Lisa tactfully suggested that he could do worse than approach some of the large firms, where he could take charge of the correspondence and keep the books. She returned to this idea again and again, and finally offered to find a position for him herself. She was gradually becoming impatient at finding him so often in her way, idle, unemployed, never knowing what to do with himself. At first this impatience was merely due to her dislike of people who do nothing to earn their keep; she had no objection as yet to his taking his meals in her house.

'I could never spend the whole day lolling about and dreaming,' she would say to him. 'That can't give you much appetite. You've got to have something to tire you out.'

Gavard, too, was on the lookout for a job for Florent, but he went about it in an extraordinary and mysterious fashion. He would have liked to find some employment that was either dramatic or bitterly ironic, something suitable for 'an outlaw'. Gavard was always against the Government. He had just turned fifty, and he boasted that he had already seen off four of them. He still shrugged his shoulders contemptuously at the thought of Charles X,* the priests and nobles and other attendant rabble, whom he had helped to sweep away. Louis-Philippe, with his 'bourgeois' following, had been an idiot, and he would tell how the citizen-king* had kept his money in woollen socks. As for the Republic of '48, it had been a farce, the workers had let him down; however, he no longer admitted that he had applauded the *coup d'état*, for he now considered Napoleon III his personal enemy, a scoundrel who shut himself away with de Morny* and others like him to indulge in orgies of gluttony. He never tired of holding forth on this subject. Lowering his voice a little, he would declare that women were brought to the Tuileries in closed carriages every evening, and that one night he had heard the sounds of an orgy as he walked across the Place du Carroussel. Gavard prided himself on being a thorn in the side of the Government. He would play all sorts of games with it and laugh about them for months afterwards. He voted for candidates who would be most likely to 'get at the ministers' in the Corps Législatif.* Then, if he could cheat the tax-collectors, or baffle the police, or bring about any kind of public disorder, he strove to give it as much of an insurrectionary character as possible. He told lies too; set himself up as a very dangerous man; talked as if 'that gang at the Tuileries' knew him well and trembled at the sight of him; and declared that half of them should be guillotined and the other half deported the next time there was 'a turnover'. These violent and voluble politics of his were fed on bragging and boasting, on cock and bull stories, demonstrating the same taste for riot and uproar that induces a Parisian shopkeeper to take down his shutters as soon as the barricades go up, so that he can get a good view of the bodies. So, when Florent returned from Cayenne, Gavard thought that he had an excellent opportunity to pull off something really big, and began to dream of how he could best make fools of the Emperor, the Government, and all men in authority down to the last *sergent de ville*.

Gavard's behaviour with Florent was altogether that of a man tasting some forbidden pleasure. He watched him out of the corner of his eye, winked at him, lowered his voice even when making the most trifling remark, and grasped his hand in a truly Masonic manner. He had at last chanced upon a real adventure; he had a friend who was really in danger; he could, without exaggeration, speak of the risks he was taking. He must certainly have felt an unacknowledged fear in the presence of this young man who had escaped from deportation and whose extreme thinness testified to the suffering he had endured; but this delicious touch of fear increased his sense of his own importance and convinced him that he was really doing something wonderful in treating a very dangerous man as a friend. Florent became a sort of sacred being in his eyes: he swore by him, and invoked him whenever arguments failed him. He wanted to crush the Government once and for all.

Gavard had lost his wife in the Rue Saint-Jacques some months after the *coup d'état*. However, he had kept on his *rôtisserie* until 1856. At that time it was rumoured that he had made a lot of money by going into partnership with a neighbouring grocer who had got a contract to supply dried vegetables to the Crimean expeditionary corps.* The truth was, however, that, having sold his shop, he lived on his capital for a year without doing anything. He did not like to talk about the real origin of his money, for that would have prevented him from expressing his opinion about the Crimean War, which he referred to as a risky business, 'undertaken simply to consolidate the throne and to line certain persons' pockets'. After a year or so he had grown utterly bored in his bachelor apartment. As he was in the habit of visiting the Quenu-Gradelles almost daily, he decided to take up residence nearer to them, and came to live in the Rue de la Cossonnerie. He loved Les Halles, with their constant noise and endless exchange of gossip, and he decided to rent a stall in the poultry market, just to give himself something to do and to fill his days with all the tittle-tattle. Thenceforth he lived a life of gossip; he knew every petty scandal in the neighbourhood, his head spinning with the incessant yapping around him. He tasted a thousand titillating delights, having at last found his true element, bathing in it voluptuously, like a carp swimming in the sunshine. Florent would sometimes go to see him at his stall. The afternoons were still warm. All along the narrow alleys sat women plucking poultry. Light streamed in between the awnings, and in the warm air, in the golden dust of the sunbeams, feathers fluttered here and there like snowflakes. A trail of calls and offers followed Florent as he walked along. 'A lovely duck, monsieur?... I've got some good fat chickens, monsieur; come and have a look!... A pair of pigeons, monsieur!' Deafened and embarrassed, he freed himself from the women, who carried on plucking as they vied for his attention; and the fine down flew about and nearly choked him, like smoke warmed and thickened by the strong smell of poultry. At last, in the middle of the alley close to the water taps, he found Gavard ranting away in shirtsleeves in front of his stall, his arms folded over the bib of his blue apron. This was where he reigned like a kind of benevolent monarch, surrounded by a group of ten or twelve women. He was the only male dealer in that part of the market. He was so fond of chin-wagging that he had quarrelled with the five or six girls he had successively engaged to look after his stall, and had therefore decided to sell his goods himself, explaining ingenuously that the silly girls spent the whole day gossiping, and this he could not tolerate. As he still needed someone to look after the stall when he went off somewhere, he took on Marjolin, who was always wandering about, having tried all the little jobs in Les Halles. Sometimes Florent stayed with Gavard for an hour, amazed by his tireless chatter and by his self-assurance among so many women. He would cut one of them short as she spoke, pick a quarrel with another ten stalls away, snatch a customer from a third, and make more noise himself than the hundred or so chattering neighbours around him, whose jabbering seemed to make the iron girders of the market resonate like so many gongs.

The poultry dealer's only remaining relatives were a sister-in-law and a niece. When his wife died, her elder sister, Madame Lecœur, who had been widowed for a year, went into the most exaggerated form of mourning, going almost every night to console the bereaved husband. She had doubtless cherished the hope that she might win his affection and step into the shoes, still warm, of his late wife. But Gavard hated thin women; he said he found it unpleasant to feel their bones under their skin, and would only stroke the fattest cats and dogs, taking great satisfaction in their plump, well-fed bodies. Madame Lecœur, her feelings greatly hurt, was furious at seeing the *rôtisser*'s money slip from her grasp; he now became her mortal enemy. When she saw him set up a stall in Les Halles, only a few metres away from the market where she sold butter, eggs, and cheese, she accused him of having 'planned it just to annoy her and bring her bad luck'. From that moment on she complained about everything, and turned so yellow and querulous that she began to lose customers. For a long time she had been looking after the daughter of one of her sisters, a peasant woman who had sent her the child and then forgotten about her. The child grew up in the markets. Her family name was Sarriet, and so she soon became known as La Sarriette. At sixteen she had developed into such an alluring young creature that men came to buy cheese at her aunt's stall just to ogle her. She had no time for gentlemen, however; with her dark hair, pale face, and eyes like fire-brands, she preferred the riff-raff. She chose as her lover a boy from Ménilmontant who did various odd jobs for her aunt. At twenty she set up in business selling fruit, with the help of money that came from a source that no one ever discovered; and from then on Monsieur Jules, as her lover was called, had spotless hands, the cleanest shirts, and a velvet cap, and only came to the markets in the afternoon, in his slippers. They lived together in the Rue Vauvilliers, on the third floor of a large house which had a disreputable café on the ground floor. Madame Lecœur became even more sour because of what she called La Sarriette's ingratitude, and she spoke of the girl in the most abusive terms. They stopped talking, the aunt exasperated, and the niece and Monsieur Jules concocting stories about the aunt, which the young man would spread around the butter market. Gavard found La Sarriette very entertaining and treated her with great indulgence. Whenever they met he would pat her cheek and say how lovely and plump she was.

One afternoon, while Florent was sitting in the *charcuterie*, tired out with the vain attempts he had made all morning to find work, Marjolin appeared. This big lad, who looked like a gentle Flemish giant, had been taken up by Lisa. She would say that he did not mean any harm; that he was a little bit stupid, but as strong as an ox, and particularly interesting because nobody knew anything about his parentage. It was she who had got Gavard to take him on.

Lisa was sitting behind the counter, annoyed by the sight of Florent's muddy boots, which were making a mess on the pink and white tiles of the floor. Twice already she had got up to scatter sawdust about the shop. She smiled, however, as Marjolin came in.

'Monsieur Gavard', began the young man, 'has sent me to ask...'

He stopped, looked round, and lowered his voice.

'He told me to make sure there was no one with you and to tell you this, which he made me learn by heart: "Ask them if it's safe and I can come and talk about they-know-what."'

'Tell Monsieur Gavard we're expecting him,' said Lisa, who was used to the poultry-dealer's mysterious ways.

But Marjolin did not move. He remained standing there, in ecstasy before the handsome mistress of the shop, looking at her with an expression of fawning humility. As if touched by this mute adoration, Lisa continued:

'Do you like working for Monsieur Gavard? He's quite nice; you should try to please him.'

'Yes, Madame Lisa.'

'But you do things you shouldn't. Yesterday I saw you climbing about on the roofs again; and you spend too much time with a lot of rough young people. You're a man now; you ought to remember that and begin to think about your future.'

'Yes, Madame Lisa.'

She broke off to serve a lady who came in to buy a pound of chops *aux cornichons*. She walked over to the chopping block at the far end of the shop. With a long, slender knife, she cut three chops from a loin of pork; then, with a small cleaver, she dealt three sharp blows that separated the chops from the loin. At each blow, her black merino dress rose slightly behind her, and the ribs of her stays showed beneath her tightly stretched bodice. She slowly picked up the chops, looking very serious as she weighed them, her eyes gleaming and her lips pursed.

When the lady had gone, and she saw how delighted Marjolin was to have seen her deal those three clean, precise blows with the cleaver, she exclaimed:

'What! Still here?'

He turned to go, but she kept him back a moment longer.

'Now, don't let me see you again with that no-good Cadine,' she said. 'Don't deny it! I saw you both this morning in the tripe market, watching them break open the sheep's heads. I can't understand what you see in a slut like her... Now go and tell Monsieur Gavard that he had better come straight away, while there's no one here.'

Marjolin, embarrassed, went off without a word.

Lisa remained standing at her counter, her head turned slightly in the direction of Les Halles. Florent gazed at her in silence, suddenly surprised to find her so beautiful. He had never looked at her properly before; indeed, he had shown no interest in women generally. He now saw her rising up over the wares on the counter. In front of her was

an array of white china dishes, *saucissons* from Arles and Lyons, slices
of which had already been cut off, tongues and pieces of boiled pork,
a pig's head in jelly, an open jar of *rillettes*, and a large tin of sardines
whose broken lid revealed a pool of oil. On the right and left, on
wooden boards, were mounds of French and Italian brawn, a common
French ham, of a pinky hue, and a York ham, whose deep red lean
stood out beneath a broad band of fat. There were other dishes too,
round ones and oval ones, containing stuffed tongue, truffled *galantine*,
and a boar's head garnished with pistachios, while, much nearer her
and within reach, stood some yellow earthenware dishes containing
larded veal, *pâté de foie gras*, and hare *pâté*. As there was no sign of
Gavard, she put away some gammon on a little marble shelf at the
end of the counter, tidied and cleaned the jars of lard and dripping,
wiped the plates of each pair of scales, and poked the fire in the
warming oven, which was getting low. Then she turned and gazed
once more at the markets. Around her rose the smell of all the cooking
meats; she was as if enveloped, in her heavy calm, by the aroma of
truffles. She looked beautifully fresh that afternoon. The whiteness
of all the dishes heightened the whiteness of her apron and sleeves,
and set off her plump neck and rosy cheeks, which had the same soft
tones as the hams and the same transparent pallor as the fats. As Florent
continued to gaze at her he began to feel intimidated, disturbed by
the dignity of her carriage; and instead of openly looking at her he
glanced furtively in the mirrors around the shop, which reflected her
from the back, the front, and the side; and the mirror on the ceiling
reflected the top of her head, with its tightly drawn bun and the little
bands over her temples. The shop seemed filled with a crowd of Lisas,
showing off their broad shoulders, powerful arms, and large breasts so
smooth and passionless that they aroused no greater desire than the
sight of a belly would. At last Florent's gaze came to rest on a particularly pleasing side view of Lisa which appeared in a mirror between
two sides of pork. All down the marble of the walls, and all down the
mirrors, sides of pork and strips of larding fat hung from hooks; and
Lisa, with her thick neck, rounded hips, and swelling bosom, looked
like the queen of all this dangling fat and meat. She leaned forward and
smiled indulgently at the two goldfish swimming round the aquarium
in the window.

  Gavard entered the shop. With an air of great importance, he went
into the kitchen to fetch Quenu. Then he installed himself on a small

marble-topped table, while Florent remained on his chair and Lisa behind the counter and Quenu leaned against a side of pork. After a few moments he announced that he had found a position for Florent. They would be very pleased when he told them what it was, and it would make the Government look really stupid.

But he suddenly stopped short, for Mademoiselle Saget, seeing such a large party gathered at the Quenu-Gradelles', had just come in. Carrying her eternal black bag on her arm, and wearing a faded dress and a black, ribbonless straw hat, which cast an ambiguous shadow over her pale face, she greeted the men with a nod and Lisa with an ironic smile. She was an acquaintance of the family and had lived in the same house in the Rue Pirouette for the last forty years, probably on a small private income, of which she never spoke. One day she talked about Cherbourg, mentioning that she had been born there. But nothing else was known about her. She talked only about other people, about all aspects of her neighbours' lives, even including the number of items they sent to the laundry each month; and she even went so far as to listen behind doors and open letters. Her gossiping tongue was feared from the Rue Saint-Denis to the Rue Jean-Jacques Rousseau, from the Rue Saint-Honoré to the Rue Mauconseil. All day long she wandered about with her empty bag, pretending that she was shopping, but in reality buying nothing, since her sole purpose was to peddle gossip and keep herself informed about the most trifling event. She had turned her brain into an encyclopedia of all the people and every household in the neighbourhood. Quenu had always accused her of having spread the story of his uncle's death on the chopping block, and had borne her a grudge ever since. She was extremely well informed about Uncle Gradelle and the Quenus; she knew everything, she would say, 'by heart'. For the last two weeks, however, Florent's arrival had greatly perplexed her, bringing her, indeed, to a fever pitch of curiosity. She became quite ill when she discovered some unforeseen gap in her knowledge. She could have sworn that she had seen that tall lanky fellow somewhere before.

She stood in front of the counter, examining the dishes one after another, and saying in her thin voice:

'I can never decide what to have. In the afternoon I can't wait for my dinner, and then, after a while, I don't feel like anything. Have you got any breaded cutlets left, Madame Quenu?'

Without waiting for an answer, she lifted one of the lids of the stove. It was the one that covered the side with the *andouilles*, sausages, and black pudding. But the stove was cold, and there was nothing inside but a left-over sausage.

'Look in the other side, Mademoiselle Saget,' said Lisa. 'I think there's a cutlet left.'

'No, I don't fancy that,' muttered the old woman, peering in the other side all the same. 'I thought I might, but a cutlet would be a bit too heavy; and I'd rather have something I don't need to heat up.'

She had turned towards Florent and stared at him; then she looked at Gavard, who was beating a tattoo with his fingers on the marble table. She gave them a smile, as if inviting them to carry on talking.

'What about a piece of *petit salé*?' asked Lisa.

'A piece of *petit salé*? Yes, that might do.'

She picked up the fork with a plated handle, which was resting on the side of the dish, and began to turn the pieces of bacon over, prodding them, tapping the bones to judge how thick they were, and studying the shreds of pink meat. As she turned them over she repeated, 'No, no, I don't fancy that.'

'Well, have some tongue, or a bit of brawn, or a slice of pickled veal,' suggested Lisa patiently.

But Mademoiselle Saget shook her head. She stayed for a few more minutes, pulling faces at the different dishes; then, seeing that they were determined to remain silent, and that she would learn nothing, she left, saying:

'No; I fancied a breaded cutlet, but the one you've got there is too fat. I'll come back some other time.'

Lisa leaned forward to watch her through the caul hanging in the window, and saw her cross the road and go into the fruit market.

'The old cow!' growled Gavard.

Then, as they were alone again, he began to tell them about the job he had found for Florent. It was a long story. A friend of his, Monsieur Verlaque, one of the inspectors in the fish market, was so ill that he had had to take some time off; and that very morning the poor man had told him that he would be very pleased if he could find someone to replace him for a while, so that he could have his job back if he recovered.

'But the thing is, you see, Verlaque won't last six months,' said Gavard, 'and Florent will be able to keep the job. It's a great idea, isn't it? And what a joke on the police! The job comes under the Préfecture, you know. It'll be so funny to see Florent being paid by those dummies!'

He burst out laughing; the idea struck him as very comical.

'I won't take it,' Florent replied bluntly. 'I swore I'd never accept anything from the Empire. I'd rather starve than work for the Préfecture. It's out of the question, Gavard!'

Gavard seemed quite put out. Quenu was looking down at his shoes, while Lisa, turning round, looked hard at Florent, her neck swollen, her bosom straining her bodice almost to bursting-point. She was about to say something when La Sarriette stepped into the shop, and there was another pause in the conversation.

'Dear me!' exclaimed La Sarriette with her soft laugh, 'I nearly forgot to get some bacon. Could you cut me a dozen slices, Madame Quenu—very thin ones? I'm making some veal olive. Jules has taken it into his head to have some. How are you, uncle?'

She filled the shop with her skirts and smiled at everyone. Her face looked fresh and creamy, and her hair was falling down on one side because of the wind that was blowing through the markets. Gavard grasped her hands, while she said cheekily,

'I bet you were talking about me. What were you saying, uncle?'

Lisa, cutting the bacon very carefully on a board, called out, 'Is this thin enough?'

She wrapped the pieces up and asked, 'Can I get you anything else?'

'Well, since I'm here,' replied La Sarriette, 'I'll have a pound of lard. I love fried potatoes, so I think I'll have a few potatoes and radishes for breakfast. Yes, a pound of lard, please, Madame Quenu.'

Lisa put a sheet of thick paper on the scales. Then she took the lard out of a jar under the shelves with a wooden spatula, adding small quantities to the greasy mound, which began to melt and run slightly. When the pan dropped, she picked up the paper, folded it, and twisted the corners.

'That'll be twenty-four sous,' she said, 'and six sous for the bacon. That makes thirty sous altogether. Would you like anything else?'

'No,' said La Sarriette, 'nothing.'

She paid, still smiling and laughing, and staring the men in the face. Her grey skirt had twisted round, and the shape of her breasts could be seen through her loose red shawl. Before she left she stepped up to Gavard again and pretended to threaten him:

'So you won't tell me what you were saying? I could see you laughing from outside. You're a crafty one! I don't love you any more!'

Then she left and ran across the road.

'Mademoiselle Saget sent her,' Lisa remarked drily.

Nobody spoke. Gavard was dismayed at Florent's reaction to his proposal. Lisa was the first to speak.

'You ought to take it, Florent,' she said in the friendliest of tones. 'You know how difficult it is to find anything, and you're hardly in a position to pick and choose.'

'I gave you my reasons,' Florent replied.

Lisa shrugged.

'You can't be serious,' she said. 'I can understand that you're not very keen on the Government, but it would be silly to let your opinions prevent you from earning a living. Besides, the Emperor isn't too bad. I don't mind you saying he is when you're talking about what happened to you. But how could he have known you were eating mouldy bread and bad meat? He can't be everywhere, and you can see that he hasn't prevented us from doing pretty well. You're not being fair, really you aren't.'

Gavard was getting very agitated. He could not bear to hear people speak well of the Emperor.

'No, no, Madame Quenu,' he interrupted, 'you're going too far. He's an absolute crook.'

'Oh, you,' exclaimed Lisa, beginning to get excited, 'you won't be satisfied until you've been robbed and attacked because of all your wild talk. Let's not discuss politics; it would only make me angry. We're talking about Florent, aren't we? Well, I say he should take the job. Don't you think so, Quenu?'

Quenu, who had not yet said a word, was annoyed to be put on the spot.

'It's a good job,' he replied non-committally.

Then, as there was another awkward silence, Florent said:

'Please, let's drop the subject. My mind's made up. I'll wait.'

'You'll wait!' cried Lisa, losing patience.

Two flames had risen to her cheeks. As she stood there in her white apron, with her wide, swelling hips, she found it hard not to lose her temper. At this point, however, another customer came in. It was Madame Lecœur.

'I'd like half a pound of mixed meats at fifty sous a pound,' she said.

At first she pretended not to notice her brother-in-law, but after a few moments she simply nodded to him, without speaking. Then she looked the three men up and down, doubtless hoping to divine their secret from the way they were waiting for her to go. She could see that she was bothering them, and this made her even more sour and angular, as she stood there in her drooping skirts, with her long spidery arms and gnarled hands, which she held clenched together under her apron. Then, as she coughed slightly, Gavard, embarrassed by the silence, asked if she had a cold.

She responded with a curt 'No'. Her taut skin was brick red on the bony parts of her face, and the dull fire burning in her eyes betrayed a vague liver complaint nurtured by feelings of bitterness and envy. She turned round again towards the counter and followed every movement Lisa made, with the distrustful look of a customer convinced that she will be cheated.

'Don't give me any saveloy,' she said. 'I don't like it.'

Lisa had picked up a thin knife and was cutting some slices of sausage. Then, her eyes fixed on the knife, she passed on to the smoked ham, and then the ordinary ham, cutting delicate slices from each, bending slightly forward as she did so. Her chubby, rosy hands, flitting about the meats with soft, gentle touches, had a kind of plump suppleness, her fingers dimpling at the joints.

'You'll have some pickled veal, won't you?' she said, pushing forward one of the dishes.

Madame Lecœur seemed to be thinking the matter over at great length; at last she said she would have some. Lisa was now digging deep into the dishes, and produced slices of pickled veal and hare *pâté* on the tip of a broad-bladed knife. Each new slice was deposited in the middle of a sheet of paper she had placed on the scales.

'Aren't you going to give me any brawn with pistachios?' asked Madame Lecœur in her querulous voice.

Lisa was obliged to give her some. Now Madame Lecœur was getting difficult to please. She wanted two slices of *galantine*; she was very fond of it. Lisa, already irritated, toyed impatiently with the handles of the knives and explained that the *galantine* was truffled and could only be served on mixed plates at three sous a pound.

Madame Lecœur, however, continued to sniff all the dishes, trying to find something else to ask for. When the mixed plate was put on the scales and weighed, she made Lisa add some jelly and gherkins. The lump of jelly, shaped like a sponge cake in the middle of a china platter, trembled beneath Lisa's hand; and she managed to make the vinegar spurt over the sides when, with her fingertips, she took a couple of large gherkins from a jar behind the stove.

'That's twenty-five sous, isn't it?' asked Madame Lecœur, who seemed in no hurry.

She was well aware of Lisa's silent irritation, and made the most of it, producing her money as slowly as possible, as if she couldn't find the right amount among all the larger coins in her pocket. She looked sideways at Gavard, relishing the embarrassed silence that her presence was prolonging, determined not to leave just because they were all hiding something from her. At last Lisa put the parcel in her hands, and she was obliged to make her departure. She left without saying a word, but with a sweeping gaze all round the shop.

When she had disappeared, Lisa burst out:

'It was that Saget woman who sent her! Is that old witch going to send the whole market here to find out what we're talking about? And they're all so cunning! Who else would buy breaded cutlets and mixed plates at five o'clock? They'd rather upset their stomachs than not know... If she sends anyone else, just watch me!'

The three men remained silent before this explosion of anger. Gavard had gone to lean on the brass rail of the window display, and was playing with one of the cut-glass knobs that had come loose on its wire rod. Then, looking up, he said:

'Well, I thought it was a great joke.'

'What was a joke?' asked Lisa, still quivering with fury.

'The job as inspector.'

She threw up her hands, gave Florent a final glance, and sat down on the upholstered bench behind the counter and said nothing more. Gavard launched into a lengthy exposition of his plan; to put it in a nutshell, it was the Government that would look stupid, because Florent would be taking their money.

'My dear fellow,' he said complacently, 'those sods left you to starve, didn't they? Well, now you can make them feed you. It's a great idea; I could see the beauty of it straight away.'

Florent smiled, but still said no. Quenu, in the hope of pleasing his wife, did his best to think of some good advice. But Lisa seemed to have stopped listening. For the last few moments she had been gazing at Les Halles. Suddenly she leapt to her feet, crying:

'Ah! It's La Normande they're sending to spy on us now! Too bad; she'll pay for the others!'

A tall dark-haired woman pushed open the door. It was the beautiful fishwife, Louise Méhudin, known as La Normande. She was a bold-looking beauty, with delicate white skin; she was almost as sturdily built as Lisa, but she had a more impudent look and more alluring breasts. She breezily made her entry, a gold chain dangling from her apron, her hair combed upwards in the latest style, and she wore a lace bow round her neck, which labelled her as one of the fashion queens of Les Halles. A vague odour of fish hung about her, and a herring scale showed like a tiny patch of mother-of-pearl near the little finger of one of her hands. She and Lisa, having at one time lived in the same house in the Rue Pirouette, were the closest of friends, made even closer by a touch of rivalry between them, which caused each to keep a constant watch on the other. People in the neighbourhood spoke of 'La Belle Normande' just as they spoke of 'La Belle Lisa'. Thus compared and contrasted, they were both compelled to maintain their reputation for beauty. If she leaned sideways a little, Lisa could see from her counter into the fish market opposite and watch the fishwife surrounded by her salmon and turbot. They kept each other under observation. La Belle Lisa drew herself in more tightly in her corsets. La Belle Normande added rings to her fingers and bows to her shoulders. When they met they were elaborately polite and most complimentary, glancing furtively at each other with half-closed eyes, in the hope of finding some flaw. They made a point of buying from each other and professed great mutual affection.

'Tell me, it's tomorrow night you make your black pudding, isn't it?' asked La Normande with a smile.

Lisa remained very cool. She seldom showed anger, but when she did she was implacable.

'Yes,' she replied drily, hardly moving her lips.

'I love it when it comes straight out of the oven,' resumed La Normande. 'I'll come and fetch some.'

She had not failed to notice her rival's lack of friendliness. She glanced at Florent, whom she seemed to find interesting; then, as she did not want to leave without having the last word, she added rather imprudently:

'I bought some off you the day before yesterday, but it didn't seem very fresh.'

'Not very fresh!' Lisa repeated, as white as a sheet, her lips quivering.

Up until now, she might have contained herself, for fear that La Normande might think she was jealous of the lace bow she was wearing; but now it was not simply a question of being spied upon, she had been insulted, and that was more than she could take. She leaned forward, planted her hands on the counter, and cried rather hoarsely:

'What? Well what about last week, when you sold me that pair of soles? Did I come and tell you in front of everybody that they were off?'

'Off! My soles off!' shouted the fishwife, very red in the face.

For a moment they remained silent, choking with anger, but glaring at each other over the array of dishes. Their studied friendliness towards each other had vanished; a simple remark had been enough to reveal what sharp teeth they had beneath their smiles.

'You really are rude!' said La Belle Normande. 'I'll never set foot in here again.'

'Get out then, get out!' said La Belle Lisa. 'We all know what you're like.'

The fishwife left the shop, thowing over her shoulder a violent curse that left Lisa trembling with rage. The whole incident had happened so quickly that the three men, quite amazed, had not had time to intervene. Almost at once Lisa recovered. She had resumed the conversation, without making any allusion to what had just occurred, when Augustine, Lisa's assistant, returned from her errands. Taking Gavard aside, Lisa told him to say nothing for the present to Monsieur Verlaque, and undertook to persuade her brother-in-law to accept the job within a couple of days at most. Quenu went back into his kitchen, while Gavard took Florent off with him. As they were about to go into Monsieur Lebigre's to have a drop of vermouth, Gavard pointed out three women standing in the covered avenue, between the fish market and the poultry market.

'Look at them, chewing it all over!' he said rather enviously.

The markets were slowly emptying, and there indeed stood Mademoiselle Saget, Madame Lecœur, and La Sarriette on the edge of the footpath. The old maid was holding forth.

'As I was saying, Madame Lecœur, your brother-in-law is always there. You saw him just now, didn't you?'

'Oh yes! He was sitting on a table. He seemed quite at home.'

'Well,' La Sarriette interrupted, 'I didn't hear anyone say anything bad. I don't know why you're making such a fuss.'

Mademoiselle Saget shrugged.

'Ah!' she answered. 'You're so innocent, my dear. Can't you see why the Quenus are always being nice to Monsieur Gavard? I bet you anything you like that he'll leave all his money to their little girl Pauline.'

'Do you really think so?' cried Madame Lecœur, pale with fury.

Then, in a mournful voice, as though she had just had a terrible setback, she continued:

'I'm all alone in the world. I've got nobody to look after me. He can just do as he pleases. His niece always sides with him, you know that. She's forgotten how much she owes me. She wouldn't lift a finger to help me.'

'No, auntie,' said La Sarriette. 'The thing is you've never been able to find anything nice to say about me.'

Almost at once they made up and kissed each other. The niece promised to stop teasing, and the aunt swore by all she held most sacred that she regarded La Sarriette as her own daughter. Mademoiselle Saget then proceeded to advise them on the best way to prevent Gavard from wasting his money. It was generally agreed that the Quenu-Gradelles were a thoroughly bad lot and should be kept under constant watch.

'I don't know what they're up to,' said the old maid, 'but it's all very fishy. What do you make of that Florent, Madame Quenu's cousin?'

They huddled together and lowered their voices.

'You know,' Madame Lecœur went on, 'we saw him one morning with his boots all split and his clothes covered in dust. He looked just like a thief… He frightens me, he does.'

'No,' murmured La Sarriette, 'he may be thin, but he's not a bad sort.'

Mademoiselle Saget thought for a while, and then said: 'I've been racking my brains for the last two weeks. Monsieur Gavard obviously knows him. I'm sure I've seen him somewhere before. But I just can't remember.'

She was still trying to remember when La Normande swept up to them like a whirlwind. She had just come away from the *charcuterie*.

'She's a rude one, that Quenu bitch!' she cried, pleased to be able to get it off her chest. 'She just told me all I sell is rotten fish! I told her where to get off, I can tell you! What a shop they've got, poisoning everybody with their rotten meat!'

'So what had you said to provoke her?' asked the old maid, quivering with excitement, delighted with the news that the two of them had quarrelled.

'Me? Nothing at all! Not a word! I just popped in to tell her very politely that I'd be going over to get some black pudding tomorrow night, and she just started shouting. Bloody hypocrite, putting on all those airs! She'll pay for this!'

They all felt that La Normande was not telling them the truth, but this did not prevent them from taking her side. They turned towards the Rue Rambuteau, throwing insults, inventing stories about the dirtiness of the Quenus' kitchens, and making the most fantastic accusations. If it had been discovered that the Quenus dealt in human flesh, their outburst could scarcely have been more threatening. The fishwife was not satisfied until she had told her story three more times.

'And the cousin, what did he say?' asked Mademoiselle Saget wickedly.

'The cousin!' repeated La Normande shrilly. 'Do you really believe he's a cousin? If you ask me, he's Lisa's lover!'

The other three cried out in disbelief. Lisa's virtue was an article of faith in the neighbourhood.

'Stuff and nonsense!' retorted La Normande. 'How do you know? Butter wouldn't melt in that woman's mouth. I'd like to see how virtuous she is without her nightdress. That husband of hers is too much of a dumbo for her not to have cuckolded him.'

Mademoiselle Saget nodded as if to say that she might be inclined to agree. She added quietly:

'What's more, that so-called cousin turned up out of nowhere, and their explanation seems very dubious to me.'

'Yes, he's her lover, there's no doubt about it!' repeated the fishwife. 'Some tramp, some good-for-nothing she picked up in the street. It's obvious.'

'Thin men always have plenty of stamina,' declared La Sarriette knowingly.

'She's dressed him up in a new set of clothes,' remarked Madame Lecœur. 'He must be costing her a fortune.'

'Yes, well, you may be right,' murmured the old maid. 'We'll have to find out a bit more.'

They all promised to keep each other fully informed about the goings-on at the Quenu-Gradelle establishment. The butter dealer declared that she wanted to open her brother-in-law's eyes to the kind of company he was keeping. In the meantime, La Normande had calmed down somewhat; a good-natured woman at heart, she went off, tired out by so much talking.

'I'm sure she said something rude,' said Madame Lecœur as soon as La Normande had disappeared. 'That's how she is. She'd do better not to talk about cousins dropping out of the sky—after all, she once found a baby in her fish shop.'

They all looked at one another and laughed. Then, when Madame Lecœur had taken her leave too, La Sarriette remarked:

'My aunt shouldn't get so involved. That's what makes her so thin. She used to give me a hiding when men showed an interest in me. But she can look as hard as she likes, she'll never find a kid under *her* pillow.'

Mademoiselle Saget laughed. When she was alone, and making her way back to the Rue Pirouette, she thought that those three silly geese weren't worth the string to hang them up with. Besides, someone might have seen her with them, and it would be bad to fall out with the Quenu-Gradelles, who were, after all, such well-to-do and respectable people. She made a detour to call in at Taboureau the baker's, in the Rue Turbigo—the best bakery in the neighbourhood. Madame Taboureau, who was a good friend of Lisa's, was an undisputed authority on everything. When it was reported that 'Madame Taboureau said this' or 'Madame Taboureau said that', that was always the end of it. So, under the pretence of finding out when the oven would be hot, so that she could bring over a dish of pears, the old woman took the opportunity to eulogize Lisa, singing the praises especially of her black pudding. Then, pleased with this moral alibi, delighted to have fanned the flames of the quarrel that had started without her involvement, she trotted home, feeling quite pleased with herself, but still trying to remember where she had come across Madame Quenu's so-called cousin.

That same evening, after dinner, Florent left the house and strolled up and down one of the covered avenues in Les Halles. A light mist was rising and the empty markets had about them a melancholy greyness, studded with the yellow lamps that hung in the air like tears. For the first time Florent felt out of place; he recognized the uncouth way in which he, thin and guileless, had fallen into this world of fat people. He admitted to himself that his presence was disturbing the whole neighbourhood, and that he was a source of discomfort to the Quenus—a false cousin of far too compromising a kind. Such thoughts made him very sad, though not because he had noticed the least harshness in the attitude of either his brother or Lisa; indeed, it was their very kindness that pained him, and he accused himself of a lack of consideration in imposing his presence upon them. He was beginning to doubt the propriety of his conduct. The memory of the conversation in the shop that afternoon troubled him. It was as if he had been overcome by the smell of meat from the counter; he had felt himself sinking into a state of extreme inertia. Perhaps he had been wrong to refuse the inspector's job. This thought gave rise to a tremendous conflict within him; he had to shake himself to reawaken his conscience. But now a damp breeze was blowing down the covered avenue. As he buttoned his coat he regained some of his calm and resolve. The wind seemed to blow away from his clothes the greasy smell of the *charcuterie*, which had made him feel so weak.

He was on his way back when he met Claude Lantier. Buttoned up in his greenish overcoat, the painter spoke in a hollow voice full of suppressed anger. He raged against painting, said it gave him a dog's life, swore he would never touch a paintbrush again. That afternoon he had kicked a hole in the study of a head he was working on, with that little pest Cadine as his model. He was prone to these temperamental outbursts, the fruit of his inability to execute the lasting, living works of which he dreamed. At such times he fell into a state of utter despair, roaming the streets and waiting for the following day as if for a resurrection. He used to say that he felt bright and cheerful in the morning and totally miserable in the evening; every day became a great struggle ending in disappointment.* Florent hardly recognized him as the carefree *flâneur* of the markets. They had met again in the *charcuterie*. Claude, who knew the fugitive's story, had grasped his hand and told him that he was a fine fellow. It was very seldom, however, that the artist called in at the Quenus'.

'Are you still at my aunt's place?' he asked. 'I don't know how you can live with all that food. The place stinks of meat. When I've been there for an hour I feel I've had enough to eat for three days.

I shouldn't have gone there this morning; that's what made me mess up my picture.'

Then, after he and Florent had taken a few steps in silence, he continued:

'But they're decent people! And amazingly healthy! I thought I might paint their portraits, but I've never been able to do that type of fat, round face... Can you imagine my aunt kicking holes in her saucepans? I'm stupid enough to have kicked one in Cadine's head! Come to think of it, the picture wasn't that bad.'

They began to talk about Lisa. Claude said that his mother* had not seen anything of her for a long time, and he gave Florent to understand that Lisa was slightly ashamed of her sister, who had married an ordinary workman; moreover, she didn't like unsuccessful people. Speaking about himself, he told Florent how a benevolent gentleman, impressed by the donkeys and old women he drew, had sent him to school when he was eight; and then he had died, leaving him a thousand francs a year, which was just enough to keep him from starving.

'All the same, I would rather have been a working man,' he continued. 'A carpenter, for example. They're very happy, carpenters. They've got a table to make, let's say; well, they make it and then go off to bed, perfectly happy. I, on the other hand, I hardly ever sleep at night. All those wretched pictures I can never finish keep swirling around in my head. I can never finish anything properly—never, never!'

He almost began to sob. Then he tried to laugh. He swore, searching for the vilest words he knew, with the cold rage of a sensitive soul full of self-doubt and who dreams of wallowing in filth. After a while he squatted down in front of one of the gratings above the cellars underneath the markets, where the gas lamps are kept continually burning. In the depths below he pointed out the figures of Marjolin and Cadine, who were quietly eating their supper, sitting on one of the stone blocks used for slaughtering the poultry. They had discovered how to hide and make themselves at home in the cellars after the gates were closed.

'What a magnificent creature!' exclaimed Claude, referring to Marjolin. 'And think how happy he is! When they've finished eating, they'll lie down in one of those big baskets full of feathers. That's the life!... Ah, you're quite right to stay at the *charcuterie*—perhaps it'll fatten you up.'

Then he suddenly walked off. Florent went upstairs to his little attic room, disturbed by Claude's nervous anxieties, which had reawakened his own uncertainty. The next morning, he avoided spending any time in the *charcuterie* and instead took a long walk along the quays of the Seine. When he returned for lunch, however, he was quite won over by Lisa's soft, gentle manner. She again spoke to him about the fish inspector's job, without undue insistence but as something that deserved consideration. As he listened to her, his plate piled high, he was affected, in spite of himself, by the prim comfort of his surroundings. The matting beneath his feet seemed very soft; the glitter of the brass hanging lamp, the yellow tint of the wallpaper, and the bright oak of the furniture filled him with a sense of appreciation for a life of well-being, which confused his notions of right and wrong. Nevertheless, he had the strength to refuse once more, repeating his reasons, though he was conscious of his apparent bad taste in making such a display of his obstinacy in Lisa's dining room. Lisa was unperturbed; on the contrary, she smiled sweetly, and this embarrassed Florent far more than the sullen annoyance she had shown the day before. At dinner they talked solely of the great winter salting,* which would keep everyone in the *charcuterie* on their toes.

The evenings were getting cold. As soon as the meal was over, they went into the kitchen, where it was very warm. The kitchen was so large that several people could easily sit together at the square table in the middle, without being at all in the way. The walls of the gaslit room were covered with blue and white tiles to the height of a man's head. On the left stood the big cast-iron stove with its three holes across the top on which three squat cooking pots were firmly set, their bottoms black with soot. At the end was a small range fitted with an oven and a smoking-place; it was used for grilling. Above the oven, high over the skimming-spoons, the ladles, and the long-handled forks, a row of numbered drawers contained grated crusts, both fine and coarse, soft breadcrumbs, spices, cloves, nutmegs, and peppers. The chopping block, a huge mass of oak, leaned heavily against the wall, its hollowed surface covered in cuts and indentations. Several items of equipment were attached to it, an injector pump, a stuffer, and a mincing machine, all of which, with their cogs and cranks, gave the place a strange, mysterious appearance, suggesting some devil's kitchen. Then, all round the walls, on wooden shelves, and even under the tables, were piles of pots and pans, dishes, buckets, plates, various tin utensils, a battery of deep saucepans, wide-mouthed funnels, racks of knives and choppers, rows of skewers and needles— a whole world drowned in fat. In spite of the excessive cleanliness, fat oozed everywhere; it sweated between the tiles, glistened on the red surface of the floor, put a greyish sheen on the stove, and gave a varnished appearance to the edges of the chopping block. In the midst of the ever-rising steam, the continuous evaporation from the three big pots, in which pork was boiling and melting, there was not a single nail from floor to ceiling that was not dripping with grease.

The Quenu-Gradelles made everything themselves. The only things they got from outside were the potted meats from well-known firms, jars of pickles and preserves, sardines, cheeses, and snails. So, when September came round, they became very busy refilling the cellar, which had emptied during the summer. They worked late into the evening, even after the shop was closed. Quenu, assisted by Auguste and Léon, filled the sausages, prepared the hams, melted down the lard, cut the gammon and the bacon. There was a tremendous noise of cooking pots and cleavers, and the smell of food spread throughout the house. But none of this impeded the daily business in fresh meats and savouries, the *pâté de foie*, the hare *pâté*, the *galantines*, the sausages, and the black pudding.

That evening, by about eleven o'clock, Quenu had begun melting down some lard and preparing the black pudding. Auguste helped him. At one corner of the square table, Lisa and Augustine sat sewing linen; while opposite them, on the other side of the table, sat Florent, his face turned towards the oven, smiling at little Pauline, who was standing on his feet and wanted to be 'jumped in the air'. Behind them, Léon was chopping up sausage meat on the oak block with slow, regular movements.

Auguste went first of all to fetch two buckets of pigs' blood from the courtyard outside. It was he who did the bleeding in the slaughterhouse. He would bring the blood and entrails of the pigs back with him, leaving the kitchen boys who scalded the carcasses to bring the prepared pigs home in their barrow. Quenu was of the view that no assistant in the whole of Paris was a finer pig-sticker than Auguste. Indeed, it was true that Auguste was a most discerning judge of the quality of the blood; the black pudding was always good when he said it would be good.

'Well, what's the black pudding going to be like this time? Good?' asked Lisa.

He put down the two buckets and said, very slowly,

'I think so, Madame Quenu—yes, I think so. I can tell mainly from the way the blood runs. If it trickles too slowly when I take the knife out, it's not a good sign, it shows the blood is poor.'

'But surely', interrupted Quenu, 'it depends on how the knife was put in.'

A smile came over Auguste's pale face.

'No, no,' he replied. 'I always stick the knife in four inches deep; that's just right. But the best sign is when the blood really runs out and I catch it in the bucket, and lash it with my hand. It's got to have a good temperature and be creamy without being too thick.'

Augustine had put down her needle. Raising her eyes, she gazed at Auguste; beneath her wiry chestnut hair her ruddy face assumed an expression of rapt attention. Lisa too, and even little Pauline, were listening with great interest.

'I beat it and beat it and beat it, you see?' the boy went on, making hand movements as if he were whipping cream. 'And then, when I take my hand out and look at it, it's got to be like it's greased with blood, a sort of red glove that's the same colour of red all over. Then you can say, without the shadow of a doubt, "the black pudding's going to be good".'

He stood there for a moment, his hand raised, in a vague attitude of complacency. The hand that lived its life in buckets of blood had bright-red nails and looked very pink above his white sleeve. Quenu nodded in approval. There was a moment's silence. Léon was still chopping the meat. Pauline, however, still looking pensive, climbed back onto her cousin's feet and cried in her clear voice:

'Tell me the story of the man who was eaten alive!'

No doubt the mention of blood flowing from the pigs had reawakened in the child's mind the idea of 'the man who was eaten alive'. Florent did not understand and asked which man she meant. Lisa laughed.

'She wants you to tell her the story of that poor man—you know who I mean—that you told Gavard one evening. She must have heard you.'

At this Florent became very serious. The little girl got up and, taking the big cat in her arms, brought it over and put it on her cousin's knees, saying that Mouton too wanted to hear the story. But Mouton jumped onto the table. He sat down, arched his back and stayed there, staring at the tall, scraggy individual before him, who for the last fortnight had seemed to him a subject for deep reflection. Pauline began to get impatient, stamping her feet and asking again for the story. As she was so insistent, Lisa said:

'Go on, tell the story; then she'll leave us in peace.'

Florent remained silent a moment longer, staring at the floor. Then, slowly raising his head, he looked at the two women plying their needles, then at Quenu and Auguste, who were preparing the pot for the black pudding. The gas was burning quietly, the warmth from the stove filled the room, and all the grease in the kitchen glistened in an atmosphere of well-being such as accompanies a good meal. Florent sat little Pauline on his knee and, smiling rather sadly, began his story:

'Once upon a time there was a poor man who was sent far away, right across the sea. On the ship that carried him away, there were four hundred convicts, and he was thrown among them. He had to live for five weeks with all these bad men, wear sail-cloth like them, and have his rations alongside them. Lice were eating him up and he sweated so much that he lost all his strength. The ship's kitchen, bakery, and engine created so much heat in the holds that ten of the convicts died. During the day they were brought up on deck fifty at a time to get some air, and as the crew were afraid of them two cannons were pointed at the little area where they took their exercise. The poor man was very glad when his turn came. He was not sweating so much now, but he could hardly eat and felt very ill. When he was back in his chains at night and the rough sea made him lurch and knock against his companions, he broke down and wept, glad that he could cry without being seen.'

Pauline was listening wide-eyed, her little hands clasped as though in prayer.

'But', she interrupted, 'this isn't the story of the man who was eaten alive. It's a different story, isn't it?'

'Wait and see,' replied Florent gently. 'I'll come to the story about that man. I'm telling you the whole story from the beginning.'

'Oh, good,' murmured the child, looking pleased.

But she remained thoughtful, obviously preoccupied by something that troubled her greatly. At last she spoke.

'But what had the poor man done,' she asked, 'to be sent away and put in the ship?'

Lisa and Augustine smiled. They were delighted by the child's intelligence, and Lisa, without giving a direct answer, took advantage of this opportunity to teach her a moral lesson: she gave her a hard smack and told her that little boys and girls who were not good were also put in a ship like that.

'So really,' Pauline remarked judiciously, 'if the poor man cried at night, it served him right.'

Lisa picked up her sewing again, bending over her work. Quenu had not been listening. He had been cutting little rounds of onion over a pot placed on the fire; and almost at once the onions began to crackle, making a clear shrill chirrup like crickets basking in the heat. It smelt so good, and when Quenu plunged his great wooden spoon into it, the pot sang even louder and filled the kitchen with the pungent smell of cooked onions. Auguste was preparing some bacon fat in a dish, and Léon's chopper fell faster and faster, scraping the block now and then to gather up the sausage meat, now almost a paste.

'As soon as they arrived,' continued Florent, 'they took the man to an island called Devil's Island. There he found himself with other men who had been deported from their own country. They were all very unhappy. At first they had to do hard labour, like convicts. The guard who watched over them counted them three times every day, to be sure that nobody was missing. Later on, they were left free to do as they liked, being merely locked up at night in a big log cabin, where they slept in hammocks slung between two bars. After a year had gone by they were going about barefoot and their clothes had become so ragged that their skin showed through. They had managed to build some huts out of tree trunks to shelter them from the sun, which is so fierce in that country that it burns everything up. But the huts did not protect them from the mosquitoes, which covered them at night with sores and swellings. Several of them died, and the others turned quite yellow, so shrivelled and bedraggled, with their long beards, that they looked the most pitiful sight.'

'Give me the fat, Auguste,' called Quenu.

Tipping the dish, he gently slid the bacon fat into the pot, spreading it out with the end of his spoon. The fat melted. Thick steam rose from the stove.

'What were they given to eat?' asked little Pauline, fascinated by the story.

'Rice full of maggots and rotten meat,' answered Florent, his voice lowering as he spoke. 'They had to take the maggots out to eat the rice. When the meat was roasted and very well done, it was just possible to eat it; but if it was boiled, it stank so badly that it made the men feel sick.'

'I'd rather eat dry bread,' said the child, after a moment's thought.

Léon, having finished with the chopper, brought the sausage meat over to the table in a dish. Mouton, who was still sitting there with his eyes fixed on Florent, as if amazed by the story, had to move back an inch or two, which he did with very bad grace. He curled up and purred, his nose nearly touching the meat. Lisa, meanwhile, could scarcely hide her disgust. The dreadful rice and the rotten meat seemed to her to be unimaginable abominations, and a disgrace to those who ate it as much as to those who offered it. Her calm, handsome face and round neck began to quiver with vague fear as she gazed at this man who had lived on such horrible food.

'No, it was not a wonderful place,' continued Florent, forgetting all about little Pauline as he stared at the steaming pot. 'Every day there were fresh torments, constant brutality, violation of all principles of justice, contempt for human charity. It drove the prisoners mad. They lived like animals, constantly on the point of being whipped. The guards would have liked to kill the poor man… You don't forget something like that, you just can't. Torture like that will one day seek revenge.'

He had lowered his voice, which was now muffled by the sound of fat sizzling cheerfully on the stove. But Lisa heard him, and was struck by the very grim expression that had suddenly come over his face. Thinking of the gentle look he usually had, she thought he must be a hypocrite.

Florent's hollow voice had stimulated Pauline's interest even further, and she wriggled with excitement on her cousin's knee.

'What about the man?' she said. 'Tell me about the man.'

Florent looked at her, seemed to remember, and smiled his sad smile again.

'The man', he continued, 'couldn't bear to be on the island. He had a single thought in his head, and that was to get away, to cross the sea and reach the mainland. On fine days they could see the white coastline on the horizon. But it wasn't easy. They had to build a raft. As some of the prisoners had already managed to escape, all the trees on the island had been chopped down so that the others would have no timber. The island was laid waste, so bare and arid under the burning sun that their lives became even more unbearable. Then the man, with two of his companions, hit on the idea of using the logs their huts were made of. So one night, they put out to sea on a few rotten beams they had tied together with dry branches. The wind carried them towards the coast. As dawn was breaking they ran aground on a sandbank with such force that the beams they had used fell apart and were carried out to sea. They almost disappeared under the sand. Two of them sank in up to their waists, and the third up to his neck, so that he had to be pulled out. After a while they managed to get to a rock, so small that there was hardly room for them to sit on it. When the sun rose they could see the coast in front of them, a line of grey cliffs stretching along the horizon. The two of them who could swim decided to make for the cliffs. They preferred to risk being drowned to starving to death on the rock. They promised their companion that they would come back for him as soon as they reached dry land and found a boat.'

'Ah, I know now!' cried little Pauline, clapping her hands in delight. 'It's the story of the man who was eaten alive.'

'They managed to reach the coast,' Florent went on, 'but the island was deserted, and it took them four days to find a boat. When they got back to the rock they saw their companion lying on his back, his hands and feet eaten away, his face gnawed, and his stomach full of crabs crawling about, making his sides shake, as if the half-eaten corpse, still fresh, was in the throes of a terrible death agony.'

A murmur of disgust escaped Lisa and Augustine, and Léon, who was preparing the pigs' intestines for the black pudding, pulled a face. Quenu stopped what he was doing and looked at Auguste, who was obviously feeling sick. Only little Pauline was smiling. The others were imagining the ravenous crabs crawling all over the kitchen, mixing their stench with the aroma of the bacon fat and onions.

'Give me the blood!' cried Quenu, who had not been following the story.

Auguste brought the two buckets over, and slowly poured the blood into the pot while Quenu stirred the mixture furiously as it began to thicken. When the buckets were empty, Quenu reached up to the drawers above the range and took some pinches of spice. He was especially liberal with the pepper.

'They left him there, didn't they?' asked Lisa. 'And they got back safely?'

'On their way back,' Florent replied, 'the wind changed and they were blown out to sea. A wave carried off one of their oars, and they shipped so much water that they had to bale it out with their hands. They were tossed about along the coast, blown out to sea by squalls and brought in by the tide. Their little store of food was gone, they had absolutely nothing to eat. This went on for three days.'

'Three days!' cried Lisa in astonishment. 'Three days without food!'

'Yes, three days without food. When the east wind finally blew them ashore, one of them was so weak that he lay all morning on the sand. In the evening he died. His companion had tried in vain to get him to chew a few leaves.'

At this point Augustine gave a little laugh. Then, embarrassed at having done so and not wishing to be considered heartless, she stammered: 'Oh, I wasn't laughing at what you said. It was Mouton. Just look at Mouton, madame.'

Now it was Lisa's turn to laugh. Mouton, who still had the plate of sausage meat under his nose, had probably begun to feel disgusted by all this food, for he had risen and was scratching the table with his paws as though he wanted to bury the dish and its contents. He then turned his back on the dish and lay down on his side, stretching out with his eyes half closed, rubbing his head in pleasure against the table. At this everyone congratulated Mouton. He never stole a thing, they said, and even a plate of sausage meat could be safely left under his nose. Pauline told how he licked her fingers and washed her face after dinner without trying to bite her.

But Lisa returned to the question of whether it was possible to go for three days without touching food. It was, she felt, impossible.

'No,' she said, 'I don't believe it. No one ever goes three days without food. When people talk about a person dying of hunger, it's just a manner of speaking. People always manage to eat, somehow or other. Otherwise they'd have to be hopeless creatures, absolute…'

She was no doubt going to say something like 'scoundrels', but, glancing at Florent, she restrained herself. But the scornful pout of her lips and her straight unflinching gaze clearly implied that in her opinion only a scoundrel could ever go without food in this ill-regulated fashion. A man capable of living without food for three days struck her as a highly dangerous character. Respectable people never put themselves in that position.

By this time Florent was almost suffocating. In front of him, the stove, which Léon had just replenished with several shovelfuls of coal, was snoring like an old chorister asleep in the sun. The heat was becoming intense. Auguste, who had taken charge of the lard melting in the pots, was sweating profusely as he watched over it, while Quenu, wiping his brow with his sleeve, was waiting for the blood to thicken. The air was heavy with an atmosphere of drowsiness and gluttony.

'When the man had buried his companion in the sand,' Florent slowly continued, 'he set off by himself, walking in a straight line. Dutch Guiana, which is where he was, is a land of forests interspersed with rivers and swamps. The man walked for more than a week without coming across the slightest sign of human life. He felt the lurking presence of death all around him. His stomach was racked by hunger, but he didn't dare to eat the brightly coloured fruit that hung from the trees; he was afraid to touch the glittering metallic berries with their knotty bumps oozing with poison. For several whole days he walked under a canopy of branches without catching the slightest glimpse of sky, struggling through the greenish gloom that was alive with horrors of all kinds. Huge birds flew overhead with a terrible beating of wings and sudden cries that rang out like death rattles; monkeys leapt about, wild animals shot through the undergrowth ahead of him, making the foliage shake and bringing down showers of leaves. But it was the snakes that made his blood run cold when he trod on the shifting surface of dry leaves and saw their flat heads sliding between a tangled mass of roots. Some corners, dank and shadowy, were alive with reptiles—black, yellow, purple, striped, speckled and streaked, some like dead reeds suddenly coming to life and slithering away. Then he would stop and look for a stone on which to take refuge from the soft earth into which he was sinking; and there he would stay for hours, terror-stricken when he suddenly glimpsed some boa on the edge of a clearing, its tail coiled, its head erect, as straight as a tree trunk, and spotted with gold. At night he slept in trees, alarmed at the slightest rustling sound, convinced that he could hear the snakes slithering about in the dark. He almost suffocated in the foliage; the shadows were heavy with an intense, oppressive heat, a clammy dankness, an unhealthy sweating, and were filled with the smell of aromatic wood and strange flowers. And when at last, after walking for many miles, the man made his way out of the forest and saw the sky again, he found himself confronted by wide rivers that prevented him from going any further. He went along their banks, keeping a watchful eye on the grey backs of the alligators and the masses of drifting vegetation, and then, when he came to a safer spot, he swam across. On the other side, the forests began again. Then there were vast plains covered in thick vegetation, in which small lakes formed distant patches of blue. The man made a wide detour and moved forward only after testing the ground with his foot, for he had nearly met his end by being buried alive beneath one of these smiling plains which he could hear cracking under his tread. The giant grass, nourished by layers of thick leaf-mould, concealed the foul-smelling marshes and depths of liquid mud; and between the expanses of grassland that spread out in sea-green immensity to the distant horizon there were only a few narrow stretches of firm ground that had to be found if the traveller was to avoid disappearing forever. One night the man sank in up to his waist. With every move he made to free himself the mud threatened to rise up to his neck. For almost two hours he remained quite still. Fortunately, as the moon rose, he was able to catch hold of a tree branch above his head. By the time he finally struck upon signs of human life, his feet and hands were bruised and bleeding, and swollen with terrible bites. He cut so piteous a figure that those who saw him were afraid of him. They tossed him some food fifty metres away from the house, whose owner kept guard at his door with a loaded gun.'

Florent fell silent, his voice choked by emotion, staring blankly in front of him. For some minutes he had seemed to be talking to himself. Little Pauline, who was beginning to feel sleepy, was almost dozing in his arms. And Quenu was beginning to get annoyed.

'Be careful, you fool,' he shouted at Léon. 'Don't you know how to hold a skin yet? Stop looking at me. It's the skin you should look at, not me! That's right, hold it like that and don't move!'

With his right hand Léon was holding aloft a long piece of sausage skin, at one end of which a large funnel had been inserted; with his left hand he coiled the black pudding round a metal bowl while Quenu filled the funnel with big spoonfuls of the meat. The mixture, black and steaming, flowed through the funnel, gradually swelling the skin, which fell back in a fat, soft curve. Since Quenu had taken the pot off the fire, both he and Léon, the child with his thin features and the man with his full broad face, stood out in the fierce light of the stove, which bathed their pale faces and white clothing in a rosy glow.

Lisa and Augustine were watching the operation with great interest—especially Lisa, whose turn it now was to scold Léon for pinching the skin too tightly; that made it bumpy, she said. As soon as the black pudding was tied up, Quenu slipped it gently into a pot of boiling water. He seemed relieved, for all he now had to do was let it cook.

'And the man? What about the man?' murmured Pauline, opening her eyes, surprised that she could no longer hear her cousin's voice.

Florent rocked her on his knee, slowing his story down even more, speaking softly as if it were a lullaby.

'The man', he said, 'came to a big town. There he was taken at first for an escaped convict and was kept in prison for several months. Then he was set free and did all sorts of work—as an accountant, teaching children to read, and so forth; one day he even signed on as a labourer at some earthworks. He still dreamed of returning to his own country. He had saved enough money when he caught yellow fever. He was thought to be dead, and his clothes were stripped off him and shared out; and then he recovered and found he had nothing left, not even his shirt. He had to begin all over again. He was in very bad health, and he was afraid to stay there. But at last he was able to leave, and he came home.'

Florent's voice had sunk lower and lower, and with a last twitch of his lips it died away altogether. Little Pauline was asleep, her head resting on her cousin's shoulder. He held her with one arm and continued to rock her on his knee, very gently, hardly moving. As no one seemed to be paying any more attention, he remained there without moving, the sleeping child in the crook of his arm.

Now came the tug of war, as Quenu said. He had to take the black pudding out of the pot. To avoid breaking it or getting it entangled, he took it out with a thick wooden pin, rolled it up, and carried it into the yard, where it dried in the sun on wicker frames. Léon gave him a hand, holding up the ends that were too long. The steaming pudding left a trail of strong smells that made the atmosphere even heavier. Auguste, taking a last look at the melting lard, had taken the lids off the two pots in which the fat was simmering, releasing with each bubble that rose to the surface a light but acrid explosion of steam. The tide of fat had been rising since the evening's work had begun, and now it was shrouding the gaslights, filling the room, running and flowing everywhere, until Quenu and the two boys, their faces flushed, were enveloped in a kind of mist. Lisa and Auguste had stood up. Everyone in the room was panting, as if they had had too much to eat.

Augustine carried the sleeping Pauline upstairs. Quenu, who liked to lock up the kitchen himself, told Auguste and Léon that they could go to bed, saying he would bring the black pudding in himself. The apprentice stole off, looking extremely red; he had slipped about a metre of pudding into his shirt and it must have been scalding him. The Quenus and Florent, left alone, remained silent. Lisa stood nibbling a little piece of the hot pudding, chewing it delicately with her front teeth, her fine lips parted to avoid being burnt. Gradually the black compound disappeared into her pink mouth.

'Well,' she said, 'La Normande made a mistake in being so rude... The black pudding is very good.'

There was a knock at the back door and Gavard came in. He spent every evening until midnight at Monsieur Lebigre's. He had dropped in for a definite answer about the inspector's job.

'The thing is,' he said, 'Monsieur Verlaque can't wait any longer; he's too ill. Florent must make up his mind. I promised to give Monsieur Verlaque an answer first thing in the morning.'

'Florent says "yes",' replied Lisa quietly, taking another little bite out of her black pudding.

Florent, who had remained sitting in his chair, overcome by a strange feeling of despondency, tried to protest.

'No, no,' Lisa went on. 'It's settled. Look, Florent, you've suffered enough already. What you've told us tonight is shocking. It's time you settled down. You're part of a good family, you've been well educated; it's not right that you should walk around like a tramp. At your age you must stop behaving like a child. You may have done some stupid things in your time—well, all that will be forgiven and forgotten. You'll come back to be with your own class, a class of decent, respectable people, and live like everyone else.'

Florent listened in amazement, quite unable to say a word. No doubt she was right. She looked so healthy and self-assured that it was impossible to imagine that she meant any harm. It was he—thin, sickly, suspect—who must be in the wrong. He no longer knew why he had resisted her.

Lisa, unstoppable, went on chiding him as if he were a naughty little boy who must be frightened by threats of the police. She assumed, indeed, a most maternal manner and found some very persuasive arguments. Then, to crown her case, she said:

'Do it for us, Florent. We need to think of our reputation in the neighbourhood. Between you and me, I'm afraid that people will begin to talk. This job will solve everything; you'll be somebody, in fact you'll be a credit to us.'

Her voice had taken on a caressing tone. Florent felt as if he were bursting, overwhelmed by all the kitchen smells, by all the nourishment floating in the air. He was falling into the state of blissful complacency created by the continuous focus on food and well-being that defined the world in which he had been living for the last two weeks. He felt, as it were, the titillation of fat forming all over his body. His whole being was slowly being invaded by the languid contentment of a shopkeeper. At this late hour, in the warmth of the Quenus' kitchen, all his bitterness and all his convictions melted away. He felt so lulled by the general atmosphere, by the smell of the black pudding and lard, and the sight of plump little Pauline asleep on his lap, that he was surprised to find himself wishing for similar evenings, an endless series of them, evenings that would make him fatter. But it was Mouton who made up his mind for him. Mouton was now fast asleep on his back, one paw resting on his nose, his tail twisted over his side as if to keep him warm. He was sleeping with such a wonderful show of feline happiness that Florent, as he looked at him, murmured,

'Yes, I know. I'll take it. Say I'll take it, Gavard.'

Lisa finished her black pudding and wiped her fingers on her apron. Then she got her brother-in-law's candle for him, while Gavard and Quenu congratulated him on his decision. A man had to settle down; risking your neck in politics didn't put food on the table. Lisa, standing with the lighted candle in her hand, gazed at Florent with an air of satisfaction, her face as serene as that of the golden calf.

CHAPTER 3

THREE days later the formalities were completed, and the Préfecture accepted Florent on the recommendation of Monsieur Verlaque almost without question, as a quite straightforward replacement. Gavard had wanted to accompany them, and did so. When he found himself alone with Florent on the pavement outside, he nudged him in the ribs, laughing without saying a word and winking most wickedly. He seemed to find something ridiculous about the *sergents de ville* they passed on the Quai de l'Horloge, for, as they went by, he hunched his shoulders and grimaced like someone doing his best not to burst out laughing in somebody's face.

The very next day Monsieur Verlaque began to induct the new inspector into the duties of his office. For a few mornings he guided him through the busy world over which it would be his responsibility to watch. Poor old Verlaque, as Gavard called him, was a pale little man, swathed in flannel, neckerchiefs, and mufflers. Constantly coughing, he made his way through the chilly atmosphere and running water of the fish market on legs as spindly as those of a sickly child.

When Florent made his appearance on the first morning, at seven o'clock, he felt quite lost, his eyes wide with fright, his head almost bursting. The women stallholders were already prowling about the auction stands, while the clerks arrived with their ledgers, and the consigners' agents, with leather bags slung over their shoulders, sat on upturned chairs next to the sale booths, waiting for their money. The fish was being unloaded and unpacked in the area closed off by the stands, right up to the footpaths. Along the roadway were piles of wicker baskets. An endless supply of crates and panniers began to appear, along with sacks of mussels piled high and dripping with water. The checkers, tremendously busy, leapt over everything, tore away the straw on top of the baskets, emptied them, and tossed them aside. Then they quickly transferred their contents in lots to bigger baskets, arranging them with a turn of the hand so that they would show to best advantage. When the baskets had been set out, it looked to Florent as if a shoal of fish had run aground on the pavement, still quivering, in pearly pink, milky white, and bloody coral, all the soft, sheeny hues of the sea.

The seaweed that lies on the ocean bed where the mysteries of the deep lie sleeping had jumbled everything into the sweep of the net: cod, haddock, flounder, plaice, dabs, and other sorts of common fish in dirty grey spotted with white; conger eels, huge snake-like creatures, with small, black eyes and muddy, bluish skins, so slimy that they seemed to be still alive and gliding along; broad flat skate, their pale underbellies edged with a soft red, their superb backs, bumpy with vertebrae, marbled to the very tips of the bones in their fins, in sulphur-red patches cut across by stripes of Florentine bronze, a sombre assortment of colours from filthy toad to poisonous flower; dogfish, with hideous round heads, gaping mouths like Chinese idols, and short fins like bats' wings, monsters who doubtless kept guard over the treasures of the ocean grottoes. Then there were the finer fish, displayed individually on wicker trays: salmon, gleaming like chased silver, whose every scale seemed to have been exquisitely chiselled on highly polished metal; mullet, with larger scales and coarser markings; huge turbot and brill, their scales pure white and closely knit like curdled milk; tuna fish, smooth and glossy, like bags of black leather; and rounded bass, with gaping mouths, as if some outsize spirit, at the moment of death, had forced its way out of the surprised creatures' bodies. Everywhere there were soles, grey or pale yellow, heaped in pairs; sand eels, thin and stiff, like shavings of pewter; herrings, slightly twisted, with bleeding gills showing on their silver-worked skins; fat bream, tinged with crimson; golden mackerel, their backs stained with greenish brown markings, their sides shimmering like mother-of-pearl; and pink gurnet with white bellies, placed with their heads together in the middle of the baskets and their tails fanned out, so that they seemed like strange flowers in a bloom of pearly white and brilliant scarlet. There were red rock mullet, too, with their exquisite flesh; boxes of whiting, like opal reflections in a mirror; and baskets of smelt—neat little baskets as pretty as punnets of strawberries and giving off a strong smell of violets. The tiny jet-black eyes of the prawns, in covered baskets, were like thousands of beads scattered across the piles of soft-toned pink and grey; the spiky lobsters and crayfish, striped with black and still alive, were dragging themselves about on their broken legs.

Florent hardly listened to what Monsieur Verlaque said. A shaft of light suddenly came through the glass roof of the covered avenue, illuminating all these precious colours, toned and softened by the waves—the iridescent flesh-tints of the shellfish, the opal of the whiting, the mother-of-pearl of the mackerel, the gold of the mullet, the shimmering of the herring, the plated silver of the salmon. It was as if the jewel boxes of some sea nymph had been emptied out on dry land—a mass of fantastic ornaments, heaps of necklaces, fabulous bracelets and gigantic brooches, primitive gems and jewels, the use of which could never be divined. On the backs of the skate and dogfish, huge stones in dark green and purple were set in black metal, while the slender sand eels and the fins and tails of the smelt appeared as delicately made as the finest jewellery.

But what struck Florent most was the freshness of the air. A salty breeze reminded him immediately of the shores of Guiana and the fine days of the crossing. He half imagined that he was gazing at some bay from which the tide had receded, with seaweed steaming in the sun, the bare rocks drying, and the beach smelling of brine. Around him the fish, all very fresh, had that excellent, rather bitter and irri-tating smell that corrupts the appetite.

Monsieur Verlaque coughed. The dampness was affecting him, and he pulled his muffler tighter round his neck.

'Now,' he said, 'let's go on to the freshwater fish.'

There, near the fruit market and backing onto the Rue Rambuteau, the auction stand was flanked by two round tanks, divided into sep-arate compartments by iron gratings. Brass taps with curved, swan-like necks were spouting thin jets of water into them. The compartments contained swarming colonies of crayfish, black-backed carp forever on the move, and tangled masses of eels con-stantly twisting and twirling. Again Monsieur Verlaque gave in to a fit of coughing. Here the air was less damp: there was the soft smell of rivers, of warm water lying dormant on a bed of sand.

That morning an unusually large number of crayfish had arrived in boxes and baskets from Germany. The market was also well stocked with fish from Holland and England. Men were unpacking shiny carp from the Rhine, with rusty metallic hues, each of their scales a miniature shaped in bronze; others were busy with huge pike, the cruel iron-grey brigands of the water, thrusting out their fearsome jaws; or with dark, magnificent tench, like red copper stained with verdigris. Amidst the metal colours of these fish were baskets of gud-geon, perch, and trout, heaps of common bleak, flatfish trawled in nets and startlingly white, their steely-blue spines gradually softening into the gentle transparency of their bellies; and fat, snow-white barbel brought a sharp note of light into this colossal still life. Sackloads of young carp were being carefully poured into the tanks. Once in the water, they turned and wriggled, lay flat for a moment, then darted off and disappeared. Baskets of little eels were emptied in a mass, falling to the bottom of the tanks like tangled knots of snakes, while the larger ones, as thick as a child's arm, lifted their heads and slipped into the water with the supple twist of a snake slithering under a bush. In the meantime, the other fish, whose death agonies had lasted all morning as they lay on the dirty wicker of the baskets, slowly expired amidst the hubbub of the auctions. Every few seconds they opened their mouths, and gasped silently for breath, their sides drawn in as if to absorb the moisture of the air.

Monsieur Verlaque led Florent back to the stalls in the sea-fish market. He walked him up and down, treating him to a recital of the minutest particulars about everything. On all three sides within the market, round the nine desks, crowds of people had gathered, their heads bobbing in every direction; above them sat the clerks, perched on stools, making entries in their ledgers.

'Do all these clerks work for the salesmen?' asked Florent.

By way of reply Monsieur Verlaque made a detour along the outside footpath, taking him into the enclosure within the auction stands. He then proceeded to explain the working of the various departments of the big yellow office, which stank of fish and was stained all over from the splashings of the baskets. Right at the top, in a little glazed compartment, the collector of the municipal dues noted the prices fetched by the different lots of fish. Lower down, sitting on stools with their elbows resting on narrow desks, were two female clerks who kept an account of business for the salesmen. At each end of the stone table in front of the office was an auctioneer who brought in the baskets and shouted the price of the fish in bulk and as single items; above him the female clerk waited, pen in hand, for the prices to be knocked down and settled. Monsieur Verlaque showed Florent the cashier, shut up in another little wooden office outside the enclosure, an enormously fat old woman whom they found stacking piles of sous and five-franc pieces.

'There's a double control, you see,' said Monsieur Verlaque. 'The Préfecture of the Seine and the Préfecture of Police. The police, who appoint the salesmen, also take responsibility for keeping an eye on them.

And the municipal authorities must be represented at every transaction in order to claim their tax.'

On he went in his flat little voice, describing at length the rivalry between the two Préfectures. Florent was hardly listening. He was gazing at one of the female clerks opposite him. She was a tall, dark woman of about thirty, with big black eyes and a very self-assured air. Her fingers were poised and careful; she had obviously been well taught.

But his attention was distracted by the jabbering of the auctioneer, who was just offering a magnificent turbot for sale.

'Going for thirty francs… thirty francs!… thirty francs!'

He repeated this phrase in every imaginable tone of voice, running up and down a curious scale of notes full of vocal somersaults. Hunchbacked and with a crooked face and dishevelled hair, he wore a big blue apron with a bib. With blazing eyes and outstretched arms, he went on shouting:

'Thirty-one! Thirty-two! Thirty-three! Thirty-three fifty! Thirty-three fifty!'

He paused for breath, turning the basket round, pushing it forward on the stone table as the fishwives all bent forward and gently touched the turbot with the tips of their fingers. Then he took up his cry again with renewed energy, throwing a figure at each bidder with his hand, spotting the smallest signs, a lifted finger, a raised eyebrow, a pout of the lips, a wink; and all this with such speed and such a flood of words that Florent, who could follow none of it, was quite at a loss when the hunchback, in a voice even more singsong than before, like a cantor coming to the final verse of a hymn, intoned:

'Forty-two! Forty-two!… A turbot going for forty-two francs!'

La Belle Normande made the final bid. Florent recognized her in a row of fishwives standing against the iron railings that surrounded the enclosure. It was a crisp morning. There stood a line of *palatines*,* a display of big white aprons stretched over stomachs and enormous breasts and shoulders. The high bun adorned with curls, the delicate white skin, and the lace bow of La Belle Normande stood out amid so much frizzy hair wrapped in scarves, drunkards' noses, sneering mouths, and faces as ugly as old pots. She too was quick to recognize Madame Quenu's cousin and was so surprised to see him there that she began whispering to her neighbours about him.

The clamour of voices had become so great that Monsieur Verlaque gave up trying to explain things. Further away, men were advertising the larger fish in prolonged cries that seemed to come from giant loudspeakers; there was one in particular who was shouting 'Mussels! Mussels!' in such a raucous voice that the roof of the market shook. As they were overturned, the sacks of mussels tumbled into baskets; others were emptied with shovels. There was a ceaseless procession of basket-trays containing skate, soles, mackerel, conger eels, and salmon, carried backward and forward by the checkers amid the ever-increasing hubbub and the pushing of the fishwives, who were pressing so hard against the iron railings that they made them creak. The hunchbacked auctioneer, now at full throttle, waved his thin arms and thrust out his chin. Eventually he climbed onto a stool, spurred on by the strings of figures he threw in handfuls to the crowd, his mouth twisted, his hair flying in the wind, no longer able to drag from his dry throat more than an unintelligible screech. Above his head the municipal tax clerk, a little old man wrapped in a coat with a collar of imitation astrakhan above which only his nose could be seen, wore a black velvet cap, and the tall, dark woman on her high wooden chair was writing away patiently, her face slightly reddened by the cold, never even batting an eyelid at the shrieks emanating from the hunchback below her.

'That man Logre is first-rate,' murmured Monsieur Verlaque with a smile. 'He's the best auctioneer in the markets. He could sell a pair of boot soles as a pair of fish!'

They went back into the market. As they again passed in front of the freshwater auction, where the buying and selling was now much less heated, Monsieur Verlaque told Florent that here the sales were falling badly, and that the whole of freshwater fishing in France was in serious danger. A blond, weasel-faced auctioneer, who scarcely moved his arms, was pricing some lots of eels and crayfish in a monotonous voice, while the checkers moved down the tanks armed with short-handled nets to catch the fish.

However, the crowd round the sales desks was growing. Monsieur Verlaque continued to play his part as Florent's instructor in a very conscientious manner, elbowing his way through the crowd and guiding his successor through the busiest parts. The main retail dealers were there, loading the porters with turbot, tuna, and salmon. The street-hawkers, who had clubbed together to buy lots of herrings and small flatfish, were sharing them out on the footpath. And there were some bourgeois folk, from further afield, who had come at four in the morning to buy fresh fish and had let themselves be persuaded to take huge amounts at knock-down prices, so that they spent the rest of the day getting their friends to take the surplus off their hands. Every now and then some violent pushing would burst open part of the crowd. A fishwife, who had got squashed, would free herself, shaking her fists and pouring out a torrent of abuse. Then the compact wall of people would re-form. Florent, who was suffocating, declared that he had seen enough and understood what was expected of him.

As Monsieur Verlaque was helping him to get clear, they suddenly found themselves face to face with La Belle Normande. She stood squarely in front of them and said in her most regal manner:

'Is it true, Monsieur Verlaque, that you're leaving us?'

'Yes, yes,' the little man replied. 'I'm going to take a rest in the country, at Clamart. Smelling fish all the time is bad for me, it seems. This is the gentleman who is going to take my place.'

He gestured towards Florent. La Belle Normande was dumbfounded. And as Florent moved away, he thought he heard her whisper to her neighbours, with a laugh: 'Well, well—we're going to have some fun.'

The fishwives were preparing their displays. Water was gushing from the taps at the corners of the marble slabs. It sounded like a sudden shower, a hiss of steady jets of water, spurting and splashing. From the edges of the sloping slabs, great drops fell with a gentle murmur, creating a maze of tiny streams that flowed along, turning holes and ruts into miniature lakes and dividing into a thousand tributaries that disappeared down the sloping street towards the Rue Rambuteau. A moist haze rose into the air, a sort of dusty rain that blew a fresh breeze in Florent's face, reminding him again of the pungent, salty breeze of the sea; and in the fish already laid out he rediscovered the pink mother-of-pearl, the blood-red coral, the milky pearl, all the sheens and colours of the ocean.

This first morning left him feeling very doubtful. He was sorry he had given in to Lisa. Ever since his escape from the greasy atmosphere of the kitchen, he had been accusing himself of cowardice so much that it almost brought tears to his eyes. But he did not dare to go back on his word. He was a little afraid of Lisa and could imagine the curl of her lips and the look of reproach on her face. He regarded her as a woman too serious-minded, too well satisfied, to be trifled with. Fortunately, Gavard made a suggestion that did much to console him. On the evening of the day Monsieur Verlaque had shown him round the auctions, he took him aside and told him, in a roundabout manner, that 'the poor devil' was in a bad way. After various remarks about a Government so fiendish that it ground the life out of its servants without even allowing them enough money to die in comfort, he ended by hinting that it would be charitable of him to give part of his salary to the old inspector. Florent was delighted with the suggestion. It was only fair, for he considered himself only a temporary replacement for Monsieur Verlaque; and besides, he had no particular needs of his own, as he boarded and lodged with his brother. Gavard added that, out of his monthly salary of one hundred and fifty francs, a share of fifty would be about right; and, lowering his voice, he added that it would not be for long, for the old man was absolutely riddled with consumption. It was thus agreed that Florent would pay a call on his wife and arrange matters with her, to avoid hurting her husband's feelings. The thought of this good deed gave him much relief; he could now accept his duties with a certain amount of pleasure, for it meant that he could return to the part he had played throughout his life. However, he made the poultry dealer promise that he would not tell a soul about this arrangement; and as Gavard was also rather afraid of Lisa, he kept the secret—which was for him a remarkable feat.

Now the entire *charcuterie* was happy. La Belle Lisa behaved in the most friendly way towards her brother-in-law. She made sure that he went to bed early, so that he would be able to rise in good time for work; she kept his lunch hot; she was no longer ashamed to be seen chatting with him in the street, now that he wore his braided cap. Quenu, delighted to see her so well disposed, had never sat so contentedly at the table, between his brother and his wife, in the evening. They often lingered over dinner until nine o'clock, leaving Augustine in charge of the shop. They digested their food in a leisurely fashion, gossiping about the neighbourhood and listening to Lisa's dogmatic opinions on politics. Florent had to report on the state of business in the fish market. Gradually he began to feel more relaxed, managing at last to taste the delights of the settled life he was now leading. The dining room, in pale yellow, had a bourgeois comfort and tidiness about it that disarmed him as soon as he crossed the threshold. The kind attentions of La Belle Lisa wrapped him in a fleecy warmth that softened every part of his mind and body. Mutual esteem and general harmony reigned supreme.

Gavard, however, felt that the household needed shaking up. He forgave Lisa her weakness for the Emperor, because, he said, one should never discuss politics with women, and La Belle Lisa was, after all, a decent person who managed her business very well. Nevertheless, he preferred to spend his evenings at Monsieur Lebigre's, where he met regularly with a group of friends who shared his opinions. As soon as Florent was appointed inspector at the fish market, he enticed him out of the house and strolled about with him for hours, saying he should lead a real bachelor's life now that he had a job.

Monsieur Lebigre kept a fine establishment, very modern in its luxury. Situated on the corner of the Rue Pirouette and the Rue Rambuteau, fronted by four little Norwegian pines in green-painted tubs, it made a worthy partner to the Quenu-Gradelles' large *charcuterie*. Through the clear glass windows you could see the interior, decorated with garlands of leaves, vine branches, and grapes, painted on the pale green walls. The floor was tiled in black and white. At the end of the room was the yawning cellar entrance, under a spiral staircase hung with red curtains, which led to the billiard room on the first floor. But it was the counter, on the right, that stood out; it looked most sumptuous, with its broad expanse of polished silver. Its wavy zinc-work overhung the red and white marble base, thus overlaying it with a silky sheen, a metal cloth, like a high altar laden with embroidery. At one end, over a gas burner, were some china jugs rimmed in copper, for punch and mulled wine; at the other end, from a lofty fountain of elaborately sculptured marble, a thin stream of water trickled into a bowl, so steady and continuous that it seemed motionless; and in the middle, at the centre of the three zinc counters, was a basin for rinsing and cooling, in which litre bottles of draught wine reared their greenish necks. Then, arranged in groups on both sides, stood the army of glasses: little glasses for brandy, thick tumblers for draught wine, cup glasses for brandied fruit, absinthe glasses, beer mugs, and tall goblets, all turned upside down and reflecting the glitter of the counter. On the left was a metal urn mounted on a pedestal, intended for tips, and on the right a similar urn bristling with a fan of small spoons.

As a rule Monsieur Lebigre was enthroned behind the counter on a bench covered with red quilted leather. Within easy reach of his hand were the liqueurs in cut-glass decanters protruding from the compartments of a stand. He would lean back against a huge mirror that covered a whole section of wall behind him; across it ran two glass shelves holding jars and bottles of every kind. On one of them, jars of preserved fruit, cherries, plums, and peaches, stood out darkly; on the other, between neatly arranged packets of biscuits, were flasks of bright green, red, and yellow, suggesting mysterious liqueurs, or exquisitely limpid flower essences. These flasks seemed suspended in the air, flashing as if on fire, in the white glow of the mirror.

To give his establishment the appearance of a café, Monsieur Lebigre had placed two small tables of bronzed iron, together with four chairs, against the wall opposite the counter. A chandelier with five arms and frosted glass bowls hung from the ceiling. On the left was a round gilt clock, on a revolving stand fixed to the wall. Then, at the back, there was a private room, a corner of the shop separated off by a partition of frosted glass with a complex design of little squares. During the day a dim light entered the room from a window that looked onto the Rue Pirouette, but in the evening the gas was lit above two tables painted to look like marble. It was here that Gavard and his political friends met every evening after dinner. They regarded the place as theirs and had prevailed upon Lebigre to reserve it exclusively for them. When the last one arrived and closed the partition door behind him, they knew that they were so safe that they could talk quite freely about 'the big clean-up'. No ordinary customer would have dared to come in.

On the first day Gavard took Florent off, he told him a few things about Monsieur Lebigre. He was a good sort and would sometimes come and have a coffee with them. They did not feel in the least inhibited, for he had told them one day that he had fought in '48.* He did not say much and seemed rather stupid. On their way through, before retiring to the back room, each of them shook his hand in silence over the glasses and bottles. Quite often a small blonde woman would sit at his side on the red leather bench, a girl he had engaged to serve at the bar in addition to the white-aproned waiter who looked after the tables and the billiard room. Her name was Rose, and she seemed a very gentle and submissive creature. Gavard told Florent with a wink that she was especially submissive to Lebigre. It was she who waited on the gentlemen in the back room, going in and out with her humble but happy look in the midst of the most stormy political discussions.

On the day when the poultry dealer introduced Florent to his friends, the only person they found in the little room was a man of about fifty, quiet and thoughtful in appearance, wearing a shabby hat and a heavy brown overcoat. He sat with his chin resting on the ivory handle of a long stick, in front of a brimming mug of beer. His mouth was so completely concealed by a thick beard that his face had a dumb, lipless appearance.

'How goes it, Robine?' asked Gavard.

Robine silently stretched out his hand, his eyes even softer now as they gave a slight smile of welcome. Then he let his chin drop again onto the handle of his stick and looked at Florent over his beer. Florent had made Gavard swear to keep his story a secret for fear of some dangerous indiscretion, but he was not displeased to detect a certain suspicion in the cautious attitude of the man with the beard. In fact he was mistaken, for Robine was always as silent as this. He was always the first to arrive, on the stroke of eight, and he always sat in the same corner, never letting go of his stick and never taking off his hat and coat. No one had ever seen him not wearing his hat. He stayed there listening to the others until midnight, taking four hours to empty his mug, looking at each one in turn as they spoke, as if listening with his eyes. When Florent asked Gavard about Robine afterwards, he gathered that the poultry dealer had a high opinion of him. He was an extremely clever man, he said; and, without explaining why, he declared that he was one of the Government's most formidable opponents. He lived in the Rue Saint-Denis, but hardly ever received visitors. Gavard said, however, that he had been there once. The polished floors were protected by green canvas runners; there were covers on the furniture, and an alabaster clock on columns. Madame Robine, whom he thought he had glimpsed disappearing through a door, appeared to be an elderly lady of genteel appearance, with her hair done in ringlets—as far as he could tell, at any rate. No one knew why they had come to live amid all the noise and bustle of a commercial neighbourhood; for Robine did absolutely nothing, spending his days no one knew how and living on no one knew what, though every evening he made his appearance as if he were tired but delighted with some excursion he had made into the higher reaches of politics.

'So, have you read the speech from the throne?'* asked Gavard, picking up a newspaper from the table.

Robine shrugged. Just at that moment, however, the door opened noisily and a hunchback entered the room. Florent recognized at once the hunchback from the fish market, though his hands were now washed and he had changed his clothes; he wore a big red muffler, one end of which hung down over his humped back like the corner of a Venetian cloak.

'Ah, here's Logre!' exclaimed the poultry dealer. 'I'm sure he'll tell us what he thought about the speech.'

Logre, it appeared, was furious. He nearly broke the hook off the wall as he hung up his hat and muffler. Then he sat down violently, thumped the table, and threw the newspaper aside.

'Do you think I read their filthy lies!' he exclaimed.

Then he burst out:

'Did you ever hear of employers treating their staff as they do! I had to wait two hours for my pay! There were at least ten of us in the office. We had to sit there until Monsieur Manoury arrived in a cab, straight from the brothel, no doubt. Those salesmen are all thieves and good-for-nothings! And even then the bastard gave me the money in small change!'

Robine expressed his sympathy with a slight movement of his eyelids. But suddenly the hunchback thought of a victim upon whom to vent his anger.

'Rose! Rose!' he cried, putting his head round the door.

As soon as the young woman stood trembling before him, he shouted: 'It's no good just staring at me! You saw me come in, didn't you? Where's my coffee?'

Gavard ordered two more coffees, and Rose hurried to bring them. Logre glared at the glasses and little sugar trays as if trying to decipher something. When he had taken a sip he seemed to calm down somewhat.

'Charvet must be getting fed up,' he said after a while. 'He's waiting outside for Clémence.'

At this point Charvet made his appearance, followed by Clémence. He was a tall, scraggy young man, close-shaven, with a pinched nose and thin lips. He lived in the Rue Vavin, behind the Luxembourg, and described himself as a teacher. In politics he was a disciple of Hébert.* He wore his hair very long, and the collar and lapels of his threadbare coat were turned back very broadly. Affecting the manner and speech of a member of the National Convention,* he would pour out such a flood of bitter words and make such a haughty display of pedantic learning that he generally got the better of his opponents. Gavard was afraid of him, though he would not admit it; when Charvet was not there, however, he would say that he went too far. Robine, for his part, expressed approval of everything with his eyebrows. Logre sometimes took issue with Charvet on the question of salaries; but Charvet was the real autocrat of the group, the most authoritative as well as the best informed. For the last ten years he and Clémence had lived together as man and wife according to a mutually agreed arrangement that was strictly observed on both sides. Florent looked at the woman with some surprise, and realized where he had seen her: it was none other than the tall, dark secretary at the fish auction, who was so well practised in the art of holding a pen.

Rose appeared on the heels of these newcomers. Without a word she put a tankard of beer in front of Charvet and a tray in front of Clémence, who then began calmly to prepare her grog, pouring hot water on a lemon, which she crushed with a spoon, adding sugar and rum by the measure so as not to exceed the right amount. Gavard now introduced Florent to the assembled company, and to Charvet in particular. He introduced them to each other as teachers, a couple of very talented men who were sure to get on well together. But it was assumed that Florent had already committed some indiscretion, for they all exchanged handshakes, gripping each other's fingers in a Masonic fashion. Charvet, for his part, was almost amiable. All of them, moreover, avoided making any allusions.

'Did Manoury pay you in small change?' Logre asked Clémence.

She said that he had, and produced some rolls of one-franc and two-franc notes, which she unfolded. Charvet watched her, following her movements as she put the rolls back in her pocket, after checking the amount.

'We'll have to settle our accounts,' he said softly.

'Yes, tonight,' she murmured. 'I think we're about square. We had lunch four times, didn't we? But I lent you a hundred sous last week.'

Florent, surprised by this exchange, discreetly turned away. And as Clémence slipped the last roll into her pocket, she took a sip of grog, leaned back against the glass partition and began to listen to the men talking politics. Gavard had again picked up the newspaper and, in a funny voice, read out some passages of the speech from the throne, which had been delivered that morning at the opening of the Chamber of Deputies. Charvet then proceeded to make tremendous fun of the official phraseology; there was not a line he did not pull to pieces. One sentence in particular amused them enormously: 'We are confident, gentlemen, that, guided by your wisdom and the conservative sentiments of our country, we shall be able to increase national prosperity day by day.' Logre stood up to declaim this sentence, doing a very good imitation of the Emperor's nasal voice.

'He's got a funny notion of prosperity,' said Charvet. 'Everyone's starving to death!'

'Trade is bad,' remarked Gavard.

'And what on earth does "guided by your wisdom" mean?' said Clémence, who prided herself on her literary knowledge.

Even Robine allowed himself a faint laugh from the depths of his beard. The conversation was warming up. They moved on to events at the Corps Législatif, about which they spoke with great severity. Logre's temper did not improve, and Florent saw that he was the same as when he was auctioning fish at the market—his jaws jutting forward, hurling his words into the air with a wave of his arms, while maintaining a crouching position like a snarling dog. He talked politics with the same ferocity as he sold a basket of soles. Charvet, on the other hand, became quieter and colder in the haze of tobacco and burning gas that filled the tiny room; his voice became dry and cutting, like the blade of a guillotine, while Robine gently nodded without raising his chin from the ivory handle of his stick. After a while, some remark of Gavard's led them to the subject of women.

'Women', declared Charvet, 'are men's equals. And as such, they should not get in his way. Marriage is a partnership. Fifty-fifty. Isn't that so, Clémence?'

'Of course,' replied the young woman, leaning back against the partition and gazing into the air.

At this point the greengrocer Lacaille came in, along with Alexandre, the burly porter, Claude Lantier's friend. For a long time the two men had always gone to sit at the other table in the room; they did not belong to the group. With the help of politics, however, their chairs had drawn closer, and they had ended by joining the company. Charvet, in whose eyes they represented 'the people', did his best to indoctrinate them, while Gavard played the host, the shopkeeper free of prejudices, and clinked glasses with them. Alexandre had the cheerful disposition of a young giant and the looks of a happy child. Lacaille, on the other hand, was quite sour; his hair was already going grey and, aching in every part of his body from his endless journeys through the streets of Paris, he would cast dubious glances from time to time at the placid figure of Robine, with his good shoes and heavy overcoat. They all ordered a small glass of brandy and the talk grew more heated now that the group was complete.

A little later Florent glimpsed Mademoiselle Saget through the half-open door. She was standing in front of the counter. She had taken a bottle from under her apron and was watching Rose as she filled it with a large measure of blackcurrant wine and a smaller one of brandy. Then the bottle disappeared again under her apron, and, her hands hidden, she started to chat, in the glow of the counter, opposite the mirror, in which the bright jars and bottles seemed to hang like Chinese lanterns. In the evening all the metal and glass seemed to light the place up. The old maid, standing there in her black skirts, seemed like some big, strange insect in the crude brilliance of the room. Seeing that she was trying to get Rose to talk, Florent suspected that she had noticed him through the half-open door. Ever since his arrival in Les Halles, he had seen her everywhere, standing in one of the covered avenues, usually with Madame Lecœur and La Sarriette. All three of them seemed always to be watching him out of the corners of their eyes, apparently surprised at his new appointment. Rose must have been slow to answer her questions, for Mademoiselle Saget turned away for a moment and seemed about to have a word with Monsieur Lebigre, who was playing cards with a customer at one of the tables. Then she managed to creep slowly up to the partition, but was suddenly spotted by Gavard, who detested her.

'Shut the door, Florent!' he said curtly. 'There's no privacy here.'

At midnight, as they were leaving, Lacaille exchanged a few private words with Monsieur Lebigre. The latter, as he shook hands with him, slipped four five-franc pieces into his palm, without anyone noticing.

'That makes twenty-two francs you'll have to pay tomorrow, okay?' he whispered. 'The person lending the money won't help any more otherwise… And don't forget, you owe three days for the cart. It's all got to be paid for.'

Monsieur Lebigre wished the company goodnight. He would certainly sleep well, he said; and he gave a slight yawn, showing his big teeth, while Rose gazed at him submissively. He gave her a push, telling her to put out the gas in the little room.

Outside on the pavement, Gavard stumbled and nearly fell. But feeling quite witty, he exclaimed:

'Damn it! Obviously I haven't got the guiding hand of wisdom.'

This seemed very amusing, and on that note the party broke up. Florent returned regularly to Lebigre's, and became quite attached to the little private room, enjoying Robine's silence, Logre's outbursts, and Charvet's ferocity. When he got home afterwards, he did not go straight to bed. He liked his attic, the girlish room where Augustine had left pieces of ribbon and other odds and ends. There were some hairpins on the mantelpiece, gilt cardboard boxes full of buttons, cut-out pictures, and empty face-cream jars still smelling of jasmine. In the drawer of the rickety deal table, there were some reels of thread, some needles, a prayer book, and a tattered copy of *La Clef des songes*.* A white, yellow-spotted summer dress hung forgotten from a hook, while on the wooden board that served as a dressing table, behind a water jug, an overturned bottle of lotion had left a big stain. Florent would have been very uncomfortable sleeping in a woman's boudoir; but this little chamber, with its narrow iron bedstead, two cane-bottomed chairs, even the faded grey wallpaper, suggested merely the naïve slow-wittedness of a fat young girl. He was happy with the purity of the white curtains, the girlishness of the gilded boxes and *La Clef des songes*, the crude coquettishness that stained the walls. He found it refreshing, and it took him back to the dreams of his youth. He would have liked it better if he had never met Augustine, with her coarse brown hair, but to have been able to imagine that he was in the room of a sister, some fine sweet girl who had arranged around him all the little signs of her budding womanhood.

It was always a great comfort for him in the evening to lean out of the attic window. In front of it was a narrow ledge with an iron railing, forming a sort of balcony, on which Augustine had been growing a pomegranate plant in a box. Since the nights had turned cold, Florent had brought the pomegranate indoors and kept it at the foot of his bed till morning. He would stand for a few minutes by the open window, breathing the fresh air wafted up from the Seine over the housetops of the Rue de Rivoli. Below him the roofs of Les Halles spread out in a confused mass. They looked like sleeping lakes, on whose surface the reflection of a window pane gleamed every now and then like a silvery ripple. In the distance the roofs of the meat and poultry markets lay in darkness, forming a shadowy mass receding towards the horizon. Florent delighted in the great stretch of sky before him, in the vastness of Les Halles which, amid the narrow streets of the city, reminded him vaguely of the seashore, of the still grey waters of a bay barely stirred by the far-off rolling of the swell. He would lose himself in dreams as he stood there; each night he would imagine some fresh coastline. It made him very sad, and at the same time very happy, to return in his mind to the eight hopeless years he had spent away from France. Then, shivering all over, he would pull the window shut. Often, as he stood in front of the fireplace taking off his collar, he was disturbed by the photograph of Auguste and Augustine. Standing hand in hand, smiling slightly, they seemed to be watching him as he undressed.

Florent's first few weeks in the fish market were extremely hard work. The Méhudins treated him with open hostility, which helped to turn the whole market against him. La Belle Normande was bent on getting her revenge on La Belle Lisa, and her cousin was a heaven-sent victim.

The Méhudins came from Rouen. Louise's mother still told the story of how she had arrived in Paris in a basket of eels. After that, she had never left the fish trade. She had married a toll-gate keeper, who had died leaving her with two little girls. It was she who, with her broad hips and glowing complexion, had earned the nickname of 'La Belle Normande', which her elder daughter had inherited. Now sixty-five, she had become flabby and shapeless, and the damp air of the market had made her voice rough and cracked and given her skin a bluish tinge. Her sedentary life had made her enormous, and her head was thrown back by the weight of her bust, by the rising tide of fat. She had never been able to give up the fashions of her day, but had kept the gaudy dress, the yellow shawl, the traditional neckerchief of the fishwife, which went well with the loud voice, the quick movements, the hands on hips, and the vulgar slang and abuse that flowed from her lips like a catechism. She missed the Marché des Innocents, talked about the ancient rights of the market 'ladies', told stories of fistfights with the police, and reminisced about her visits to Court in the time of Charles X and Louis-Philippe, dressed in silks and carrying large bouquets. Mère Méhudin, as she was called, had for a long time been the standard-bearer of the Sisterhood of the Virgin at Saint-Leu. For processions in the church she wore a dress and a bonnet of tulle decked with satin ribbons, and she held on high in her puffy fingers the gilded staff of the silk standard, embroidered with a figure of the Mother of God.

According to local gossip, Mère Méhudin must have made a great deal of money, though the only sign of it was the solid gold jewellery she loaded on her neck, arms, and bosom on important occasions. Her two daughters did not get on well together as they grew up. The younger one, Claire, a lazy, fair-haired girl, complained of the ill-treatment she received at the hands of her sister Louise, saying in her slow voice that she would never agree to be her sister's servant. As they would certainly have ended by coming to blows, their mother separated them. She gave her stall in the fish market to Louise, while Claire, who was subject to fits of coughing at the smell of skate and herrings, took a stall to sell freshwater fish. And their mother, although she swore that she had retired altogether, went from one stall to the other, interfering in the selling of the fish, and causing her daughters continual trouble because of the insolent way she spoke to the customers.

Claire was a curious person, very gentle and sweet, and yet constantly quarrelling with others. People said she was very headstrong. In spite of her dreamy, girlish face, she had a kind of dumb obstinacy, a spirit of independence that prompted her to live apart; she never saw things as other people did, scrupulously fair one day but monstrously unjust the next. Sometimes she would throw the market into confusion by suddenly raising or dropping prices at her stall for no apparent reason. By the time she was thirty, her delicate physique and fine skin, which the water in the tanks seemed to keep continually fresh and soft, her small-featured face, and her supple limbs, were all destined to become heavy and coarse, until she looked like some faded saint that had stepped down from a stained glass window into the degraded world of the markets. But at twenty-two, in the midst of her carp and eels, she was, as Claude would say, as fresh as a Murillo—a Murillo with dishevelled hair, heavy shoes, and chunky dresses that made her appear quite shapeless. There was nothing flirtatious about her, and she became quite contemptuous when Louise, flaunting her ribbons and bows, teased her about her badly knotted shawls. It was said that the son of a rich shopkeeper in the neighbourhood had gone abroad in despair after failing to win her heart.

Louise, La Belle Normande, was different. She had been engaged to a man in the corn market; but the poor fellow had broken his back in an accident with a sack of flour. Seven months afterwards, however, she had given birth to a boy. In the Méhudin circle she was looked upon as a widow. The old fishwife would sometimes say: 'When my son-in-law was alive…'

The Méhudins were a real power in the markets. When Monsieur Verlaque had finished instructing Florent in his new duties, he advised him to be very prudent in his dealings with certain of the stallholders, unless he wished to make life intolerable for himself; he was even prepared to teach him the little tricks of the trade—when it was important to turn a blind eye, when he should feign displeasure, when he should be prepared to accept gifts. A market inspector is at once a policeman and a magistrate; he has to maintain order and cleanliness, and also settle disputes between buyers and sellers. Florent, whose character was weak, became artificially stiff when he was obliged to exercise his authority; and he also had to cope with the bitterness born of long suffering, the sombre spirit of an outcast.

The tactics of La Belle Normande were to involve him in quarrels. She had sworn that he would not keep his job for more than two weeks.

'Well,' she said to Madame Lecœur one morning, 'that fat Lisa's much mistaken if she thinks she can dump her left-overs on us!… We've got better taste. That man of hers is hideous.'

After the auctions, as Florent began his round of inspection, picking his way along the pathways running with water, he would see La Belle Normande watching him with an impudent smile on her face. Her stall, in the second row on the left, near the freshwater fish, faced the Rue Rambuteau. She would turn round and make fun of him with her neighbours, without ever taking her eyes off him. Then, as he walked past, slowly examining the slabs, she pretended to be in the highest of spirits, slapping her fish all over the place, and turning on her tap so that the water flooded the pathway. Florent remained unperturbed.

But one morning, inevitably, war broke out. When Florent arrived at La Belle Normande's stall, he was met by an unbearable stench. There, on the marble slab, lay a superb salmon cut to reveal the light pink of its flesh; some creamy white turbot; conger eels, pierced with black pins to mark off the portions; several pairs of soles, and some bass and red mullet—in fact, quite a display. But in the middle of all these bright-eyed fish whose gills were still spilling blood, there lay a large reddish skate, marbled with dark stains and resplendent in its strange colourings. Unfortunately, the skate was rotten; its tail was falling off and the ribs of its fins were breaking through the skin.

'You must throw that skate away,' said Florent, as he approached.

La Belle Normande laughed. Looking up, Florent saw her standing before him, leaning against the bronze lamp post which lit up the four stalls in her section. She was standing on a box to protect her feet from the water and seemed very tall as he looked up at her. She pursed her lips, looking even more beautiful than usual, with her hair arranged in little curls, her head lowered, and her red hands standing out against her big white apron. Florent had never seen her wearing so much jewellery. She had long earrings, a chain round her neck, a brooch, a set of rings on two fingers of her left hand and one finger of her right.

As she continued to stare at him, without replying, he repeated:

'Do you hear? You must get rid of that skate.'

He had not noticed Mère Méhudin sitting on a chair in a corner. She now got up, however, ready for battle; planting her fists on the marble slab, she exclaimed insolently:

'And why should she throw her skate away? You're not proposing to buy it, I suppose?'

Florent suddenly understood what was happening. The women at the other stalls were tittering, and he felt all around him a latent feeling of revolt. He restrained himself and pulled the rubbish can from underneath the stall and dropped the skate into it. Mère Méhudin had already put her hands on her hips; but La Belle Normande, who had not uttered a word, laughed maliciously as Florent strode away amid a chorus of jeers, which he pretended not to hear.

Every day there was something new. He had to walk through the market as if he were in enemy territory. He was splashed with water from the sponges used to clean the slabs; he slipped and almost fell because of the rubbish spread under his feet; and even the porters contrived to hit him in the neck with their baskets. One morning, when he rushed up to prevent a fight between two of the fishwives, he had to duck to avoid being pelted by a shower of little dabs that flew over his head. There was much laughter at this, and he always believed that the two fishwives were in league with the Méhudins. However, his experience as a teacher had armed him with the patience of an angel, and he was able to maintain a schoolmasterly calm even when he was boiling with anger and his whole being was quivering with humiliation. But the children in the Rue de l'Estrapade had never been as fierce as the ladies of Les Halles, a relentless mob of enormous women, whose bellies and bosoms shook with delight when-ever he fell into one of their traps. Red faces stared at him insolently. In their ribald voices, the aggressive swing of their hips, their swelling throats and thighs, and the gesturing of their hands, he could read something of the torrent of abuse that was directed at him. Gavard would have been in his element amid all these petticoats and would have administered a few good slaps if they had got too close. But Florent had always been afraid of women, and he began to feel as if he were having a nightmare in which giant women, prodigiously well endowed, were closing in on him, shouting and brandishing their bare, prizefighters' arms.

Among this horde of women, Florent had one friend. Claire made a point of declaring that she thought the new inspector a fine man. When he walked by, braving the vulgar taunts of her neighbours, she gave him a smile. She sat nonchalantly behind her stall with locks of blonde hair falling over her neck and temples, her dress crookedly fastened. Usually he saw her there with her hands in the tanks, transferring the fish from one compartment to another, amusing herself by turning on the brass taps, shaped like little dolphins whose mouths poured forth streams of water. This trickling water gave her the quivering grace of a bather at the edge of a stream, who has just slipped on her clothes.

One morning in particular she was very friendly. She called Florent over to show him a huge eel which had been the wonder of the market when exhibited at the auction. She removed the grating which she had been sensible enough to put over the basin in which the eel seemed to be sound asleep.

'Look,' she said. 'Watch this.'

Then she gently slipped her arm into the water. It was a slender arm on which the soft blue veins showed through the silken skin.

As soon as the eel felt her touch, it turned and twisted and seemed to fill the tank with its glistening greenish coils. As soon as it had settled down again, Claire stirred it once more with her fingertips.

'It's huge,' Florent felt bound to say. 'I've rarely seen anything like it.'

Claire confessed that she used to be terrified of eels; but now she had learned how to tighten her grip so that the eel couldn't wriggle out of her hands. She took a smaller one from the next tank. It began to wriggle with head and tail as she held it in the middle with both hands. It made her laugh. She let it go, then grabbed another, stirring up the tank and disturbing the whole heap of serpent-like creatures with her slim fingers.

She paused for a moment to chat about business, which was rather slack. The stallkeepers along the footpath in the covered avenue were doing them a lot of harm. As she was talking, her bare arm, which she had not bothered to dry, was still dripping wet. Large drops were falling from her fingers.

'Oh,' she said suddenly, 'I must show you my carp!'

She removed a third grating and, with both hands, took out a carp, which began to flap its tail and gasp. She looked for a smaller one, and this she was able to hold in one hand, which was forced open a little each time the fish gasped. She thought it would be fun to put her thumb into its gaping mouth.

'It doesn't bite,' she murmured, laughing softly. 'It's quite harmless. So are the crayfish; I'm not at all frightened of them.'

She plunged her arm into the water again and brought up from a compartment full of confused activity a crayfish that had caught her little finger in its claws. She gave it a shake, but it was holding on very tightly; she grew red and snapped its claw with a quick, angry gesture, without losing her smile.

'By the way,' she said, to cover her embarrassment, 'I wouldn't trust a pike. It would cut my fingers off like a knife.'

She then showed him some big pike arranged in order of size on some clean scrubbed boards, next to some bronze-coloured tench and some small heaps of gudgeon. By now her hands were quite slimy with handling the carp; as she stood there in the dampness rising from the tanks, she held them out over the wet fish on the stall. She seemed enveloped in an odour of spawn, that heavy smell that rises from reeds and water lilies when the eggs fill the bellies of fish to bursting point as they bask in the sunlight. Then she wiped her hands on her apron, still smiling the placid smile of a girl who knew nothing of passion as he stood gazing at the icy shivers of the dying fish before her.

Claire's friendliness was small consolation to Florent. By stopping to chat with her he only attracted more jeers. She shrugged and said her mother was an old hag and her sister not much better. The injustice of the market people towards Florent made her angry. But the campaign against him became more vicious every day. Florent had serious thoughts of giving up the job; he would not have stuck it for a day if he had not been afraid of seeming cowardly to Lisa. He was worried about what she might think and say. She was well aware, of course, of the great battle raging between the fishwives and their inspector, for everyone in Les Halles was talking about it, and each fresh incident attracted endless comment.

'Oh well,' she would often say after supper at night, 'I'd never put up with their nonsense! They're all filthy sluts. I wouldn't touch any of them with a barge-pole! La Normande is the absolute limit... I'd soon show her what's what! You should use your authority, Florent. Your approach isn't right. If you put your foot down, they'll behave.'

The battle soon reached a terrible climax. One morning Madame Taboureau, the baker's wife, sent her servant to the market for a brill. La Belle Normande, who had seen her wandering around, began to make overtures to her:

'Come over here. I'll fix you up. Would you like a pair of soles or a lovely turbot?'

When at last the maid came up and sniffed at a brill with that dissatisfied expression customers have when they are trying to get something very cheaply, La Belle Normande continued:

'Just feel the weight of this,' and handed her the brill wrapped in a sheet of thick yellow paper.

The maid, a timid little thing from the Auvergne, weighed the fish in her hand and examined its gills, still frowning. Then, in a reluctant tone, she asked:

'How much?'

'Fifteen francs,' replied La Belle Normande.

The maid hastily put the brill back on the stall. She was about to walk off, but La Belle Normande held her back.

'Well, what do you want to pay?'

'No, no, it's too dear.'

'Just make me an offer.'

'Eight francs?'

Mère Méhudin seemed to wake up at this point and gave a contemptuous laugh. Did people think that she and her daughter got their fish by stealing them?

'Eight francs for a brill that size!' she exclaimed. 'You'll want one for nothing next, to keep your skin fresh at night!'

La Belle Normande had turned away as though insulted. But the maid came back twice, offering nine francs and then going up to ten.

'All right, then—give me the money,' cried the fishwife, seeing that she was about to depart for good.

The maid stood in front of the stall, chatting amicably with Mère Méhudin. Madame Taboureau was so fussy! She had some people coming to dinner, some cousins from Blois, a lawyer and his wife. Madame Taboureau's family, she added, was very respectable, and she herself, though only a baker's wife, had had an excellent education.

'You'll clean it out for me, won't you?' she added, pausing for a moment.

La Belle Normande had emptied the brill with a flick of her finger and thrown the guts into a bucket. She slipped a corner of her apron into the gills to remove a few grains of sand. Then, putting the fish in the girl's basket, she said:

'There, my dear, you'll come back and thank me for this.'

A quarter of an hour later, the maid did indeed come back, her face flushed. She had been crying and her little body was shaking with anger. Tossing the brill onto the stall, she pointed to a broad gash in its belly that went right to the bone. Then a flood of disjointed words poured out of her.

'Madame Taboureau doesn't want it. She says she can't serve it. She said I was stupid and I'd let myself be cheated by anyone. Look at it, it's spoilt. I never thought of looking at it underneath. I trusted you. Give me my ten francs back.'

'You should look at what you buy,' replied La Belle Normande calmly.

Then, as the maid raised her voice, Mère Méhudin stood up and said:

'Will you please go away! We're not taking back a fish that's been in other people's houses. How do we know you didn't drop it and damage it yourself?'

'Me! Me!' The little maid was choking with indignation. 'You're a couple of thieves!' she cried, sobbing. 'Yes, thieves! Madame Taboureau warned me about you.'

The scene became terrible to watch. Mother and daughter, livid with rage, brandishing their fists, fairly exploded. The little maid, dazed and bewildered, trapped between the hoarse voice of the one and the shrill voice of the other, like a ball being hit backwards and forwards, sobbed louder and louder.

'Clear off! Your Madame Taboureau isn't perfect—she'd definitely have to be patched up before being served!'

'A whole fish for ten francs! What will she want next!'

'And those earrings of yours—how much did they cost? We know how you earned them—on your back!'

'That's right—she uses the corner at the end of the Rue de Mondétour.'

Florent, who had been fetched by the market keeper, arrived in the thick of the fight. The whole market seemed in a state of revolt. The fishwives, who would leap at each other's throats over the sale of two sous' worth of herrings, were only too ready to defend one another against the customers. They were chanting: 'The baker's wife has heaps of crowns, which cost her precious little.'* They were stamping their feet, egging on the Méhudins as if they were encouraging animals to bite. Some of them, at the other end of the alley, even left their stalls and rushed up as if they were going to leap at the bun at the back of the little maid's hair. She was lost, swamped, almost drowned in the flood of insults.

'Give Mademoiselle her ten francs,' said Florent sternly, when he had been told what had happened.

But Mère Méhudin had her blood up.

'You can sod off, you little…! This is how I'll give her back her ten francs!'

She threw the brill as hard as she could at the girl, who took it full in the face. Her nose began to bleed, and the brill fell to the ground with a thud, like a wet dishcloth. This act of violence made Florent furious. La Belle Normande felt frightened and stepped back as he shouted:

'You're suspended for a week! I'll have your licence withdrawn!'

Then, as the fishwives were jeering, he turned round with such a threatening air that they suddenly fell silent and tried to assume an expression of innocence. When the Méhudins had given back the ten francs, he made them pack up their stall immediately. The old woman was speechless, while her daughter went as white as a sheet. She, La Belle Normande, driven from her stall! Claire murmured in her gentle voice that it served her right, a remark which nearly brought the two sisters to blows that evening in the Rue Pirouette. However, when the Méhudins returned to the market at the end of the week, they were well behaved, curt, and filled with a cold fury. They found the market calm and restored to order. From that day onwards La Belle Normande dreamed of wreaking her revenge. She felt that she had Lisa to thank for what had happened. She had met her the morning after the fight, and her head was held so high that she swore she would make her pay for her look of triumph. Endless confabulations took place in various corners of Les Halles with Mademoiselle Saget, Madame Lecœur, and La Sarriette; but when they eventually tired of their wearisome tales of Lisa's shameless conduct with her cousin and the hairs in Quenu's sausages, she could think of nothing further. She longed for a stroke of genius that would devastate her rival.

Her child was being allowed to grow up freely in the fish market. From the age of three he sat about on a piece of rag in the midst of the fish. He would fall asleep next to the big tuna fish as if he were one of them, and wake up alongside mackerel and whiting. He smelt so strongly of the fish barrel that people wondered if he had actually come into the world from the belly of some huge fish. For a long time his favourite game, whenever his mother's back was turned, was to build walls and houses with the herrings; he also played at soldiers on the marble slab, lining up the red gurnets against each other, marching them forward and smacking their heads together, making drum and trumpet sounds with his lips, and finally throwing them all into a heap again, saying that they were dead. When he grew a little older he would play around his aunt Claire's stall, trying to get hold of the bladders of the carp and pike she had emptied out; he would put them on the ground and make them burst—a game that delighted him. At the age of seven he ran up and down the alleys, crawled under the counters and among the wooden boxes reinforced with tin, and became the spoilt child of all the women. Whenever they showed him something new, he would clap his hands and exclaim ecstatic-ally: 'Oh, it's so *muche*!'* He used this word so often that it stuck to him as a nickname. Muche here, there, and everywhere. They all called out to him. He seemed to be everywhere, in the sales offices, among the piles of oyster baskets, in between the dustbins. He was like a young barbel, fresh and rosy, frisking about and slipping past as though swimming in clear water. He was as fond of running water as any little fish. He dragged his feet through the puddles and stood under the drops from the tables, and when no one was looking he would turn on one of the taps, delighted by the splashing of the jet. But he was to be found most often at the fountains near the cellars. This was where his mother went to fetch him in the evenings; she led him away soaked to the skin, his hands blue, his shoes, even his pockets, full of water.

At seven Muche was as pretty as an angel and as coarse in his manners as any carter. He had curly chestnut hair, beautiful soft eyes, and an innocent-looking mouth from which issued words that would have stuck in the throat of the toughest gendarme. Brought up amidst the filth of Les Halles, he could rattle off the catechism of the fish trade with his hand on his hip, just like Mère Méhudin in full flight. At such times, phrases like 'slut' and 'whore', 'Give it to him, then', and 'How much do you charge for it?' streamed from his lips in a voice of such crystalline purity that you might have thought that it belonged to a choirboy. He would even try to assume a roughness of tone, to degrade the exquisite freshness of childhood that made him resemble the Babe smiling in the Virgin's lap. The fishwives laughed till they cried. Thus encouraged, he never put two words together without popping in a 'God Almighty!' at the end. But in spite of all this he was still adorable, ignorant of the filth he was uttering, kept in vigorous good health by the fresh breezes and strong smells of the fish market, reciting his foul catechism with a kind of exalted delight, as if he were saying his prayers.

Winter was on its way, and that year Muche felt the cold. As soon as the colder weather set in, he became very interested in the inspector's office. This was situated in the left-hand corner of the market, on the same side as the Rue Rambuteau. It was furnished with a table, a set of pigeonholes, an armchair, two other chairs, and a stove. It was the stove that attracted Muche. Florent adored children, and when he saw the little fellow, his legs soaking wet, looking at him through the window, he asked him in. His first conversation with the boy gave him a great surprise. Muche sat down in front of the stove and said very naturally: 'I'll just warm me pins for a while. It's bloody cold out there.'

Then he started to laugh, and added:

'My Auntie Claire looks a bit down in the dumps this morning. Is it true, mister, that you go and warm her toes for her at night?'

Flabbergasted, Florent began to take a strange interest in the little fellow. La Belle Normande was as surly as ever, but let Muche visit Florent in his office without a word of objection. Thus Florent thought that he had her permission to receive the boy, and encouraged him to come in the afternoons, slowly forming the idea that he would make a well-mannered young person out of him. It was as if his brother Quenu had grown little again and they were back together in the Rue Royer-Collard. His secret dream was to devote himself to someone young who would never grow up, whom he could go on teaching for ever, and through whose innocence he would be able to love all mankind. On the third day he brought an alphabet to the office, and the lad delighted him with the intelligence he showed. He learned his letters with all the flair of a Paris street urchin, and was very tickled by the woodcuts illustrating the alphabet. He had a wonderful time in the little office, although the stove remained the chief attraction. First of all there were potatoes and chestnuts to be roasted on it, but that soon seemed tame. He then stole some gudgeons from his Aunt Claire, which he cooked one at a time, on the end of a piece of string, which he held in front of the fire; he ate them with relish, but without bread. One day he even brought a carp, but it refused to cook and made such a smell in the office that they had to open the door as well as the window. When the smell of all this cooking became too much for him, Florent would throw the fish into the street, but as a rule he just laughed. After two months Muche had begun to read quite fluently, and his copybooks were very neat.

In the evenings, however, the boy drove his mother mad with stories about his great friend Florent. His great friend Florent had drawn him pictures of trees and men in huts. His great friend Florent had waved his arm and said that men would be better off if they could all read. La Normande heard so much about Florent that it was almost as if she were living with the man she would gladly have strangled. One day she locked Muche in the house so that he would not go to the inspector's, but he cried so much that the next day she had to set him free. She was very weak, despite her size and her cheeky airs and attitudes. When the child told her how nice and warm he had been, and came home with dry clothes, she felt vaguely grateful, satisfied to know that he had found a place to shelter, where he could sit with his feet in front of a fire. She was very touched later on when he read aloud to her a few words from a scrap of dirty newspaper wrapped round a slice of conger eel. Little by little she came round to the view, though without admitting it, that Florent was perhaps not such a bad sort. She respected his learning, and her respect was mixed with growing curiosity about what he was really like. Then, quite suddenly, persuading herself that she was working towards her revenge, she found an excuse for getting to know more about him. She would make friends with Florent and set him against Lisa— what fun that would be.

'Does your friend Florent ever say anything about me?' she asked Muche one morning while she was dressing him.

'No,' he replied. 'We just have fun.'

'Well, you can tell him I've forgiven him, and I'm very grateful that he's taught you to read.'

From then on the child was given some message every day. He went backwards and forwards, bearing friendly words, and questions and answers, which he repeated without knowing what they meant. He could easily have been made to say the most monstrous things. But La Belle Normande was afraid of appearing shy, and so one day she went in person to the office and sat on one of the chairs while Muche was having a writing lesson. She was very quiet and very polite. Florent was even more embarrassed than she was. They talked only about the child. When Florent expressed his fear that he might not be able to continue the lessons in the office, she invited him to come to their home in the evening. She then mentioned money; but at this he blushed, and said that he certainly would not come if there was any talk of that kind. She resolved that she would pay him in kind, with the finest fish she had.

Thus peace was declared. La Belle Normande even took Florent under her protection. He was in any case becoming accepted by everyone; the fishwives found him, despite the odd look in his eyes, a better man than Monsieur Verlaque. Only Mère Méhudin shrugged her shoulders; she still bore a grudge against 'the beanpole', as she called him. But one morning, a strange thing happened. As Florent stopped with a smile by Claire's tanks, the young woman dropped the eel she was holding, her face almost purple, and turned her back on him. Florent was so taken aback that he mentioned it to La Normande.

'Oh, never mind her,' said the young woman. 'She's got a screw loose. She likes to be different. She probably behaved like that just to annoy me.'

La Normande was exultant, preening herself at her stall and becoming more coquettish than ever, arranging her hair in the most elaborate manner. When she met La Belle Lisa one day, she returned her contemptuous look and even burst out laughing in her face. Her conviction that she was driving Lisa to despair by taking her cousin away from her made her laugh quite heartily, her plump white neck shaking as she did so. At the same time she hit on the idea of dressing Muche up very prettily in a little tartan jacket and a velvet cap. Until now the boy had never worn anything but a tattered shirt. It unfortunately happened, however, that at this time he again became very fond of the taps under the cellar stairs. The ice had melted and the weather was quite mild. Letting the taps run at full cock, he soaked the tartan jacket up to his elbows. He called this 'playing at gutters'. His mother finally caught him with two other street children, watching two little fishes swimming in his velvet cap, which he had filled with water.

Florent lived for about eight months in Les Halles as though in the grip of a constant need for sleep. After emerging from his seven years of suffering, his life had become so calm and regular that he hardly felt he was alive at all. He drifted along without thinking about it, always surprised to find himself each morning in the same armchair in the same little office. He liked the room because of its bareness and its resemblance to a wooden hut. It was a refuge from the endless din and bustle of the markets, which made him think of some surging sea spreading around him and cutting him off from the rest of the world. But little by little a vague feeling of anxiety began to prey upon him; he was unhappy and accused himself of faults he could not define, and began to rebel against the emptiness he felt more and more acutely in mind and body. And the foul smells of the fish market made him feel nauseous. By degrees he was becoming unhinged, his vague sense of emptiness developing into nervous overexcitement.

All his days were alike. He walked through the same sounds and the same smells. In the morning the loud buzz of the auctions resounded in his ears like a distant pealing of bells; and sometimes, when there was a delay in the delivery of the fish, the auctions did not finish until very late. In that case he would stay in the market until midday, constantly disturbed by quarrels and disputes, which he tried to settle with the utmost scrupulousness. It might take him hours to resolve some petty matter that was disturbing the entire market. He would pace up and down amidst the crush and uproar of the sales, moving from one avenue to the next, sometimes stopping in front of the stalls that fringed the Rue Rambuteau. These were piled high with shiny pink prawns and baskets of boiled lobsters with their tails tied together, while live ones, sprawled on the marble slabs, were slowly dying. Here he would watch gentlemen in silk hats and black gloves bargaining with the fishwives and eventually going off with a cooked lobster wrapped in newspaper, which they stuffed into one of their coat pockets. Further along, standing before the trestle tables where the commoner sorts of fish were sold, he would recognize the women of the neighbourhood, coming bareheaded at the same time every day to make their purchases. Sometimes his interest would quicken at the sight of a well-dressed lady trailing her lace petticoats over the wet cobblestones, accompanied by a servant in a white apron; he would follow her at a slight distance and observe how the fishwives shrugged their shoulders at her expressions of disgust. The hurly-burly of hampers, baskets, and bags, and the procession of skirts flitting along the wet alleyways occupied him until lunchtime. He took pleasure in the running water and the distinctive smells, which ranged from the acrid smell of the shellfish to the sharp tang of the salted fish. He would always end his tour of inspection with the sea fish. The cases of red herrings, the Nantes sardines laid out on beds of leaves, the rolled cod on display in front of fat, faded fishwives, all made him dream of some great sea voyage necessitating a vast supply of salted provisions. In the afternoons the markets became quieter and fell asleep. Florent then shut himself in his office and brought his paperwork up to date; this was the happiest hour of his day. If he happened to go out and cross the fish market, he found it almost deserted. There was no longer the pushing and shoving and uproar of ten o'clock in the morning. Sitting comfortably behind their empty stalls, the fishwives were knitting at their ease, and a few late shoppers were moving about, gazing at the remaining fish with the calculating stare and pursed lips of women working out the price of their dinner to the nearest sou. At last dusk came, there was a noise of boxes being moved, and the fish were laid out for the night on beds of ice. Then, after supervising the locking of the gates, Florent went off, taking the fish market with him in his clothes, his beard, and his hair.

For the first few months he was not particularly worried by this penetrating smell. The winter was harsh; ice turned the alleyways into slippery mirrors, and icicles hung like lace from the water taps and the marble slabs. In the mornings little braziers had to be placed under the taps before a drop of water could be drawn. The fish, frozen hard, their tails twisted, dull and hard like ground metal, broke with a cracking sound like thin sheets of cast iron. Until February the market looked mournful and desolate, shaggy in its shroud of ice. But then the thaw came and milder weather, the fog and rain of March. The fish became soft again, and the stench of rotting flesh mingled with the smell of mud in the neighbouring streets. The smells were as yet a vague presence in the air, a sweet, nauseous clamminess dragging low along the ground. At last the blazing afternoons of June arrived, and then the stench rose and the air grew heavy with the hot air of plague. Upper windows were opened and large blinds of grey canvas were hung under the burning sky. A rain of fire poured down over the markets, heating them as if they were a great boiler, and not a breath of air came to waft away the stench of rotten fish. Steam rose from the stalls.

The masses of food amongst which Florent lived now began to cause him the greatest discomfort. The disgust he had felt in the *charcuterie* came back even more strongly. He had experienced smells as terrible as these, but they had never come from the belly. His own small stomach, the stomach of a thin man, was sickened as he passed by the displays of fish, which, despite all the water lavished upon them, turned bad at the first sign of warm weather. They assailed him with their powerful smells and took his breath away, as though they had given him indigestion. Even when he shut himself in his office, the loathsome smell followed him and crept in through the badly joined woodwork of the door and the window. On days when the skies were grey the little room remained in darkness; it was like a long twilight in the depths of some evil-smelling bog. He was often seized by fits of nervous anxiety, which he tried to dispel by taking walks; he would then go down into the cellars by the large staircase in the middle of the market. In the stuffy air down below, in the dim light provided by a few gas jets, he found the freshness of pure water. He would stop in front of the big tank where the reserve stock of live fish was kept and listen to the incessant song of the four little streams of water falling from the four corners of the central urn, then spreading into a broad stream and running in a sheet under the locked gratings of the basins. This underground spring, murmuring in the gloom, had a tranquillizing effect on him. He also enjoyed, in the evenings, the glorious sunsets that sharply silhouetted the fine lace-work structure of Les Halles against the red glow of the sky; the five o'clock evening light, the dust dancing in the last sunbeams, poured in through the bay windows, through the chinks between the wooden shutters; and the whole was like a luminous transparency on which he could see, minutely outlined, the slender shafts of the pillars, the elegant curves of the girders, the geometrical tracery of the roofs. Florent feasted his eyes on this immense design washed in Chinese ink on phosphorescent parchment, and began to dream once more of some colossal machine with all its cogs and levers and balances glimpsed in the crimson glow of the fires burning beneath its boilers. At each hour of the day the changing play of light would alter the appearance of Les Halles, from the pale blue of early morning and the black shadows of noon to the fire of the setting sun and the ashen grey of dusk. But on these nights of flaming skies, when the foul smells arose and forced their way across the broad yellow beams like clouds of hot smoke, he began to feel sick again, and his dream changed as he imagined the markets to be giant ovens or a knacker's boiling-house where the fat of an entire nation was being melted down.

He was ill at ease in this vulgar neighbourhood, among people whose words and behaviour seemed redolent of the very smells of the place. But he was good-natured and would not allow himself to be shocked; still, the women embarrassed him, though he did feel quite at home with Madame François, whom he had seen again. She took such obvious pleasure in knowing that he had a job and was happy and out of trouble (as she put it) that he was most touched. Lisa, La Normande, and the others all worried him with their laughter; but he would have told Madame François anything. There was not a trace of mockery in the way she laughed; when she did laugh, it was in simple pleasure at the happiness of others. And she was resilient, too; her work was hard in winter when the frost was about, and in rainy weather it was even harder. Florent saw her some mornings when it had been raining solidly since the day before. Between Nanterre and Paris the wheels of her cart had sunk up to the axles in mud, and Balthazar was caked in it up to his belly. There she was, however, patting him and making a fuss of him as she wiped him down with some old aprons.

'These creatures are very fragile,' she said. 'They catch a cold as soon as look at you. Poor old Balthazar! I thought we'd fall into the Seine when we were coming over the Pont de Neuilly, it was raining so hard!'

Balthazar was stabled at the inn, while Madame François remained in the pouring rain to sell her vegetables. The footpath had become a river of mud. The cabbages, carrots, and turnips were splashed by dirty rainwater, quite drowned by the muddy torrent that gushed down the middle of the road. Gone was the splendid greenery of the bright mornings. The market gardeners, huddled in their greatcoats beneath the downpour, cursed the authorities, who, after an inquiry, had declared that rain did the vegetables no harm and that therefore there was no need to erect shelters.*

The rainy mornings made Florent desperately sad. He thought of Madame François, and always managed to slip away for a few words with her. But he never found her in low spirits. She shook herself like a poodle and said that she was used to it; she was not made of sugar and would not melt with a few drops of rain. He insisted that she should shelter for a little while in one of the covered avenues, and several times he even took her to Monsieur Lebigre's to have some mulled wine. As she looked at him with her pleasant, friendly face, he felt quite delighted with the healthy scent of the fields she brought with her into the foul atmosphere of Les Halles. She smelt of earth and hay, fresh air and open skies.

'You must come to Nanterre,' she said. 'I'll show you my garden. I've put borders of thyme everywhere. Paris stinks!'

And she went off, soaking wet. Florent felt quite refreshed by her company. He also tried his best to work, as a way of warding off his nervous depression. He was very methodical and sometimes allotted his time to certain tasks with a strictness that bordered on mania.

He shut himself up two evenings a week in order to write a great work on Cayenne. His attic room was excellent, he thought, for soothing his spirits and encouraging him to work. He would light his fire and make sure that the pomegranate plant at the foot of his bed was faring well; then, installing himself at the little table, he would work until midnight. He had put the prayer book and *La Clef des songes* in the drawer, which was filling up with notes, papers, and manuscripts of all kinds. The book on Cayenne proceeded slowly, however, as it was constantly being interrupted by other projects, plans for enormous undertakings which he sketched out in a few words. He successively drafted an outline for a complete reform of the administrative system of Les Halles, a scheme for transforming the city dues, levied on produce as it entered Paris, into a tax on sales, a new system for distributing provisions to the poorer neighbourhoods, and finally, a vague humanitarian scheme for the common warehousing of the produce brought to the markets, with the aim of ensuring that every household in Paris would receive a minimum daily supply. As he sat there, with his head bent over his table and his mind engrossed in all these weighty matters, his gloomy figure cast a great black shadow across the room. Sometimes a chaffinch he had picked up one snowy day in the market would mistake the lamplight for daylight and break the silence, disturbed only by the scratching of Florent's pen on the paper before him.

As though driven by fate, Florent returned to politics. He had suffered too much at its hands not to accept it as the great luxury of his life. With a different background and in different circumstances, he would have become a good provincial schoolteacher, happy in some peaceful little town. But he had been treated as a threat to society, and now felt that he had been marked out by his exile for some fighting task. His nervous anxiety was only the reawakening of his Cayenne dreams, his brooding bitterness at his undeserved suffering, and his vow one day to avenge people put to the whip and trodden underfoot. The giant markets, overflowing with food, had brought things to a head. They seemed like some satiated beast, embodying Paris itself, grown enormously fat, and silently supporting the Empire. He seemed surrounded by huge breasts, monstrous hips, and round faces, like never-ending arguments against his martyr-like thinness and his sallow, discontented face. Les Halles were the shopkeepers' belly, the belly of respectable petit bourgeois people, bursting with contentment and well-being, shining in the sun, and declaring that everything was for the best, since respectable people had never before grown so wonderfully fat. It was then that Florent felt his fists clench. He was now ready to begin the struggle, more angered by the thought of his exile than at any time since his return to France. Once again hatred filled his heart. Often he let his pen fall from his hand and became lost in dreams. The dying flames of the fire cast a bright glow over his face; the smoking lamp spluttered, while the chaffinch went to sleep again on one leg, its head tucked under its wing.

Sometimes Auguste, on coming upstairs at eleven o'clock and seeing the light shining under the door, would knock before going to bed. Florent, in some impatience, would open the door. The boy would sit down in front of the fire, not saying much, and never giving a reason for knocking. He would stare at the photograph of Augustine and himself holding hands in their Sunday best. Florent came to the conclusion that the young man liked sitting in the room because it had been occupied by his sweetheart; and one evening he asked him with a smile if he had guessed right.

'Perhaps,' replied Auguste, surprised at the discovery he was now making. 'I never thought about it. I don't really know why I came. If I told Augustine, she'd laugh. When you're going to be married in any case, you don't think about those things.'

When he was in a talkative mood, he would always return to the eternal subject of the *charcuterie* he would open with Augustine in Plaisance. He seemed so confident that he could arrange his life as he wanted that in the end Florent felt a kind of respect for him, mingled with irritation. In fact, stupid though he may have looked, the boy was very bright; he was making straight for the goal he had set himself and would doubtless reach it in perfect assurance and contentment of mind. On the evenings of these visits from the apprentice, Florent could not settle down to work again; he went to bed in a bad mood, which did not improve until he thought to himself: 'What a pest that Auguste is!'

Every month he went to Clamart to see Monsieur Verlaque. It was almost a pleasure for him. The poor man was hanging on, to Gavard's surprise, for he had given him no more than six months. Each time Florent went to see him, Verlaque would tell him that he was feeling better and was keen to go back to work. But the days passed and his health slowly declined. Florent sat on the edge of his bed and chatted about the fish market in an attempt to lift his spirits a little. He would place on the bedside table the fifty francs he gave the inspector each month; and the old inspector, though the payment had been agreed upon, always protested, making as if to refuse the money. Then they would begin to talk about something else, and the money would remain lying on the table. When Florent left, Madame Verlaque accompanied him to the door. She was a gentle little woman, and often tearful. All she ever talked about was the expense occasioned by her husband's illness, the chicken broth, the red meat, Bordeaux wine, medicine, and doctors' fees. Her doleful conversation embarrassed Florent. At first he did not understand. Then, as the poor woman seemed always to be in a state of tears, and kept saying how happy they had been on the eighteen hundred francs from the inspector's job, he timidly offered to give her something without her husband's knowledge. She refused, but at once assured him that fifty francs were enough. In the course of the next month she wrote numerous times to Florent, whom she called their saviour. Her handwriting was small and fine, yet she would contrive to fill three pages of letter-paper with easy, humble phrases in request for ten francs; and this she did so regularly that before long nearly the whole of Florent's hundred and fifty francs found its way to the Verlaque household. No doubt the husband did not know about it, but the wife gratefully kissed Florent's hands. This charity gave him the greatest pleasure, and he concealed it like some secret act of self-indulgence.

'That devil Verlaque is making a fool of you,' Gavard would sometimes say. 'He's having a cushy time while you earn his money for him.'

One day Florent replied:

'It's agreed. Now I'm only giving him twenty-five francs.'

The fact was that Florent had little need of money. The Quenus still gave him board and lodging. The few francs he had were enough to pay for drinks at Monsieur Lebigre's in the evening. Little by little his life had become as regular as clockwork. He worked in his room, he continued with little Muche's lessons twice a week from eight o'clock until nine, and, giving one evening over to La Belle Lisa so as not to offend her, he spent the rest of his time with Gavard and his friends in the little back room.

He would appear at the Méhudins with the rather strait-laced gentility suitable to a teacher. He liked the old house in the Rue Pirouette.

Downstairs he passed through the subtle aromas of a cooked herb shop; bowls of spinach and jars of sorrel were cooling in a little court-yard. Then he climbed the winding staircase, whose worn, narrow steps sloped in a most disturbing manner. The Méhudins occupied the whole of the second floor. Even when they had become more prosperous, the mother had refused to move, despite the entreaties of her daughters, who dreamed of living in a new house in a wide street. But the old woman was not to be moved; she had lived there, she said, and meant to die there. She was happy, in any case, with a dark little closet of a room, leaving the larger rooms to Claire and La Normande. The latter, with the authority of the elder born, had taken possession of the room that overlooked the street; it was the best and largest room. Claire was so vexed that she refused to have the room next door, whose window overlooked the courtyard, and decided that she would sleep on the other side of the landing, in a sort of garret, which she would not even allow to be whitewashed. She had her own key and she was free; whenever the slightest thing displeased her, she locked herself in.

When Florent arrived, the Méhudins would be finishing dinner. Muche would jump up at him. He sat down for a few moments, the child chattering away between his legs. Then, when the oilcloth had been wiped, the lesson began at one corner of the table. Le Belle Normande always welcomed him warmly. She would knit or sew, drawing her chair up to the table to work by the light of the same lamp; and she often put down her needle to listen to the lesson, which filled her with surprise. Very soon she held this young man who knew so much in high esteem; he was as gentle as a woman and as patient as an angel. She no longer found him ugly; indeed it was not long before she grew almost jealous of La Belle Lisa. She drew her chair up and smiled at Florent.

'Eh, maman, you're knocking my elbow, I can't write,' Muche would say crossly. 'Look, you've made me make a blot! Move out of the way!'

Soon La Normande took to spreading unpleasant stories about Lisa. She claimed that she concealed her age, and laced herself in corsets to the point of suffocation; and that, if she came down in the morning looking so neat and well presented, it must be because she looked so hideous in a state of undress. Then she would lift her arms just enough to show that she did not wear a corset; and she continued to smile as she breathed in to show off her superb bust, which was so easy to imagine beneath her thin, badly fastened shift. At these times the lesson was interrupted, and Muche, most interested, watched his mother as she lifted her arms. Florent listened and laughed a little, thinking to himself that women were very strange creatures. The rivalry between La Belle Normande and La Belle Lisa amused him.

Meanwhile Muche completed his page of writing. Florent, whose handwriting was very neat, prepared the models—strips of paper on which he wrote, in both capitals and script, very long words which took up a whole line. He gave particular emphasis to such words as 'tyranically', 'liberticide', 'unconstitutional', 'revolutionary'; either that, or he made the child copy sentences like the following: 'The day of justice will come… The suffering of the just is the condemnation of the oppressor… When the bell tolls, the guilty will fall.' In writing out these models, he was ingenuously expressing his own obsessions; he forgot Muche, La Belle Normande, and his surroundings. Muche might just as well have copied out *The Social Contract*.* He wrote column after column, covering page after page, with 'tyranicallys' and 'unconstitutionals', forming each letter with the utmost care.

As long as the tutor remained there, Mère Méhudin kept fidgeting round the table, muttering to herself. She still bore Florent a terrible grudge. According to her, it made no sense to make the child work in this way in the evenings, when children ought to be in bed. She would certainly have turned that 'beanpole' out of the house if La Belle Normande, after a stormy exchange, had not bluntly said that she would go and live somewhere else if she was not free to receive whoever she liked in her own home. But the quarrel broke out again every evening.

'You can say what you like,' the old woman kept saying, 'he looks shifty… He's skinny, and you can never trust skinny men. You can't put anything past them. I've never come across a decent one yet. His stomach must have slipped down to his bum—he's as flat as a board. And he's ugly, as well! I'm over sixty-five, but I wouldn't fancy wakin' up next to 'im.'

She said all this because she had a shrewd idea of how things were likely to turn out. Then she went on to speak glowingly of Monsieur Lebigre, who had always shown a keen interest in La Belle Normande. Apart from the fact that he had his eye on a fat dowry, he thought that the young woman would do beautifully behind his counter. The old woman never missed an opportunity to sing his praises; he wasn't a bit skinny, he must be as strong as an ox, with legs like tree trunks. But La Normande simply shrugged and snapped back:

'I couldn't care less about his legs. I'm not interested in anybody's legs. In any case, I'll do what I want.'

And if the old woman became too insistent, her daughter would shout:

'Anyway, it's none of your business, and it's not true either. And even if it was, do you think I'd ask you what you think? Leave me alone!'

She would then go off into her room, slamming the door behind her. She had assumed a certain power in the house and had now taken to abusing it. During the night, imagining that she had heard some noise or other, the old woman would get out of bed and listen barefoot at her daughter's door to find out whether or not Florent was in her room. But he had another, even worse enemy at the Méhudins. As soon as he arrived, Claire would get up without saying a word, and, with a candle in her hand, withdraw to her room on the other side of the landing. She could be heard double-bolting the door in sullen anger. One evening when her sister had asked Florent to dinner, she prepared her own food on the landing and ate it in her bedroom. Often she shut herself away to such an extent that nothing was seen of her for a whole week. She was as soft-hearted as ever, but had sudden fits of temper, her eyes blazing from under her tawny hair like a wild animal. Mère Méhudin, thinking that she could relieve her feelings in Claire's presence, only enraged her further by talking about Florent. Then in exasperation the old woman told everyone who cared to listen that she would have got out for good had she not been afraid that if they were left alone together her daughters would tear each other to pieces.

As Florent was leaving one evening, he walked past Claire's door, which stood wide open on the landing. She stared at him, her face very red. Her hostility troubled him, but his timidity with women held him back from seeking an explanation. He would have entered her room that evening, had he not caught a glimpse of the little white face of Mademoiselle Saget leaning over the banisters of the floor above. He continued on his way and had not walked down more than half a dozen steps before Claire's door slammed violently behind him, making the whole staircase shake. It was this episode that convinced Mademoiselle Saget that Madame Quenu's cousin slept with both the Méhudins.

In fact, Florent scarcely gave a thought to these beautiful young women. His general behaviour towards women was that of a man who had never enjoyed the least success with them. Too much of his virility was expended in dreams. He had come to feel a genuine friendship for La Normande; she was a good-hearted creature when her temper did not get the better of her. But he never went any further than that. In the evening, when she drew up her chair under the lamp and leaned forward as if to look at Muche's copybook, he felt a certain uneasiness to feel her warm, powerful body so close to his own. She seemed huge, very heavy and almost disturbing, with her large breasts. He moved his sharp elbows and thin shoulders away, perhaps afraid of digging them into her; a feeling of anguish passed through his thin, bony body at the sight of her breasts. He looked down and sank even lower in his chair; the odours from her body made him feel uncomfortable. Whenever her shift hung open, he seemed to see a breath of health and life rise up from between her two white breasts and float past his face, still warm, as if mingling for a moment with the stench of Les Halles on a hot July evening. It was a lingering scent that clung to her smooth, silky skin, a sweaty, fishy secretion from her splendid breasts, her regal arms, and supple waist, bringing a sharp tang to her female smell. She had tried every kind of aromatic oil, she washed in running water, but as soon as the freshening effect of her bathing wore off, her blood again impregnated her skin with the faint odour of salmon, the musky perfume of smelts, and the pungency of herring and skate. Her skirts, as she moved about, exhaled these fishy smells; she walked as through an evaporation of slimy seaweed. With her goddess-like figure and her purity of form and complexion, she was like an ancient marble statue that had rolled about in the depths of the sea and had been brought to land in some fisherman's net. Florent was troubled by her. He felt no desire for her, for his senses were repelled by his afternoons in the fish market; and he found her irritating, too salty, too bitter to the taste, too fulsome in her beauty, too intense in her smell.

Mademoiselle Saget, for her part, swore by all the gods that he was her lover. She had quarrelled with La Belle Normande over ten sous' worth of dabs. Ever since this squabble she had been very friendly towards La Belle Lisa, for she hoped in this way to find out sooner about what she called 'the plots and plans' of the Quenus. But Florent continued to remain a mystery, and she told her friends that she felt like a body without a soul, though she was careful not to reveal the cause of her discontent. A young girl infatuated with a hopeless passion could not have been in greater distress than this terrible old woman at finding herself unable to solve the mystery of the Quenus' cousin. She spied on him, followed him, undressed him with her eyes, scrutinized him from head to foot, enraged beyond words at her failure to satisfy her rampant curiosity. Since he had begun to visit the Méhudins, she was forever haunting the stairs and landings. She soon realized that La Belle Lisa was extremely annoyed to see Florent frequenting 'those women', so every morning she called in at the *charcuterie* with a ration of information about the goings-on in the Rue Pirouette. She entered the shop shrivelled and shrunk by the frosty air, and, putting her hands on the warming-stove, stood in front of the counter, never buying anything, but repeating in her thin little voice:

'He was there again yesterday; he seems to live there now. I heard La Normande call him "my love" on the stairs.'

She told a few lies like this in order to stay and warm her hands a little longer. The day after she imagined seeing Florent coming out of Claire's room, she ran straight to Lisa and managed to make the story last a good half-hour. It was a shocking business; Lisa's cousin was now going from one bed to the other.

'I saw him,' she said. 'When he's had enough of La Normande, he creeps across the landing to cuddle up to the little sister. Yesterday he was just leaving the young one, no doubt to rejoin the older one, when he saw me. That stopped him in his tracks. And to think that Mère Méhudin sleeps in a closet just behind her daughters' rooms!'

Lisa, who wore a look of contempt, said very little, encouraging Mademoiselle Saget's tittle-tattle by her silence. But she listened to every word. When the details were on the point of becoming sordid, she would murmur:

'Oh no, no. I don't want to hear… No woman would do that.'

Thereupon Mademoiselle Saget would tell Lisa that unfortunately not all women were as decent as she was. And then she pretended to find all sorts of excuses for Florent: men can't help themselves;

he was a bachelor, no doubt? In this way she asked questions without appearing to do so. But Lisa never passed judgement on her cousin, she simply shrugged and pursed her lips. When Mademoiselle Saget had gone, she threw a look of disgust at the lid of the warming-stove, on which the old woman had left the dirty imprint of her two small hands.

'Augustine,' she called, 'bring a cloth and wipe the stove. It's filthy.'

The rivalry between La Belle Normande and La Belle Lisa became intense. La Belle Normande was convinced that she had stolen her enemy's lover, while La Belle Lisa was furious with this dreadful creature, who, by luring Florent to her home, would surely end up by getting them all into trouble. Each displayed her hostility according to her temperament: the one remained calm and scornful, like a lady who holds up her skirts to protect them from the mud; while the other, more outspoken, shouted insolently and took up the whole width of the footpath, swaggering like a duellist looking for a fight. Their encounters would become the talk of the fish market for a whole day. Whenever La Belle Normande saw La Belle Lisa standing at the door of her shop, she would go out of her way to walk past her and brush against her with her apron; their black looks crossed like swords, with the cut and thrust of polished steel. On the other hand, when La Belle Lisa went to the fish market, she affected an expression of disgust as she approached the stall of La Belle Normande; she would choose some big fish, a turbot or a salmon, from a neighbouring fishwife, and then spread out all her money on the slab, having noticed that this so annoyed the 'dreadful creature' that she stopped laughing. To listen to them, one might have thought that the fish and sausages they sold were unfit for human consumption. But their main battlefields were, for La Belle Normande, her stall, and for La Belle Lisa, her counter, and from these two strongholds they would glower fiercely at each other across the Rue Rambuteau. They sat in state in their big white aprons, dressed up to the nines and covered in jewels. Battle would commence with the first light of day.

'Look! The fat cow's got up!' La Belle Normande would exclaim. 'She's done up as tight as her sausages! Well, well, she's still wearing the collar she had on Saturday and the same old poplin dress!'

At the same time, on the other side of the street, La Belle Lisa was saying to her assistant:

'Just look at that creature staring at us, Augustine! She's almost deformed. It must be the life she leads… Can you see those earrings? She's wearing those big pendants, isn't she? It's a shame to see that jewellery on a girl like that!'

'Considering what it costs her,' replied Augustine dutifully.

When either of them had a new piece of jewellery, it was a victory; the other one would seethe with resentment. All morning they would scrutinize and count each other's customers, most peeved if they thought that 'that great lump over there' was doing better business. Then they spied on what each other had for lunch. Each knew what the other ate and even watched to see how she digested it. In the afternoon, the one sitting among her cooked meats, the other in the midst of her fish, they struck poses and gave themselves airs, as if they were paragons of beauty. It was then that the day's victory was decided. La Belle Normande embroidered, and chose very difficult needlework of a kind that exasperated Lisa.

'She'd do a lot better', she would say, 'to mend her boy's socks. He runs about barefoot. Just look at her playing the lady, with her hands all red and stinking of fish!'

Lisa usually knitted.

'She's still on the same sock,' La Normande would observe. 'She falls asleep; she eats too much. That poor cuckold of hers will have to wait a long time to get his feet warm.'

They would carry on like this, implacably, until evening, taking note of every customer and showing such keen eyesight that they could pick out the smallest detail of each other's person, while other women at that distance declared that they could see nothing at all. Mademoiselle Saget expressed great admiration one day for Madame Quenu's eyesight when she succeeded in making out a scratch on the fishwife's left cheek. 'With eyes like yours,' she said, 'you must be able to see through doors.' When night fell, victory was often uncertain; sometimes one of them was temporarily crushed, but would take her revenge the next day. Bets were made in the neighbourhood, some backing La Belle Lisa and others La Belle Normande.

They reached the point of forbidding their children to talk to each other. Pauline and Muche had been good friends, notwithstanding the girl's stiff petticoats and ladylike demeanour, and the lad's dishevelled appearance, coarse language, and rough manners. They would play together on the wide footpath in front of the market. But one day, when Muche came to fetch her as usual, La Belle Lisa shut the door in his face, saying that he was a dirty little street urchin.

'You never know', she said, 'with these badly brought up children... This one has been set such bad examples that I'm not happy when he's with my daughter.'

The child was seven. Mademoiselle Saget, who happened to be there, said:

'Yes, you're quite right. He's always up to no good with all the little girls... They found him in the cellars with the coal merchant's daughter.'

When Muche came home in tears and told his story, La Belle Normande flew into a terrible rage. She wanted to go over at once to the Quenu–Gradelles' and smash everything up in their shop, but she contented herself with giving Muche a good hiding.

'If you ever go back there,' she shouted, 'you'll have me to answer for it!'

But the real victim of the two women was Florent. It was he, in truth, who had brought them into this state of war, and they fought only because of him. Since his arrival in Les Halles, things had gone from bad to worse. He had compromised, angered, and upset a world that had previously lived in perfect peace and harmony. La Belle Normande would gladly have scratched his eyes out when he lingered too long at the Quenus'; it was the heat of battle that made her want so badly to win him for herself. La Belle Lisa maintained a judicial attitude to the bad behaviour of her brother-in-law, whose relations with the two Méhudins were the talk of the neighbourhood. She was extremely annoyed, but forced herself not to show her jealousy, that particular kind of jealousy which, despite her contempt for Florent and a coldness she judged appropriate for a respectable woman, exasperated her every time he left the *charcuterie* to go to the Rue Pirouette and every time she imagined the forbidden pleasures he tasted there.

Dinner at the Quenus' had now become a less pleasant occasion. The neatness of the dining room seemed to have assumed a chilling severity. Florent felt a certain reproach, a kind of condemnation, in the bright oak, the lamp that was too clean, the carpet that was too new.

He scarcely dared to eat for fear of dropping crumbs on the floor or dirtying his plate. At the same time there was a guileless simplicity about him which prevented him from seeing things as they really were. Everywhere he spoke highly of Lisa's kindness. She was indeed still very kind to him. She would say with a smile, as if joking:

'It's strange, you eat quite a lot these days, but you're not getting any fatter... The food doesn't seem to be good for you.'

At this Quenu would laugh and tap his brother on the stomach, claiming that the entire *charcuterie* could pass through it without leaving enough fat to cover a coin. But there was in Lisa's insistence the dislike and distrust of thinness which La Méhudin expressed more crudely; and behind it, too, there was a veiled allusion to the disreputable life Florent was supposedly leading. Never, indeed, did she refer to La Belle Normande in his presence. Quenu had made a joke about it one evening, but she received it so icily that he had not ventured to refer to the matter again. They would remain seated at the table for a few minutes after dessert, and Florent, who had noticed his sister-in-law's reaction if he went off too soon, made an attempt at conversation. She sat quite close to him. He did not find her, like the fishwife, warm and alive, nor did she exude the same whiff of the sea, tasty and spice-blown; she smelt, rather, of fat and good meat. Not a quiver passed across her tight-fitting bodice to crease or wrinkle it. Contact with the firm bodily presence of La Belle Lisa disturbed his bony frame even more than the obvious overtures of La Belle Normande. Gavard had once said to him, in the strictest confidence, that Madame Quenu was certainly a beautiful woman, but he preferred them 'less armour-plated'.

Lisa avoided speaking to Quenu about Florent. She prided herself on her patience, and in any case thought it wiser not to come between the two brothers without a good reason to do so. As she said, she was very good-natured, but should not be pushed too far. She had reached the stage of courteous tolerance, the expressionless face, the affected indifference, the strict politeness. She carefully avoided anything that might have told Florent that, although he ate there and slept there, they never even caught a glimpse of his money. Not that she would have accepted any payment, she was above that; but the least he could do, surely, was to eat lunch somewhere else.

'We never seem to be alone now,' she remarked to Quenu one day. 'If we want to talk to each other we have to wait until we're in bed.'

And one night she said to him, when they were in bed:

'Your brother earns a hundred and fifty francs a month, doesn't he? It's funny he can't put a bit aside to buy a few clothes. I've just had to give him three more of your old shirts.'

'Oh, that's all right,' Quenu replied. 'He's no trouble. Let him do what he wants with his money.'

'Yes, of course,' murmured Lisa, without taking her point any further. 'I didn't mean that... Whether he spends his money well or badly is his affair.'

She was sure that his money disappeared at the Méhudins'. Only on one occasion did she lose her poise, her perpetual mood of calculated reserve. La Belle Normande had made Florent a present of a magnificent salmon. Florent, embarrassed to have the fish, but not daring to refuse it, had presented it to Lisa.

'You can make a pie with it,' he suggested ingenuously.

White-lipped, she stared at him coldly, and then, trying to control herself, said:

'Do you think we haven't got enough food here? I think we've got quite enough, thank you! Take it back!'

'But cook it for me, at least,' said Florent, surprised at her outburst. 'I'll eat it.'

Then she exploded.

'This isn't a hotel! Ask whoever you got it from to cook it! I won't let my saucepans stink with it! Take it back!'

She was ready to grab it and throw it into the street. He took it to Monsieur Lebigre's, where Rose was ordered to make a pie of it. And so, one evening, it was eaten in the little back room. Gavard bought oysters all round. Florent began to spend more and more time at Monsieur Lebigre's, until he hardly stirred from the place. He found there an overheated atmosphere in which his passion for politics could be freely indulged. At times, now, when he shut himself up in his attic to work, the tranquillity of the room irritated him; his theoretical research into liberty was not enough for him, and he was forced to go over to Monsieur Lebigre's to seek satisfaction in the grand declarations of Charvet and the wild outbursts of Logre. During his first visits, he had found their noisy talk offputting; he still had a sense of the emptiness of it all, but at the same time felt a need to be intoxicated and excited by it, to be inspired to make some extreme resolution that would soothe his troubled spirit. The atmosphere of the little room, reeking with the smell of spirits and warm with tobacco smoke, transported him, prompting a kind of abandonment of himself which made him willing to acquiesce in the wildest ideas. He came to love those he met there, and looked forward to each meeting with a pleasure that increased with habit. The gentle, bearded features of Robine, the serious expression of Clémence, Charvet's pallor, Logre's hump, Gavard, Alexandre, Lacaille, all of them became part of his life and occupied an ever more important place in it. He took a sensual delight in the meetings. As he took the brass doorknob of the little room in his hand, he seemed to feel it respond to his touch, to become quite warm, and turn of its own accord. He could not have felt a greater thrill if he had been caressing the soft fingers of a woman.

In fact, serious things were happening in that little back room. One evening, Logre, who had been thundering away even more violently than usual, banged his fist on the table and declared that if they were real men they would make a clean sweep of the Government. And he added that it was vital to take an immediate decision if they were to be ready when the time for action came. Then, bending forward and lowering their voices, they decided to form a little group, to be prepared for any eventuality of that kind. From that day forward, Gavard saw himself as a member of a secret society, engaged in a conspiracy. The little circle would receive no new members, but Logre promised to put them in touch with other groups; later, when they had Paris in their grasp, the Tuileries* would beg for mercy. A series of endless discussions thus began, lasting for months: questions of organization, tactics, strategy, and future government. As soon as Rose had brought Clémence's grog, Charvet's and Robine's beer, coffee for Logre, Gavard, and Florent, and little glasses of brandy for Lacaille and Alexandre, the door was carefully fastened and the session began.

Charvet and Florent were naturally those whose utterances were listened to with the greatest attention. Gavard had been unable to hold his tongue and had gradually given away the whole story of Cayenne; Florent thus acquired a halo of martyrdom. His words were received as articles of faith. One evening, Gavard, annoyed at hearing his friend attacked behind his back, cried:

'Leave him alone! He was at Cayenne!'

But Charvet was nettled by this advantage.

'Cayenne, Cayenne,' he muttered under his breath. 'They weren't treated that badly over there!'

And he tried to prove that exile meant nothing and real suffering lay in remaining in one's own oppressed country, watching, with a gag over one's mouth, the triumph of despotism. Besides, it was not his fault if he had not been arrested on 2 December. He even hinted that those who had got themselves arrested were idiots. This secret jealousy of his made him Florent's perpetual adversary. Every discussion always finished as a battle between the two of them. They talked for hours while the others remained silent, neither of them ever admitting that he was beaten.

One of their favourite subjects was the reorganization of the country once victory was achieved.

'We're bound to win, aren't we?' Gavard would begin.

Victory being taken for granted, each of them would put forward his own personal opinion. There were two schools of thought. Charvet, who was a disciple of Hébert, was supported by Logre and Robine. Florent, still wrapped up in his humanitarian dreams, called himself a socialist,* and was backed by Alexandre and Lacaille. Gavard, for his part, was not at all averse to violent action; but, as people sometimes reproached him for his money, with no end of sarcastic comments that upset him, he was, he said, a communist.

'We'll have to make a clean sweep of everything,' Charvet would curtly say, as if he were wielding an axe. 'The trunk is rotten, we'll have to cut it down.'

'Yes! Yes!' cried Logre, standing up to make himself seem taller, making the partition shake with the excited motion of his hump. 'Everything will be levelled to the ground. That's clear. Then we'll see.'

Robine wagged his beard in approval. His silence had something joyous about it when the proposals really became revolutionary. His eyes assumed a great gentleness at the mention of the guillotine. He half closed them as if to visualize the scene, and the sight of it moved him greatly; then he would rub his chin lightly with the knob of his stick, purring with satisfaction.

'Just a minute,' Florent would then say, his voice betraying a touch of sadness. 'If you cut down the tree, you'll have to keep cuttings. I take the other view, that we ought to preserve the tree in order to graft new life onto it. The political revolution is over now, you see. Today we must think of the working man, the labourer. Our movement must be purely social. You must not deny the demands of the people. They're tired of waiting, they want their share.'

These words fired Alexandre with enthusiasm. Beaming, he declared that it was true, the people were tired of waiting.

'And we want our share too,' added Lacaille, looking more threatening. 'All the revolutions so far have been for the bourgeois. They don't need any more. The next one will be for us.'

It was at this point that disagreement set in. Gavard offered to make a division of his property, but Logre declined, saying that it wasn't simply a matter of money. Then little by little Charvet prevailed over the tumult, until he alone was left speaking.

'Class self-interest is one of the most powerful allies of tyranny,' he said. 'It's wrong of the people to be self-interested. If they help us, they'll have their share... Why should I fight for the workers if the workers won't fight for me? Anyway, that's not the question. It takes ten years of revolutionary rule to get a country like France used to the exercise of liberty.'

'Particularly', said Clémence sharply, 'because the workers aren't ready for it yet, and must be governed.'

She hardly ever spoke. This tall, serious-looking girl, lost in the midst of all these men, listened to the endless political talk with the air of a schoolteacher. She leaned back against the partition and every now and then sipped her grog as she gazed at the speakers, frowning or dilating her nostrils in a dumb show of approval or disapproval that bore witness to her understanding and her very definite ideas about the most complex matters. Sometimes she would roll a cigarette, blowing thin streams of smoke from the corners of her mouth as she grew more and more attentive. It was as though the battle was taking place in her honour, and in the end she would present the prizes. She certainly believed that, as a woman, she should keep her opinions to herself and not get carried away like the men. Only at the height of battle would she occasionally throw in a phrase or even, as Gavard put it, 'shut Charvet up'. In her heart of hearts she considered herself much cleverer than the men. Robine was the only one she respected, and she watched over his silence with her big black eyes.

Florent paid no more attention to Clémence than the others did. They treated her as if she were a man, shaking hands with her so roughly that they nearly broke her arm. One evening Florent witnessed the periodic settlement of accounts between her and Charvet.

She had just received her pay, and Charvet wanted to borrow ten francs; but she said no, insisting that first of all they must reckon up how things stood between them.* They lived together on the basis of free marriage and free income; they were both very strict about paying their own expenses, with the result, so they said, that they owed each other nothing and had never become slaves to each other. The rent, food, laundry, and amusements were all noted down and added up. On that particular evening, Clémence, having done the sums, showed that Charvet owed her five francs. She then gave him the ten francs, saying:

'Remember, that makes fifteen francs you owe me now, and you'll pay me back on the fifth when you get paid for teaching the Léhudier boy.'

When Rose brought the bill, they all pulled money from their pockets to pay for what they had drunk. Charvet laughingly dubbed Clémence an aristocrat because she drank grog; he claimed she wanted to make him feel small by making him realize that he earned less than she did, which was indeed the case. But, beneath his laughter, there was a feeling of bitterness that Clémence should be better off than himself, in spite of his theory of the equality of the sexes.

If the discussions reached no conclusion, they served to exercise their lungs. An appalling racket rose from the room; the frosted glass vibrated like the skin of a drum. Sometimes the noise became so loud that Rose, languidly pouring a drink for some fellow outside, would cast an anxious glance at the partition.

'God, they seem to be tearing each other apart in there,' the customer would say, putting his glass down on the counter and wiping his mouth with the back of his hand.

'Oh, not at all,' Monsieur Lebigre would calmly reply. 'It's just some gentlemen talking.'

Monsieur Lebigre, extremely strict as far as other customers were concerned, allowed the politicians to shout their heads off. He would sit for hours on the plush bench behind the counter, wearing his cardigan, his big head propped back against the mirror as he watched Rose uncorking bottles or wiping the bar with a cloth. When he was in a good mood and she was standing in front of him washing glasses with her sleeves rolled up, he would pinch her in the fleshy parts of her legs without anyone noticing, and she would accept this with a smile of pleasure. She did not even give a start; when he had pinched her almost black and blue, she would simply say that she wasn't ticklish.

In spite of the soporific atmosphere, Monsieur Lebigre would monitor the noise coming from the little room. When the voices grew louder, he went over to lean against the partition, and sometimes he pushed open the door and sat down for a few minutes, giving Gavard a friendly slap on the thigh. On these occasions he nodded his approval of everything. Gavard was of the view that although Lebigre was not born to be an orator, he could be counted on when 'the day of reckoning' came.

One morning in Les Halles, when a tremendous row broke out between Rose and one of the fishwives over a basket of herrings Rose had accidentally knocked over, Florent heard Lebigre called a 'dirty spy' and 'in the pay of the police'. As soon as he had re-established order, he was treated to all sorts of stories about Monsieur Lebigre. Yes, he was in the pay of the police; the whole neighbourhood knew that. Mademoiselle Saget, before becoming a customer of his, had said that she had bumped into him one day on his way to give evidence; and he was also quite well off, a moneylender who lent petty sums by the day to greengrocers and hired out carts to them, demanding a scandalously high rate of interest. Florent was greatly disturbed by all this and felt it his duty, that evening, to tell the assembled company what he had heard. They simply shrugged their shoulders and laughed.

'Poor old Florent!' said Charvet. 'Just because he's been to Cayenne, he thinks the entire police force is breathing down his neck.'

Gavard gave his word of honour that Lebigre was 'absolutely sound'. But Logre became really annoyed. He declared that it was impossible to carry on like this; if everyone was going to be accused of being a police spy, he would rather stay at home and have nothing more to do with politics. Wasn't it the case that people had dared to suggest at one time that even he, Logre, was mixed up with the police, he who had fought in 1848 and 1851 and who, on two occasions, had narrowly escaped being deported! As he shouted this, he thrust his jaws out and glared at the others as if he wanted to convince them forcibly that he was not 'in with the police'. Under his furious gaze, the others made gestures of protestation. Meanwhile Lacaille, on hearing Monsieur Lebigre called a moneylender, lowered his head.

The incident was soon forgotten. Monsieur Lebigre, ever since Logre had launched the notion of a conspiracy, had taken to exchanging even heartier handshakes with the regulars in the little room. Their custom could hardly have been worth his while, for they never ordered more than one round of drinks. They drained the last drops as they rose to leave, having been careful to keep a little in their glasses, even during their most heated arguments. They shivered as they went out into the chilly night. They stood for a moment on the footpath, their eyes dazzled and their ears buzzing, as if taken by surprise by the silence and darkness of the street. Rose, in the meantime, was closing the shutters. Then, exhausted, incapable of uttering another word, they shook hands and went their separate ways, mulling over the evening's discussion, regretting that they could not ram their particular theories down each other's throats. Robine, with his bent back, disappeared in the direction of the Rue Rambuteau, while Charvet and Clémence walked off through Les Halles towards the Luxembourg, their shoes echoing on the paving stones, never taking each other by the arm, still discussing some question of politics or philosophy.

The plot was slowly ripening. At the beginning of the summer, they were still only speaking of the need to 'do something'. Florent, who had at first been very sceptical, had now come to believe in the possibility of a revolutionary movement. He gave most careful thought to the matter, making notes and planning it all out on paper, while the others did nothing but talk. Little by little he became obsessed with this idea, which made his brain throb night after night; at last he even took his brother with him to Monsieur Lebigre's quite as a matter of course, not meaning any harm by it. He still regarded Quenu as in some degree his pupil and even thought it his duty to point him in the right direction. Quenu was an absolute novice in politics, but after five or six evenings in the little room he found himself quite in accord with the others. He was extremely docile and, when Lisa was not present, showed something approaching respect for his brother's opinions. What really seduced him, however, was the mild dissipation of leaving the shop and coming to shut himself up in a little room full of shouting, and where the presence of Clémence, in his opinion, gave a tinge of rakishness and romance to the proceedings. He would hurry through his sausages so that he would get there as early as he could, anxious not to miss a word of the discussions, which seemed to him so weighty and important, even though he was not always able to follow them. La Belle Lisa soon noticed his hasty departures, but refrained from any comment. When Florent came to fetch him, she stood on the doorstep, pale and severe, and watched them go into Monsieur Lebigre's.

One evening, from her attic window, Mademoiselle Saget recognized Quenu's shadow on the frosted glass of the window of the little room that faced the Rue Pirouette. She found her attic an excellent lookout, as it overlooked the milky transparency of the window, on which were drawn the silhouettes of the figures within, with noses suddenly appearing and disappearing, jutting jaws springing abruptly into sight and then vanishing, and huge arms, apparently unattached to any bodies, gesticulating violently. This extraordinary dislocation of limbs, these dumb and agitated profiles, were dramatic signs of the fierce discussions taking place in the little room, and kept the old maid riveted at her curtains until the transparency turned black. She suspected they were 'up to no good'. By continual watching she had come to identify the different silhouettes from hands, hair, and clothes. As she gazed at the confusion of clenched fists, angry heads, and swaying shoulders, which all seemed to have become detached and to be rolling about one on top of the other, she would cry out: 'There's that daft cousin, there's that old miser Gavard, there's the hunchback, and there's that tall Clémence girl too.' Then, when the action of the shadow-play became more pronounced, and they all seemed to have lost control of themselves, she felt an irresistible urge to go downstairs and see what was happening. She now bought her blackcurrant wine in the evening, saying that she felt 'out of sorts' in the morning and had to take a sip as soon as she got out of bed. The day she saw Quenu's massive head outlined on the transparency, superimposed on the nervous gesticulations of Charvet's skinny arm, she arrived at Monsieur Lebigre's quite out of breath, and made Rose rinse out her little bottle to gain time. She was just about to leave again when she heard Quenu exclaim with a sort of childish candour:

'It's time… We'll make a clean sweep of all those bloody deputies and ministers! The whole lot of them!'

The next morning Mademoiselle Saget was at the *charcuterie* at eight o'clock sharp. There she found Madame Lecœur and La Sarriette, dipping their noses into the warming-stove and buying hot sausages for their lunch. As the old woman had managed to draw them into her quarrel with La Belle Normande over the ten sous' worth of dabs, they had both lost no time in making friends again with Lisa, and they now had nothing but contempt for La Normande and her sister, whom they dismissed as dirty sluts only interested in fleecing men for their money. Mademoiselle Saget had given Madame Lecœur to understand that Florent sometimes passed one of the sisters on to Gavard and the four of them had wild parties at Baratte's, at Gavard's expense of course. Madame Lecœur was deeply saddened.

That morning the old girl directed all her malice at Madame Quenu. She fidgeted about in front of the counter and then murmured in her sweetest voice:

'I saw Monsieur Quenu last night. They seem to have a high old time in that back room at Lebigre's, judging from the racket they make.'

Lisa looked out at the street, not wanting to show that she was listening very carefully to what was being said. Mademoiselle Saget paused, hoping for a question. Then, almost whispering, she said:

'They had a woman with them. Oh, not Monsieur Quenu, I don't mean with him. I don't know…'

'That would be Clémence,' interrupted La Sarriette. 'A tall, scraggy thing who gives herself airs because she went to a boarding school. She lives with a shabby-looking schoolteacher. I've seen them together. They always look as if they're taking each other to the police station.'

'That's right, that's right,' replied the old woman, who knew everything about Charvet and Clémence, and had only wanted to make Lisa worried.

But Lisa didn't bat an eyelid. She seemed to be watching something very interesting over in the markets. Mademoiselle Saget therefore became more pointed in her remarks. Looking at Madame Lecœur, she said:

'I've been meaning to tell you, you should tell your brother-in-law to be more careful. Last night they were shouting the most dreadful things in there. Men really seem to lose their heads when they get involved in politics. If anyone had heard them, they might have got into serious trouble.'

'Gavard always goes his own way,' sighed Madame Lecœur. 'But that would be dreadful. I'd die of shame if he was sent to prison.'

As she said this, her eyes gleamed. But La Sarriette laughed and shook her head, her little face as fresh as could be in the morning air.

'You should hear what Jules says about people who speak against the Empire,' she said. 'They should all be thrown into the Seine, because, as he said, there isn't a single decent man among them.'

'There's no harm as long as it's only people like me who hear their nonsense. I'd sooner have my tongue cut out... But last night Monsieur Quenu was saying...'

Again she paused. Lisa made a slight movement.

'Monsieur Quenu was saying that the ministers and deputies, and all the rest, should be shot.'

This time Lisa turned round, as white as a sheet, her hands clenched under her apron.

'Quenu said that?' she asked curtly.

'And other things I can't remember. But no one else heard. Don't worry, Madame Quenu. You know you can trust me not to say anything. I'm old enough to know the trouble it would cause. It's safe with me.'

Lisa had recovered somewhat. She took pride in the harmony and respectability of her home; and she would not acknowledge that there had ever been the slightest difference between herself and her husband. So she shrugged and murmured with a smile:

'It's all silly nonsense.'

As soon as the three women were outside on the footpath, they agreed that La Belle Lisa had looked quite put out. They agreed that the odd goings-on of the cousin, the Méhudins, Gavard, and the Quenus would end badly. Madame Lecœur asked what happened to people who got arrested 'for politics'. All Mademoiselle Saget knew was that they disappeared and were never heard of again; which led La Sarriette to suggest that they were probably thrown into the Seine, as Jules had said.

Lisa avoided all reference to the matter at lunch and dinner; and when Florent and Quenu went off to Monsieur Lebigre's, she seemed to have lost the very serious look she had had earlier on. On that particular evening, however, they debated the new constitution they would draw up, and it was one o'clock before the company finally left the little room. The shutters were up and they had to leave by the little side door, bending down as they went. Quenu walked home with an uneasy conscience. He opened as quietly as possible the three or four doors on his way to bed, walking on tiptoe through the sitting room, feeling his way so as not to bump into the furniture. The house lay asleep. When he reached the bedroom, he was most put out to see that Lisa had left the candle alight; it was burning in the deep silence with a tall, mournful flame. As he took off his shoes and put them in a corner, the clock struck half past one in such resounding tones that he looked at it in alarm, almost afraid to move, and looked angrily at the gilt Gutenberg with his finger on a book. All he could see of Lisa was her back; her head was buried in her pillow, but he knew quite well that she was not asleep, that her eyes were probably wide open and staring at the wall. Her broad back, very fleshy round the shoulders, was pale and smooth; it bulged out, seeming to carry all the weight of an unanswerable accusation. Abashed by the extreme severity of this back, which seemed to be scrutinizing him with the steady glare of a judge, Quenu slipped under the bedclothes, blew out the candle, and lay very still. He stayed on the edge of the bed, to avoid touching his wife. He could have sworn that she was awake. At last he fell asleep, in despair at her silence, not daring to say goodnight, feeling powerless against this implacable back which protected the bed against anything he might wish to say in self-defence.

He slept late the following morning. When he awoke, spread-eagled across the bed with the eiderdown up to his chin, he saw Lisa sitting at the desk arranging some papers. He had slept so deeply that he had not heard her get up. He now took courage and spoke to her, from the depths of the alcove:

'Why didn't you wake me up? What are you doing?'

'I'm sorting these drawers out,' she replied in her usual, calm way.

Quenu felt relieved. But she added:

'You never know what might happen. If the police come...'

'What! The police?'

'Yes. You've got very involved in politics, after all.'

He sat up, taken totally by surprise.

'Me, involved in politics! Me, involved in politics!' he repeated. 'But it's no concern of the police. I've done nothing wrong.'

'No,' replied Lisa, with a shrug of her shoulders. 'You just talk about having everybody shot.'

'Me? Me?'

'Yes. And you shout it out loud in a bar. Mademoiselle Saget heard you. The whole neighbourhood must know by now that you're a Red.'

Quenu fell back in bed again. He was still not fully awake. Lisa's words resounded in his ears as though he could already hear the clatter of policemen's boots on the stairs. He looked at her, tight in her corset and her hair already done, her usual meticulously tidy self, and was all the more bewildered to find her so neat and proper in such extraordinary circumstances.

'You know I respect your freedom,' she continued after a while, still sorting out the papers. 'I don't want to wear the trousers, as the saying goes. You're the master; it's your position in life you're jeopardizing, our good name you're compromising, our business you're ruining... My main concern is to make sure that Pauline doesn't come to any harm.'

He began to protest, but she silenced him with a gesture of the hand.

'No, don't say anything,' she continued. 'I don't want a quarrel or even an explanation. If only you had asked me, we could have talked it over together. It's wrong to say that women don't understand politics... Shall I tell you what my politics are?'

She had risen to her feet and moved from the bed to the window, removing with her finger the specks of dust she saw on the polished mahogany of the wardrobe and dressing table.

'It's what responsible people understand by politics... I'm grateful to the Government when business is doing well, when I can eat my meals in peace, when I can sleep without being woken up by gunfire. It was a fine mess in 1848, wasn't it? Uncle Gradelle—he was a good man, you know—showed us his books for that year. He lost more than six thousand francs. Now that we've got the Empire, though, business is good. We're doing well. You can't deny that. So what is it you want? How will you be better off when you've had everybody shot?'

She stood with her arms folded before the bedside table, opposite Quenu, who had disappeared under the eiderdown. He tried to explain what his companions wanted, but he got entangled in the social and political systems of Charvet and Florent. He could only mutter a few confused words about the advent of democracy and the regeneration of society, muddling everything up in such a funny way that Lisa shrugged her shoulders, not understanding a word of what he said. At last he wriggled out of it by attacking the Empire: it was a regime of debauchery, scandal, and armed robbery.

'You see,' he said, recalling a phrase Logre often used, 'we are the victims of a gang of adventurers who are plundering, violating, and murdering the whole of France… They must go!'

Lisa still shrugged her shoulders.

'Is that all you've got to say?' she asked in her wonderfully cool way. 'What has all that got to do with me? Even if it were true, what then? Have I ever suggested that you should be dishonest? Have I ever told you not to pay your bills, or cheat your customers, or make a pile of money the wrong way? You're going to make me really angry in a minute! We're decent, honest people. We don't plunder or murder anybody. That's all there is to it. Other people can do what they like!'

She looked quite majestic. She began walking about, drawn up to her full height, still speaking.

'Do we have to give up our business to please those who haven't got any money of their own? Of course I take advantage of good times and support a government that helps business. If it does anything dishonourable as well, I don't need to know. I know that *I* don't commit any crimes and that no one in the neighbourhood can point a finger at me. Only fools go tilting at windmills. You remember when Gavard told us, at the last elections, that the Emperor's candidate had been declared bankrupt after getting mixed up in some shady business? It may have been true, I don't know. But it didn't stop you from voting for him, and quite right too, because that wasn't the point; you weren't being asked to do business with him or lend him money, but just to show the Government you were satisfied with how well the *charcuterie* was doing.'

At this point Quenu remembered one of Charvet's pronouncements and began to recite it: 'the bloated bourgeois and fat shopkeepers, who support a government of universal gormandizing, should be the first to go to the wall.' It was thanks to them, thanks to their selfish worship of the belly, that the country was being corrupted by despotism. He was trying to get to the end of this declaration when Lisa cut him short.

'That's enough! My conscience is clear. I don't have any debts, I've never got mixed up in anything that's not above board, I buy and sell good quality things, I don't charge more than other

people… What you say may apply to our cousins, the Saccards.*
They pretend they don't even know I'm in Paris; but I'm prouder
than they are and I couldn't care less about their millions. They say
that Saccard speculates in property development and cheats everybody.* It wouldn't surprise me; he was always like that. He loves
money. He wants to wallow in it and then throw it out of the
window like a lunatic… I agree it's not hard to find fault with people
like that, who pile up too much money for their own good. If you
want to know, I don't think much of Saccard. But us? We mind our
own business, we'll need fifteen years to save enough to be independent, we never get involved in politics, we just want to bring up
our daughter properly and make sure that our business does well.
We're decent and honest!'

She walked over and sat on the edge of the bed. Quenu was shaken.

'Listen to me,' she resumed in an even more serious tone. I don't
suppose you want your shop raided, your cellars emptied, and your
money stolen, do you? If those men who meet at Monsieur Lebigre's
got what they wanted, do you imagine you'd still be lying nicely
tucked up in bed? And when you went downstairs to the kitchen, do
you think you'd get on quietly with making your *galantines*, as you
will in a few minutes? No, you know you wouldn't. So why talk about
overthrowing the Government, which looks after you and lets you
save money? You've got a wife and daughter, and they're your first
duty. It would be very wrong of you to put their happiness at risk.
It's only homeless people, who've got nothing to lose, who want to
see the shooting start. You don't want to put your life at risk for their
sake, do you? So stay at home, you silly thing, sleep well and eat well,
make money, have a clean conscience, and tell yourself that France
will deal with her own problems, even if the Empire does worry her
a bit. France doesn't need *you*!'

She laughed her lovely laugh, and Quenu was quite convinced by
what she had said. Yes, she was right; and she looked very beautiful,
he thought, as she sat there on the edge of the bed, even at this early
hour so neat and clean in her white linen. As he listened to her, his
eyes fell on their portraits on each side of the mantelpiece. Yes, it was
true that they were decent and honest; they looked most respectable
in their black clothes and gilded frames. The room itself now seemed
the bedchamber of people who were of some account in the world.
The lace squares seemed to give a dignified appearance to the chairs,

and the carpet, the curtains, and the vases decorated with painted landscapes—all spoke of their hard work and their love of comfort. He wriggled further down under the eiderdown, where he lay as if in a hot bath. He began to realize that at Monsieur Lebigre's he had only just managed to avoid losing all this—his enormous bed, his cosy room, his *charcuterie*. He was now filled with remorse. And from Lisa, from the furniture, from everything around him, he derived a sense of well-being that seemed a little claustrophobic, but delightfully so.

'Silly thing!' said Lisa, seeing that she had won. 'You took a wrong turning there, I must say. But you would have had Pauline and me to deal with... You can stop bothering about the Government now. All governments are the same anyway. If we didn't have one, we'd have another. The main thing is that, when you get old, you've got some savings to live on and you know you worked hard for them.'

Quenu nodded. He wanted to make some excuses.

'It was Gavard,' he murmured.

But Lisa began to look very serious again and interrupted him.

'No, it wasn't Gavard... I know who it was; and it would be a lot better if he thought about his own safety before starting to put others at risk.'

'You mean Florent?' Quenu asked timidly, after a pause.

Lisa did not answer at once. She got up and went back to the desk, as if trying to control herself. Then she said crisply:

'Yes, Florent... You know how good-natured I am. Nothing in the world would make me want to come between you and your brother. Family bonds are sacred. But I really think I've had enough. Ever since your brother arrived, things have gone from bad to worse. But I don't want to talk about it now; it's better not to.'

There was another pause. Quenu stared at the ceiling in some embarrassment. Then she continued:

'You've got to admit it—he doesn't seem to realize what we do for him. We've really put ourselves out for him. We've given him Augustine's room, and the poor girl sleeps without a word of complaint in a cramped little room where she can hardly breathe. We feed him morning, noon and night, we look after him... But he takes it all for granted. He's earning money, but what he does with it nobody knows; or rather, everybody knows only too well.'

'There's his share of the inheritance,' Quenu ventured to say, pained at hearing his brother criticized in this way.

Lisa suddenly stiffened, as if stunned. Her anger vanished.

'Yes, you're right, there's his share of the inheritance. Here are the details, in the drawer. He didn't want it. You were there, don't you remember? That just shows how brainless and hopeless he is. If he had anything about him, he would have done something by now with that money. I'd just as soon not have it; it would be a big relief. I told him so twice, but he won't listen to me. You should persuade him to take it. Try to talk to him about it.'

Quenu grunted in reply, and Lisa did not insist; she felt that she had done everything she could to argue her case.

'He's not like other men,' she resumed. 'Let's face it, it's a worry to have him in the house. I'm only saying that because we're talking about him. I'm not concerned with his conduct, but he's got the whole neighbourhood talking about us. He can eat here and sleep here and get in our way, if he likes; we can put up with that. But what I won't tolerate is for him to get us mixed up in his politics. If he gives you any more funny ideas, or looks as if he's going to get us into any sort of trouble, I'll turn him out of the house straight away. I'm warning you.'

Florent was doomed. Lisa was making a great effort not to vent all her pent-up resentment towards Florent. He offended all her instincts, he disturbed her, and made her really unhappy.

'A man who has had the most dreadful adventures,' she murmured, 'and who's never even been able to set up a home of his own... No wonder he wants the shooting to start. He can go off and get himself shot, if that's what he wants; but let him leave decent people and their families alone. Anyway, I don't like him! He smells of fish when he comes back for dinner! It puts me off my food. He doesn't miss a mouthful—for all the good it does him! He can't even fatten himself up a bit, he's so eaten away by all those unhealthy ideas of his.'

She had moved across to the window and suddenly saw Florent crossing the Rue Rambuteau on his way to the market. There were endless deliveries of fish that morning; the baskets were full of glittering silver, and the auction rooms were deafening. Lisa kept her eyes on her brother-in-law's narrow shoulders as he became enveloped in the pungent smells of the market, stooping a little as they hit him; her expression as she watched him was that of a woman bent on combat and determined to be victorious.

When she turned round, Quenu was getting up. Standing in his nightshirt, still warm from the eiderdown and with his feet in the fleecy carpet, he looked pale and distressed by the gulf between his wife and his brother. But Lisa gave him one of her lovely smiles, and he was most touched when she handed him his socks.

CHAPTER 4

MARJOLIN had been found in the Marché des Innocents, lying asleep in a pile of cabbages, underneath an enormous white one which covered his rosy face with one of its broad leaves. Nobody ever knew what poverty-stricken mother had left him there. He was already a sturdy little fellow of two or three, very plump and lively, but so backward and dense that he could hardly stammer more than a word or two, though he knew how to smile. When one of the vegetable stallholders discovered him under the cabbage, she uttered such a cry of surprise that her neighbours rushed up to see what was the matter. The child, still in its baby clothes and wrapped in a piece of old blanket, stretched out its arms. He couldn't tell them who his mother was. His eyes were wide with surprise as he clung to the shoulder of a fat tripe-seller who had picked him up. The whole market fussed around him all day. He soon felt safe, ate some slices of bread and butter, and smiled at all the women. The fat tripe-seller looked after him for a while; then he passed him on to a neighbour; a month later he was living with someone else. When they asked him where his mother was, he waved his little hand in the direction of all the women in sight. He was the child of Les Halles, always clinging to the skirts of one woman or another, always finding a corner of a bed and a bowl of soup somewhere. Somehow, too, he managed to find clothes, and even had a few sous in the depths of his ragged pockets. A handsome redhead who sold medicinal herbs christened him Marjolin, but no one knew why.

Marjolin was nearly four when Mère Chantemesse came upon a little girl who had been left on the footpath in the Rue Saint-Denis at the corner of the market. The child might have been about two, but she chattered away like a magpie, mixing up her words in her childish babble; Mère Chantemesse was able to gather from her, however, that her name was Cadine and that the previous evening her mother had left her on a doorstep and told her to wait until she returned. The child had fallen asleep and did not cry, because she said she was beaten at home. She was happy to follow Mère Chantemesse and was delighted with this vast place where there were so many people and so many vegetables. Mère Chantemesse, a retail dealer by trade, was a crusty but kind woman getting on for sixty; she loved children, having lost three boys before they were out of the cradle. She thought that the little thing she had found 'was far too lively not to make it', and so she adopted her.

One evening, however, when Mère Chantemesse was walking along holding Cadine by her right hand, Marjolin came up and without more ado took her left hand.

'Well now, what's this?' said the old woman, stopping. 'That place is already taken. Have you given up Thérèse, then? You're a terrible flirt, aren't you?'

He looked at her, smiling, but would not let go. He looked so pretty with his curly hair that she could not resist.

'Come on, then,' she said. 'I'll put you in the same bed.'

So she arrived in the Rue au Lard, where she lived, with a child clinging to each hand. Marjolin made himself quite at home there. When they became too unruly, she gave them both a slap, pleased to be able to shout and be angry, clean their faces and pack them away under the same blanket. She had fixed up a little bed for them in a greengrocer's cart which had long since lost its wheels and shafts. It was like a huge cradle, rather hard and still smelling of the vegetables which it had long kept fresh and cool under damp cloths. Cadine and Marjolin, at the age of four, slept there in each other's arms.

Thus they grew up together and were always to be seen arm in arm. At night Mère Chantemesse could hear them quietly chatting away. Cadine's clear treble continued for hours, punctuated occasionally, in a deeper tone, by Marjolin's expressions of surprise. She was a mischievous creature and invented stories just to frighten him, telling him, for instance, that one night she had seen a man dressed all in white, looking at them and sticking out a big red tongue, at the foot of the bed. Marjolin was beside himself with fear and asked for more details, and she would then begin to make fun of him and call him a 'silly ass'. At other times they got carried away and kicked each other under the bedclothes. Cadine pulled her legs up to her chest and tried not to giggle as Marjolin, lunging out with all his might, missed her and hit the wall. When this happened, Mère Chantemesse had to get up and straighten the bedclothes, and sent them off to sleep with a box round the ears. For a long time their bed was a sort of playground. They had toys in it and ate stolen turnips and carrots there; and every morning their adopted mother was surprised at the curious assortment of objects she found in the bed—pebbles, leaves, apple cores, dolls made out of bits of rag. When it was bitterly cold she left them asleep, Cadine's black mop mingling with Marjolin's sunny curls, their mouths so close together that they seemed to keep each other warm with their breathing.

This room in the Rue au Lard was a big, dilapidated attic, with a single window, the panes of which were made dirty by the rain. The children would play hide and seek in the tall walnut wardrobe and under Mère Chantemesse's huge bed. There were also two or three tables, under which they would crawl on all fours. It was a lovely playground for them, because so dimly lit, and cluttered with vegetables. The Rue au Lard was fun too. It was a narrow street without much traffic, with a wide arcade opening onto the Rue de la Lingerie. Their house was next to the arcade, and it had a low door which could only be opened halfway because of the greasy winding staircase behind it. The house, which had a pent roof and a bulging front, was dark with damp and had a greenish casing round the drainpipes. It, too, became a huge toy. They spent their mornings throwing stones, trying to land them in the gutters; when they succeeded, the stones clattered down the drainpipes, making a merry sound. They succeeded, however, in breaking two panes of glass and filling the drainpipes with so many stones that Mère Chantemesse, who had lived in the house for forty-three years, was nearly asked to leave.

Cadine and Marjolin then turned their attention to the carts, barrows, and drays drawn up in the deserted street. They climbed onto the wheels, swung on the chains, and clambered over the boxes and baskets. The commission agents' premises in the Rue de la Poterie backed onto this street; huge, gloomy warehouses, filled and emptied every day, provided a constant supply of new hiding-places, where they could get lost amidst the odour of dried fruit, oranges, and fresh apples. When they got tired of playing there, they went off to look for Mère Chantemesse in the Marché des Innocents, crossing streets arm in arm and laughing their way through the traffic, without the least fear of being run over. They knew the footpaths well and waded knee-deep through the vegetables; they never slipped, and laughed themselves silly when some porter in heavy boots trod on an artichoke stem and went head over heels. They were the rosy-cheeked tutelary spirits of the streets, and were seen everywhere. On rainy days they trotted soberly about under a huge ragged umbrella with which La Mère Chantemesse had protected her wares for twenty years; they set it up in a corner of the market and called it 'their house'. When the sun shone they ran about so much that by the evening they were exhausted; they paddled in the fountain, dammed up the gutters, or covered themselves up in piles of vegetables and stayed there in the cool, chattering to each other as they did in bed at night. Passers-by often heard muffled voices coming from a mountain of lettuces, and if the greenery was parted they could be seen lying together on their bed of leaves, bright-eyed, like startled birds in a hedge. As time went by, Cadine could not bear to be without Marjolin, and Marjolin began to cry when he lost Cadine. If they happened to be separated for some reason, they looked for each other behind the skirt of every stallholder in Les Halles, in all the boxes and under all the cabbages. It was mostly under the cabbages that they grew up and came to love each other.

Marjolin was nearly eight, and Cadine six, when Mère Chantemesse began to chide them for their laziness. She said she would make them partners in her vegetable business and pay them a sou a day if they would help her to clean and peel the vegetables. For the first few days they were very keen. They squatted down on each side of the stall armed with little knives, and worked away energetically. Mère Chantemesse specialized in peeled vegetables; on her stall, covered with a strip of damp black cloth, she laid out rows of potatoes, turnips, carrots, and white onions, arranged in pyramids of four, with three for the base and one for the top, all ready to be popped into the saucepans of housewives who wanted to save time. She also had bundles tied up ready for the soup pot—four leeks, three carrots, one parsnip, two sticks of celery; not to mention the freshly cut julienne, finely chopped on sheets of paper, cabbages cut in quarters, heaps of tomatoes, and slices of pumpkin, which were like red stars and golden crescents against the white of the other vegetables, washed as they were in running water. Cadine proved to be much better at it than Marjolin, even though she was younger. She cut such thin peels of potato that you could see the light through them; she tied up the bundles for the soup pot so artistically that they looked like bouquets; and she had a way of arranging small clutches of vegetables to make them look bigger, with just three carrots or turnips. The passers-by would stop and smile when she called out in her shrill little voice: 'Come on, ladies! Two sous a pile!'

She had her regular customers, and her little pyramids were well known. La Mère Chantemesse, sitting between the two children, would laugh until she almost burst at seeing them take their work so seriously. She religiously gave them each their daily sou. But eventually they grew bored with their little piles of vegetables. They were growing up, and their thoughts turned to more lucrative occupations. Marjolin remained a child much longer than Cadine, and this irritated her. He had no more brains than a cabbage, she said. Indeed, try as she would to think up ways for him to earn money, he wasn't even capable of running an errand. She, on the other hand, was clever. When she was eight she joined forces with one of those women who sit on a bench near Les Halles with a basket of lemons, which a band of street-girls sell under their orders; carrying the lemons in her hands and offering them at two or three sous each, Cadine ran after every woman who passed, thrusting her wares under their noses, coming back to fetch more when her hands were empty. For every dozen lemons she sold she received two sous, which on good days earned her five or six sous. The following year she hawked bonnets at nine sous apiece and her profits were greater; but she had to keep a sharp lookout, since street trading of this kind is forbidden. She could scent a *sergent de ville* a hundred metres away, and the bonnets would be bundled under her skirt while she innocently munched an apple. Then she took to selling cakes, cherry tarts, gingerbread, and dry biscuits, thick and yellow, on wicker trays. Marjolin, however, ate up nearly all the profits. At last, when she was eleven, she fulfilled an ambition which had been tormenting her for some time. In a couple of months she put by four francs, bought a small basket she could carry on her back, and set up as a dealer in bird food.

It was really big business. She got up early in the morning and bought her supply of chickweed, millet, and bird-cake from the wholesalers. Then she set off across the river and did the rounds of the Latin Quarter, from the Rue Saint-Jacques to the Rue Dauphine and even to the Luxembourg Gardens. Marjolin went with her, but she would not let him carry her basket. He was only fit to call out, she said; and so, in his thick, heavy voice, he would shout: 'Chickweed for pet birds!'

Then Cadine herself, with her flute-like voice, would take up the call, starting on a strange scale of notes and ending in a clear, protracted alto: 'Chickweed for pet birds!'

They each took one side of the street, looking upwards as they walked along. Marjolin wore a big red jacket that came down to his knees and had originally belonged to Monsieur Chantemesse, who had been a cabdriver. Cadine wore a dress in blue and white check, made from an old piece of tartan that belonged to Mère Chantemesse. All the canaries in the garrets of the Latin Quarter knew them; and, as they walked along, repeating their cry, each echoing the other's voice, the birdcages burst into song.

Cadine also sold cress. 'Two sous a bunch! Two sous a bunch!' And Marjolin went into the shops offering 'Fine fresh watercress! Very healthy!' Les Halles had just been built, and the little girl would stand gazing in ecstasy at the avenue of flower stalls that ran through the fruit market. From end to end, on either side, the stalls were like borders along a garden path, blossoming like splendid bouquets. It was a harvest of perfumes, two thick hedges of roses, between which the girls in the neighbourhood loved to walk, smiling and a little over-come by the powerful scents. Above the displays there were artificial flowers, paper leaves with drops of gum that looked like dew, and funeral wreaths made of black and white beads that glittered with blue reflections. Cadine would dilate her nostrils like a cat, lingering there as long as possible and taking with her as much of the perfume as she could. When her hair bobbed under Marjolin's nose, he would say that it smelt of carnations. She claimed that she no longer needed to use anything for her hair; all she had to do was walk down the avenue. She used all her guile to secure a job with one of the stall-holders; Marjolin then declared that she smelt sweet from head to foot. She lived in the midst of roses, lilacs, wallflowers, and lilies of the valley; and Marjolin would playfully sniff her skirt, breathe in, furrow his brow, and exclaim: 'Lily of the valley!' Then he would sniff her waist and bodice: 'Wallflowers!' Then her sleeves and wrists: 'Lilac!' Then the back of her neck, all round her throat, cheeks, and lips: 'Roses!' Cadine laughed and called him an idiot, and told him to stop because he was tickling her with the end of his nose. Her breath was like jasmine. She was a bunch of flowers, full of warmth and life.

She now got up at four o'clock every morning to help her mistress with her purchases. Every day they bought armfuls of flowers from suppliers in the suburbs, and bunches of moss, fern, and periwinkle for the bouquets. Cadine loved the jewels and fine lace worn by the daughters of the great gardeners of Montreuil, who came to the mar-kets amidst their roses. On the feast days of Saint Mary, Saint Peter, and Saint Joseph, the saints most generally celebrated, the sale of flowers began at two o'clock. More than a hundred thousand francs worth of cut flowers would be sold on the footpaths, and some of the retailers would make as much as two hundred francs in a few hours. On these days Cadine's curly locks were all that could be seen of her above the bunches of pansies, mignonette, and daisies. She was drowned in the mass of flowers, and would spend the whole day mounting posies on bamboo canes. In just a few weeks she acquired a great deal of skill, a real flair for graceful arrangements. Her bouquets did not please everyone. Sometimes they made people smile, and sometimes they appeared quite disturbing. Red was the dominant colour, violently cut across by blues, yellows, and purples, creating a barbaric beauty. On the mornings when she pinched Marjolin and teased him until she made him cry, she made fierce-looking bouquets, reflecting her own bad temper, with strong smells and bright colours. At other times, when her mood was affected by some sorrow or some pleasure, her bouquets would be silvery grey, soft and subdued in tone, and delicately perfumed. Then there were the roses, blood-red like open hearts, lying in lakes of white carnations; the savage glare of gladioli, their flaming sprays shooting up from the terrified foliage; Smyrna tapestries of complicated design, constructed in a pattern flower by flower, as on a canvas; silken fans, spreading out as delicately as lace. Sometimes she made a posy of delicious purity, sometimes a fat nosegay, whatever one might dream of for the hand of a marchioness or a fishwife; all the charming fantasies, in short, which the brain of a twelve-year-old girl, already budding into womanhood, could devise.

There were only two flowers that Cadine now respected: white lilac, which in the winter cost between fifteen and twenty francs for a bunch of eight or ten sprays; and camellias, which were even more expensive, and arrived in boxes of a dozen, resting on a bed of moss and covered with a blanket of cotton wool. She handled them as if they were jewels, not daring to breathe for fear of dimming their lustre; then, with infinite care, she attached their short stems to cane sticks. She spoke of them with reverence. She told Marjolin that a pure white camellia was a very rare and lovely thing. One day, when she was holding one up for him to admire, he exclaimed:

'Yes, it's pretty, but I prefer your neck. It's much softer and more transparent than your camellia... It's got little blue and pink veins which are just like the veins in a flower petal.'

He caressed her with the tips of his fingers, then he sniffed her and murmured:

'You smell of orange blossom today.'

Cadine was very self-willed. She could not accept the role of a servant. So at last she set up her own little business. As she was only thirteen, and could not hope for a big business and a stall in the flower market, she sold one-sou bunches of violets stuck in a bed of moss on a wicker tray slung round her neck. She roamed about all day in and around Les Halles, carrying with her this little hanging garden. She loved to be constantly on the move, for it exercised her legs after the long hours spent kneeling, on a low chair, making bouquets. She prepared her violets with marvellous deftness as she walked along, twiddling them like spindles. She counted out six or eight flowers, according to the season, folded a strand of raffia in two, added a leaf, twisted some damp thread round the whole, and broke off the thread with her strong young teeth. So rapidly did she perform this trick that the little bunches seemed to grow of their own accord on the moss in the tray. Along the footpaths, through the jostling of the crowd, her nimble fingers sprouted flowers, though she gave them not a glance, but boldly scanned the shops and passers-by. Sometimes she rested for a few moments in a doorway; and alongside the gutters, greasy with kitchen slops, she would bring, as it were, a hint of springtime, of green woods and fresh blossoms. Her flowers still betokened her frame of mind, her fits of bad temper and her moments of tenderness. Sometimes they bristled and glowered with anger amidst their crumpled bed of leaves; at other times they spoke only of love and tranquillity as they smiled in their neat collars. Wherever she went, she left a sweet perfume behind her. Marjolin followed her in a trance of joy. Now, from head to foot, she smelt of only one thing. When he took hold of her and sniffed her from her skirt to her bodice, from her hands to her face, he said that she was herself a big, lovely violet. He smothered his face in her, and repeated:

'Do you remember the day we went to Romainville? You smell just like that, especially there, in your sleeve... Don't ever change your job again. You smell too nice.'

She never did change her job. It was her final choice. But the two children were growing up, and often she would forget her tray and run about the neighbourhood. The building of Les Halles, which was still in progress, was a constant source of entertainment for them. They climbed into the building sites through a gap in the fencing; they went down into the foundations that were being excavated, and scaled the first iron pillars to go up. Every hole being dug, every piece of the new structure, witnessed their games and their quarrels. The markets grew up under their little hands. From this grew their affection for the great markets, and which the markets seemed to return. They were on intimate terms with this gigantic edifice, as old friends who had seen the smallest bolt driven home. They were not afraid of the monster; they patted it and treated it like a friend; and Les Halles seemed to smile on these two urchins, who were their song, their shameless idyll.

Cadine and Marjolin no longer slept together in the greengrocer's cart at Mère Chantemesse's. The old woman, who continued to hear them chattering away at night, made up another bed for the little boy on the floor in front of the wardrobe; but the next morning she found him, as usual, with his arm round Cadine, under the same blanket. Then she sent him out to a neighbour's to sleep. This made the children very unhappy. In the daytime, when Mère Chantemesse wasn't about, they would lie down fully dressed on the footpath in each other's arms, as though it were a bed. Later they began to misbehave; they sought out the dark corners of the bedroom and often hid in the warehouses in the Rue au Lard, behind sacks of apples and crates of oranges. They were as free as birds and quite without shame, like sparrows mating on the rooftops.

It was in the cellars under the poultry market that they found a way of continuing to sleep together. Near the slaughtering blocks were some big baskets of feathers in which they could stretch out. As soon as night fell they went down and spent the evening there, warm in their soft bed, with the down up to their eyes. Usually they would drag their basket away from the gaslight; they were alone in the strong smell of poultry, kept awake by the sudden crowing of cocks in the dark. They laughed and kissed, full of affection which they were not sure how to express. Marjolin was very stupid. Cadine would beat him, furious at him without knowing why. But gradually she taught him things; eventually, in their basket of feathers, they came to know every pleasure. It was a game. The hens and cockerels that slept so close to them could not have been more innocent.

Later still, they filled Les Halles with their carefree sparrow love. They lived as young animals live, instinctively, satisfying their appetites in the midst of mountains of food, in which they had grown like plants. At sixteen Cadine was a dark gypsy of the streets, greedy and sensual. Marjolin, at eighteen, was a tall, strapping lad, quite without intelligence, living by his senses. She often left her bed to spend the night with him in the poultry cellars, and the next day would laugh cheekily at Mère Chantemesse, dodging out of reach of her broom, saying that she had stayed out 'to see if the moon had horns'. As for Marjolin, he lived like a tramp. On nights when Cadine did not visit him, he stayed with the orderly left by the market guards; he slept on sacks or boxes or in some convenient corner. In the end neither of them ever left Les Halles for more than a few minutes at a time. The markets became their home, their aviary, their stable, the manger where they lived and loved, on a great bed of meat, butter, and vegetables.

But they always remained especially fond of the big baskets of feathers. They returned there to make love. The feathers were all mixed up—turkey's feathers, long and black; goose quills, white and smooth, which tickled their ears when they turned over; the down from ducks, like cotton wool; and golden chicken feathers, which flew up in a cloud each time they breathed, like a swarm of flies buzzing in the sunlight. In winter there was the purple plumage of pheasants, the ashen grey of larks, the mottled silk of grouse, quail, and thrush. The feathers, freshly plucked, were still warm with their own smell, and the children often imagined, in their cosy nest, that they were being carried aloft by a great bird with huge, flapping wings. In the morning Marjolin had to look for Cadine, lost in the depths of the basket as if under a snowdrift. Her hair tousled, she stood up, shook herself, and emerged from a cloud of feathers.

They discovered another little paradise in the market where dairy produce was sold wholesale. Every morning enormous walls of empty baskets were piled up, and they would find a way to slip through the wall and hollow out a hiding-place. As soon as they had made room for themselves inside, they closed it in by drawing in one of the baskets. They made themselves thoroughly at home there. What amused them was that only a thin wicker partition separated them from the market crowd, whose loud voices rang out all around. They often shook with laughter when people stopped to talk just a few feet away. They would then make little peepholes. When cherries were in season, Cadine threw stones at the old women who passed by—a pastime that amused them greatly because the women, frightened out of their wits, had not the faintest idea where the hail of stones came from. They also prowled about in the cellars. They knew the darkest corners and could squeeze through even the most carefully locked gates. One of their favourite games was to get onto the tracks of the underground railway, the plan of which was to connect with the various goods' stations of the city. Sections of this track passed underneath the covered avenues, between the cellars of the various markets; the work, indeed, had reached such an advanced stage that turntables had been put into position at all the junctions in readiness for use. Cadine and Marjolin had eventually discovered, in the fencing that protected the track, a loose plank which allowed them to pass in and out at will. There they were quite cut off from the world, though they could hear the continuous rumble of traffic above them. The track stretched out into the darkness, its deserted galleries stained with daylight seeping through iron gratings, while in some dark corners gas jets burned. They wandered about as though in a castle of their own, confident that no one would disturb them, happy in this rumbling silence, with its murky glimmers of light and its atmosphere of secrecy, which gave their wanderings a touch of melodrama. From neighbouring cellars, across the fencing, came all kinds of smells: the musty smell of vegetables, the pungency of fish, the overpowering smell of cheese, the reek of poultry.

At other times, on clear nights, they would climb onto the roofs, ascending the steep ladders up the turrets that were placed at the corners of each of the markets. At the top they found fields of lead, endless walks and open spaces, whole stretches of undulating countryside that belonged to them. They roamed over the square roofs, following the long covered avenues, climbing up and down the slopes, getting lost on endless journeys. When they got bored with the foothills, they climbed higher, venturing up the iron ladders on which Cadine's skirt flapped like a flag. Then, high in the sky, they ran along the second tier of roofs. Above them they had only the stars. All sorts of sounds rose up from the markets below, sounds like thunderclaps or a distant storm in the night. At this height the morning breeze swept away the stale smells, the foul breath of the awakening markets. The first rays of the sun turned their faces pink. Cadine laughed with delight at being so high, her throat rippling like a dove's; Marjolin leaned over to see the streets below, still full of shadows, his hands clutching the edge of the roof like the claws of a pigeon. When they climbed down again, excited by their excursion, they would say that they had just come back from the country.

It was in the tripe market that they first met Claude Lantier. They went there every day, thirsting for blood, with all the cruelty of urchins who love to see heads cut off. Streams of blood flowed along the gutters round the market; they would dip their toes in it and block it up with leaves, creating big pools. They loved to watch the slaughterhouse carts arrive; they stank to high heaven and had to be washed out with water. They watched the unpacking of sheep's feet, which were heaped on the ground like dirty cobblestones, big stiffened tongues, which showed where they had been torn bleeding from the animals' throats, and ox hearts as solid as church bells. But what thrilled them most were the huge baskets dripping with blood and full of sheep's heads, greasy horns, and black snouts on which scraps of woolly skin still clung to the livid flesh. They had visions of a guillotine casting into the baskets the heads of countless animals. They followed the baskets down into the cellar, watching them slide down the rails laid over the steps, and listening to the sound of these wicker wagons, like a scythe cutting grass. Down below there was a scene of exquisite horror. They were met by the stench of a charnel house and walked through dark puddles in which purple eyes seemed now and then to blink and glitter. Their shoes became sticky. They splashed through the wet, apprehensive and yet delighted by the horrible sludge underfoot. The gas jets burned very low, like bloodshot eyes. Near the water taps, in the pale light that filtered through the gratings, they came to the butcher's chopping blocks. It was here that they loved to watch the tripe dealers, their aprons stiff with blood, breaking open the sheep's heads one by one with a single blow of the mallet. They stayed there for hours, waiting until all the baskets were empty, riveted to the spot by the cracking of bones, unable to tear themselves away, watching until the end the tearing out of tongues and the removal of brains from the splintered skulls. Sometimes a cleaner passed behind them, washing the floors with buckets of water. Sheets of water crashed to the floor like a dam bursting; the force of it disturbed the flagstones, but was unable to remove the stains and stench of the blood.

Cadine and Marjolin were sure to meet Claude in the afternoon, between four and five, at the sale of offal. He would be standing there among the tripe dealers' carts with the crowd of men in blue dungarees and white aprons, jostled on all sides and deafened by the shouts of the bidding. But he never felt the elbows digging into him, he stood in ecstasy before the lungs and lights that hung from the auction hooks. He often explained to Cadine and Marjolin that there was no sight more beautiful than this. The lights were a tender rose-pink, deepening gradually and turning at the lower edges to a bright crimson. Claude compared them to watered satin, finding no other term to describe the silken softness of the flowing lengths of flesh which fell in folds like the caught-up skirts of a dancer. He thought, too, of gauze and lace that revealed a woman's skin underneath. And when a ray of sunlight fell across the offal and gave it a golden hue, an expression of rapture came into his eyes, and he felt happier than if he had been privileged to see Greek goddesses filing past in their splendid nudity, or the *châtelaines* of romance in their brocaded robes.*

The painter became the great friend of the two children. He loved beautiful animals, and such they were. For a long time he dreamt of painting a huge picture of Cadine and Marjolin as lovers in Les Halles, among the vegetables, the fish, and the meat. He would have depicted them sitting on their bed of food, their arms round each other, exchanging an idyllic kiss. In this idea he saw an artistic manifesto, positivism* in art—modern art, experimental and materialist. And he saw in it, too, a satiric comment on intellectual painting, a blow against the old schools. But for almost two years he kept repeating his sketches, never able to strike quite the right note. He tore up about fifteen canvases. His failure frustrated him deeply, but he continued to see his two models quite often out of a kind of hopeless love for his abortive picture. When he met them wandering about in the afternoon, he too took to strolling round Les Halles, his hands thrust deep in his pockets, fascinated by the life of the streets.

All three of them walked along, dragging their heels and spreading themselves across the footpath, forcing other people into the roadway. They breathed in the odours of Paris, their noses tilted in the air. They could have recognized every corner with their eyes shut, simply because of the smell of alcohol from the wine merchants, the warm puffs from the bakers and confectioners, and the musty odours from the fruiterers. They would walk for hours. They enjoyed going through the circular hall of the corn market, a massive stone cage where sacks of flour were piled up on every side, and where their footsteps echoed in the silence of the vault. They were fond, too, of little narrow streets that had become as deserted, dark, and desolate as an abandoned town: the Rue Babille, the Rue Sauval, the Rue des Deux Écus, and the Rue de Viarmes. The Rue de Viarmes was very pallid because of its proximity to the millers' stores, and became very lively at four o'clock because of the corn exchange that was held there. It was generally from this point that they started on their round. They made their way slowly along the Rue Vauvilliers, glancing as they went at shady eating houses, nudging each other and laughing when they went past a house with its blinds drawn.* In the bottleneck of the Rue des Prouvaires, Claude screwed up his eyes as he saw, at the end of one of the covered avenues, framed as by a railway station, a side door of Saint-Eustache, with its *rosace* and two rows of mullioned windows. Then, with an air of defiance, he would say that the whole of the Middle Ages and the whole of the Renaissance were less mighty than Les Halles. As they walked down the wide new streets, the Rue du Pont-Neuf and the Rue des Halles, he explained to the two urchins something of the new life of the city, with its fine pavements, tall houses, and luxurious shops. He predicted, too, a new form of art, which he knew was on its way, but which, to his great frustration, he felt he could not describe. Cadine and Marjolin, however, preferred the provincial tranquillity of the Rue des Bourdonnais, where they could play at marbles without fear of being run over. Cadine preened herself as they passed the wholesale hatters and glove shops, while at every shop doorway the young assistants, their pens behind their ears and looking bored, stared after her. They also preferred those parts of old Paris that remained standing: the Rue de la Poterie and the Rue de la Lingerie, with their butter, egg, and cheese dealers; the Rue de la Ferronerie and the Rue de l'Aiguillerie, the best examples of former times, with their small dark shops; and especially the Rue Courtalon, a dank, dirty lane running from the Place Saint-Opportune to the Rue Saint-Denis, riddled all the way down with stinking alleys where they had played when they were younger. The Rue Saint-Denis brought them to the world of sweets and chocolate. They smiled at the toffee apples, the sticks of liquorice, the prunes and sugar candy in the windows of grocers and sweet shops. Their wanderings always culminated in the idea of delicious things to eat, and a wish to devour with their eyes all the goods on display. For them this neighbourhood was like a large table always laid, an everlasting dessert into which they would have loved to plunge their fingers. They wasted little time visiting the other cluster of tumbledown houses in the Rue Pirouette, the Rue de Montadour, the Rue de la Petite-Truanderie, and the Rue de la Grande-Truanderie, where their interest was only mildly stimulated by the dealers in snails and cooked vegetables, the tripe sellers, and wine merchants. But in the Rue de la Grande-Truanderie there was a soap factory, smelling so sweetly in the midst of all the foul odours, outside which Marjolin always came to a halt, waiting for someone to go in or come out so that he could smell the perfume through the door. Then, with all speed, they returned to the Rue Pierre Lescot and the Rue Rambuteau. Cadine was extremely fond of salted provisions and stood in admiration before the bundles of herrings, the barrels of anchovies and capers, and the casks of gherkins and olives, with wooden spoons standing in them. The smell of vinegar titillated her throat; the pungent odour of rolled cod, smoked salmon, bacon and ham, and the sourish waft of a basket of lemons, made her mouth water. She also loved to feast her eyes on the piles of sardine tins, assembled in metallic columns among all the sacks and boxes. In the Rue Montorgueil and the Rue Montmartre were other grocers' shops and restaurants, with appetizing smells always wafting up through their gratings, wonderful displays of poultry and game, and shops selling preserved food, at the doors of which were crates overflowing with yellow sauerkraut that looked like old lace. Then, in the Rue Coquillière, they were lost in the odour of truffles. Here there was a large provision merchant's that exhaled such a strong perfume that Cadine and Marjolin, when they closed their eyes, could imagine that they were eating the most exquisite foods. These perfumes, however, distressed Claude. He said that it made him feel empty, and he returned to the corn market, via the Rue Oblin, inspecting the salads being sold in doorways and the cheap pottery spread out on the footpath, leaving the 'two animals' to finish their wanderings in this scent of truffles, the keenest aroma to be found anywhere in the neighbourhood.

Such were their walks together. When Cadine was selling her violets she added details to the itinerary, lingering at certain shops she particularly liked. She was especially fond of the Taboureau bakery, in which a whole window had a cake display. She would go along the Rue Turbigo, walking up and down it a dozen times to look at the almond cakes, the *savarins*, the flans and fruit tarts, the rum *babas*, the *éclairs* and cream puffs; and she was also very fond of the big jars full of biscuits, macaroons, and *madeleines*. This bright shop, with its big mirrors, its marble and gilt, its wrought-iron bread bins, and its second window, in which long brown-varnished loaves lay slantwise, with one end resting on a crystal shelf while above they were held up by a brass rod, was so warm and smelt so pleasantly of baked dough that she would go in and buy herself a *brioche* for a couple of sous. There was another shop, opposite the Square des Innocents, that also awoke her greedy curiosity. This shop specialized in pies and pasties. In addition to ordinary pies, there were fish pasties and pies of *foie gras* with truffles, and she would stand there in a dream, saying to herself that one day she would really have to eat one of them.

Cadine also had her moments of vanity. On such occasions she would imagine buying herself some of the magnificent dresses displayed in the windows of Aux Fabriques de France,* which decked out the Pointe Saint-Eustache with immense swathes of material, hung and draped from the *entresol* right out to the footpath. A trifle encumbered by her tray among the market women in dirty aprons gazing at future Sunday dresses, she would feel the woollens, flannels, and cottons, to make sure of the texture and suppleness of the material. She promised herself a dress of brightly coloured flannel or printed cotton or scarlet poplin. Sometimes she even chose from the windows, from the pieces displayed by the boy assistants, some soft sky-blue silk or apple green, which she imagined herself wearing with pink ribbons. In the evenings she would go and stand in front of the glittering windows of the big jewellery shops in the Rue Montmartre. This terrible street deafened her with its interminable flow of traffic, and the endless crowds never stopped jostling her, but nothing could shift her from her position as she stood gazing at the splendours set out in the window, under the row of lamps hung outside the front of the shop. On one side were the smooth expanses of white, with the bright glitter of silver: rows of watches, chains hanging down, forks and spoons laid crossways, mugs, snuffboxes, napkin rings, and combs laid out on shelves. She was fascinated by the silver thimbles, dotted round a porcelain stand with a glass shade. Then, on the other side, was the tawny glow of gold. A cascade of long chains was suspended from above and rippled with ruby gleams; small ladies' watches, with the backs of their cases displayed, shone like fallen stars; wedding rings were threaded on thin pieces of wire; bracelets, brooches, and expensive jewels glimmered on the black velvet of their cases; rings sparkled with little flames of blue, green, yellow, or mauve; and on all the shelves, in two or three rows, were earrings, crucifixes, and lockets, hanging down like the fringes of an altar cloth. The reflection of all this gold lit up half the street. Cadine believed that she was in the presence of something holy, or on the threshold of the Emperor's treasure chamber. She scrutinized the heavy jewellery for fishwives, carefully reading the price tickets inscribed with large figures that accompanied each article. She decided on some earrings, pendants made of artificial coral dangling from golden roses.

One morning Claude came upon her standing in ecstasy before a hairdresser's window in the Rue Saint-Honoré. She was gazing at the hair with a look of intense envy. Hung high up in the window there was a profusion of long manes, soft wisps, loose tresses, frizzy falls, wavy comb-curls, a flood of silky and bristling hair, in flaming red, dark black, or pure blonde, and even in snowy white for old lovers of sixty. Lower down in the window, neat fringes, crisp ringlets, combed and scented coils and knots, were lying asleep in cardboard boxes. And in the middle, in a sort of shrine* beneath these hanging locks, was the revolving bust of a woman. She wore a red satin scarf, fastened between her breasts by a copper brooch, and a very tall bridal headdress decorated with sprigs of orange blossom, and smiled with her doll's mouth. Long lashes were planted stiffly round her pale blue eyes, and its waxen cheeks and shoulders bore evident traces of the heat and smoke of the gas. Cadine waited for her to come round again with her smiling face, and her delight increased as its profile could be seen more distinctly and it slowly turned from left to right. Claude was indignant. He shook Cadine and asked her what she was doing there looking at 'that dreadful thing, that corpse-like tart picked up at the Morgue!' He flew into a rage over the dummy's cadaverous face and shoulders, this disfigurement of the beautiful, and said that artists painted nothing but that type of woman nowadays. Cadine was unconvinced; she considered the woman very beautiful. Then, freeing her arm from the painter's grip, and scratching her black mop of hair in annoyance, she pointed to an enormous tail of red hair which had been torn from some handsome mare, and told him that she would like to have that sort of hair.

When all three of them, Claude, Cadine, and Marjolin, went on their long walks around Les Halles, they caught a glimpse of the great iron giant at the end of every street. At every turn they saw it differently, from unexpected angles; the horizon was always bounded by it, but it constantly assumed different forms. Claude was perpetually turning round to look at it, especially in the Rue Montmartre after they had passed the church. From there the markets, seen obliquely in the distance, filled him with enthusiasm. A huge arcade, a gaping doorway, would open to his gaze; and the markets seemed to crowd up one on top of the other, with their two lines of roof, their countless shutters and blinds. It seemed that the outlines of houses and palaces had been superimposed to create a vast Babylonian structure of metal, wonderfully delicate in its workmanship, and criss-crossed by hanging gardens, aerial galleries, and flying buttresses.* They always came back there, to this city through which they roamed, never straying more than a hundred metres from it. They went back to it during the hot afternoons, when the shutters were closed and the blinds drawn. In the covered avenues everything seemed to be asleep, the ash-grey air streaked by yellow bars of sunlight falling from the high windows. A subdued murmur was all that could be heard, along with the footsteps of a few passers-by hurrying along; while the porters, wearing their badges, sat in a row on the stone ledges at the corners of the markets, and took off their boots to nurse their aching feet. This was the peace and calm of a colossus at rest, interrupted occasionally by the crowing of a cock from the cellars below. They would often go to see the empty baskets being loaded on to the drays that came every afternoon to collect them and take them back to the suppliers. These baskets, labelled with black letters and numbers, were stacked up in enormous piles in front of the second-hand shops in the Rue Berger. The porters arranged them symmetrically, in tiers, on the vehicles. But when the tower on the dray got as high as the first floor, the man on the ground who was balancing the next batch of baskets had to take a wide swing to hurl them up to his mate perched on the top with his arms outstretched. Claude, who enjoyed feats of strength and skill, would stand for hours watching these wicker missiles flying through the air, laughing when too vigorous a throw sent them flying over the top of the load into the street on the other side. He was also fond of the footpaths of the Rue Rambuteau and the Rue du Pont-Neuf, at the corner of the fruit market, where the retail dealers congregated. The sight of the vegetables in the open air, on trestle tables covered with damp black cloths, delighted him. At four o'clock the whole of this nook of greenery was aglow with sunshine; and Claude walked down the avenues, noting the different-coloured faces of the vendors: the younger women, their hair in nets, already had ruddy complexions because of the hard lives they led; the older ones were bent and shrivelled, their faces quite red under their yellow headscarves. Cadine and Marjolin refused to go with him when they saw Mère Chantemesse shaking her fist at them, angry to see them larking about together. He would rejoin them on the opposite side of the street, where he found a splendid subject for a painting: the stallkeepers under their big faded umbrellas, red, blue, and mauve, which, mounted on poles, formed little humps of colour throughout the market, catching the fiery glow of the setting sun, before it faded away over the carrots and turnips. One vendor, an old woman of about a hundred, was sheltering three scrawny lettuces under a battered umbrella of pink silk.

One day Cadine and Marjolin made the acquaintance of Léon, the apprentice at the Quenu-Gradelles', when he was delivering a pie to one of the houses in the neighbourhood. They saw him carefully raise the lid of the pie-dish in a secluded corner of the Rue de Montdétour and take out a rissole. They grinned at each other, for this gave them a wonderful, mischievous idea. Cadine thought of a plan to fulfil at least one of her greatest ambitions. When she next met Léon with his dish, she was extremely friendly and managed to get herself offered a rissole. She laughed as she licked her fingers, but she was a little disappointed, having imagined that it would taste much nicer. But she took a fancy to the youth, with his sly, greedy face and his white apron, which made him look like a girl going to her first communion. She invited him to an enormous lunch, which she gave in the baskets of the butter market. The three of them, Marjolin, Léon, and herself, shut themselves away within four walls of wicker. The table was laid on a big flat basket. There were pears, nuts, cream cheese, prawns, fried potatoes, and radishes. The cheese came from a fruiterer in the Rue de la Cossonnerie and was a present. A fried-food man in the Rue de la Grande-Truanderie had sold them two sous' worth of fried potatoes on credit. The rest of the meal, the pears, the nuts, the prawns, and the radishes, had been stolen from various parts of Les Halles. It was a wonderful banquet. Léon was keen to return the compliment, and invited them to dinner in his room at one in the morning. He offered them cold black pudding, slices of *saucisson* and *petit salé*, gherkins and goose fat. The Quenu-Gradelle *charcuterie* had provided everything. But that was not the end of it. Magnificent suppers alternated with fine lunches, and the flow of invitations never ceased. Three times a week there were great feasts, either amid the baskets or in Léon's attic room, where Florent, on the nights when he lay awake, could hear until dawn the muffled sound of eating and laughing.

The love of Cadine and Marjolin now took another turn. He played the gentleman and, just as another might entertain his *innamorata* at a champagne supper in the private room of a fine restaurant, he took her to dine in some quiet corner of the market cellars, where they munched apples or pieces of celery. One day he stole a herring, which they devoured with great pleasure on the roof of the fish market, sitting on the edge of the gutter. There was nowhere in the whole of Les Halles where they had not had one of their secret feasts. The neighbourhood, with its rows of open shops full of fruit and cakes and preserves, was no longer a forbidden paradise, in front of which they paraded their hunger. As they walked past the shops, they stretched out their hands and pinched a prune or a handful of cherries or a piece of cod. They also stocked up in the markets themselves, keeping a sharp lookout as they made their way along the avenues, picking up whatever fell to the ground, and indeed often helping things to fall with a jerk of the shoulder. But despite their plundering, terrible bills began to mount up with the fried-food man in the Rue de la Grande-Truanderie. This man, whose booth was propped against a tumbledown house supported by beams green with moss, kept a stock of cooked mussels in large earthenware bowls filled to the brim with clear water, dishes of little yellow dabs in too thick a coating of pastry, squares of tripe simmering in a pan, and grilled herring, black and charred, as hard as wood. Some weeks Cadine owed as much as twenty sous, which required her to sell an incalculable number of violets, because it was quite out of the question to count on Marjolin for anything. Besides, she felt compelled to return Léon's hospitality, and she even felt a little ashamed at never being able to offer him a scrap of meat. In the meantime, he had taken to stealing whole hams. His usual technique was to stuff everything inside his shirt. At night, when he went up to his room, he produced from his chest pieces of sausage, slices of *pâté de foie*, and pieces of pork rind and crackling. There was no bread and nothing to drink. One evening Marjolin caught Léon kissing Cadine between two mouthfuls. But he only laughed. He could have knocked the lad cold with a single blow. He was not jealous, however; he treated Cadine as a friend he had known for years.

Claude did not take part in these feasts. Having caught Cadine one day stealing a beetroot from a little basket lined with straw, he had boxed her ears and given her a scolding. It was so typical of her, he said. But, in spite of himself, he could not help feeling a sort of admiration for these sensual, pilfering, greedy creatures, who preyed upon everything that lay about, picking up the crumbs that fell from the giant's table.

Marjolin was now working for Gavard, happy enough with nothing to do but listen to his master's endless stories. Cadine still sold her violets, quite accustomed by this time to the constant grumbling of Mère Chantemesse. They were still like children, indulging their appetites without the slightest shame. They were like the vegetation that sprang from the greasy footpaths of Les Halles, where, even in fine weather, the mud is still black and sticky. However, as Cadine walked along the footpaths, twisting her bunches of violets, she began to have disturbing dreams; and Marjolin, too, felt an uneasiness which he could not explain. Sometimes he would wander off on his own and even miss a feast in order to go and gaze at Madame Quenu through the windows of the *charcuterie*. She was so beautiful, so plump and round, that he was happy just to look at her. He felt full and satisfied whenever he looked at her, as though he had eaten something good. And when he went off, a sort of hunger and thirst to see her again soon came upon him. This had lasted now for several months. At first he had looked at her with the respect he showed for the window displays of grocers and provision dealers. Then, when he and Cadine had taken to general pilfering, he began to dream, when he saw her, of taking her thick waist in his arms, just as he plunged them into barrels of olives or casks of dried apples.

For some time Marjolin had seen La Belle Lisa every morning. She walked past Gavard's shop and stopped for a few moments to chat. She did her own shopping, she said, to make sure she wasn't cheated. The truth, however, was that she was trying to win Gavard's confidence. At the *charcuterie* he was cautious, but at his stall he held forth endlessly and told anybody anything they wanted to know. She thought that she was bound to find out through him exactly what went on at Monsieur Lebigre's; for she had no great confidence in her secret agent, Mademoiselle Saget. She had obtained from this terrible old gossip a jumble of alarming information. Two days after her confrontation with Quenu, she came back from the market looking extremely pale. She gestured to her husband to follow her into the dining room. She shut the door and said:

'So your brother wants to see us on the scaffold, does he? Why didn't you tell me everything?'

Quenu declared that he knew nothing. He swore that he had not returned to Monsieur Lebigre's and that he never would.

'That's just as well,' she said, 'unless you want to end up dead... Florent is up to something dreadful, I'm sure of it. I've found out enough to know where he's headed. He's going back to prison! Mark my words!'

Then, after a pause, she continued more calmly:

'The fool! He had everything here he could possibly want. He could easily have become a decent citizen again; he had nothing but good examples in front of him. But no, it's in his blood! He'll come to a bad end with his politics! I want it all to stop, do you hear? I warned you!'

She stressed these last words. Quenu bowed his head, as if awaiting sentence.

'To begin with,' she continued, 'he won't eat here any more. It's bad enough that he sleeps here. But since he earns money he can feed himself.'

Quenu seemed on the point of protesting, but his wife cut him short, adding with some emphasis:

'You've got to choose between him and us. If he stays here, I swear I'll leave and take my daughter with me. If you want to know the truth, he's capable of anything; and he's come here to wreck our home. But I'll put things right, you can be sure of that. That's all I have to say: it's either him or me.'

Then, leaving her husband silent and confused, she went back into the shop, where she served a customer with her usual affable smile. The fact was that Gavard, in the course of a political argument which she had cleverly engineered, had become so excited that he had told her that things would be happening quite soon, that there was going to be a takeover, that two determined men like her brother-in-law and himself could easily get the ball rolling. This was the dreadful business she had alluded to, a conspiracy Gavard was always hinting at with a grin and a sly laugh, which he clearly intended to be most meaningful. She had visions of *sergents de ville* breaking into the *charcuterie*, seizing all three of them—Quenu, Pauline, and herself—and throwing them into some dark dungeon.

That evening, at dinner, her manner was icy. She made no attempt to serve Florent, and several times she remarked:

'It's funny how much bread we've been getting through lately.'

Eventually Florent understood. He felt that he was being treated like a poor relation being shown the door. For the last two months Lisa had been dressing him in Quenu's old trousers and coats, and as he was as thin as his brother was fat these ragged garments looked very odd on him. She had also given him Quenu's old linen, handkerchiefs that had been darned a dozen times, torn towels, sheets which were only fit to be made into dusters and dishcloths, and frayed shirts stretched by Quenu's corpulent figure and so short that they could have been used as jackets. Moreover, he no longer felt around him the friendly atmosphere of earlier times. The whole household seemed to be turning its back on him, following Lisa's example. Auguste and Augustine ignored him, and little Pauline, with the cruel frankness of childhood, made remarks about the stains on his coat and the holes in his shirt. Meals were particularly painful. He hardly dared to eat when he saw mother and daughter staring at him as he cut a piece of bread. Quenu kept his eyes on his plate, to avoid taking any part in what was happening. But what tortured Florent was the fact that he did not know how to leave. For nearly a week he turned over and over in his mind a sentence expressing his resolve to take his meals elsewhere, but he could not bring himself to utter it.

Florent had such a gentle nature that he lived in a world of illusion. He was afraid that he might hurt the feelings of his brother and sister-in-law if he no longer ate at their table. It had taken him more than two months to notice Lisa's veiled hostility, and even so he sometimes thought that he might be mistaken and that she was perfectly well disposed towards him. His lack of selfishness made him forget his own needs; this trait of his character was no longer a virtue, but utter indifference to self, a complete lack of personality. Even when he saw that he was being gradually turned out of the house, he never gave a thought to his share of old Gradelle's money or the accounts that Lisa had worked out. He had already planned his budget for the future: he calculated that, with the money Madame Verlaque left him out of his salary and the thirty francs for lessons that La Belle Normande had arranged for him, he would have eighteen sous for his lunch and twenty-six sous for dinner. This, he thought, would be ample. At last, one morning, he took the plunge, saying that the new lessons he was giving would make it impossible for him to be at the *charcuterie* at mealtimes. He blushed as he pronounced this flagrant lie, and began making excuses:

'I'm sorry, but the boy is only free at those times… Don't worry, I can easily get a bite to eat somewhere. I'll come and say goodnight later on.'

La Belle Lisa remained extremely cold towards him, and that made him even more uncomfortable. She had not wanted to turn him out, preferring to wait until he left of his own accord—that way she would have no cause for self-reproach. So she avoided any show of friendliness that might hold him back. Quenu, however, was not unmoved, and exclaimed:

'Don't worry, eat out if it's more convenient. We won't turn you out! Come and have a bite to eat on Sundays, when you can!'

Florent hurried off with a heavy heart. When he had gone, La Belle Lisa did not dare to reproach her husband for his weakness in inviting Florent to come on Sundays. The victory was still hers. She breathed a sigh of relief in the light oak dining room and would have liked to burn some sugar to drive away the odour of perverse leanness she thought she could still smell in the air. She remained, however, on the defensive; and after a week she was beginning to have thoughts of an even more disturbing kind. Seeing Florent only occasionally, she imagined that terrible things were happening, that he was constructing an infernal machine in his room, or sending out signals from the balcony so that barricades would be set up throughout the neighbourhood. Gavard had become very gloomy; he just nodded or shook his head when she spoke to him, and left Marjolin in charge of his stall for days on end. La Belle Lisa resolved to get to the bottom of things. She knew that Florent had a day off and was going with Claude to visit Madame François at Nanterre. As he would be leaving early in the morning, and would not return until the evening, she hit on the idea of inviting Gavard to dinner. He would be sure to talk freely with a meal in front of him. But throughout the morning she could not find him anywhere, and so in the afternoon she went back to the markets.

Marjolin was at the stall alone. He dozed there for hours, resting after his endless wanderings. Usually he sat in one chair with his legs up on another. In the winter the display of game was a source of endless fascination for him: the roebucks hanging head downwards, their front legs broken and twisted round their necks; the larks festooning the stall like garlands; large russet-coloured hares, speckled partridges, bronze-grey waterfowl, grouse from Russia which arrived in a packing of straw and charcoal, and the pheasants, magnificent in their scarlet hoods, their throat-pieces of green satin, their mantles of enamelled gold, and their flaming tails flaring out like an evening gown. All this plumage made him think of Cadine and their nights in the cellars.

That afternoon La Belle Lisa found Marjolin sitting in the midst of the poultry. It was a warm afternoon, and a few breaths of hot air passed along the narrow alleys of the market. She had to bend down before she could see him stretched out beneath the bare flesh of the birds. Above his head, fat geese were hanging from spiked bars, the hooks sunk into bleeding wounds in their long, stiff necks, while their huge bellies, reddish beneath a fine down, ballooned out obscenely between their linen-white tails and wings. Also hanging from the bar were grey rabbits, their legs parted as though in readiness for some gigantic leap, their ears lying flat, with a tuft of white tail, and their heads, with sharp teeth and dim eyes, grinning with the grin of death. On the counter plucked chickens displayed their fleshy breasts, stretched taut on the spit; pigeons, packed tightly together on wicker trays, seemed to have the soft skin of newborn babies; ducks, with rougher skin, splayed out their webbed feet; and three magnificent turkeys, shadowed with blue like a clean-shaven face, their throats sewn up, slept on their backs in the broad black fans of their tails. On plates close by were giblets, livers, gizzards, necks, feet, and wings; while in an oval dish was a skinned and cleaned-out rabbit, its four legs wide apart, its head bespattered with blood and its belly slit to reveal its kidneys; a trickle of blood, running down to its tail, had fallen drop by drop, staining the white dish. Marjolin had not even bothered to wipe the carving board, next to which the rabbit's paws were still lying. His eyes were half closed, and he was surrounded, on the three shelves at the back of the stall, by further piles of dead birds, birds in paper wrappers like bouquets, such a regular pattern of folded legs and rounded breasts that they confused the eye. Amid all this food, with his large frame, his cheeks and hands and powerful neck seemed as soft as the flesh of the turkeys and as plump as the breasts of the geese.

As soon as he saw La Belle Lisa, he jumped up, blushing at having been caught lounging about. He was always timid and nervous in her presence; and when she asked him if Monsieur Gavard was there, he stammered:

'Oh, I don't know. He was here just now, but he's gone again.'

Lisa looked at him, smiling. She had always been very fond of him. Suddenly, feeling something warm against her hand, she gave a little cry. Some rabbits, in a box under the counter, were sniffing at her skirt.

'Oh,' she said, laughing. 'It's your rabbits—they're tickling me.'

She bent down and tried to stroke a white rabbit, which at once took refuge in a corner of the box. Then, straightening up, she said:

'Will Monsieur Gavard be back soon, do you think?'

Marjolin again replied that he did not know. His hands were trembling a little. Then he said, with some hesitation:

'He might be in the storeroom. I think he said he was going down there.'

'In that case I'll wait for him,' said Lisa. 'Perhaps you could go and tell him I'm here. Or I could go down and see him. Yes, that's a good idea. I've been meaning to go down and have a look at the cellars these last five years. Will you take me down and show me?'

He had become very red. Jumping up, he walked in front of her, leaving the stall to look after itself.

'Of course,' he said. 'Whatever you want, Madame Lisa.'

The air in the cellars was almost too much for her. She paused on the last step and looked up at the vaulted ceiling of red and white bricks, in semicircular arches, veined with iron joints and supported by small pillars. What made her stop was the intense, warm smell rather than the gloom—the smell of live animals, which irritated her nose and throat.

'What a smell!' she exclaimed. 'It must be very unhealthy down here.'

'It doesn't do me any harm,' replied Marjolin. 'It's not bad when you get used to it. And it's nice and warm in winter.'

She followed him, saying that the smell made her feel quite sick, and that she wouldn't be able to eat chicken again for two months. The storerooms, the small cubicles where the stallholders kept their livestock, stretched into the distance in straight regular lanes, intersecting each other at right angles. The gaslights were few and far between, and the little alleys seemed wrapped in sleep, like the lanes of a village when everyone is in bed. Marjolin told Lisa to feel her way with the wire mesh; and as she made her way along one of the lanes, she read the names of the owners, which were written on blue labels.

'Monsieur Gavard's storeroom is right at the end,' said Marjolin.

They turned to the left and came to a dead end, a dark cavern where no light had ever penetrated. Gavard was not there.

'Never mind,' said Marjolin. 'I'll show you the birds all the same. I've got a key.'

Lisa followed him into the darkness. Then suddenly she found him all tangled up in her skirts. She thought she must have gone too far and bumped into him, so she stepped back and said, laughing:

'I don't think I'll be able to see them in the dark...'

He said nothing; then he mumbled that there was always a bit of candle in the storeroom. He was fumbling about with the lock and seemed unable to find the keyhole. As she tried to help him, she felt his hot breath on her neck. And when at last he had opened the door and lit the candle, she saw that he was trembling.

'You silly boy!' she exclaimed. 'Getting yourself into a state because a door won't open! You're just like a girl, in spite of those big fists!'

She stepped inside. Gavard had rented two storerooms, which he had made into a chicken-run by removing the partition between them. The larger birds—geese, turkeys, and ducks—were paddling about in the manure; above them, on three rows of shelves, were flat open-work boxes that contained the hens and rabbits. The wire netting was so coated in dust and cobwebs that it seemed covered with grey blinds. The urine of the rabbits had corroded the lower panels and birdlime had stained the floorboards. But Lisa did not want to disappoint Marjolin with further comments, and said nothing. She poked her fingers through the holes in the boxes, bemoaning the fate of the hens, so cooped up that they could not even stand upright. She stroked a duck crouching in a corner with a broken leg, and Marjolin told her that it would be killed that evening in case it died during the night.

'But what do they do for food?' asked Lisa.

He explained to her that birds never want to eat in the dark, and that the poulterers had to light a candle and wait there until they had finished their meal.

'I like watching them,' he continued. 'I often stay here with a light for hours. You should see them pecking away. When I hide the candle in my hand, they all stand still with their necks streched out, as if the sun had set. It's against the rules to leave a lighted candle here and go away. One woman, Mère Palette—you know her,

don't you?—nearly burned the whole place down the other day.*
One of the hens must have knocked the candle over in the straw.'

'Well, fancy that,' said Lisa. 'Lighting the chandeliers for them every
time they have a meal!'

This made him laugh. Then she stepped out of the storeroom,
wiping her feet and holding up her skirt to keep it from getting too
dirty. He blew out the candle and locked the door. Lisa felt nervous
at finding herself in the dark again with this big youth; so she hurried
on ahead so that she would not feel him touching her again.

'I'm pleased I came,' she said, when he caught up. 'There are things
you'd never imagine under the markets. Thank you for showing me.
I really must go now. They'll be wondering what's happened to me.
If Monsieur Gavard turns up, tell him I'd like a word straight away.'

'He must be in the slaughter-house,' he said. 'We can go and have
a look if you want.'

She did not answer. She felt oppressed by the heavy atmosphere.
She was quite flushed, and her bodice, generally so still and lifeless,
began to heave. The sound of Marjolin's steps behind her made her
feel uneasy. She stood aside and let him pass. The lanes of the underground village were still fast asleep. Lisa noticed that Marjolin was
taking the long way round. When they came out in front of the railway line, he told her that he wanted to show her the track, and they
stood there for a moment, looking through the gaps in the fencing.
He offered to take her on to the line, but she refused, saying that it
was not worth it, because she could see what it was like from where
they were. On the way back they came across Mère Palette in front
of her storeroom, untying the thick string round a big square basket,
in which a furious fluttering of wings and scraping of feet could be
heard. When she had undone the last knot, the lid flew open, as though
activated by a spring, and some big geese appeared. In wild alarm,
they made their escape, craning their necks, and filling the dark cellars
with a frightful noise of hissing and clacking. Lisa could not help
laughing, in spite of the lamentations of the old woman, who was
swearing like a trooper as she caught hold of two of the geese, which
she dragged back by the neck. Marjolin, in the meantime, had set off
in pursuit of a third goose. He could be heard running along the
lanes, thoroughly enjoying the chase. Then, in the distance, there
was the sound of a scuffle, and a few moments later he reappeared,
holding the goose. Mère Palette, a sallow-faced old woman, took it in

her arms and clasped it for a moment to her bosom, in the classical attitude of Leda.*

'Well,' she said, 'I don't know what I'd have done if you hadn't been there. The other day I had a fight with one of them. But I had my knife with me and cut its throat.'

Marjolin was out of breath. When they came to the slaughtering blocks, where the gas burnt more brightly, Lisa could see that he was sweating, and his eyes were shining in a way she had not seen before. She thought he looked very handsome like that, with his broad shoulders, flushed face, and curly hair. She gazed at him with that special look of admiration women feel they can safely express with young boys. He became very shy again.

'Well, Monsieur Gavard isn't here either, is he?' she said. 'You're wasting my time.'

Marjolin, however, began rapidly explaining the business of slaughtering. There were five huge stone blocks stretched out along the Rue Rambuteau under the yellow light from the gratings and the gas burners. At one end there was a woman bleeding chickens, which led him to remark that this woman was plucking the poultry while they were still alive, because it was easier that way. Then he wanted her to feel the feathers lying in heaps on the blocks, and informed her that they were sorted out and then sold for up to nine sous a pound, according to their quality. She was also made to sink her arms into the big baskets full of down. Then he turned on the water taps that were fixed to every pillar. There was no end to the information he gave. The blood, he said, ran along the blocks and made puddles on the flagstones. Every two hours the cleaners came to wash the place down, scrubbing away the red stains with thick brushes. When Lisa stooped over the drain which carries everything away, there was another lengthy explanation; when there was a storm, he said, the water came up through the drain and flooded the cellars. On one occasion it had risen thirty centimetres and they had had to evacuate the poultry to the other end of the cellars, which sloped upwards. He laughed as he recalled the noise the birds had made. But now he had finished and could think of nothing else to show her, until he remembered the ventilator. He took her right to the end and told her to look up, and inside one of the corner turrets she saw a sort of escape pipe, through which the foul-smelling air of the storerooms escaped to the surface.

Marjolin fell silent as they stood there, surrounded by foul smells. The air had the alkaline coarseness of guano. But he seemed wide awake, stimulated. His nostrils were quivering and he was breathing hard, as though rediscovering some bold desire within him. For the quarter of an hour he had been in the cellars with Lisa, he had grown drunk with the warm animal smells. Now he was timid no longer, he was full of the rut that heated the dung in the chicken-roosts, under the heavy vaulted ceiling, black with shadows.

'Well,' said La Belle Lisa, 'it was nice of you to show me all this… When you come to the *charcuterie*, I'll give you something.'

She had taken his chin in her hand, as she often did, forgetting that he was no longer a child. She was somewhat affected, in fact, by her underground excursion and by quite tender feelings she was pleased to feel, and which were perfectly normal and innocent. She might have allowed her hand to linger a little longer than usual under his chin, so soft to the touch. At all events, Marjolin was thrilled by the caress and gave way to a sudden impulse; glancing round to make sure they were alone, he threw himself on La Belle Lisa with the strength of a bull. Grabbing her by the shoulders, he pushed her backwards into a basket of feathers, where she fell in a heap, her skirts round her knees. He was about to grab hold of her waist, just as he did with Cadine, with all the brutality of an animal following its instincts, when, without a sound and quite pale with the suddenness of this attack, she leapt out of the basket. She raised her arm as she had seen them do in slaughterhouses, clenched her beautiful woman's fist, and knocked Marjolin senseless with one blow between the eyes. He fell backwards, smashing his head against the edge of one of the stone blocks. Just at that moment the raucous crowing of a cock could be heard in the darkness.

La Belle Lisa remained perfectly composed. Her lips were pursed and her bosom had once again assumed the solid, rounded shape that made it look like a belly. Above her head she could hear the rumble of Les Halles, and the sounds of the pavement could be heard through the gratings on the Rue Rambuteau. She reflected that her powerful arms had saved her. She shook out the few feathers that still clung to her skirts. Then, afraid of being discovered, she hurried off, without even giving Marjolin a last glance. As she climbed the stairs, and passed through the grated entrance to the cellars, the light of day brought her a great sense of relief.

She returned to the *charcuterie*, very calm but a little pale.

'You've been out a long time,' Quenu said.

'I've been looking for Gavard. I can't find him anywhere,' she replied. 'We'll have to have our leg of lamb without him.'

Then she had the lard pot filled and cut some chops for her friend Madame Taboureau, who had sent her maid for them. The strokes of the chopper falling on the block reminded her of Marjolin down there in the cellars. But she felt that she had done nothing wrong. She had acted as a decent woman. She had no intention of disturbing her peace of mind for a boy like him; she was too well off with her husband and daughter. However, she glanced at Quenu. He had rough reddish skin on the back of his neck, and his shaven chin was as rough as gnarled wood, whereas Marjolin's chin and neck were as soft as satin. It was better not to think about it. In any case, she would never touch him again. It was a small pleasure she had allowed herself, and now regretted, and she could not help thinking that children nowadays grow up much too fast.

The colour had returned to her cheeks, and Quenu thought she was looking extremely well. He came and sat down with her at the counter.

'You ought to go out more often,' he said. 'It does you good. If you like, we'll go to the theatre one of these evenings, to the Gaîté.* Madame Taboureau has been to see the play that's on there; she said it was very good.'

Lisa smiled and said they would see about it. Then she disappeared once more. Quenu thought how good it was of her to run after Gavard. In point of fact, however, she had just gone upstairs to Florent's room, the key to which hung from a nail in the kitchen. Since Gavard had failed her, she hoped to discover something by inspecting her brother-in-law's room. She went slowly round it, examining every inch. The window onto the little balcony was open, and the budding pomegranate plant was bathed in the golden light of the setting sun. The room looked as if Augustine had never left it and had still been sleeping there the night before. There seemed to be nothing masculine about it. This surprised her, for she had expected to find some suspicious-looking boxes and crates under lock and key. She went to feel Augustine's summer dress, which was still hanging against the wall. Then she sat down at the table and read a sheet of paper half covered with writing, in which the word 'revolution' occurred twice. This alarmed her, and she opened the drawer, which she found full of papers. But her honesty reasserted itself in the face of this secret, so badly kept by the rickety little table. She stood there for a minute, bent over the papers, trying to understand them without actually touching them, in a state of great emotion, when the shrill cry of the chaffinch made her start. She shut the drawer. What she was doing was very wrong, she thought.

As she lingered by the window, wondering whether she should ask Father Roustan for his advice, she saw a crowd of people round a stretcher in the roadway below. Night was falling, but she could easily make out Cadine, who was crying, while Florent and Claude stood talking earnestly at the edge of the footpath. She hurried downstairs, surprised to see them back so soon. She hardly had time to reach the counter before Mademoiselle Saget came in.

'It's that hopeless creature Marjolin they've just found in the cellars, with his head split open,' she explained. 'Are you coming to have a look, Madame Quenu?'

Lisa crossed the road. Marjolin was lying on the stretcher, very pale. His eyes were closed and a lock of his hair was clotted with blood. The general view was that he would be all right and he probably had himself to blame anyway, for he was always playing around in the cellars. They assumed that he had been trying to jump over one of the stone blocks, a favourite game of his, and had fallen and knocked his head.

'That little devil probably pushed him,' muttered Mademoiselle Saget, pointing to Cadine. 'They're always horsing around.'

Marjolin, revived by the fresh air, opened his eyes. He looked round at everybody, and then, seeing Lisa bending over him, smiled at her gently, with an expression of humility and affection. He seemed not to remember. Lisa, relieved, said that he ought to be taken straight to hospital, and said she would take him some biscuits and oranges. Marjolin's head had fallen back. When the stretcher was taken away, Cadine followed it, her basket still round her neck, tears rolling down her cheeks and falling onto her bunches of violets. But she did not think for a moment of the flowers.

As Lisa went back to the shop, she heard Claude say, as he said goodbye to Florent with a shake of the hand:

'Ah, the devil! He's spoilt my day! But we had a really good time, didn't we?'

Claude and Florent had returned, tired but happy, from their trip to Nanterre, bringing back with them the fresh smell of the country air. By daybreak that morning Madame François had sold all her vegetables, and the three of them had gone to fetch the cart from the Compas d'or in the Rue Montorgueil. There, in the middle of Paris, was a patch of coutryside. Behind the Restaurant Philippe,* with its frontage of gilt woodwork rising to the first floor, was a kind of farmyard, dirty and teeming with life, reeking with the smell of hot manure and fresh straw. Chicken were pecking at the soft ground. Sheds green with mould, stairways, galleries, and broken roofing, leaned against the old houses, and at the far end, under a crudely constructed shelter, Balthazar was waiting in his harness, eating the oats in his nosebag. He went along the Rue Montorgueil at a slow trot, looking pleased to be going home so soon. But the cart was not empty. Madame François had struck a bargain with the people who cleaned out Les Halles, and twice a week she carried off a cartload of leaves, pitchforked out of the heaps of rubbish that cluttered up the streets in the area. It made excellent manure. In a few minutes the cart was full. Claude and Florent stretched out on this bed of greenery; Madame François took the reins and Balthazar shambled off, his head bent under the effort of pulling so many people.

The outing had been planned for a long time. Madame François laughed with pleasure. She liked the two men, and promised them an *omelette au lard* that simply could not be had in 'that terrible city'. They revelled in the thought of this day of relaxation, which had not yet even begun to dawn. Nanterre seemed like some distant paradise.

'Are you comfortable?' asked Madame François as the cart turned into the Rue du Pont-Neuf.

Claude said that it was 'as soft as a bridal bed'. Lying on their backs with their hands crossed under their heads, they looked up at the pale sky, in which the stars were beginning to fade. All along the Rue de Rivoli they were silent, waiting until there were no more houses, listening to Madame François as she talked to Balthazar, telling him softly:

'Take your time, old boy. There's no hurry. We'll get there in the end.'

On the Champs-Élysées, when the painter could see only the tops of the trees on either side, and the great green sweep of the Tuileries gardens in the distance, he seemed to wake up and became quite talkative.

As they passed the Rue du Roule, he caught a glimpse of the side entrance to Saint-Eustache, which could be seen far off under the giant curve of one of the covered avenues of Les Halles. He kept talking about this view of the church, which he saw as a symbol.

'It's an odd mixture,' he said, 'that section of the church framed by an avenue of cast iron. The one will destroy the other.* The iron will kill the stone. The time is not far off now. Do you believe in chance, Florent? I don't think it was some chance need for symmetry that put one of the rose windows of Saint-Eustache right in the middle of Les Halles. No, it's an entire manifesto in itself! It's modern art, realism, naturalism—whatever you want to call it! And it has grown up in the face of traditional art, don't you agree?'

As Florent remained silent, Claude went on:

'Besides, that church is a piece of bastard architecture, made up of the death agony of the Middle Ages and the birth pains of the Renaissance. Have you noticed the sort of churches they're building nowadays? They look like just anything—libraries, observatories, dovecotes, barracks; and surely nobody could possibly think they are the houses of God. The old Christian masons are all dead, and it would surely be best to stop building these dreadful stone constructions that mean nothing to anybody... Since the beginning of this century, only one original building has been built that has not been copied from somewhere else and has sprung naturally from the spirit of the times, and that is Les Halles. Do you realize, Florent? It's a brilliant creation, although it only gives us a vague understanding of what we'll see in the twentieth century! But that's why Saint-Eustache is done for! There it is with its rose windows, and without a congregation, while Les Halles keep growing next to it. They're full of life! That's how I see it, my friend!'

'Well, well,' said Madame François, laughing. 'You're quite an orator, Monsieur Claude! Even Balthazar is pricking up his ears. Giddyup, Balthazar!'

The cart was slowly making its way up the slope. At this early hour of the morning the avenue, with its double lines of iron chairs on each pathway, and its lawns dotted with flower beds and shrubbery, stretching away under the blue shadows of the trees, was deserted. At the Rond-Point a man and a woman on horseback trotted past. Florent, who had made himself a pillow with a bundle of cabbage leaves, was still gazing up at the sky, across which the pink light of morning was slowly spreading. Every now and then he would close his eyes the better to smell the freshness of the air, so happy to be leaving Les Halles to enjoy purer air that he hardly listened to what Claude was saying.

'And those chocolate box artists, what jokers they are!' resumed the painter. 'They're always saying the same thing: "You can't create art out of science"; "Industry kills poetry", and so on. Then they wail about the fate of the flowers, as if anybody wished the flowers any harm!... It makes me sick. I'd love to answer those snivelling fools with something really bold. I'd love to shock them. Do you know what my best work has been so far, the one that gives me the greatest satisfaction? It's quite complicated... On Christmas Eve last year, when I was staying with my Aunt Lisa, that idiot apprentice boy—you know, Auguste—was setting up the window display. Well, he nearly drove me mad with the unimaginative way he was doing it. I told him to get out of the way and let me do it really well, like a painting. I had plenty of strong colours to work with—the red of the tongues, the yellow of the hams, the blue of the paper shavings, the pink of the things that had been cut into, the green of the sprigs of heather, and the black puddings—a magnificent black, which I've never managed to produce on my palette. And, of course, the caul, the sausages, the *andouilles*, and the crumbed trotters gave me a very subtle range of greys. With all that I created a real work of art. I took the dishes, plates, pots, and jars, and arranged all the colours very carefully; it made a fantastic still life, running up and down the whole scale of colours and shades, from the most delicate to the most brilliant. The red tongues seemed to be on fire, and the black puddings, set among the grey sausages, suggested a terrible night of indigestion. What I did, you see, was produce a picture symbolizing the gluttony of Christmas Eve, when people meet at midnight after hymns and gorge themselves on empty stomachs after all the singing. At the top I put a huge turkey with a white breast, marbled under its skin by the black truffles. It was magnificent, like a huge belly, and with something so primitive and ironic about it that people stopped to look, alarmed by such a vivid display of colour. When my Aunt Lisa came back from the kitchen, she was terrified, and thought for a moment that I'd set the fat on fire. She thought the turkey was so obscene that she threw me out, and Auguste rearranged everything in his own stupid way. People like that will never learn the trick of putting a spot of red next to a spot of grey. Never mind! That was my masterpiece. The best thing I've ever done.'*

He fell silent, smiling at his own description. The cart had now reached the Arc de Triomphe. Strong gusts of wind swept across the broad expanse from the various avenues. Florent sat up and breathed in the smell of grass from the fortifications. He looked round, turning his back on Paris and straining to see the meadows in the distance. At the corner of the Rue de Longchamp, Madame François pointed out the spot where she had picked him up. This made him very thoughtful, and he gazed at her as she sat there, so healthy and relaxed, her arms slightly extended so as to hold the reins. She looked even more beautiful than La Belle Lisa, with her neckerchief round her head, her weather-beaten face, and her bluff, friendly expression. She clicked her tongue, whereupon Balthazar pricked up his ears and quickened his pace.

When they arrived at Nanterre, the cart turned to the left into a narrow lane between blank walls and came to a halt at a dead end. They had reached the end of the world, as Madame François would say. The first job was to unload the cabbage leaves. Claude and Florent would not hear of the garden boy, who was busy planting lettuces, leaving his work, and so they armed themselves with pitchforks and proceeded to toss the leaves into the manure pit. It was great fun. Claude had quite a liking for manure. Vegetable peelings, the mud of Les Halles, the refuse that had fallen from that giant table, were still alive, and they were now being returned to the place where the vegetables had first sprung from the ground, to nourish new generations of cabbages and carrots and turnips. They would rise again as perfect produce, and return once more to be spread out along the footpath. Paris made everything rot and returned everything to the earth, which never wearied of repairing the ravages of death.

'Ah!' exclaimed Claude, as he plied his fork one last time, 'here's a cabbage stalk I'm sure I've seen before. It has sprouted up at least a dozen times over there by the apricot tree.'

This made Florent laugh. But he soon became serious again, and walked slowly round the kitchen garden while Claude made a sketch of the stable and Madame François made some breakfast. The garden was a long strip of ground, divided down the middle by a narrow path. It was on a gentle slope, at the top of which, if you looked up, you could see the low barracks of Mont-Valérien. Green hedges separated it from other plots of land, and these high walls of hawthorn seemed to draw a green curtain over the horizon in such a way that in all the surrounding countryside Mont-Valérien alone seemed to stand on tiptoe to peer into Madame François's garden. A great sense of peace came from the invisible countryside. The May sun shone throughout the garden, the silence disturbed only by the buzzing of insects, and there was a pleasant atmosphere of drowsiness and fertility. Every now and then a faint cracking sound, or a soft sigh, suggested that one could actually hear the vegetables being born and beginning to grow. The patches of spinach and sorrel, the strips of radishes, carrots, and turnips, the beds of potatoes and cabbages, were spread out evenly across the black soil, in the green shadows cast by the trees. Further on, lettuces, onions, leeks, and celery were planted in rows, and looked like little regiments of soldiers on parade; while the peas and beans were beginning to unfurl their thin stems and to curl up a forest of sticks, which in June would become trees thick with leaves. Not a single weed could be seen. The garden was like two parallel carpets with a geometrical pattern of green on a reddish background, carefully brushed every morning. Borders of thyme added a grey fringe to each side of the path down the middle.

Florent paced up and down amid the scent of thyme warmed by the sun. He felt profoundly happy in the peace and cleanliness of the garden. For the past year or so he had only seen vegetables bruised by the jolting of the carts, pulled out of the earth the previous night and still bleeding. Now he rejoiced at finding them in their proper place, living happily in the earth, healthy in every limb. The cabbages shone with well-being, the carrots looked bright and cheerful, and the lettuces lounged about with an air of carefree indolence. Les Halles now seemed to him like a huge ossuary, a place of death, littered with the remains of things that had once been alive, a charnel house reeking with foul smells and putrefaction. He began to walk more slowly, resting in the garden as if after a long and difficult journey. The noise and dampness of the fish market had left him. He was reborn in the pure air. Claude was right, he thought. Les Halles were a world of death; the earth was life, the eternal cradle, the health of the world.

'The omelette's ready!' cried Madame François.

When they were all sitting round the kitchen table, the door open to the sun, they ate so merrily that Madame François looked at Florent in wonder, saying after every mouthful:

'You've changed so much. You look ten years younger. It's that dreadful Paris that makes you so gloomy. Now you've got some

sunshine back in your eyes… Big cities are no good. You should come
and live here.'

Claude laughed and said Paris was a wonderful place. He defended
it down to the last brick, at the same time admitting a great liking for
the country. In the afternoon Madame François and Florent found
themselves alone at the bottom of the garden, among a few fruit
trees. They were sitting on the ground, chatting to each other quite
seriously. She asked him endless questions about his life and what he
proposed to do later on, and told him never to forget that he could
always count on her if he felt she could help in any way. He was very
touched. No woman had ever spoken to him like that. She seemed
like some hardy plant that had grown up with the vegetables in the
fertile soil of the garden; while the Lisas, the Normandes, and all the
other market women, seemed like mutton dressed up for the shop
window. Here he enjoyed several hours of perfect well-being, freed
from the sickening smell of food, and restored to life in the fertile
atmosphere of the country, like the cabbage stalk Claude said he had
seen sprout up a dozen times.

At about five o'clock they took their leave of Madame François.
They wanted to walk back to Paris. She went with them to the end of
the lane, and for a moment held Florent's hand in hers.

'Don't forget what I said, if anything happens to you,' she said
gently.

For a quarter of an hour Florent walked in silence, already feeling
sad, reflecting that he had left his health behind him. The road to
Courbevoie was white with dust. They both liked tramping long
distances, and hearing the sound of their heavy boots on the hard
ground. Little clouds of dust rose up behind their feet with every
step they took, while the evening sunlight slanted across the avenue,
lengthening their shadows so much that their heads reached the
other side of the roadway and travelled along the opposite footpath.

Claude, swinging his arms, and taking long, regular strides, watched
the two shadows while enjoying the rhythmical cadence of his steps.
After a while, as if emerging from a dream, he asked:

'Do you know "The Battle of the Fat and the Thin"?'

Florent, surprised, said that he didn't. Thereupon Claude began to
talk very enthusiastically about this series of prints.* He mentioned
certain scenes: the Fat, big enough to burst, preparing their evening
orgies; the Thin, doubled up with hunger, staring in from the street

like envious stick figures; and then again, the Fat, sitting at table, their cheeks bulging with food, chasing away a Thin man who has had the temerity to insinuate himself into their midst in all humility, and looks like a ninepin in a nation of bowls. In these pictures Claude saw the entire drama of human life; and he ended by dividing everyone into Fat and Thin, two hostile groups, one of which devours the other and grows fat and sleek and endlessly enjoys itself.

'Cain', he said, 'was a Fat man and Abel a Thin one. Ever since that first murder, the big eaters have sucked the lifeblood out of the small eaters. The strong constantly prey on the weak; each one swallows his neighbour and then gets swallowed up in turn. Beware of the Fat, my friend!'

He relapsed into silence, still watching their shadows as they lengthened across the street in the light of the setting sun. Then he murmured:

'We're Thin, you and I. Just look and tell me if we take up much room in the sunlight, with stomachs as flat as ours.'

Florent looked at the two shadows and smiled. But this annoyed Claude.

'It's not funny,' he said. 'I know I suffer from being Thin. If I were Fat, I would paint happily, have a nice studio, and sell my pictures for their weight in gold. But, instead of that, I'm Thin; and I have to wear myself out trying to get the Fat to take notice. It'll kill me in the end. And you! You're an amazingly Thin man, the king of the Thin people, in fact! Do you remember your quarrel with the fishwives? It was magnificent: all those huge breasts flying at you! They were behaving instinctively; they were chasing one of the Thin just as a cat chases a mouse. Fat people, you see, hate Thin people so much that they have to drive them out of their sight, with a bite or a kick. That's why I'd be very careful if I were you. The Quenus are Fat people, and so are the Méhudins; in fact you're surrounded by them!'

'What about Gavard, and Mademoiselle Saget, and your friend Marjolin?' asked Florent, still smiling.

'Well, if you like, I'll go through all the people we know,' replied Claude. 'I've been keeping their faces in my studio for a long time, with notes on the category they belong to. It makes a whole lesson in natural history. Gavard is Fat, but the sort that pretends to be Thin. That type is quite common. Mademoiselle Saget and Madame Lecœur are Thin, but the kind to beware of—Thin people desperate to be Fat.

My friend Marjolin, little Cadine, La Sarriette, they're all Fat. They don't know it yet, because they're so young and innocent. It must be said that the Fat, before they get older, are charming creatures. Monsieur Lebigre is Fat, isn't he? And your political friends are mostly Thin—Charvet, Clémence, Logre, Lacaille. I'd only make an exception for that fat fool Alexandre, and that strange creature Robine. He has given me a lot of trouble.'

Claude carried on in this vein, all the way from the Pont de Neuilly to the Arc de Triomphe. He went back on himself and finished off certain portraits with a few characteristic touches. Logre, he said, was a Thin man who carried his belly between his shoulder-blades; La Belle Lisa was all belly and La Belle Normande all breasts; Mademoiselle Saget, in her younger days, must have missed an opportunity to get fat, because she despised both the Fat and the Thin; and Gavard was always risking his position as a Fat man and would end up as thin as an earwig.

'And what about Madame François?' Florent asked.

Claude seemed quite embarrassed by this question. He thought for a while and then stammered:

'Madame François, Madame François—well, I don't know. I never thought about classifying her. But she's a good old soul, and I think that's enough. She's neither one nor the other!'

But Florent had stopped smiling. Paris had recaptured him, the Paris that frightened him now, after costing him so many tears in Cayenne. By the time he arrived at Les Halles, night was falling, and the smells were stifling. He lowered his head as he returned once more to the nightmare of endless food, with the bitter-sweet memory of this day of health and sunlight caught in the perfume of thyme.*

CHAPTER 5

THE next day at about four o'clock, Lisa went to Saint-Eustache. She had dressed very carefully for the short walk across the square, in black silk, with a woven shawl round her shoulders. La Belle Normande, from her stall in the fish market, watched her until she vanished into the church.

'Ha! So she's going in for priests now, is she?' she sneered. 'Well, some holy water might calm her down a bit.'

She was wrong, for Lisa was not in the least devout. She did not usually go to church, but simply said that she did her best to live decently. At the same time, she did not like to hear people speak ill of religion, and she would often silence Gavard, who loved stories about the misdemeanours of priests and nuns. Talk of that sort seemed to her quite improper. Everyone had a right to his own beliefs, the right to demand respect for his scruples. Besides, priests were generally fine people. She knew Father Roustan at Saint-Eustache, a man of distinction and good counsel, upon whose friendship she knew she could rely. She always said that religion was essential to the great majority of people; she saw it as a kind of police force that helped to keep order and without which no government could possibly function. When Gavard went too far and said that priests should be turned into the streets and the churches closed down, she shrugged and replied:

'A lot of good that would do! After a few weeks they'd be killing each other in the streets, and they'd have to invent some other God. That's what happened in '93.* You know I don't have much to do with priests, but I do think they're necessary; we couldn't do without them.'

When Lisa entered a church, she did so with reverence. She had bought a handsome prayer book, which she never opened, for the times when she had to attend a wedding or a funeral. She knelt down and stood up at all the right places, and made a point of conducting herself with the utmost propriety. She assumed a sort of official demeanour, such as all respectable tradespeople should adopt in their dealings with religion.

As she entered Saint-Eustache that afternoon, she let the double door, covered in green baize, faded and worn by the touch of many pious hands, close softly behind her. She dipped her fingers in the holy water and crossed herself in the correct fashion. Then she made her way discreetly to the chapel of Saint Agnes, where the kneeling figures of two women were waiting with their faces in their hands, while the blue skirts of a third protruded from the confessional. Lisa seemed rather put out by the presence of these three women, and, addressing a verger who happened to be shuffling past wearing a black skull cap, she asked:

'Is it Father Roustan's day for confessions?' she asked.

The verger replied that Father Roustan had only two more penitents waiting, and would not take very long; she had only to take a seat and her turn would come almost immediately. She thanked him, without admitting that she had not come to confess. She decided to wait and walked slowly up and down the aisle, as far as the main door, where she stood looking down the nave, tall and severe between the brightly coloured side aisles. Looking up, she examined the high altar, which she found too plain for her taste; she did not like the cold grandeur of the stonework, but preferred the gaudy reds and golds of the side chapels. On the side of the Rue du Jour, these chapels looked almost grey in the light that filtered through the dusty windows, while on the other side the setting sun lit up the stained glass, sharpening the delicate colours, especially the greens and yellows. It reminded Lisa of the liqueur bottles on the shelf in front of Monsieur Lebigre's mirror. She came back along this side, which seemed to be warmed by the glow of light, and looked for a moment at the shrines, the altar decorations, and the wall paintings splashed with prismatic reflections. The church was empty, quivering with the silence that fell from its vaulted roof. Here and there a woman's dress made a dark stain against the yellow of the chairs; and the sound of whispering came from the closed confessionals. As she again approached the chapel of Saint Agnes, she saw that the blue dress was still kneeling at the feet of Father Roustan.

'I could say everything in ten seconds, if I wanted to,' she thought, proud of her absolute decency.

She walked to the end of the church. Behind the high altar, in the shadows of a double row of pillars, the chapel of the Blessed Virgin is dark and silent. In the stained windows, you can only make out the robes of the saints, in large folds of red and purple, burning like flames of mystic love in the solemn adoration of the darkness. It is a place of mystery, like some twilit corner of paradise, lit only by the gleaming stars of two candles. The four candelabra with brass lamps hanging from the vaulted roof are not lit and are almost invisible. Between the pillars women are always to be seen, kneeling on their chairs, engulfed in the voluptuous gloom.

Lisa stood gazing calmly about her. She was not at all nervous. She thought it was wrong not to light the candelabra, as it would have been much more cheerful with lights. There was also something almost indecent about the darkness, an atmosphere of alcoves that did not seem to her at all appropriate. The candles burning in a candelabrum by her side warmed her face, and an old woman was scraping some of the wax away with a big knife. In the gentle quiver of holiness that passed through the chapel, the dumb and swooning atmosphere of adoration, she could hear the rumble of carriages turning the corner of the Rue Montmartre, behind the red and purple saints on the windows. The distant, muffled sounds of Les Halles came to her ears.

As Lisa was about to leave the chapel, she saw the younger of the Méhudin sisters come in, Claire, the dealer in freshwater fish. The girl lit a candle, and then went to kneel behind a pillar, on the hard flagstones, her face so pale under her loose fair hair that she looked like a corpse. Thinking she was hidden, she gave way to her feelings and wept, praying with such fervour that she bowed down as if bent by a strong wind. Lisa watched in amazement, for the Méhudins were not known to be in any way pious; indeed, Claire usually spoke of religion and priests in a way that made one's hair stand on end.

'What's got into her?' she wondered, as she went back to the chapel of Saint Agnes. 'She must have poisoned some man or other, I'll be bound.'

Father Roustan finally emerged from the confessional. He was a handsome man of about forty, with a kindly air. When he saw Madame Quenu, he clasped her hands, called her 'dear lady', and led her to the vestry, where he took off his surplice and said that he was entirely at her disposal. They returned to the church, the priest in his cassock, bareheaded, and Lisa strutting along in her shawl. They paced up and down in front of the side chapels on the side of the Rue du Jour, conversing in hushed tones. The sunlight was fading from the windows, the church was growing dark, and the footsteps of the last few worshippers made a rustling sound on the flagstones.

Lisa explained her problem. Never did any question of religion arise between them. She never confessed and only sought his advice in moments of difficulty, because he was shrewd and discreet, and she preferred him, she would sometimes say, to shady businessmen who smelt of prison. His desire to help her had proved unfailing. He looked up points of law for her in the Code,* told her about good investments, resolved her moral difficulties with great tact, recommended tradespeople, and invariably had an answer for any question she asked, however difficult it might be. He supplied all this help quite naturally, without ever bringing God into it or trying to gain an advantage for himself or his faith. A word of thanks and a smile were all he asked. He seemed delighted to oblige beautiful Madame Quenu, about whom his housekeeper spoke very respectfully, as of a person highly regarded in the neighbourhood.

But on this occasion the consultation was particularly delicate. Lisa was anxious to know what steps she might reasonably take, as a woman of principle, in respect to her brother-in-law; whether she had a right to keep an eye on him to prevent him from compromising her husband, her daughter, and herself; and how far she could go if the situation became desperate. She did not ask these questions point blank, but asked them in such a skilful, roundabout way that the priest was able to answer without making personal allusions. The conclusion he came to was that a good and honest citizen had the right, and even the duty, to thwart evil, and was justified in using whatever means were necessary to ensure the triumph of good.

'That is my opinion, dear lady,' he said. 'The question of means is always very difficult. It is often a snare for souls of average virtue... But I know that you have a very good conscience. If you weigh carefully everything you do, and there is nothing you find repugnant, then proceed. Decent people have that wonderful gift of always knowing how to do the right thing.'

Then, changing his tone, he continued:

'Please give my regards to Monsieur Quenu. When I'm passing your way, I'll call in and give little Pauline a kiss. Goodbye, my dear lady. And please remember, I'm always ready to help.'

He went back into the vestry. On her way out, Lisa was curious to see if Claire was still praying, but she had gone back to her eels and carp; and in front of the chapel of the Blessed Virgin, which was already shrouded in darkness, there were just a number of chairs overturned by the ardour of the women who had knelt there.

When La Belle Lisa crossed the square again, La Normande, who was looking out for her, recognized her in the dusk by the shape of her skirt.

'Heavens!' she exclaimed. 'She's been in there for over an hour! When the priests clear away her sins, the choirboys have to line up with buckets to throw all the muck out into the street!'

The next morning Lisa went straight up to Florent's room and settled down in complete peace of mind. She was sure that she would not be disturbed; moreover, if Florent were to return, she had decided to lie, to say that she had come to see if his sheets needed changing. While in the shop, however, she had seen him very busy with his work in the fish market. Sitting down at the little table, she pulled out the drawer, put it on her knees, and began to examine its contents, taking the greatest care to put everything back in the same place. To begin with, she found the opening chapters of the book about Cayenne; then the drafts of Florent's various projects, his schemes for converting municipal dues into a sales tax, the reform of the administrative system of Les Halles, and so on. These pages of small writing, which she tried to read, bored her completely, and she was about to put the drawer back, convinced that Florent had hidden elsewhere the proof of his evil intentions, when she came across a photograph of La Normande in an envelope. It was rather dark. La Normande was pictured standing, her right arm resting on a broken pillar. She was wearing all her jewels, a new silk dress, and a cheeky smile. Lisa forgot all about her brother-in-law, her fears, and what she had come to do. She became lost in her examination of the photograph. She had never had the opportunity to study her rival at such close quarters. She scrutinized her hair, her nose, her mouth, she held the photograph away from her, then brought it closer. Then, with pursed lips, she read on the back, written in a big, ugly scrawl: 'From Louise to her friend Florent.' This shocked her—it was a confession. She felt an urge to take the photograph and keep it as a weapon against her enemy. But she slowly put it back in the envelope, telling herself that it would do no good, and, anyway, she could always come back for it.

Then, as she again began leafing through the papers, it occurred to her to look at the back of the drawer, where Florent had pushed Augustine's needles and thread; and there, between the prayer book and the *Clef des songes*, she discovered what she was really after, the incriminating notes, all simply concealed under a sheet of grey paper. The idea of an insurrection, of an armed uprising to overthrow the Empire, as suggested one evening at Monsieur Lebigre's by Logre, had slowly ripened in Florent's feverish brain. He soon came to see it as a duty, a mission. This was the object, finally revealed to him, of his escape from Cayenne and his return to Paris. Believing that he was destined to avenge his thinness upon a city that had grown fat while the defenders of justice starved to death in exile, he had taken upon himself the role of arbiter, and dreamt of rising up in Les Halles and sweeping away the reign of gluttony and drunkenness. In a sensitive nature like his, this idea had quickly taken root. His surroundings assumed huge dimensions, the wildest fancies sprang up in his mind. He imagined that the markets had taken possession of him on his arrival, to sap his strength and poison him with smells. Then he imagined that Lisa wanted to cast a spell over him; he would avoid her for two or three days at a time, as if she were some dissolving agency that would destroy his will if he went too close. These crises of puerile fear, these wild feelings of rebellion, always resulted in a rush of tenderness, a need to love, which he concealed with a boyish shame. It was in the evenings especially that his mind was filled with these imaginings. Depressed by his day's work, his nerves frayed, but not wishing to sleep because of his fear of what dreams might come, he would stay even later at Monsieur Lebigre's or the Méhudins', and when he returned he would still not go to bed, but would sit up writing and preparing for the great insurrection. Little by little a strategy emerged. He divided Paris into twenty sections, one for each *arrondissement*,* each with a leader, a sort of general, who would have in his command twenty lieutenants in charge of twenty companies of affiliated members. Every week these leaders would hold a meeting, every time in a different *arrondissement*, and, to ensure secrecy, the affiliated members would only know the lieutenant, who himself would deal exclusively with the leader of the section. It occurred to Florent that it would be useful if these companies believed themselves to be engaged on an imaginary mission, for this would have the effect of throwing the police off the scent. As for putting these forces to work, that would be a simple matter. They would wait for a complete formation of their ranks, and then take advantage of the first public disturbance. As they would doubtless only be equipped with a few old hunting guns, they would first of all take control of the police stations, disarm the fire brigade, the Paris guards, and the soldiers of the line, with as little fighting as possible, since they would all be invited to make common cause with the people. Then they would march on the Corps Législatif, and from there proceed to the Hôtel de Ville. This plan, to which Florent returned night after night as if to the script of a drama that relieved his overexcited nerves, was so far written only on scraps of paper, full of crossings-out, which showed how its author was still feeling his way, and revealing each phase of his scientific yet puerile project. When Lisa had glanced through these notes, without understanding all of them, she sat trembling, not daring to touch them further for fear of seeing them explode in her face like home-made bombs.

A final note frightened her more than all the rest. It was half a sheet of paper on which Florent had drawn the badges that would distinguish the leaders and the lieutenants, and, alongside, the pennants of the various companies. Diagrams in pencil denoted the colours of the pennants for all of the twenty sections. The leaders were to be distinguished by a red sash and the lieutenants by red armbands. To Lisa this seemed like an immediate realization of the uprising; she saw all these men with their red badges running past the *charcuterie*, firing bullets into the marble and the mirrors, stealing sausages and *andouilles* from the window. The dastardly schemes of her brother-in-law were surely directed against her and her happiness. She closed the drawer and looked round the room, thinking that it was she who had provided this man with a home, that he slept between her sheets and used her furniture. She was particularly exasperated by the thought that he had concealed his infernal plan in that rickety little table, which she herself had used before her marriage.

She stood there for a while, wondering what to do. There was no point in saying anything to Quenu. It occurred to her to confront Florent with the whole business, but she was afraid that he would go and commit his crime further away, and still compromise them out of malice. She gradually calmed down and decided that it would be best just to watch him. At the first sign of danger she would think again. She already had enough evidence to send him back to the galleys.*

When she went back into the shop, she found Augustine in quite a state. Little Pauline had disappeared more than half an hour before, and to Lisa's anxious questions she could only reply:

'I don't know, Madame... She was here just now, with a little boy... I was watching them. Then I cut some ham for a gentleman, and they had disappeared.'

'I bet it was Muche!' cried Lisa. 'That dreadful boy!'

It was indeed Muche. Pauline, who was wearing a new dress that day, with blue stripes, had wanted to show it off. She had stood outside the shop, on her best behaviour, wearing the serious expression of a little woman of six who is anxious not to get dirty. Her short, starched petticoats stood out like the skirts of a ballet dancer, displaying her smooth white stockings and shiny sky-blue bootees, while her pinafore, which hung low round her neck, had a narrow embroidered flounce round the shoulders, below which her pretty little arms appeared, bare and pink. She was wearing turquoise earrings, a little gold crucifix, and a blue velvet ribbon in her well-brushed hair. She combined her mother's plumpness and softness with the graceful, fashionable look of a new doll.

Muche had spotted her from the market. He was amusing himself by dropping into the gutter some dead little fish, following them along the curb as the water carried them off, and declaring that they were having a nice swim. But the sight of Pauline standing outside the shop, looking so smart and pretty, made him cross over to her, with his torn shirt, his trousers slipping down to reveal his vest, and his whole appearance that of a young street urchin. His mother had forbidden him ever to play with 'that silly fat girl whose parents stuff her fit to burst'. So he stood hesitating for a few moments, then went up to Pauline and asked if he could feel her pretty striped dress. Pauline, flattered at first, pouted rather prudishly and stepped back, murmuring in a tone of displeasure:

'Leave me alone… Mummy said I mustn't.'

Muche, who was very bold, simply laughed.

'Ha!' he snorted. 'What does it matter what your mummy said? Let's play a game.'

It was obvious that he wanted to get Pauline dirty. But, seeing him getting ready to give her a push in the back, she retreated, as if to go back into the shop. Muche then adopted a cajoling tone. With the air of a man of the world, he hitched up his trousers, and said:

'You're stupid, aren't you? It's just for fun… You look nice like that. Is that little cross your mother's?'

Pauline drew herself up and said it was hers. Then he led her off to the corner of the Rue Pirouette, touching her skirts and expressing his amazement at their wonderful stiffness. This pleased Pauline immensely. All the time she had been preening herself on the footpath she had been peeved that nobody had taken the slightest notice of her. But in spite of Muche's compliments, she still refused to leave the footpath.

'Little tart!' he shouted suddenly, becoming very crude again. 'I'll push you into the gutter if you don't look out, Miss Fancy Pants!'

She took fright. He grabbed her by the hand, but, seeing how badly she reacted, he once more became cajoling and began to fumble in his pocket.

'I've got a sou,' he said.

The sight of the coin had a calming effect on Pauline. He held it between his fingertips, to such effect that she stepped into the road without noticing. Little Muche was now getting somewhere.

'What do you like best?' he asked.

She gave no immediate answer. She didn't know, there were so many things she liked. He suggested a whole lot of different things: liquorice, treacle, gobstoppers, and sherbet. The sherbet made her think for a while. Then, making up her mind, she said:

'I like screws best.'

Muche then took her by the arm and she let him lead her away. They crossed the Rue Rambuteau, followed the broad footpath skirting the markets, and went as far as the grocer's in the Rue de la Cossonnerie, which was famous for its screws. 'Screws' are small paper packets used by grocers for the left-overs of their sweet displays—broken *dragées*, *marrons glacés* falling to pieces, all the dregs of their sweet jars. Muche was a real gentleman; he allowed Pauline to choose her screw, a blue one, and made no attempt to snatch it from her as he paid his sou. Outside, on the footpath, she emptied the miscellaneous collection of scraps into both pockets of her pinafore; and they were such little pockets that they were soon full. Then she began to munch the fragments one by one, delighted, wetting her finger to catch the fine powder, with the result that the sweets dissolved and two brown stains soon appeared on her pinafore. Muche laughed slyly to himself. He had his arm round her waist and rumpled her dress as he whisked her round the corner of the Rue Pierre Lescot, in the direction of the Place des Innocents.

'Let's play at something now,' he said. 'It's nice, what you've got in your pockets, isn't it? You see I didn't mean any harm.'

Thereupon he stuck his own hands into his pockets, and they entered the square together. It was to this spot, no doubt, that he had intended to lure his victim all along. He did her the honours of the square, as if it were his own private property. Pauline had never been so far from home, and she would have wept like a young lady who had been abducted had it not been for the sweets in her pockets. The fountain spurted and sheeted down in the middle of the lawn, and Jean Goujon's nymphs, very white against the grey stonework, tilted their urns and displayed their nude graces in the grimy air of Saint-Denis. The two children walked round the fountain, watched the water fall into the basins, took an interest in the grass, and thought, no doubt, of crossing the central lawn or crawling under the clumps of holly and rhododendrons that bordered the railings of the square. Little Muche, who had now managed to crumple Pauline's dress very badly at the back, said with his sly smile:

'Let's play at throwing sand now.'

Pauline had given in completely. They began to throw sand at each other, closing their eyes. The sand got into Pauline's low-cut bodice and ran down into her stockings and bootees. Muche was very pleased to see her white pinafore become quite yellow. But he must have considered it still too clean for his taste.

'Let's go and plant some trees!' he exclaimed suddenly. 'I know how to make nice gardens.'

'Real gardens!' murmured Pauline, very impressed.

Then, as the keeper of the square was nowhere to be seen, he got her to kneel down and dig some holes in one of the flower beds. Soon she was lying at full length in the soft earth, her arms buried up to her elbows. In the meantime, he began to gather pieces of wood and broke branches off the trees. These were the garden trees which he planted in the holes Pauline had been digging. He kept saying, however, that the holes were not deep enough and, like a demanding employer, called her a bad worker. When she stood up, she was black from head to foot. She had soil in her hair, her face was smeared, and she looked such a sight with her coal miner's arms that Muche clapped his hands with glee, and exclaimed:

'Now we'll have to water them. They won't grow if they're not watered.'

This was the final blow. They left the square, scooped up the water from the gutters, and ran back to pour it over the bits of wood. On the way, Pauline, who was so fat that she could not run properly, let the water drip down onto her dress, so that by the time the sixth journey had been made she looked as if she had been rolling in the gutter. Muche chuckled with delight on seeing how thoroughly dirty she was. He made her sit down next to him under a rhododendron near the garden they had made. Taking her by the hand and calling her his little wife, he told her that the garden was already growing.

'You're not sorry you came, are you?' he said. 'Instead of staying there on the footpath, looking so bored. You can have such fun in the streets. We must do this again. But you mustn't say anything to your mother. If you do, I'll pull your hair the next time I go past the shop.'

Pauline agreed to everything. And as a final act of gallantry, he filled both pockets of her pinafore with earth. He squeezed her tight, trying to hurt her now with urchin cruelty. Now all the sweets had gone, she had stopped playing, and was getting worried. When he started to pinch her, she burst into tears and said she wanted to go home. But at this he only grinned and said he would not take her home at all. She grew even more alarmed and sobbed like a maiden on the point of being seduced. Muche would certainly have begun to punch her to make her be quiet if a shrill voice, the voice of Mademoiselle Saget, had not cried out:

'Goodness me, it's Pauline! Leave her alone, you wicked thing!'

The old woman took Pauline by the hand, amazed at the state of her clothes. Muche was not greatly perturbed, but followed them, giggling at his handiwork, and saying that it was Pauline who had wanted to go with him and had fallen down. Mademoiselle Saget often went to the Square des Innocents. Every afternoon she would spend a good hour there, to keep up to date with all the gossip of that particular little community. On both sides of the square, there is a long semicircular row of benches placed end to end. The people from the slum dwellings round about gather there in groups: frail, shrivelled old women in tattered bonnets, young women in camisoles with their skirts badly fastened, bareheaded and already looking tired and prematurely aged; and a few men, neat-looking grandfathers, porters in greasy jackets, suspicious individuals in black silk hats; while the children play around on the footpath, dragging toy carts that have lost their wheels, filling buckets with sand, shouting and quarrelling—a ragged, snotty-nosed collection of brats, running everywhere like vermin. Mademoiselle Saget was so thin that she always managed to find room on one of the benches. She would listen, and then start a conversation with her neighbour, some sallow-faced worker's wife who might be mending linen, every now and then producing handkerchiefs and stockings full of holes from a little basket patched up with string. She knew some of the women. In the midst of the shrieking of the children and the rumble of traffic in the Rue Saint-Denis, the tittle-tattle never ended—endless stories about tradespeople, grocers, butchers, bakers, enough to fill the columns of a local newspaper, soured and distorted by the refusal of credit and the frustrated longings of the poor. From these poor creatures she learnt the most terrible things, the gossip of squalid lodging houses and concierges' lodges, all the filthy stories that circulated in the neighbourhood—which tickled her appetite enormously. As she sat looking towards the markets, she had in front of her the square and its three blocks of houses. She did her best to see into the windows, seeming somehow to grow taller as she examined the various floors, right up to the attic windows. She stared at the curtains, reconstructing a whole drama from the sight of a head appearing between two shutters; and in the end she had come to know the stories behind the tenants of every house simply by watching from the outside. The Restaurant Baratte interested her particularly, with its wine merchant's shop and the fretted golden awning above it. She liked the pale blue wash, the yellow columns, the inscribed pillar topped by a shell, the frontage like a cardboard temple, the whole tumbledown building; and the way the effect was completed by a balcony of roughly coloured tin at the edge of the roof. Behind red-striped window blinds she pictured fine lunches, delicate suppers, and feasts fit for kings. She even lied to herself: it was here, she declared, that Florent and Gavard came to carouse with the two Méhudin sisters; she did not dare to say what happened after the dessert.

Meanwhile, Pauline cried even louder now that Mademoiselle Saget had taken her by the hand. The old lady was on the point of taking her out through the gate of the square when the girl seemed to have second thoughts. She sat down on a bench and tried to make the child stop crying.

'Now, stop crying, or the *sergents de ville* will come and get you,' she said to Pauline. 'I'm going to take you home. You know me, don't you? Come on, let's have a smile.'

The tears, however, were choking her and she wanted to go. Mademoiselle Saget let her cry, waiting until she had finished. The poor child was shaking; her petticoats and stockings were wet through; and as she wiped her tears away with her hands, her whole face became dirty. When at last she calmed down a little, the old woman continued in a wheedling voice:

'Your mummy is very nice, isn't she? She loves you, doesn't she?'

'Yes,' said Pauline, still sobbing.

'And your daddy, he's very nice too, isn't he? He doesn't hit you or quarrel with your mummy, does he? What do they say at night when they go to bed?"

'I don't know. I'm asleep then.'

'Do they talk about your cousin Florent?'

'I don't know.'

Mademoiselle Saget pretended to look very serious and got up as if to go away.

'You don't tell stories, do you?' she said. 'You know you mustn't tell stories. I'll just leave you here if you tell stories, and Muche will come back and pinch you.'

Muche, who had been hovering about, intervened at this point and said in his clear, manly voice:

'Oh, she's too stupid to know. But I do know that Florent looked very excited yesterday when mummy said he could kiss her if he wanted to!'

Pauline had begun to cry again at the threat of being abandoned.

'Be quiet, can't you!' muttered the old woman, giving her a shake. 'Look, I won't go away. I'll even give you a piece of barley sugar! You don't like your cousin Florent, do you?'

'No, mummy says he's not nice.'

'So your mummy does say something.'

'One night when I was in bed with Mouton, she said to Daddy: "Your brother has only escaped from the galleys to take us all back there with him."'

Mademoiselle Saget uttered a cry. She stood up, trembling. It had just dawned on her. Then, without a word, she took Pauline by the hand and took her straight back to the *charcuterie*. At the corner of the Rue Pirouette, Muche prudently disappeared. Lisa was in a dreadful state. When she saw her daughter so bedraggled, she turned her round and round, looking at her from every angle.

'She's been with Muche,' said Mademoiselle Saget. I found them in the square. I don't know what they were up to. But that boy is capable of anything.'

Lisa was speechless. She did not know where to take hold of her daughter, so great was her disgust at the sight of the muddy bootees, the dirty stockings, the torn skirts, and the filthy hands and face. The blue velvet ribbon, the earrings, and the little crucifix were all coated in mud. But the last straw for Lisa were the pockets full of earth. She knelt down and emptied them, regardless of the pink and white tiles. As she dragged Pauline away, she could only gasp:

'You filthy thing!'

Mademoiselle Saget, who had found the whole scene most enjoyable, fairly skipped across the Rue Rambuteau. She knew at last! For nearly a year she had been dying to find out, and here she suddenly was—in full possession of the facts, and of Florent. It was unimaginably satisfying, like being cured of a disease, for she really felt that Florent would have seen her to her grave had he continued to frustrate her curiosity. Now the whole neighbourhood of Les Halles belonged to her. Now there was nothing she did not know. She could have told the tale of every street, shop by shop. She uttered little sighs of delight as she entered the fruit market.

'Hello, Mademoiselle Saget,' cried La Sarriette from her stall. 'What are you smiling about? Have you won first prize in the lottery?'

'No, no. Ah, if you only knew!'

La Sarriette, untidy and dishevelled as usual, looked charming in the midst of her fruit. Her frizzy hair fell over her forehead like vine branches. Her bare arms and neck, in fact each bare and rosy part of her body that was visible, had the freshness of cherries and peaches. Just for fun she had hung cherries in her ears, black cherries that dangled against her cheeks as she bent down, laughing. She was eating some redcurrants, and what amused her was the way she was smearing her face with them. Her lips were bright red, glistening with the juice from the fruit, as if they had been painted and perfumed with some middle eastern cosmetic. A smell of plums rose from her skirts. Her loosely tied shawl smelt of strawberries.

Fruit of every kind was piled up around her behind her narrow stall. On the shelves at the back were rows of melons, cantaloupes covered in wart-like knots, *maraîchers* whose skin was covered with grey lace-like netting, and *culs-de-singe*, with their smooth bumps. In front was an array of choice fruits, carefully arranged in baskets. They looked like full, round cheeks half hidden from view, or the faces of beautiful children glimpsed through a curtain of leaves; especially the peaches, the blushing Montreuil peaches with their soft, clear skin like girls from the north, and the yellow, sun-burnt peaches from the south, tanned like the women in Provence. The apricots lying in their moss took on the colour of amber, like the sunset glow on the necks of dark-haired girls just where the little hairs begin to curl. The cherries, arranged in rows, were like the lips of Chinese girls drawn into a tight smile: the Montmorencies, suggesting the fleshy lips of fat women; the English ones, much longer and more serious; the common black ones, which looked as if they had been bruised by kisses; the bigaroons, speckled with pink and white, which seemed to be smiling with a mixture of merriment and anger. The apples and pears stood in symmetrical piles, often in pyramids, showing the light flush of developing breasts, golden shoulders and hips, a discreet style of nudity among the sprays of fern. They all had different skins: the lady-apples soft like a baby, the raddled Rambourgs, the Calvilles in their white dresses, the ruddy Canadas, the blotchy crab-apples, the freckled pippins. Then came the pears: the white pears and English pears, the Beurrés, the Messire-Jeans, and the Duchesses— some dumpy, some with slender swan-like necks, others with heavy shoulders, their green and yellow bellies marked at times by a splash of carmine. Next to them the transparent plums were like pale, anaemic virgins: the greengages were like innocent flowers, while the mirabelles were like the golden beads of a rosary lying forgotten in a box with sticks of vanilla. The strawberries exhaled the fresh perfume of youth, especially the smaller ones, those that are picked in woods, and are much more aromatic than the big garden strawberries that smell of watering cans. Raspberries added their bouquet to this pure aroma. The redcurrants and the blackcurrants smiled knowingly, while the grapes, in heavy bunches laden with intoxication, lay languorously in their baskets, some of them dangling over the edge, scorched by the voluptuous heat of the sun.

La Sarriette lived and worked here, as if in an orchard, in a rapture of intoxicating smells. The cheaper fruit—cherries, plums and strawberries—were piled up in front of her in baskets lined with paper, bruised each other's bodies and stained the stall with juice, a rich juice that steamed in the heat. On hot July afternoons she would feel quite giddy, when the melons enveloped her with their powerful aroma of musk. Then, tipsy, with her loosened shawl showing more of her breasts, fresh as she was with the springtide of life, she pouted her lips, tempting all who saw her to kiss them. It was she—her arms and neck—that gave such sensuous life to her fruit, such silky feminine warmth. At the next stall an old woman, a hideous old drunkard, displayed nothing but wizened apples, pears as flabby as herself, and cadaverous apricots as vile and sallow as a witch. But La Sarriette's stall spoke of love and passion. It seemed that her lips had placed the cherries there like kisses, one by one; that the silken peaches had fallen gently from her body; that the plums had been supplied with the softest parts of her skin; that some of her own blood had flowed into the veins of the redcurrants. The heat of her youth and beauty excited these fruits of the earth, these seeds whose love had reached its climax on a bed of leaves, in the alcoves spread with moss deep in the baskets. The avenue of flowers behind her stall seemed to have a dull smell in comparison with the vital aroma that rose from her open baskets and her low-slung shawl.

That day she was very excited by a huge consignment of plums. She could see that Mademoiselle Saget had some important news and that she wanted to stop and talk. But the old woman stamped her foot and said:

'No, no, I haven't got time. I'm on my way to see Madame Lecœur. But I've got some amazing news. You can come with me, if you like.'

In fact, her sole purpose in going through the fruit market was to entice La Sarriette to go with her. La Sarriette could not resist the temptation. Monsieur Jules was there, wriggling about on his chair.

'Look after the shop for a minute, will you?' she asked. 'I'll come straight back.'

Jules, however, stood up and shouted after her:

'Hey, no! I'm going! I don't want to hang about here for an hour, as I did the other day. Besides, these plums give me a headache.'

He strode off, his hands in his pockets, and the stall was left to look after itself. Mademoiselle Saget trotted along so fast that La Sarriette had to run to keep up. At the butter market, a neighbour told them that Madame Lecœur was in the cellars. La Sarriette went down to fetch her, while the old woman sat down among the cheeses.

The cellar under the butter market is a very gloomy spot. The rows of storerooms are protected by very fine wire meshing, as a safeguard against fire; and the gas burners, which are few and far between, make dull yellow splodges, in the heavy, nauseous atmosphere beneath the low roof. Madame Lecœur was working her butter on one of the tables that lay under the Rue Berger; the gratings allowed a pale light to filter through. These tables, constantly washed down with water from the taps, are as white as if they were new. With her back to the water pump at the far end, Madame Lecœur was kneading her butter in an oak box. She took some of the different kinds that lay behind her and mixed them together, correcting the result with the addition of one or another, just as is done in the blending of wines. Bent almost double, with her pointed shoulders, and her thin, knotty arms like poles, she was thrusting her fists furiously into this greasy paste, which was beginning to look white and creamy. She was sweating, and uttered a sigh with every effort she made.

'Mademoiselle Saget would like a word, auntie,' said La Sarriette.

Madame Lecœur halted and pushed her bonnet back over her hair with her greasy fingers, not seeming to mind making a mess of it.

'I've finished,' she replied. 'Ask her to wait a minute.'

'She's got something very interesting to tell you.'

'Just a minute.'

Once more she plunged her arms into the butter, up to her elbows. Softened beforehand in warm water, it oiled her parchment-like skin and made the thick blue veins bulge out on her arms. La Sarriette was quite disgusted by the sight of these ugly arms, slaving away in the depths of the melting mass of butter. But she remembered what it was like: at one time she too had kept her pretty little hands in the butter for whole afternoons. It had even replaced her hand cream, an unguent that had kept her skin white and her nails pink, and had seemed to give her fingers their extreme suppleness.

'I don't think that butter will be very good, auntie,' she continued, after a pause. 'Your butter is too strong.'

'I know,' said Madame Lecœur, between two groans. 'But what can I do? Everything's got to be used. Some people want cheap butter, so that's what they get… It's always too good for the customers, anyway.'

La Sarriette thought that she wouldn't like to eat butter worked by her aunt's arms. Then she glanced at a little pot full of a red dye.

'Your *raucourt* is too light,' she murmured.

The *raucourt* is a colouring matter used to give the butter its fine shade of yellow. The butter women imagine that its secret is known only to themselves, though it is simply made from annatto,* and sometimes from carrots and marigolds.

'Are you coming or not?' said the young woman, who was not used to the foul smell of the cellar and was getting impatient. 'Mademoiselle Saget may have gone again. I think she's got some important news about Uncle Gavard.'

On hearing this, Madame Lecœur stopped work abruptly. She left the butter and the *raucourt* and did not even bother to wipe her arms. With a little tap she once more adjusted her bonnet and climbed the steps behind her niece, repeating anxiously:

'Do you really think she's gone again?'

She was pleased to see Mademoiselle Saget sitting among the cheeses. The old woman had not dreamed for a moment of going away. The three of them sat behind the stall, so close together that their noses almost touched. Mademoiselle Saget remained silent for two whole minutes, and then, seeing that the others were dying of curiosity, she said in her shrill little voice:

'You know that Florent? Well, I can tell you where he was before he came here.'

For a moment longer she kept them in suspense. Then, in a deep, melodramatic voice, she said:

'He was in prison.'

All around them the cheeses were stinking. On the two shelves at the back of the stall were huge blocks of butter: Brittany butter overflowing its baskets; Normandy butter wrapped in cloth, looking like models of bellies on to which a sculptor had thrown some wet rags; other blocks, already cut into and looking like high rocks full of valleys and crevices. Under the display counter of red marble veined with grey, baskets of eggs shone like white chalk; while on layers of straw in boxes were *bondons* placed end to end, and *gournays* arranged like medals, forming darker patches tinted with green. But for the most part the cheeses stood in piles on the table. There, next to the one-pound packs of butter, a gigantic *cantal* was spread on leaves of white beet, as though split by blows from an axe; then came a golden Cheshire cheese, a *gruyère* like a wheel fallen from some barbarian chariot, some Dutch cheeses suggesting decapitated heads smeared in dried blood and as hard as skulls—which has earned them the name of 'death's heads'. A *parmesan* added its aromatic tang to the thick, dull smell of the others. Three *bries*, on round boards, looked like melancholy moons. Two of them, very dry, were at the full; the third, in its second quarter, was melting away in a white cream, which had spread into a pool and flowed over the thin boards that had been put there in an attempt to hold it in check. Some *ports-saluts*, shaped like ancient discuses, bore the printed names of their makers. A *romantour* in silver paper suggested a bar of nougat or some sweet cheese which had strayed into this realm of bitter fermentations. The *roqueforts*, too, under their glass covers, had a princely air, their fat faces veined in blue and yellow, like the victims of some shameful disease common to rich people who have eaten too many truffles; while on a dish next to them stood the *fromages de chèvre*, about the size of a child's fist, hard and grey like the pebbles which the rams send rolling down stony paths as they lead their flock. Then came the strong-smelling cheeses: the *mont-d'ors*, pale yellow, with a mild sugary smell; the *troyes*, very thick and bruised at the edges, much stronger, smelling like a damp cellar; the *camemberts*, suggesting high game; the *neufchâtels*, the *limbourgs*, the *marolles*, the *pont-l'évêques*, each adding its own shrill note in a phrase that was harsh to the point of nausea; the *livarots*, tinted red, as irritating to the throat as sulphur fumes; and finally, stronger than all the others, the *olivets*, wrapped in walnut leaves, like the carcasses of animals which peasants cover with branches as they lie rotting in the hedgerow under the blazing sun. The warm afternoon had softened the cheeses; the mould on the rinds was melting and glazing over with the rich colours of red copper verdigris, like wounds that have badly healed; under the oak leaves, a breeze lifted the skin of the *olivets*, which seemed to move up and down with the slow deep breathing of a man asleep. A *livarot* was swarming with life; and behind the scales a *géromé* flavoured with aniseed gave off such a pestilential smell that all around it flies had dropped dead on the marble slab.

This *géromé* was almost under Mademoiselle Saget's nose. She recoiled and leaned her head against the big sheets of white and yellow paper that hung down from a corner at the back of the stall.

'Yes,' she repeated with an expression of disgust. 'He was in prison. So, you see, those Quenu-Gradelles have no reason to put on such airs!'

Madame Lecœur and La Sarriette made noises of consternation. It couldn't be true. What could he have done to be sent to prison? Who could possibly think that Madame Quenu, whose virtue was renowned throughout the neighbourhood, would choose a convict as a lover?

'You don't seem to understand!' cried the old woman impatiently. 'Listen to me... I was sure I'd seen that great beanpole somewhere before.'

She proceeded to tell them Florent's story. She had recalled a vague rumour about a nephew of old Gradelle being transported to Cayenne for killing six gendarmes at a barricade. She had even seen this nephew once in the Rue Pirouette. Well, the nephew and the cousin were one and the same! Then she began to bemoan her waning powers. Her memory was going, she said; she would soon be unable to remember anything. She mourned her loss of memory like a scholar who sees his notes, his life's work, being blown away by the wind.

'Six gendarmes!' murmured La Sarriette in admiration. 'He must be incredibly strong.'

'And he's done away with plenty of others,' added Mademoiselle Saget. 'I wouldn't like to meet him on a dark night!'

'What a villain!' stammered Madame Lecœur, quite stunned.

The sun was slanting into the market, the cheeses stank even more. The smell of the *marolles* seemed strongest; it released powerful whiffs into the air, like the stink of stable litter. Then the wind changed, and suddenly the deathly presence of the *limbourg* struck the three women, pungent and bitter, like the last gasps of a dying man.

'But', Madame Lecœur went on, 'if he's that fat Lisa's brother-in-law, then he could hardly have slept with her.'

They looked at each other. This aspect of the case took them by surprise. They were loath to give up their original theory. Mademoiselle Saget, shrugging her shoulders, suggested:

'Well, that wouldn't stop him... Although, I must say, it would be a bit much... Still, I wouldn't put it past him.'

'But, in any case, that must be ancient history, because, as you said, he's spending all that time with the Méhudin girls.'

'He certainly is,' said Mademoiselle Saget irritably, feeling that her word was doubted. 'He's there every evening. But it's not our concern, is it? We're decent, aren't we? What he gets up to makes no difference to us!'

'Quite right,' agreed the other two. 'He's an absolute villain.'

The story was almost turning tragic. La Belle Lisa seemed spared, but they consoled themselves for this by prophesying that Florent would bring about some terrible catastrophe. Of course he had evil designs; people like that only escape in order to burn everything down, and if he had come back to Les Halles it must be to hatch some plot. Then they began to imagine the most extravagant scenarios. The two tradeswomen declared that they would put extra padlocks on the doors of their storerooms; and La Sarriette remembered that she had had a basket of peaches stolen the previous week. Mademoiselle Saget, however, really frightened the other two by telling them that the 'Reds' didn't work like that: their concern was not with baskets of peaches; they formed into companies of two or three hundred to kill everyone in sight and plunder and pillage at will. That was 'politics', she said, with the superior air of a woman who thought she knew what she was talking about. Madame Lecœur was feeling quite ill. She could already see Florent and his henchmen hiding in the cellars, and rushing out at night to set fire to Les Halles and sack Paris.

'By the way,' exclaimed Mademoiselle Saget, 'now that I come to think of it, there's old Gradelle's money. Dear me, the Quenus must be really worried!'

She now looked very happy again. The gossiping continued. They fell to talking about the Quenus, and she told the story of the treasure discovered in the salting tub, which she knew down to the last detail. She could even quote the precise amount, eighty-five thousand francs, though neither Lisa nor her husband could recall confiding it to any living soul. Anyway, the point was that the Quenus had not given 'the beanpole' his share. He was too badly dressed for that. Perhaps he didn't even know about the salting tub. They were all thieves in that family. Then they bent their heads together, lowered their voices, and decided that while it was probably dangerous to attack La Belle Lisa, they should certainly 'deal with that Red', so that he wouldn't eat up any more of poor Monsieur Gavard's money.

A silence fell at the mention of Gavard. They all looked at each other cautiously. As they were all rather short of breath by this time, it was the *camembert* they could smell. This cheese, with its gamy odour, had overpowered the milder smells of the *marolles* and the *limbourg*; its power was remarkable. Every now and then, however, a slight whiff, a flute-like note, came from the *parmesan*, while the *bries* came into play with their soft, musty smell, the gentle sound, so to speak, of a damp tambourine. The *livarot* launched into an overwhelming reprise, and the *géromé* kept up the symphony with a sustained high note.

'I saw Madame Léonce,' said Mademoiselle Saget with a meaningful look.

At this the other two became extremely attentive. Madame Léonce was the concierge at Gavard's place in the Rue de la Cossonnerie. It was an old house standing back from the street, its ground floor occupied by an orange and lemon distributor who had had the front distempered in blue up to the second floor. Madame Léonce acted as Gavard's housekeeper, kept the keys of his cupboards, and took him *tisanes* when he happened to catch cold. She was a dour woman in her fifties, who spoke slowly but at endless length. She had been rather put out one day when Gavard had pinched her round the waist, but this had not prevented her from putting leeches on him in a rather delicate spot after a fall. Mademoiselle Saget, who went to have coffee with her every Wednesday night, became even friendlier with her when Gavard came to live in the house. They would talk about him for hours; they were both attached to him, and were very concerned for his health and happiness.

'Yes, I saw Madame Léonce,' repeated the old woman. 'We had coffee yesterday... She seemed very worried. Apparently Monsieur Gavard never comes home these days before one in the morning. On Sunday she took him some broth, because she thought he looked in a bad way.'

'Oh, I'm sure it's not his health she's interested in,' exclaimed Madame Lecœur, who was somewhat concerned by Madame Léonce's attentions to Gavard.

Mademoiselle Saget thought she ought to defend her friend.

'You're quite wrong... Madame Léonce is a better woman than her position might make you think. She's quite a lady. If she'd wanted to help herself to handfuls of Monsieur Gavard's things, she could have done so long ago. Apparently he leaves everything just lying about. I wanted to talk to you about that. But not a word to anyone, please.'

They swore that they would not breathe a word, and craned their necks to hear what Mademoiselle Saget had to say:

'Well, Monsieur Gavard has been behaving very strangely recently. He has been buying firearms, one of those big revolvers. Madame Léonce says that it's horrible, the pistol is always on the mantelpiece or the table, and she doesn't dare to do any dusting any more. But that's not all. His money...'

'His money!' echoed Madame Lecœur, with blazing cheeks.

'Well, he's got no shares left, he's sold them all. All he's got now is a pile of gold in a cupboard.'

'A pile of gold!' cried La Sarriette, becoming most excited.

'Yes, a big pile of gold. A whole shelf-full. It's dazzling. Madame Léonce told me he opened the cupboard one morning when she was there, and it nearly blinded her.'

There was another silence. The three women were blinking, as if they had the gold in front of them. La Sarriette was the first to burst out laughing, and murmured:

'If my uncle gave it all to me, I'd have a wonderful time with Jules. We'd never get up; we'd have fine food brought in from the restaurant.'

Madame Lecœur, however, seemed stunned by the revelation, crushed beneath the weight of the gold which she could not stop imagining. She felt deeply envious. At last she raised her skinny arms and dry hands, her fingernails still covered in butter, and stammered in a distressed tone:

'I mustn't think of it! It's too painful!'

'It would all be yours if anything happened to him,' said Mademoiselle Saget. 'If I were in your shoes, I'd put myself first... That gun is a very bad sign. Monsieur Gavard has got into bad company. I'm afraid it'll all end badly.'

Then the conversation turned once more to Florent. They tore him to pieces even more violently than before. And then, with perfect composure, they began to discuss what was likely to happen to Florent and Gavard, given all these goings-on. They'd certainly be done for if there was any gossiping. So, they swore to keep their mouths shut, not because that rat Florent deserved any favours, but because Monsieur Gavard had to be protected at all costs. They stood up, and Mademoiselle Saget was turning as if to go when Madame Lecœur said: 'But if anything does happen to him, do you think Madame Léonce could be trusted? Perhaps she's got the key to the cupboard.'

'Now that's going a bit far,' replied the old woman. 'I think she's perfectly decent; but, of course, there's no telling... Some people... Anyway, I've given you all due warning. Now it's up to you.'

As they stood there taking their leave of each other, the cheeses seemed to stink even more. They all seemed to stink together, in a foul cacophony: from the oppressiveness of the heavy Dutch cheeses and the *gruyères* to the sharp alkaline note of the *olivet*. From the *cantal*, Cheshire, and goat's milk came the sound of a bassoon, punctuated by the sudden, sharp notes of the *neufchâtels*, the *troyes*, and the *mont-d'ors*. Then the smells went wild and became completely jumbled, the *port-salut*, *limbourg*, *géromé*, *marolles*, *livarot*, and *pont-l'évèque* combining into a great explosion of smells. The stench rose and spread, no longer a collection of individual smells, but a huge, sickening mixture. It seemed for a moment that it was the vile words of Madame Lecœur and Mademoiselle Saget that had produced this dreadful odour.

'I'm very grateful,' said Madame Lecœur. 'If I ever get rich, I won't forget you.'

The old woman picked up a cream cheese, inspected it, and put it back on the marble slab. Then she asked how much it was.

'To me,' she added with a smile.

'To you, nothing,' replied Madame Lecœur. 'It's yours.'

And again she added: 'If only I was rich!'

Mademoiselle Saget assured her that one day she would be rich. The cheese had already disappeared into her bag. Madame Lecœur went back to the cellar, while Mademoiselle Saget walked back with La Sarriette to her stall. There they stopped for a moment and talked about Monsieur Jules. The fruit around them had a fresh springtime smell.

'It smells much nicer here than at your aunt's,' said the old woman. 'I was beginning to feel quite ill just now. I don't know how she can stand it. But here everything smells nice. It makes you look quite rosy, my dear.'

La Sarriette began to laugh. She loved compliments. Then she sold a woman a pound of plums and told her they were like sugar.

'I'd like some plums too,' murmured Mademoiselle Saget, when the woman had gone. 'But I only need one or two... Living by myself, you know...'

'Take a handful,' said La Sarriette. 'It won't ruin me. Tell Jules to come back if you see him. He's probably smoking a cigar on the first bench on the right as you come out of the avenue.'

Mademoiselle Saget took the biggest handful of plums she could, and they followed the cheese into the bag. Then she pretended to leave the markets, but in reality made a detour through one of the covered avenues, walking slowly and thinking that the plums and a cheese would not make much of a dinner. When she did not manage, during her afternoon foraging, to wheedle the stallkeepers into filling her bag, she was reduced to making a meal out of scraps. So she crept back to the butter market, where, on the side of the Rue Berger and behind the offices of the oystermongers, there were some cooked-meat stalls.

Every morning little closed box-like carts, lined with zinc and fitted with air vents, drew up in front of the larger Parisian kichens and carried away the left-overs from restaurants, embassies, and ministries. The left-overs were then sorted out in the market cellars, and by nine o'clock plates of food were displayed for sale at three or five sous apiece: slices of meat, scraps of game, fish heads and tails, vegetables, bits of *galantine*, and, by way of dessert, cakes scarcely cut into, and other confectionery. The half-starved, small-time workers and women shivering with fever would queue up to buy them, and sometimes the street urchins would make fun of them, especially the pale old skinflints who would glance round nervously when they bought something, to make sure nobody was watching them. Mademoiselle Saget slipped in front of a stall whose keeper boasted that what she sold came only from the Tuileries. One day she had persuaded the old woman to buy a slice of lamb by assuring her that it had come straight from the plate of the Emperor himself; and this piece of meat, consumed with some pride, still tickled her vanity when she thought of it. Her secretive approach was explained by her desire not to put out the neighbouring shopkeepers, whom she was always visiting without ever buying anything. Her method was to pick a quarrel with the shopkeepers as soon as she knew all about them; then she would bestow her patronage on others, desert them in turn, and gradually make friends again with those with whom she had quarrelled. In this way she made the rounds of Les Halles, making herself known in every shop. Anyone would have thought that she consumed vast amounts of provisions, whereas, in fact, she lived off presents and the few scraps she had to buy when all else failed.

That evening only an old man was standing in front of the stall. He was sniffing at a plate of mixed meat and fish. Mademoiselle Saget began to sniff at a plate of cold fried fish. It was offered at three sous. She bargained and got it for two. The fish was swallowed up in her bag. Other customers arrived and with one accord bent down to sniff the plates. The smell of the stall was nauseating, an odour of greasy dishes and filthy sinks.

'Come and see me tomorrow,' the stallkeeper said to the old woman. 'I'll keep something nice for you... There's a big dinner at the Tuileries tonight.'

Mademoiselle Saget was about to promise to come, when, turning round, she saw Gavard, who had been listening. She turned very red, and hurried away, pretending not to have recognized him. But he followed her for a moment, shrugging and muttering to himself that he wasn't at all surprised at how malicious the old bat was, seeing that she 'poisoned herself with the filth they carted off from the Tuileries'.

The very next day vague rumours began to circulate in the markets. Madame Lecœur and La Sarriette still maintained that they were sticking to their vows of secrecy. Mademoiselle Saget had been particularly clever; she had held her tongue, leaving it to the others to spread the story about Florent. At first only a few small details were hawked about in whispers; then various versions of the story began to emerge, incidents were exaggerated, and gradually a legend grew up in which Florent played the part of a bogey man. He had killed ten gendarmes at the barricade in the Rue Grenéta; he had returned to France on a pirate ship whose crew massacred every living thing on the seas; and since his arrival in Paris he had been seen at night prowling about the streets with suspicious-looking characters, of whom he was obviously the leader. From that point on the imagination of the market women knew no bounds. They spawned the most melodramatic ideas. There was talk of a band of smugglers in the heart of the city, and of a vast organization that masterminded all the thefts committed in Les Halles. Much pity was expressed for the Quenu-Gradelles, mixed with malicious allusions to Gradelle's money. The money was what obsessed them. It was generally thought that Florent had returned to claim his share. But as it was rather hard to explain why the division had not yet been made, they put forward the theory that he was waiting for an opportunity to pocket the lot. The Quenu-Gradelles were bound to be found murdered one morning; and a rumour spread that dreadful quarrels took place every night between the two brothers and La Belle Lisa.

When these stories reached the ears of La Belle Normande, she shrugged her shoulders and burst out laughing.

'Don't be silly,' she said. 'You don't know him as I do... He's as gentle as a lamb.'

She had recently refused the hand of Monsieur Lebigre, who had at last ventured to make a formal proposal. For the last two months he had been giving the Méhudins a bottle of liqueur every Sunday. Rose took the bottle round, with her usual submissive air. She was always entrusted with a compliment for La Normande, some pretty speech which she faithfully repeated, without appearing in the slightest degree embarrassed. When Monsieur Lebigre was rejected, to show that he took no offence and was still hopeful, he sent Rose the following Sunday with two bottles of champagne and a big bunch of flowers. She duly gave all this to the beautiful fishwife, reciting as she did so Monsieur Lebigre's prose madrigal:

'Monsieur Lebigre invites you to drink this to his health, which has been greatly shaken by you know what. He hopes that one day you will be willing to cure him, as you remain as pretty and as sweet as these flowers.'

La Normande was much amused by the enraptured look on Rose's face. She kissed her and talked to her about her master, who was very hard to please, or so people said. She asked her if she was fond of him, whether he wore braces and snored at night. Then she made her take back the champagne and the bunch of flowers.

'Tell Monsieur Lebigre not to send any more. You are too good, my child. It annoys me to see you being made to come here with bottles of champagne. Why don't you slap him across the face, that master of yours?'

'What? But he wants me to come,' replied Rose, as she left. 'You shouldn't upset him. He's very kind.'

La Normande had been completely won over by Florent's gentle nature. She still followed his lessons with Muche, under the lamp in the evening, dreaming that one day she would marry this man who was so good with children; she would keep her fish stall going, while he would doubtless rise to a position of high authority in the administration of Les Halles. This dream was hardly in keeping, however, with Florent's very respectful attitude towards her. He would greet her formally, keeping his distance, whereas she would have liked to laugh with him, be flirtatious, and love as she knew how to love. Florent's passive resistance was the reason why she kept toying with the idea of marriage. She imagined the boost it would give to her self-esteem. Florent, however, lived on a loftier plane. Perhaps he would have succumbed if he had not been so attached to little Muche; and also, the thought of having a mistress in that house, so close to the sister and mother, filled him with horror.

She was greatly surprised when she learnt the history of the man she loved. He had never breathed a word about these things, and she reproached him for it. But his extraordinary adventures only increased her affection for him, and, for whole evenings, she made him relate everything that had happened to him. She trembled to think that the police might discover him; but he reassured her, saying that the matter was now too old for the police to bother about. One evening he told her about the woman in the Boulevard Montmartre, the woman in the pink bonnet whose blood had run onto his hands. He still often thought about that poor creature. In his nights of anguish in Cayenne her image had often appeared before him; and he had returned to France with the mad notion of seeing her walking down the street in broad daylight, although he had never stopped feeling the weight of her body across his legs. And yet, he thought, she might perhaps have recovered. Sometimes, when he was walking in the street, he had the sudden impression that he had seen her, and his heart almost stopped; and he sometimes followed pink bonnets and shawl-draped shoulders with a wildly beating heart. When he closed his eyes, he could see her walking towards him; but she would let her shawl slip, showing the two red stains on her bodice; and then he saw her waxen face, her empty eyes, and her mouth twisted in pain. For a long time his great sorrow had been not to know her name, and being forced to see her as a mere shadow. Whenever the idea of a woman arose in his mind, it was her image that appeared before him, as the one pure, tender creature he knew. He often caught himself imagining that she was looking for him on the boulevard where she had fallen, and that she would have given him a whole lifetime of happiness if she had met him a few seconds sooner. He wanted no other woman; indeed, no other woman existed for him. His voice trembled so much when he spoke about her that La Normande, with the instinct of a woman in love, understood, and was jealous.

'Well,' she murmured unkindly, 'it's good that you won't see her again. She can't be very pretty now.'

Florent turned pale with horror at the vision these words evoked. His love was rotting in her grave. He could not forgive La Normande for this cruel remark, which from that moment made him see the grinning jaws and hollow eyes of a skeleton under the lovely pink bonnet. When La Normande tried to tease him about 'the woman he had slept with on the corner of the Rue Vivienne', he became quite angry, and shut her up immediately.

What struck La Belle Normande most in the course of these revelations was that she was wrong to think she was enticing a lover away from La Belle Lisa. This diminished her feeling of triumph so much that for a week or so her love for Florent abated. She found some consolation in the story of the inheritance. La Belle Lisa was no longer a prude, but a thief who was denying her brother-in-law what was rightfully his. Every evening now, while Muche had his handwriting lesson, the conversation turned to Gradelle's money.

'What an idea!' the fishgirl would exclaim with a laugh. 'He must have wanted to salt his money. Why else would he put it in a salting tub? Eighty-five thousand francs! That's a tidy sum! Especially when you think that the Quenus probably lied. Perhaps there was two or three times that much. If I were you, I'd insist on having my share. Straight away.'

'I don't need anything,' Florent kept saying. 'I wouldn't know what to do with the money anyway.'

At that, she would become quite angry.

'You're not much of a man, I must say. It's pitiful! Can't you see that the Quenus are making a fool of you? The fat thing even gives you her husband's old clothes. I don't want to hurt your feelings, but everybody comments on it… That old pair of trousers you've got on, everybody's seen your brother in them for the last three years. If I were you, I'd throw all that rubbish back at them and insist on my rights. It's forty-two thousand francs they owe you, isn't it? I'd insist on every cent!'

Florent tried to explain that his sister-in-law had offered to give him his share, and was keeping it on one side for him, but he simply did not want it. He went into the whole business in the minutest detail, trying to convince her of the Quenus' honesty.

'Pull the other one!' she would scoff. 'We know all about their honesty. That fat thing folds it up every morning and puts it away in her wardrobe so as not to get it dirty. Really, I feel sorry for you. It's so easy to pull the wool over your eyes. You're like a child. She'll put the money in your pocket one day, and take it out the next. As easy as that! Do you want me to go and ask for the money for you? It would be interesting to see what would happen. I'd either get the money or smash the place up—you can be sure of that!'

'But it's no business of yours,' said Florent, quite alarmed. 'We'll see. Perhaps I'll need some money soon.'

She shrugged and muttered something about him being far too weak. Her great aim now was to bring him into conflict with the Quenu-Gradelles, and she used for this purpose every means at her disposal—anger, mockery, and affection. And there was something else she dreamed of. When she had succeeded in marrying Florent, she would pay Lisa a visit and give her a good slap across the face if she refused to hand over the money. As she lay awake at night, she imagined the whole thing: walking straight into the *charcuterie*, sitting down in the middle of the shop at the busiest time of day, and making a terrible scene. She became so obsessed with this idea that she would have been prepared to marry Florent just to be able to go and lay claim to the forty-two thousand francs.

Mère Méhudin, exasperated by La Normande's rejection of Monsieur Lebigre, began to tell everybody that her daughter was mad and that 'that beanpole' must have slipped her some terrible drug. When she heard the story about Cayenne, she flew into a rage, called him a convict and a murderer. She said it was no wonder that his villainy had kept him so thin. Her versions of Florent's story were the most monstrous of all. At home she kept fairly quiet, simply grumbling and making a show of locking up the drawer where the silver was kept whenever Florent appeared. One day, however, after a quarrel with La Normande, she exclaimed:

'It can't go on like this! That dreadful man is turning you against me. Don't push me too far, or I'll go and tell the police about him, as sure as I'm standing here!'

'You'd tell the police!' echoed La Normande, clenching her fists and trembling. 'You'd better not! If you weren't my mother…'

At this, Claire, who had witnessed the quarrel, burst out laughing, with a nervous laugh that seemed to stick in her throat. For some time now she had been behaving even more oddly than ever; her eyes were often red and her face very pale.

'Well, what would you do?' she asked. 'Would you hit her? And would you hit me too, your sister? That's how it'll end up, you know. I'll certainly get him out of our house. I'll go to the police myself and save mother the trouble.'

Then, as La Normande choked with rage and stammered out threats, Claire added:

'You won't have to bother with me. I'll throw myself in the river when I come back over the bridge.'

Tears were rolling down her face. She ran into her bedroom and slammed the door. La Mère Méhudin never spoke again of denouncing Florent to the police, although Muche reported to his mother that he had seen her talking to Monsieur Lebigre several times in the neighbourhood.

The rivalry between La Belle Normande and La Belle Lisa now became more silent and disturbing in character. In the afternoons, when the pink-striped canvas awning was drawn down at the front of the *charcuterie*, the fishwife would call out that the fat woman inside was afraid and was hiding. The shop also had a window blind, which maddened her when it was down; it bore a picture of a hunting lunch-eon in a forest glade, with gentlemen in black and bare-shouldered ladies sitting on the yellow grass and eating a red pie almost as big as themselves.* Of course La Belle Lisa was not afraid. As soon as the sun went down, she raised the blind; as she sat knitting behind her counter she gazed serenely across at the concourse in front of Les Halles, where a swarm of urchins were poking about in the soil under the gratings that protected the roots of the plane trees; porters were smoking their pipes on the benches; and at either end of the foot-path was a billposting pillar covered with theatre posters, alternately green, yellow, red, and blue, like a harlequin's costume. While pre-tending to be interested in the traffic, Lisa kept a constant eye on La Belle Normande. Sometimes she would lean forward as if following, right up to the stop at the Pointe Saint-Eustache, the bus which ran between the Bastille and the Place Wagram; but this was only to get a better view of the fishwife, who, to avenge the business of the blind, covered her head and her fish with large sheets of brown paper, on the pretext of warding off the rays of the setting sun. At present La Belle Lisa had the upper hand. She remained very calm as the day of reckoning drew near, whereas her rival, despite her attempt to appear similarly detached, invariably lapsed into some crude insult, which she immediately regretted. La Normande's ambition was always to appear 'ladylike'. Nothing irritated her more than to hear people extolling the good manners of her rival. Mère Méhudin had noticed this weak spot, and now she used it to attack her daughter.

'I saw Madame Quenu standing outside her shop this afternoon,' she would sometimes say. 'It's amazing how young she looks. And she's so refined, a real lady. It's the counter that does it, that's what keeps her up to the mark and makes her so concerned about her appearance.'

In this remark there was a veiled allusion to Monsieur Lebigre's proposal. La Belle Normande would say nothing, but sat for a moment lost in thought. She pictured herself at the other end of the

Rue Pirouette, behind the counter, forming a pendant, as it were, to La Belle Lisa. This was the first wavering in her affection for Florent.

The truth was that Florent was becoming very hard to defend. The whole neighbourhood was up in arms against him. Everyone seemed to have a special reason for wanting to destroy him. Some swore that he was in the pay of the police, while others claimed to have seen him in the butter cellars, trying to make holes in the wire netting, so that he could throw lighted matches into the storerooms. The slander increased, turning into a flood of abuse, the source of which no one really knew. The fish market was the last to rise up in revolt. The fishwives liked Florent for his gentleness, and for a while they defended him; but, under the influence of the women in the butter and fruit markets, they finally gave in. Then the battle began again: the thin figure of Florent on one side, the huge breasts and bellies of the women on the other. Once more he became lost in swirling skirts, beset by bursting bodices. But he noticed nothing, and carried on regardless with his plan.

At every hour of the day, and in every corner of the market, Mademoiselle Saget's black hat could be seen bobbing about in the midst of all this activity. Her pale little face seemed everywhere. She had sworn revenge on the company which met in Monsieur Lebigre's back room. She blamed them for spreading the story of how she lived on scraps. The fact of the matter was that one evening Gavard had told them how the 'old nanny goat' who came to spy on them fed herself on the filth tossed away by that Bonapartist clique. Clémence felt sick when she heard this, while Robine gulped down a mouthful of beer, as if to rinse his throat. Gavard, however, repeated his witticism:

'Stuff the Tuileries have belched on...'

He pulled a hideous face as he pronounced these words. To him the pieces of meat scraped off the Emperor's plate were so much political ordure, vile left-overs from all the foul deeds of the regime. It was thus that, at Monsieur Lebigre's, Mademoiselle Saget came to be regarded with the utmost distaste. She was looked upon as some kind of unclean animal that battened upon corruption. Clémence and Gavard hawked the story round the markets so efficiently that the old woman's relations with the shopkeepers were seriously affected; when she haggled over prices and gossiped away without buying anything, they told her curtly to go off to the scrap stalls. This cut down her supply of information, and on some days she did not have the faintest idea what was happening. She wept with frustration, and in one moment of anger she said point-blank to La Sarriette and Madame Lecœur:

'You've pushed me far enough. I'll see to your Gavard now!'

The two women were rather taken aback, but did not protest. The next day, however, Mademoiselle Saget had calmed down, and once more she expressed her sympathy for that poor Monsieur Gavard who was so ill advised and was positively rushing to his doom.

Gavard was certainly compromising himself. Ever since the conspiracy had begun to take shape, he had been carrying about in his pocket the revolver that had so alarmed Madame Léonce. It was a big, impressive-looking weapon, which he had bought at the best gunmaker in Paris, veiling the whole transaction in the deepest mystery. He showed it to all the ladies in the poultry market, just like a schoolboy who keeps a forbidden novel in his desk. He let the gun stick out of his pocket, and drew attention to it with a wink. Then he affected a mysterious reticence, indulged in vague hints and insinuations— played, in short, the part of a man revelling in feigning fear. The revolver made him feel very important, placed him definitely among the most dangerous men in Paris. Sometimes, when he was safe inside his stall, he would consent to take it out of his pocket altogether and show it to two or three women. He asked the women to stand in front of him so that they would, as he said, hide him with their skirts. Then he cocked it, played around with it, and took aim at a goose or a turkey hanging on display. The women's fright delighted him; in the end he always reassured them by telling them it was not loaded. But he carried a supply of cartridges about with him, in a box which he opened with the most elaborate precautions. When they had handled the cartridges, he at last decided to put away his arsenal. Then, with arms folded, he would chatter away jubilantly for hours.

'A man's a man when he's got a weapon like that,' he would say in the most swaggering way. 'I couldn't care less about the police now. On Sunday I went with a friend to try it out on the Plaine Saint-Denis. Of course, it doesn't do to tell everybody you've got one of these playthings. But, lo and behold, we shot at a tree, and I hit it every time! You'll see, you'll see. It won't be long before you hear a lot more about Anatole.'

Anatole was the name he had bestowed on the revolver. Within a week everyone in the market knew about the weapon and the cartridges.

His friendship with Florent, however, seemed suspicious. He was too rich and too fat to attract the hatred that was directed at Florent, but he lost the respect of the shrewdest among them and succeeded in frightening the timid ones. This pleased him immensely.

'It's not wise to carry firearms about,' said Mademoiselle Saget. 'It'll get him into trouble in the end.'

At Monsieur Lebigre's, Gavard was in his element. Since he had stopped eating with the Quenus, Florent virtually lived in the little back room. He lunched and dined there, and constantly shut himself away there. He had almost turned it into a room of his own, a study where he left his old coats and books and papers lying about. Monsieur Lebigre offered no objection; he had even removed one of the tables to make room for a kind of wall-sofa, which Florent could use, if the need arose, to sleep on. Whenever Florent expressed any qualms about taking advantage of Monsieur Lebigre's kindness, the landlord told him not to worry and said the place was entirely at his disposal. Similarly, Logre was extremely friendly towards him. He had appointed himself his 'lieutenant', and would talk to him constantly about 'the affair', keeping him informed of his actions and giving him the names of new members. He had assumed responsibility for organising things; it was his task to bring the various plotters together, forming the different sections, and weaving each mesh of the huge net into which Paris was to fall once the signal was given. Florent, however, remained the leader, the moving spirit behind it all. Much as the hunchback appeared to toil, however, he achieved no appreciable result. Although he had sworn that he knew two or three groups of staunch supporters in every district, similar to the group that gathered at Monsieur Lebigre's, he had so far failed to pass on any precise information about them; he had merely mentioned a few names and spoken of secret expeditions and the wonderful enthusiasm for the cause of the people he had met. He made a big point of the handshakes he received. So-and-so, whom he knew very well indeed, had pumped his hand and said he could be counted on. At the Gros-Caillou, a tall chap who would make an excellent section leader had almost dislocated his arm in his enthusiasm. In the Rue Popincourt a whole group of working men had embraced him. It sounded as if a hundred thousand men could be raised overnight. When he arrived, looking exhausted and dropping onto the bench in the little room, he would launch into fresh variations on his usual reports, while Florent took notes and said that he was relying on him to bring it all to fruition. Soon, in Florent's pocket, the plot came to life. The notes became realities, the ideas indisputable; and since it was on these notes and ideas that the entire plan was constructed, it was now simply a question of waiting for the right moment. Logre, with his impassioned gestures, declared that it would all go like clockwork.

Florent was extremely happy. He was walking on air, as though borne aloft by his burning desire to dispense justice. He had the credulity of a child and the confidence of a hero. He would not have been surprised if Logre had told him that the figure of Liberty on the Colonne de Juillet* had come down from his pedestal to march at their head. In the evenings, at Monsieur Lebigre's, his eloquence was infinite; he spoke of the imminent battle as of a celebration to which all right-thinking people would be invited. But at this, although Gavard was enraptured and began to play with his revolver, Charvet became more snappish than ever and sneered and shrugged his shoulders. His rival's assumption of the group's leadership had annoyed him beyond measure, and had destroyed his interest in politics. One evening, when he had arrived early and found himself alone with Logre and Lebigre, he took the opportunity to unburden himself.

'He's just a boy,' he said. 'He hasn't got the faintest idea about politics. He would have done better to get a job teaching composition in a girl's school. It would be a tragedy if he succeeded, because, with his sentimentality, we'd have all those blasted workmen on our hands. That'll be his downfall. We don't need any more snivelling humanitarian poets,* people who throw their arms round each other at the slightest scratch. But he won't succeed! He'll get himself locked up, that's all.'

Logre and the wine merchant did not react. They let Charvet have his say.

'And he'd have been locked up long ago', he continued, 'if he was anything like as dangerous as he wants to make out. The airs he puts on just because he's been to Cayenne! It makes you sick. But I'm sure the police knew he was here the moment he arrived. They left him alone because they couldn't care less.'

At this Logre gave a slight start.

'They've been keeping tabs on me for the last fifteen years,' he went on, with a measure of pride. 'But I don't go shouting it from the rooftops… I for one won't get mixed up in this riot he's organizing.

I'm not going to let myself get nabbed like a fool. I dare say he's got half a dozen spies at his heels, just waiting to grab him as soon as they're given the word.'

'Oh dear, no! What an idea!' said Monsieur Lebigre, who usually never said a word. He was a little pale, and looked at Logre, who was gently rubbing his hump against the partition.

'They're just conjectures,' murmured the hunchback.

'Conjectures if you like,' replied the teacher. 'But I know how these things work. Whatever happens, I'm not going to let myself be caught by the police. You can do what you like, but if you want my advice—especially you, Monsieur Lebigre—I wouldn't put your business at risk. They'd make you close it down.'

At this Logre could not suppress a smile. Several times Charvet spoke to them in this vein, as if he wanted to prize them away from Florent by putting the fear of God into them. He was greatly surprised by the calmness and confidence they continued to show. But he still came quite regularly in the evenings with Clémence. She no longer worked as a clerk in the fish market—Monsieur Manoury had dismissed her.

'Those agents are all crooks,' growled Logre when he heard of the dismissal.

Clémence, lolling back against the partition and rolling a cigarette between her long, slender fingers, responded sharply:

'Well, it's fair enough. We don't have the same political views, you see. Manoury is making loads of money. He'd lick the Emperor's boots if he had to. If I were an auctioneer, I wouldn't keep him on my staff for a minute.'

The truth was that her weird sense of humour had got her into trouble. One day she had amused herself by writing up on the sales boards, next to the dabs and skate and mackerel to be sold in the auction, the names of the most prominent ladies and gentlemen of the Court. The piscine names given to high dignitaries, the offer of countesses and barons for sale at thirty sous apiece, had shocked Monsieur Manoury. Gavard was still laughing about it.

'Never mind,' he would say, patting Clémence on the arm. 'You're a real man, you are!'

Clémence had discovered a new method of mixing her grog. First she filled the glass with hot water; then, after adding some sugar, she poured the rum drop by drop onto the slice of lemon floating there, in a way that avoided mixing the rum with the water; then she lit it with a match and watched it burn, as she slowly smoked her cigarette, her face green in the leaping flames of the alcohol. Grog, however, was an expensive luxury, which she had to give up after she lost her job. Charvet would say to her, with a supercilious laugh, that she wasn't rich any more. She supported herself by giving French lessons, at a very early hour of the morning, to a young woman who lived at the top of the Rue Miromesnil, who was improving her education in such secrecy that even her maid did not know about it. Thus, all Clémence ordered in the evening was a glass of beer, which she drank, moreover, most philosophically.

The evenings in the little back room were now far less noisy than they had been. Charvet would suddenly lapse into silence, pale with suppressed anger when the others ignored him to listen to his rival. The thought that he had once reigned supreme and, before Florent's arrival, had exercised despotic power over the group, gnawed at his heart, making him feel like a dethroned monarch. If he continued to come, it was because he felt strangely attached to the little room, in which he remembered so many happy hours lording it over Gavard and Robine. In those days, even Logre's hump had been his property, along with Alexandre's brawny arms and Lacaille's gloomy face. He had done what he liked with them, stuffed his opinions down their throats, broken his sceptre over their backs. But now he was too embittered; he had stopped talking, simply shrugging his shoulders and whistling disdainfully, not deigning to respond to the absurdities pronounced in his presence. What hurt him most was the gradual way in which he had been ousted from his position of dominance, so gradual that he had not noticed. He could not see that Florent was in any way his superior. After listening to him speak for hours, in his gentle, melancholic voice, he would say:

'The boy's really a priest! All he needs is a skull-cap!'

The others seemed to lap up everything Florent said. When Charvet saw Florent's clothes hanging from every peg, he pretended not to know where he could put his hat to prevent it from getting dirty. He pushed back the papers that lay about and said that they could no longer feel at home now that 'the gentleman' had taken the place over. He even complained to Monsieur Lebigre, asking him if the room belonged to one customer alone or to the group. This invasion of his realm was the last straw. Men were mere brutes. He held humanity in contempt when he saw Logre and Lebigre hanging on Florent's every word. Gavard irritated him with his revolver. Robine, who sat silently behind his glass of beer, seemed to him the only sensible person in the group, and one who judged people on their merits and was not blinded by empty rhetoric. As for Alexandre and Lacaille, they confirmed him in his view that 'the people' are stupid and require ten years of revolutionary dictatorship to learn how to behave.

Meanwhile, Logre declared that the sections would soon be organized. Florent began to assign responsibilities. Then one evening, after a discussion in which he again came off worst, Charvet got up, grabbed his hat, and said:

'A very good night to everyone. You can get your heads beaten in if you want... But not me! I've never been in the business of furthering one person's ambition!'

Clémence, who had also stood up and was putting on her shawl, added simply:

'The plan's absurd.'

Then, as Robine watched them about to leave, Charvet turned and asked if he was coming with them. But Robine, who had not quite finished his beer, thought it enough to stretch out his hand to be shaken. Charvet and Clémence never went back. Lacaille told the group one day that they now frequented a beer house in the Rue Serpente. He had seen them through the window, surrounded by a group of young people, gesticulating fiercely.

Florent was never able to enlist Claude among his supporters. At one time he had entertained the idea of making him a disciple, an assistant in his revolutionary task; and to initiate him he had taken him one evening to Monsieur Lebigre's. Claude, however, spent the whole evening making a sketch of Robine, with his hat and brown coat, and his beard resting on the handle of his stick.

'Really, you know,' he said to Florent as they came away, 'all that stuff you were saying in there doesn't interest me in the least. It's all very fine, I'm sure, but it's not for me. But that man in there, Robine, he's absolutely fascinating. I'll come back, but not for the politics. I'll do a sketch of Logre and one of Gavard, and put them with Robine in a wonderful picture I was thinking about while you were discussing—what was it?—the problem of the Two Chambers. I can just see it, Gavard, Logre, and Robine talking politics, with their glasses of beer in front of them! It would be the success of the Salon, a huge success, a truly modern painting!'

Florent was upset by the artist's scepticism about politics; so he asked him up to his room and kept him talking on the little balcony, opposite the great blue mass of the markets, until two in the morning, lecturing him and telling him that he wasn't a man unless he showed an interest in the well-being of his country.

'You may be right,' replied Claude. 'I'm selfish. I can't even say I paint for my country, for one reason because my sketches horrify everybody who looks at them, and for another because, when I paint, it's for my own pleasure. When I'm painting, it's as if I were tickling myself; it makes my whole body feel good… I can't help it, that's just the way I am. Anyway, as my Aunt Lisa says, France doesn't need me. And—can I be frank?—the reason why I like you is because you're devoted to politics in the same way that I'm devoted to painting. You titillate yourself, just like me.'

Florent protested, but Claude went on:

'Yes, yes. You're an artist in your own way. You dream about politics. I bet you spend whole evenings here, gazing at the stars, imagining that they are the ballot papers of infinity. You titillate yourself with your ideas about truth and justice. It's obvious. Your ideas, like my paintings, frighten bourgeois people. Between you and me, do you think that if you were Robine I'd enjoy being your friend? You're a poet!'

Then he began to joke about it, saying that politics did not bother him at all and he had got used to hearing politics being talked about in beer shops and artists' studios. He mentioned a café in the Rue Vauvilliers, on the ground floor of the building where La Sarriette lived. This smoky place, with its benches upholstered in frayed plush and marble tables yellowed by the smudges of coffee laced with brandy, was where the young people of Les Halles usually gathered. Monsieur Jules lorded it over gangs of porters, shop assistants, and men in white smocks* and velvet caps. His side-whiskers grew in two little locks glued to his cheeks like kiss-curls. Every Saturday he had his hair tidied up with a razor at a barber's in the Rue des Deux-Écus, where he had credit by the month. At the café it was he who set the tone, especially when he played billiards—with studied grace, half lying across the green baize in order to show off his figure. When the game was over, they would sit round and chat. They were very reactionary and took great interest in the doings of 'society'. Jules read the fashionable newspapers. He knew the performers at the smaller theatres, seemed on first name terms with celebrities, and always knew whether a play which had just had its first night was a success or a failure. He also had a weakness for politics. His hero was Morny,* as he simply called him. He read about the sessions at the Corps Législatif and laughed with delight at the slightest words that fell from Morny's lips. Morny could easily handle those dreadful republicans! And he would go on to say that only the scum of the earth detested the Emperor, for His Majesty wished for the happiness of all decent people.

'I call in at that café sometimes,' said Claude to Florent. 'They're very funny, that lot, with their pipes, discussing Court balls as if they'd been invited. La Sarriette's young man was making great fun of Gavard the other night. He calls him Uncle. When La Sarriette came downstairs to fetch him, she had to pay his bill. It came to about six francs, because he had lost a lot of drinks playing billiards... She's a fine girl, La Sarriette, isn't she?'

'You have a good time,' murmured Florent, smiling. 'Cadine, La Sarriette, and all the others, eh?'

The painter shrugged his shoulders.

'No, you're quite wrong,' he replied. 'I'm not interested in women, they disturb me too much. I wouldn't know what to do with one; I've never tried... Goodnight, sleep well. If ever you become a minister, I'll give you a few ideas for beautifying Paris.'

Florent was obliged to give up his plan of making a disciple out of Claude. This saddened him, for, blinded though he was by his fanaticism, he was becoming aware of the ever-increasing hostility around him. Even at the Méhudins he found his welcome less warm. The old woman would snigger at him; Muche no longer obeyed him; La Belle Normande cast impatient glances at him when he failed to respond in any way when she moved her chair closer to his. She told him once that he seemed cross with her, and when he only replied with an embarrassed smile she got up and went to sit on the other side of the table. At the Quenus' too he had lost the friendship of Auguste. The assistant no longer called in on his way up to bed. He was alarmed by the rumours going around about this man, with whom he had dared to spend so much time late at night. Augustine had made him swear never again to be so imprudent. But it was Lisa who turned him into Florent's sworn enemy by asking him and Augustine to defer their marriage until Florent had vacated his room; she wanted to avoid putting the new assistant in the little closet on the first floor. From that moment Auguste longed for the 'convict' to be taken away. He had found the *charcuterie* of his dreams, not at Plaisance, but a little further away, at Montrouge. Trade was much improved, and Augustine, with her silly, girlish laugh, said she was ready. So every night, whenever some slight noise woke him up, Auguste felt a surge of delight, as he imagined for a moment that the police had come to arrest Florent.

No mention was made in the *charcuterie* of the rumours that were circulating. There was a tacit understanding among the staff that they would say nothing in front of Quenu. Quenu, saddened by the quarrel between his brother and his wife, sought solace in stringing his sausages and salting his pork. Sometimes he would go and stand at the door of the shop, his red face shining brightly above his white apron, stretched tight over his bulging stomach; but not for a moment did he suspect the sudden surge of gossip that his appearance caused in Les Halles. Some of the women felt sorry for him, and, even though he was enormous, thought that he might have lost some weight; others blamed him for not having grown thin with shame at having a brother like Florent. He, like a deceived husband who is always the last to hear of his misfortune, lived in happy ignorance and excellent spirits as he stopped some neighbour on the footpath to ask her how she had liked his brawn or his truffled boar's head. The neighbour would assume a rather pained expression and seemed, in her reply, to be offering him her sympathy, as if all the pork on his premises had become infected.

'What's the matter with all those women?' he asked Lisa one day. 'Why do they behave as if they were at a funeral? Do I look ill?'

She reassured him and said he looked as fresh as a rose; for he had a terrible fear of illness, groaning and making a tremendous fuss whenever he had the slightest ailment. But it was a fact that the *charcuterie* was becoming a very gloomy place; the mirrors seemed pale, the marble was as white as ice, and the cooked meats on the counter stagnated in their yellow fat or in dark pools of jelly. One day, even, Claude came into the shop to tell his aunt that the window display looked 'sad'. It was true. The tongues, on their bed of blue paper shavings, had the whitish appearance of sick people; and the once chubby hams seemed to be wasting away, and their green pompons looked quite mournful. Moreover, in the shop itself, a customer never asked for a piece of black pudding, ten sous' worth of bacon, or half a pound of lard, without lowering her voice as though in the presence of someone at death's door. There were always two or three mournful-looking female customers in front of the warming oven, which had grown cold. La Belle Lisa discharged the duties of chief mourner with silent dignity. Her white apron fell more primly than ever over her black dress. Her hands, scrubbed clean and gripped at the wrists by long sleeves, and her face, with its appropriate expression of sorrow, plainly told the neighbourhood, and all the gossips who passed through the shop from morning to night, that they were the victims of an undeserved misfortune, but that she knew the cause of it and would soon regain the upper hand. Sometimes she would bend down to look at the two goldfish, who also seemed ill at ease as they swam listlessly round the tank in the window, and her look seemed to promise them better days.

La Belle Lisa now allowed herself only one pleasure. She could stroke Marjolin under his satin chin with perfect impunity. He had just come out of hospital. His skull had healed, and he was as fat and jolly as ever, but even more stupid than before, in fact an idiot. The crack in his skull must have affected his brain, for he was now a mere animal. He had the mind of a five-year-old and the body of Hercules. He laughed and lisped, failed altogether to pronounce certain words, and was as docile as a lamb. Cadine took entire possession of him again. Surprised, at first, at the alteration in him, and then delighted at this superb beast with whom she could do as she liked; she would bed him down in the feather baskets, take him out to gambol and play in the streets, use him according to her whims, treating him as a dog or a puppet or a lover. He belonged to her like a piece of fine food, something nice taken from Les Halles, a body she used as she wanted to give her pleasure. But although she squeezed everything out of him and kept him following at her heels like some submissive giant, she could not prevent him returning to Madame Quenu's. She would thump him, but he never seemed to notice. As soon as she had slung her tray round her neck and was off down the Rue du Pont-Neuf or the Rue de Turbigo with her violets, he went to prowl about in front of the *charcuterie*.

'Come in!' Lisa would shout.

Usually she gave him some gherkins, which he loved. He would eat them, laughing like a child, as he stood in front of the counter. The sight of this beautiful woman made him clap his hands in joy.

Then he would skip about the shop uttering little cries, like a child looking at something nice. At first she had been afraid that he would remember.

'Does your head still hurt?' she asked.

He said that it didn't, dancing about and laughing merrily. Then she asked:

'What happened? Did you fall?'

'Yes, I fell, fell, fell,' he sang, tapping his skull.

Then, as if he were in a kind of ecstasy, he repeated more and more slowly, as he gazed at her: 'Beautiful, beautiful, beautiful!' This quite touched Lisa. She had prevailed upon Gavard to keep him in his service. When he sang his little song of adoration, she stroked him under his chin, telling him he was a good lad. He closed his eyes in satisfaction, like a pet being fondled. In order to make excuses to herself for the very decent pleasure she took in him, Lisa told herself that she was making up for the blow with which she had felled him in the cellars.

The *charcuterie*, however, remained under a cloud. Florent sometimes ventured in to see his brother, while Lisa looked on in glacial silence. Occasionally he would even dine there on a Sunday night; Quenu would make great efforts at gaiety, but never succeeded in bringing any warmth to the meal. He ate badly and became irritable. One evening, after one of these family dinners, he said to his wife, almost in tears:

'What can be the matter with me? Is it true that I'm not ill? Have I changed? I feel as if I've got a heavy weight pressing down on me. And I feel unhappy, too, without knowing why... Can you tell me why?'

'Just a bad mood, I dare say,' replied Lisa.

'No, no, it's been going on too long for that. It's really getting me down. The business isn't doing badly, I've got nothing to be upset about, and I'm carrying on as usual... But you, too, my dear, you don't seem well, you seem miserable the whole time... If it goes on like this, I'll have to call the doctor.'

Lisa looked at him gravely.

'There's no need for a doctor,' she said. 'It'll pass. There's an ill wind at the moment. Everybody in the neighbourhood is sick.'

Then, as if giving in to a feeling of maternal concern, she added:

'Don't worry, my dear. We can't let you fall ill. That wouldn't do at all.'

Usually she sent him back to the kitchen, knowing that the sound of the choppers, the fizzing of the fat, and the clattering of the saucepans had a cheering effect on him. She also now avoided the indiscretions of Mademoiselle Saget, who had taken to spending whole mornings in the *charcuterie*. The old woman seemed bent on giving Lisa a shock and forcing her at last to take decisive action. She began by worming her way into her confidence.

'There really are a lot of nasty people about,' she said. 'People who would do far better to mind their own business. If only you knew, Madame Quenu—but no, really, I shouldn't tell you...'

As Lisa declared that she was quite above gossip, which had no effect on her at all, Mademoiselle Saget leaned across the table and whispered:

'Well, they say that Monsieur Florent isn't your cousin at all...'

Little by little she revealed that she knew the whole story, thus showing that she had Lisa at her mercy. When Lisa confessed the truth, also for tactical reasons, simply to have someone who would keep her up to date with the gossip, the old woman swore that she would be as quiet as a mouse about it and would deny everything, even if her head was on the block. She then began to take intense delight in this drama. Every day she arrived with some fresh piece of disturbing news.

'You must be careful,' she murmured. 'I heard two women in the tripe market today talking about you know what. I can't interrupt people and tell them they're telling lies, can I? But the story has got around, and it's spreading. It can't be stopped now. The truth will have to come out.'

A few days later she returned to the attack. She arrived looking very flustered and waited impatiently until there was no one in the shop. Then she hissed:

'Do you know what they're saying now? Those men who meet at Monsieur Lebigre's, well, they've all got guns and are just biding their time until they can start another revolution as they did in '48. It's such a shame to see a man like Monsieur Gavard, so rich and respectable, getting mixed up with that lot! I wanted to let you know, because of your brother-in-law.'

'It's all nonsense, surely,' said Lisa, to urge her on.

'Nonsense! Well, if you walk down the Rue Pirouette in the evening, you can hear them shouting in the most dreadful way. They don't hold back, I can tell you. You know how they tried to rope your husband in? And the bullets I can see them making from my window, are they nonsense? I'm only telling you this for your own good!'

'Oh, I know, thank you. But so many things are made up.'

'Yes, but this isn't made up, I'm afraid. The whole neighbourhood is talking about it. They say that if the police find out, a lot of people will be in trouble—Monsieur Gavard, for example.'

Lisa shrugged as if to say that Gavard was an old fool and it would serve him right.

'I'm just taking Monsieur Gavard as an example. I might just as well take your brother-in-law,' the old woman slyly continued. 'Your brother-in-law seems to be the leader, in fact... That's extremely embarrassing for you, and I feel very sorry for you, because if the police came here they might take Monsieur Quenu as well. Two brothers are like two fingers on the same hand.'

La Belle Lisa said she did not agree, but she turned very pale, for Mademoiselle Saget had touched a sensitive spot. From that day on the old woman brought endless stories of innocent people who had been thrown into prison for harbouring criminals. In the evening, after she went to fetch her blackcurrant liqueur from the wine merchant's, she prepared a little dossier of information for use the following morning. Rose, however, was not very forthcoming. The old woman had to rely on her own eyes and ears. She had been struck by Monsieur Lebigre's friendliness towards Florent, the care he took to retain his custom, the courtesies which were so inadequately rewarded by the money the young man spent in the bar. She was all the more surprised by Lebigre's behaviour because she was well aware of the situation between the two men with regard to La Normande.

'Anyone would think', she thought, 'that he's fattening him up for sale. Whom does he want to sell him to, I wonder?'

One evening, when she was in the bar, she saw Logre throw himself down on the bench in the back room and heard him start talking about his journeys through the working-class districts, which had left him dead beat. She glanced at his feet and saw that there was not a speck of dust on his boots. She smiled to herself and went off with her blackcurrant liqueur.

Then, sitting at her window, she would complete her report. The window was very high up, commanding a view of all the neighbouring houses, and it gave her endless pleasure. At all hours of the day she would install herself there, as though it were an observatory from which she kept watch on everything that went on below her. She was familiar with all the rooms opposite, both on the right and left, down to the smallest items of furniture; she could have given an account, without omitting a single detail, of the habits of the tenants, whether their households were happy or not, how they washed their faces, what they had for dinner, and even who came to call on them. She also had a view across Les Halles, which meant that there was not a woman in the neighbourhood who could walk across the Rue Rambuteau without being seen by her; she could say for certain, without ever making a mistake, where the woman came from, where she was going, what she had in her basket, in short everything about her, her husband, her clothes, her children, and her means. 'That's Madame Loret, over there, she's giving her son a fine education; there's poor Madame Hutin, so neglected by her husband; and that's Mademoiselle Cécile, the butcher's daughter, whom no one will marry because she's so moody.' She could have continued like this for days, rehearsing endless bits of biographical information, keeping herself entertained with absolute trivia. But, from eight o'clock onwards, she had eyes only for the frosted glass window, on which she could see the shadows of those gathered in the little back room. She guessed that Charvet and Clémence had broken with the group, when she noticed that their shadows no longer appeared on the window. Not an incident occurred in that room without her guessing it eventually by some sudden movement of arms and heads. She became a highly skilled interpreter, able to divine the meaning of elongated noses, parted fingers, gaping mouths, and shrugging shoulders, and thus was able to follow the progress of the conspiracy step by step, in such a way that she could tell day by day how matters stood. One evening the terrible outcome of it all was revealed to her. She saw the shadow of Gavard's revolver, a huge silhouette with pointed muzzle outlined in black against the glimmer of the window. It kept appearing and disappearing so rapidly that it seemed as though the room was full of revolvers. These were the firearms of which Mademoiselle Saget had spoken to Madame Quenu. Then, on another evening, she was very puzzled when she thought she saw endless lengths of material being measured out, and came to the conclusion that the men were making cartridges. The following morning she went into the bar on the pretext of asking Rose if she could lend her a candle, and, glancing furtively into the little room, she spotted a heap of red material lying on the table. This greatly alarmed her, and her manner was extremely grave when she made her report the following day.

'I don't want to frighten you, Madame Quenu,' she said, 'but it's looking very serious. I'm really afraid. You must swear not to tell a soul what I'm going to tell you. They'd cut my throat if they knew.'

When Lisa had sworn that she would not tell a soul, she told her about the red material.

'I can't think what it can be for. There was a big pile of it. It looked like rags dipped in blood. Logre—you know, the hunchback— went off with some of it over his shoulder. He looked like a hangman. Something's brewing, for sure.'

Lisa made no reply, but seemed deep in thought as she played with a fork and arranged slices of *petit salé* on a tray.

'If I were you,' Mademoiselle Saget continued, 'I'd take it very seriously, I'd want an explanation… Why don't you go upstairs and have a look in your brother-in-law's room?'

At this Lisa gave a start. She put the fork down and looked at the old woman, who went on:

'After all, it would be fully justified. There's no knowing what trouble your brother-in-law might get you into, if you let him. We were talking about you yesterday at Madame Taboureau's. You've really got a good friend in her. She said you were much too easygoing, and that if she were in your shoes she would have put an end to it all long ago.'

'Is that what she said?' Lisa murmured thoughtfully.

'She did indeed, and Madame Taboureau is a woman worth listening to. You should try to find out what all that red material is. I'd really like to know.'

But Lisa was no longer listening. She was gazing at the snails and the Gervais cheeses between the strings of sausages in the window. She seemed lost in an inner struggle, which brought two little furrows to her brow. The old woman, in the meantime, was sniffing at the dishes on the counter. As if talking to herself, she murmured:

'Ooh, some sliced *saucisson*… It must get very dry, when it's been cut up for a long time. And that black pudding has burst. It's been stuck through with a fork. It shouldn't be there, it's making a mess of the dish.'

Still looking very distracted, Lisa gave her the black pudding and the *saucisson*, saying:

'That's for you, if you like.'

It all disappeared into the shopping bag. Mademoiselle Saget was so used to being given things that she no longer offered thanks. Every morning she took away all the scraps from the *charcuterie*. Now she went off with the aim of collecting her dessert from La Sarriette and Madame Lecœur, in exchange for a few titbits of gossip about Gavard.

When at last she was alone, Lisa sat down on the bench behind the counter, as if she thought that she would be able to come to a better decision if she were comfortably seated. For a whole week now she had been very anxious. One evening Florent had asked Quenu, quite casually, for five hundred francs. Quenu referred him to his wife. This displeased Florent, and he felt rather uneasy as he put his request to La Belle Lisa. But she went straight up to her room and returned with the money, which she gave him without a word. She simply remarked that she had made a note of the payment on the inheritance account. Three days later he took a thousand francs.

'I don't know why he bothered to make himself out to be so disinterested,' Lisa said to Quenu when they were going to bed. 'I was right to keep those accounts. I must write down today's thousand francs.'

She sat down at the desk and read over the page of figures. Then she added:

'And I was right to leave some extra space. I'll put the withdrawals in the margin… He'll fritter it all away in dribs and drabs… I've been expecting this to happen.'

Quenu said nothing, but climbed into bed feeling very disgruntled. Every time his wife opened the desk, the flap gave a sad little squeak which made him feel quite depressed. He even thought of taking his brother to task, to prevent him from ruining himself with the Méhudins; but when the opportunity arose, he drew back. Two days later Florent asked for another fifteen hundred francs. One evening Logre had expressed the view that, if they could only find some money, things would move much faster. The next day he was delighted to find his comment, made quite casually, result in his being handed a little pile of gold, which he pocketed with a snigger, his hump heaving with pleasure. From that moment onwards, there was a constant flow of requests for money: one section wanted to hire a meeting room, while another felt compelled to provide for various patriots in need; then there were arms and ammunition to be purchased, men to be enlisted, and private police expenses. Florent would have paid for anything.

He remembered the inheritance and La Normande's advice. So he went to the source in Lisa's desk, restrained only by his vague fear of her forbidding face. Never, as it seemed to him, could he spend his money in a holier cause. Logre, bubbling with enthusiasm, began to sport amazing pink neckties and patent leather boots, the sight of which made Lacaille glower darkly.

'That makes three thousand francs in seven days,' Lisa remarked to Quenu. 'What do you think of that? Pretty good, isn't it? If he carries on at that rate, his fifty thousand won't last more than four months... So much for old Gradelle, who took forty years to accumulate his money!'

'It's your fault!' cried Quenu. 'You didn't have to tell him about the money!'

She looked at him severely and said:

'It's his money, he can take it all. It isn't giving it to him that upsets me; it's knowing that he's probably making bad use of it. I've been telling you long enough. It's time it stopped.'

'Do whatever you want; I won't try to stop you,' Quenu finally declared, tortured though he was by his avarice.

He still loved his brother, but the thought of fifty thousand francs frittered away in four months was something he could not bear. Lisa, after listening to Mademoiselle Saget, guessed where the money was going. As the old woman had ventured to refer to the inheritance, Lisa took advantage of this opportunity to let it be known in the neighbourhood that Florent was taking his share and disposing of it as he wanted. The following day the story of the strips of red material impelled her to take action. She stood in the shop for a little while, still struggling with herself, looking round at the dismal appearance of the place: the sides of pork hung sulkily from their hooks; Mouton, sitting near a jar of dripping, had the ruffled coat and dull eyes of a cat no longer able to digest his food in peace. Then she called Augustine to look after the counter and went upstairs to Florent's room.

When she entered, she got quite a shock. The bed was covered in red sashes that trailed down to the floor. On the mantelpiece, between the gilded boxes and the old pots of face cream, were several red armbands and bundles of rosettes. They looked like big pools of blood. Hanging from every nail and hook stuck in the faded grey wallpaper were pieces of bunting, and flags, in squares of yellow, blue, green, and black, which Lisa recognized as the colours of the twenty sections.

The childish simplicity of the room stood in sharp contrast to all this revolutionary decoration. The sense of guileless stupidity left behind by the shop assistant, the white innocence of the curtains and furniture, seemed to have caught the reflections of a fire; the photograph of Auguste and Augustine looked white with terror. Lisa walked round the room, examining the flags, the armbands, and the sashes, but did not touch any of them, as though afraid that the dreadful things might burn her. She told herself that she had not been mistaken to think that it was on these and similar things that Florent had been spending his money. To her it was an abomination, something she could hardly believe, and which repelled her completely. Her money, the money she had earned so honestly, was being used to organize and finance an insurrection! She stood gazing at the open flowers of the pomegranate on the balcony—which seemed to her like another set of crimson rosettes—and listening to the shrill notes of the chaffinch, which sounded in her ears like the distant echo of gunfire. Then the idea occurred to her that the insurrection was planned to begin the next day, perhaps even that very evening. Suddenly she saw the banners unfurled and the sashes marching in line, and heard a sudden roll of drums. She hurried downstairs, without even glancing at the papers spread out on the table. She stopped on the first floor and went to dress.

At this grave hour La Belle Lisa arranged her hair most carefully and with a steady hand. She was firm in her resolve, there was not a quiver in her face, only a sterner expression than usual in her eyes. As she fastened her black silk dress, stretching the material with all the strength in her fingers, she remembered what Father Roustan had said. Her conscience told her that she was about to do her duty. Drawing her thick shawl round her broad shoulders, she felt that she was about to perform an act of the greatest integrity. She put on a pair of dark purple gloves, and attached a thick veil to her hat. Before leaving, she double-locked the desk, with a hopeful expression on her face, as if to say that that poor piece of furniture would at last be left in peace.

Quenu was airing his great white belly at the door of the *charcuterie*. He was surprised to see her going out all dressed up at ten o'clock in the morning.

'Hello, where are you off to?' he asked.

She pretended that she was going out with Madame Taboureau and added that she would call in at the Théâtre de la Gaîté to buy some tickets. Quenu ran after her to ask her to buy seats in the middle if possible, so that they would be sure to have a good view. Then, as he went back to the shop, she made her way to the cab rank by the side of Saint-Eustache, climbed into one of the cabs, pulled down the blinds, and told the driver to take her to the Théâtre de la Gaîté. She was afraid of being followed. When she had bought her tickets, she directed the cabman to take her to the Palais de Justice. There, in front of the gate, she paid and let him go, and slowly made her way through the halls and corridors to the Préfecture de Police.

Finding herself lost in a noisy crowd of *sergents de ville* and men in long frock coats, she gave a man ten sous to take her to the office of the *préfet*. She found, however, that, to gain access to him, a letter of introduction was necessary. She was shown into a small room, fitted out like a boarding house parlour, where a fat, bald individual dressed in black received her with surly coldness. She was invited to speak. So, lifting her veil and telling him her name, she related the whole story quite bluntly, hardly pausing for breath. The bald individual, still looking weary, listened to her in silence. When she had finished, he simply said:

'You are this man's sister-in-law, are you not?'

'Yes,' Lisa replied. 'We are respectable people, and I don't want my husband to get into trouble.'

The official shrugged, as if to say how boring he found the whole affair.

'Do you know', he said impatiently, 'that I've been pestered with this business for more than a year now? I've received denunciation after denunciation, and I'm continually being told to deal with the matter. You will understand that, if I haven't taken any action yet, it's because I prefer to wait. We have our reasons. Here's the file.'

He placed before her a big bundle of papers in a blue folder. Lisa leafed through them. They were like individual chapters of the story she had just been telling. The *commissaires de police* at Le Havre, Rouen, and Vernon had all announced Florent's arrival. Then came a report confirming his installation at the Quenu-Gradelles', and after that, his appointment in Les Halles, the life he led, his evenings at Monsieur Lebigre's, and so on; not a detail was omitted. Lisa, flabbergasted, noticed that the reports were in duplicate, and must therefore have come from two different sources. Finally she came to a collection of anonymous letters, of all shapes and sizes, and in all kinds of handwriting. She recognized a thin scrawl, the writing of Mademoiselle Saget, denouncing the group who met in the little back room at Lebigre's. There was a big sheet of greaseproof paper, stained with Madame Lecœur's beating sticks, and a sheet of creamy notepaper, decorated with a yellow pansy, covered with the scrawls of La Sarriette and Monsieur Jules. Both letters warned the Government to beware of Gavard. She also recognized the scurrilous style of Mère Méhudin, who in four almost indecipherable pages repeated all the wildest stories about Florent that had circulated in the markets. But she was particularly affected by the sight of one of her own invoices, with the letterhead *Charcuterie Quenu-Gradelle*, on the back of which Auguste had betrayed the man he considered to be an obstacle to his marriage.

The official had shown her the file for a purpose.

'Do you recognize any of the handwriting?' he asked.

'No,' she stammered, rising to her feet, overwhelmed by what she had just learnt. She lowered her veil to hide the blush of embarrassment she felt rising to her cheeks. Her silk dress rustled, and her dark gloves disappeared beneath her shawl.

'You see, Madame,' said the bald man with a faint smile, 'your information has come a little late. But you can be assured that your visit will not be forgotten. Tell your husband to do nothing. Something may happen quite soon which…'

He did not finish his sentence but, half rising from his chair, nodded a brief farewell. This was her dismissal. She left at once. In the anteroom, she found Logre and Monsieur Lebigre, who quickly looked away. But she was more embarrassed than they were. She made her way through the halls and along the corridors, feeling as if she had been caught in the grip of this police world which, it now seemed to her, saw and knew everything. At last she emerged into the Place Dauphine. She walked slowly along the Quai de l'Horloge, refreshed by the cool breeze from the Seine.

She now understood the utter pointlessness of what she had done. Her husband was in no danger at all. This was a relief to her, even though she felt a twinge of remorse. She was angry with Auguste and the women who had put her in such a ridiculous position. She began to walk even more slowly, gazing at the Seine as it flowed past.

Barges, black with coal dust, moved through the greenish water on their way downstream, while along the banks anglers were casting their lines. So it was not she who had denounced Florent to the police. This thought struck her all of a sudden and surprised her. Would she have been guilty of a wicked action if she had been his betrayer? She felt confused, surprised by the possibility that she had been misled by her conscience. The anonymous letters definitely seemed wicked. She, on the other hand, had gone quite openly and given her name, in order to save everyone. When suddenly she thought of old Gradelle's money, she sounded her conscience and found she was quite prepared, if necessary, to throw it all in the river to cure the *charcuterie* of its sickness. No, she wasn't mean, it wasn't the money that had made her go to the police. As she crossed the Pont au Change, she calmed down completely, recovering all her wonderful equanimity. It was much better that the others had been to the Préfecture before her. Now she would not need to deceive Quenu, and she would sleep with an easier conscience.

'Did you get the tickets?' Quenu asked when she got home.

He wanted to see them and made Lisa explain exactly where they would be sitting in the dress circle. Lisa had imagined that the police would rush to the house as soon as she had tipped them off, and her proposal to go to the theatre had only been a crafty ploy to get Quenu out of the way while the police arrested Florent. She had thought of taking him for an outing in the afternoon—one of the little jaunts they occasionally allowed themselves. They would take a cab to the Bois de Boulogne,* dine in a restaurant, and then spend a little while at a *café-concert*. But now there was no need to go out. She spent the day as usual behind her counter, with a rosy glow on her face, and seemed brighter and more cheerful, as if she had just recovered from an illness.

'I told you you needed some fresh air,' said Quenu, 'and I was right. Your walk this morning did you the world of good.'

'Rubbish!' she said after a pause, once more looking at him sternly. 'The streets of Paris are not very good for your health.'

That evening at the Gaîté they saw *La Grâce de Dieu*.* Quenu, in a frock coat and grey gloves, his hair carefully brushed and combed, spent most of the time hunting for the names of the performers in the programme. Lisa was superb with her bare shoulders, resting her hands, in their tight-fitting white gloves, on the red plush of the balcony.

They were both profoundly moved by the misfortunes of Marie. The commander, they thought, was certainly a terrible villain, and Pierrot made them laugh from the moment he appeared. Lisa wept. The death of the child, the prayer in the maiden's bedchamber, the return of the poor mad creature, moistened her eyes with tears, which she brushed away with little dabs of her handkerchief. But the evening became a positive triumph for her when, looking up, she caught sight of La Normande and her mother in the upper gallery. That made her swell with pride; she sent Quenu to buy some caramels at the buffet, and played with her fan, a magnificent object in mother-of-pearl with touches of gold. The fishwife was defeated; she lowered her head to listen to her mother, who was whispering something to her. At the end of the performance, as they left, La Belle Lisa and La Belle Normande greeted each other in the foyer with a vague smile.

That day Florent had dined early at Monsieur Lebigre's. He waited for Logre, who was to come and introduce him to a retired *sergent*, a capable man with whom they would discuss the plan of attack on the Palais-Bourbon and the Hôtel de Ville. Night fell, and a fine rain which had started in the afternoon covered Les Halles with a grey shroud. The markets stood out in black against the smoky red of the sky, while ragged clouds as dirty as dishcloths drifted past almost on a level with the roofs, as though caught and torn by the tips of the lightning conductors. Florent was depressed by the muddy streets and the streaming yellowish rain that seemed to wash the twilight away and extinguish it in the mire. He watched the people taking refuge along the footpaths in the covered avenues, the umbrellas flitting past in the downpour, and the cabs clattering along the almost deserted streets. Then the weather cleared for a moment. A red glow appeared in the west. Then a whole army of sweepers came into view at the end of the Rue Montmartre, pushing before them with their brooms a lake of liquid mud.

Logre did not turn up with the *sergent*. Gavard had gone to have dinner with some friends in the Batignolles district, and so Florent was reduced to spending the evening alone with Robine. He talked the whole time and ended up feeling quite depressed. His companion merely wagged his beard and stretched out his arm every quarter of an hour to raise his glass of beer to his lips. Florent became bored and went to bed. But Robine, though left alone, stayed there, frowning pensively and staring at his glass. Rose and the waiter, who had hoped to shut up early since the group in the back room were not there, were forced to wait another half an hour before he decided to leave.

Once in his room, Florent was afraid to go to bed. He was gripped by one of the nervous attacks that sometimes gave him horrible nightmares until dawn. At Clamart, the day before, he had attended the funeral of Monsieur Verlaque, who had died after much suffering. He still grieved at the thought of the little coffin being lowered into the ground; and he kept seeing Madame Verlaque, who would not stop following him, complaining about the coffin that still had to be paid for, and the cost of the funeral, which she had no idea how to cope with as she had not a sou in the place, because the day before the chemist had insisted on the settlement of his account on hearing that the patient was dead. Florent was thus obliged to advance the money for the coffin and the funeral; he even tipped the undertakers. Just as he was leaving, Madame Verlaque looked at him with such a heartbroken expression that he gave her twenty francs.

The death of Monsieur Verlaque was a cause of concern to Florent, for it raised once more the question of his position in the markets. He might lose the job, or be considered for a permanent position. In either case these were complications that might involve the police. He would have liked the insurrection to break out the next day, so that he could then hurl his braided cap into the street. His head full of these troubling thoughts, he stepped out onto the balcony, as if hoping that a cold breeze would cool his fevered brow. The rain had made the wind drop; the blue, cloudless sky was still full of a thundery heat. Les Halles, washed by the downpour, spread out below him, the same colour as the sky, and, like the sky, studded with the yellow stars of their gas burners.

Leaning on the iron balustrade, Florent reflected that sooner or later he would be punished for agreeing to accept the inspector's job. It was like a blot on his life. He figured in the accounts of the Préfecture, he had perjured himself by serving the Empire, in spite of everything he had sworn to himself during his exile. His desire to please Lisa, his charitable disposal of the money earned, the honest way in which he had tried to fulfil his duties, none of these things seemed to him a strong enough argument to excuse his betrayal of his principles. If he suffered in the midst of all that sleek fatness, it served him right. Before him rose a vision of the terrible year he had been through, his persecution by the fishwives, the sick feeling in his stomach on rainy days, the chronic indigestion that had afflicted him in his thinness, and the latent hostility he had felt growing around him. All these things he accepted as due chastisement. The heavy rumble of hostility, the cause of which he never knew, must forebode some catastrophe that already made him bow his shoulders, with the shame of one who knows that he must expiate a sin. Then, at the thought of the popular uprising he was preparing, he became furious with himself, reflecting that he was no longer pure enough to achieve success.

How many dreams he had dreamt up there, gazing at the endless expanse of roofs! Usually he saw them as grey oceans that spoke to him of faraway countries. On moonless nights they grew darker, becoming dead black lakes, stagnant and foul. The clear nights changed them into shimmering fountains of light; the moon streamed across the two levels of the roofs, pouring down the vast sheets of metal, running over the edges of those immense superimposed basins. In cold weather the roofs were stiff and frozen, like the fjords of Norway where the skaters fly; while the hot nights of June lulled them into a deep sleep. One evening in December, when he opened his window, he had found them white with snow, so lustrously white that they lit up the coppery sky. Unmarked by a single footprint, they stretched out like Arctic wastes; and they lay in the loveliest of silences, as gentle as an innocent giant. As the panorama before him changed, Florent's thoughts would become tender or violent. The snow calmed him, the vast sheet of whiteness seemed to him a veil of purity thrown over the filth of the markets. The clear nights, with their shimmering moonlight, carried him away into a land of fairy tale. It was only on dark nights that he suffered, the burning nights in June, which spread before him a kind of evil-smelling marsh, the stagnant water of some accursed sea. And the same nightmare always returned.

Les Halles were always there. He could not open his window or lean on the balustrade without seeing them in front of him, filling the horizon. He would leave the markets in the evening, only to see once more the endless expanse of roofs when he went to bed. They cut him off from the rest of Paris, imposed their massive presence upon him, intruded into his life at every hour of day and night. That night the nightmare returned, made even worse by his vague forebodings. The rain in the afternoon had filled the markets with a malodorous dampness. They breathed their foul breath in his face, a breath that had rolled round the town as a drunkard rolls under the table with the last bottle he drinks. It seemed to him that a thick vapour was rising from each of the markets. In the distance the meat and tripe markets reeked of blood; the vegetable and fruit markets exhaled odours of sour cabbages, rotten apples, and greenery tossed out into the street; the butter and cheese gave off a dreadful stench; the smell from the fish market was acrid; while from the ventilator in the tower of the poultry market just below him came a blast of hot air, a stench that poured out like soot from a factory chimney. All these exhalations formed into a single great cloud over the rooftops, spread to the neighbouring houses, and seemed to fill the sky over the whole of Paris. It was as if Les Halles were bursting out of their iron belt and enveloping the gorged city with their foul breath.

Down below, on the footpath, Florent heard the sound of people talking and laughing. The side door was closed noisily. Quenu and Lisa had returned from the theatre. Feeling dizzy, as if drunk with the air he had breathed, Florent went inside, fearing the storm he felt gathering overhead. The source of his discomfort was there, in the markets, which were still hot from the day's excesses. He slammed the window shut, and left them sprawling in the darkness, naked, sweating, displaying their swollen bellies, and relieving themselves under the stars.

CHAPTER 6

A WEEK later, Florent thought that at last he was going to be able to take action. An outburst of public discontent provided an opportunity for unleashing his insurrectionary forces on Paris. The Corps Législatif, divided on a law on senatorial annuities,* was now discussing the introduction of a highly unpopular tax, and the working-class districts were beginning to growl about it. The Government, fearing defeat, was fighting for all its worth. There would probably be no better pretext for action for a long time.

One morning, at dawn, Florent went to reconnoitre the Palais-Bourbon. He forgot all about his duties in the market and stayed there, studying the place from all angles, until eight o'clock, without for a moment thinking that his absence must have caused an uproar in the fish market. He wandered round all the neighbouring streets, the Rue de Lille, the Rue de l'Université, the Rue de Bourgogne, the Rue Saint-Dominique; he even went as far as the Esplanade des Invalides, stopping at certain crossroads and measuring distances by taking long strides as he went along. Then, back at the Quai d'Orsay, sitting on the parapet, he decided that the attack should be directed from all sides at once: the Gros-Caillou contingent should arrive along the Champ de Mars; the sections from the north of Paris would come down past the Madeleine, while those from the west and south would follow the *quais** or join battle in small groups along the streets of Saint-Germain. But he was worried by the Champs-Élysées, with their wide avenues, on the other side of the river; he could see that cannon would be positioned there to sweep the *quais*. Thereupon he modified several details of his plan, and marked the combat positions of the various sections in a notebook. The main offensive must certainly be made from the Rue de Bourgogne and the Rue de l'Université, while a diversion would be created along the Seine. The eight o'clock sun warmed the nape of his neck, shone brightly on the wide pavements, and gilded the columns of the large building opposite. Already he could see the fighting, the groups of men clinging to those columns, the gates burst open, the peristyle invaded, and scraggy arms suddenly appearing at the top and planting a flag there.

At last he slowly returned homewards, gazing at the ground. All at once he heard a cooing sound, and looked up. He saw that he was crossing the Tuileries gardens. A group of pigeons was strutting across one of the lawns, puffing out their breasts. He leaned for a moment on the tub of an orange tree, looking at the grass and the pigeons bathed in sunshine. The chestnut trees opposite cast black shadows. The garden was wrapped in a warm silence, broken only by the distant rumbling of the Rue de Rivoli on the other side of the railings. The smell of greenery moved him, for it reminded him of Madame François. A little girl ran past, chasing a hoop, and frightened the pigeons. They flew off and settled in a row on the arm of a marble statue of a classical wrestler in the middle of the lawn, still cooing and puffing out their breasts, but more gently now.

As Florent was walking back to Les Halles along the Rue Vauvilliers, he heard the voice of Claude Lantier calling out to him. The painter was going down into the cellars underneath the poultry market.

'Hello!' he called. 'Come with me! I'm looking for that devil, Marjolin.'

Florent followed, glad to forget his thoughts and to defer for a few moments longer his return to the fish market. Claude said that now his friend Marjolin had nothing more to desire, he had become an animal. He was toying with the idea of making him pose on all fours with that childlike grin of his. Whenever he lost his temper over some disappointing sketch, he would go and spend a few hours in the idiot's company, not saying a word, but trying to catch his expression when he smiled.

'He'll be feeding his pigeons, I expect,' he murmured. 'But I don't know where Monsieur Gavard's storeroom is.'

They groped their way round the gloomy cellar. In the middle some water was trickling from a couple of taps. The storerooms in this part of the cellars were reserved exclusively for pigeons. All along the wire netting they heard faint cooings, like the song of birds nestling in leaves at dusk. Claude laughed when he heard this music.

'It sounds as if all the love-birds in Paris are kissing in there, doesn't it?' he said.

None of the storerooms were open, and he had begun to think that Marjolin wasn't in the cellars after all when the sound of kissing, loud, smacking kisses, pulled him up sharply before a half-open door.

He pushed it open and saw Marjolin the animal, whom Cadine had made to kneel on the straw-covered ground in such a way that the boy's face was exactly at the level of her lips. She was kissing him gently, everywhere. She parted his long fair hair to kiss him behind his ears, she went beneath his chin, round his neck, coming back to his eyes and mouth, taking her time, covering his face with tiny caresses, as though it were some delicious possession of hers, which she was using to give herself pleasure. He obediently stayed just as she had placed him. He was hardly aware of what she was doing. He offered her his body, not even afraid of being tickled.

'So this is what you're up to!' said Claude. 'Don't mind us! Aren't you ashamed, teasing him like that in all this dirt? Look, he's absolutely filthy.'

'So what?' said Cadine brazenly. 'He doesn't care. He likes being kissed, because he gets frightened now in places where it's dark… It's true, isn't it? You do get frightened, don't you?'

She made him stand up. He put his hands to his face, as if feeling for the kisses she had given him. He stammered something about being frightened, while she continued:

'Anyway, I came to help him feed the pigeons.'

Florent looked at the poor creatures. All along the shelves were boxes without lids in which the pigeons, squeezed in, showed their mottled plumage. Every now and then a tremor ran across the moving mass of feathers; then they would settle down again, huddled even closer together, and nothing could be heard but their muffled cooing. Next to Cadine was a saucepan full of water and seeds; she filled her mouth, picked up the pigeons one at a time, and blew a mouthful into their beaks. They struggled and nearly choked, and fell back white-eyed into the boxes, stunned by this force-feeding.

'The poor things!' murmured Claude.

'Oh, that's too bad!' said Cadine when she had finished. 'They're much nicer to eat when they've been well fed. In a couple of hours we'll give those over there some salty water. It makes their flesh white and tender. And a couple of hours after that they'll be bled. If you want to see, there are some here that are ready. Marjolin can do it in no time.'

Marjolin carried off a box containing about fifty pigeons. Claude and Florent followed him. He squatted on the ground next to one of the water taps, put the box next to him, and placed a wooden frame covered with fine mesh on a kind of zinc trough. Then he began the process. The knife working swiftly between his fingers, he picked the birds up by the wings, stunned them with a blow on the head with the knife handle, and stuck the point in their throat. They quivered for a few seconds and ruffled their feathers as Marjolin laid them in rows with their heads in the netting on the wooden frame over the zinc trough, into which their blood fell drop by drop. He kept repeating the operation like clockwork, from the crack on the head to the pendulum-like movement of his hand as he took the live birds from one side and laid them down dead on the other. He went faster and faster, taking pleasure in the slaughter, crouched with shining eyes like an enormous, excited mastiff. In the end he burst out laughing, and began to sing 'Tic-tac, tic-tac, tic-tac', clicking his tongue to the rhythm of the knife, making a noise like a mill grinding heads. The pigeons hung like little pieces of silk.

'You like that, don't you, you great animal?' said Cadine, laughing too. They look so comical like that when they pull their heads in to hide their necks! But they're horrible things, you know; they'd give you a nasty peck if they could.'

Laughing at Marjolin's feverish movements, she added:

'I've tried to do it as fast as him, but I can't. Once he bled a hundred in ten minutes.'

The wooden frame was nearly full; they could hear the drops of blood falling into the zinc trough. Then Claude, turning round, saw that Florent was extremely pale, and hurried to get him outside. When they reached the street, he made him sit down on a step.

'What's the matter?' he said, tapping him on the shoulder. 'Here you are, fainting like a woman.'

'It's the smell down there,' mumbled Florent, feeling rather ashamed of himself.

The pigeons, made to swallow seeds and salty water and then taken by the throat and slaughtered, had reminded him of the birds he had seen in the Tuileries gardens, strutting in their rippling satin coats over the sunlit grass. He saw them cooing on the arm of the classical wrestler in the silence of the garden, while in the dark shadows of the chestnut trees the little girls were bowling their hoops. It was then that he had begun to feel faint, when he saw that great blond brute massacring the birds, stunning them with the handle of his knife and driving its point into their throats, in the foul-smelling cellar; his legs had almost given way beneath him, and his eyelids quivered.

'Well, you'll never make a soldier!' said Claude, when Florent came round. 'I must say, whoever sent you to Cayenne must have been a funny one to have been afraid of you! If you ever got involved in an uprising, you wouldn't dare fire a shot. You'd be too afraid of killing anyone.'

Florent got to his feet without answering. He looked very grim, and his face was drawn. He walked off, leaving Claude to go back to the cellar on his own. As he made his way back to the fish market, he thought once more about his plan of attack and the armed bands that would invade the Palais-Bourbon. Cannon would roar from the Champs-Élysées; the gates would be broken down; there would be blood on the steps and skulls smashed against the pillars. A vision of the battle flashed through his mind. He saw himself in the thick of it, deadly pale, hiding his face in his hands, not daring to look.

As he was crossing the Rue du Pont-Neuf, he thought he saw the pale face of Auguste peering round the corner of the fruit market. He must have been on the lookout for someone, his eyes almost popping out of his head in excitement. Suddenly he disappeared, and ran back to the *charcuterie*.

'What's the matter with him?' Florent wondered. 'Is he frightened of me, perhaps?'

That morning there had been some very serious developments at the Quenus-Gradelles'. At daybreak, Auguste had run to Madame Quenu in a state of great excitement with the news that the police had come to arrest Monsieur Florent. Then, stammering even more, he gave a garbled account of how Florent had already left, doubtless to avoid being apprehended. La Belle Lisa, uncorseted and in her nightdress, not worrying about anyone or anything, rushed upstairs to her brother-in-law's room, where she took the photograph of La Normande, after a quick look round to make sure there was nothing there that might compromise her and Quenu. On her way down, she came upon the police on the first floor. The *commissaire* asked her to accompany them to Florent's room. After speaking to her for a few moments in hushed tones, he installed himself with his men in the room, advising her to open the shop as usual, to avoid arousing anyone's curiosity. The trap was laid.

Lisa's only concern throughout was the shock poor Quenu was going to have. She was afraid, moreover, that he might ruin everything by bursting into tears as soon as he knew the police were in the house. For this reason she made Auguste swear to keep absolutely quiet about it, then went back upstairs, put on her corsets, and explained the noise away to Quenu, who was still half asleep. Half an hour later she was standing at the door of the *charcuterie*, brushed and combed and corseted as usual, her face pink and smooth. Auguste was quietly setting up the window display. Quenu appeared on the pavement for a moment, yawning and stretching in the fresh morning air. There was nothing to indicate the drama that was about to unfold upstairs.

It was the *commissaire* himself who put the neighbourhood on the alert by paying a visit to the Méhudin household in the Rue Pirouette. He was in possession of the most precise information. In the anonymous letters received by the Préfecture, much was made of the view that Florent slept on a regular basis with La Belle Normande. Perhaps he had taken refuge there. The *commissaire*, accompanied by two of his men, proceeded to knock at the door in the name of the law. The Méhudins had only just got up. The old woman opened the door in a fury, but soon calmed down and began to snigger, when she saw what the position was. She sat down and fastened her clothes, and told her visitors:

'We're decent people, we have nothing to be afraid of. You can look wherever you like.'

As La Normande was slow to open her door, the *commissaire* told his men to break it open. She was half-naked, an underskirt held between her teeth; this unceremonious entry, which she did not understand, enraged her. Flushing more with anger than with embarrassment, she let go of the underskirt and was about to throw herself at the men in her shift. The *commissaire*, confronted by this imposing, naked woman, stepped forward to protect his men, repeating in his cold voice:

'In the name of the law! In the name of the law!'

She dropped into a chair, and began to sob uncontrollably at finding herself so powerless and not understanding what they wanted. Her hair had fallen loose, her shift did not even reach her knees. The policemen shot sidelong glances to get a good look at her. The *commissaire* threw her a shawl that was hanging on a peg, but she ignored it; she sobbed all the more, watching the men roughly searching her bed, slapping the pillows and running their hands down the sheets.

'But what have I done?' she stammered at last. 'What are you looking for in my bed?'

The *commissaire* mentioned Florent's name, and as Madame Méhudin had remained standing in the doorway, her daughter cried:

'The old witch! It's all her doing!' and rushed at her mother.

She would have hit her if she could, but the men held her back and wrapped her in the shawl. She struggled and said, choking:

'What do you take me for? That Florent has never been in this room! There was nothing between us. They're just trying to get me a bad name in the neighbourhood; I'd like them to come here and accuse me to my face. They can send me to prison, I don't care! And as for Florent, I can do better than him. I can marry whoever I like, and whoever sent you here can go to hell.'

This flood of words seemed to calm her. Her anger now turned against Florent, the cause of all the trouble. She turned to the *commissaire*, in an effort to justify herself:

'I had no idea what he was really like, monsieur. He had such a mild manner that he fooled us all. I didn't want to listen to what people said, because they can be so nasty. He only came here to give lessons to my little boy, and always left straight away afterwards. I made him a meal now and then, and sometimes gave him a really good fish as a present. That's all. But this will be a warning. I'll never let my kindness get the better of me again.'

'Didn't he give you some papers to look after?' asked the *commissaire*.

'No, certainly not. In any case, I'd hand them over if he had. I've had about enough of all this! I don't like seeing you rummaging through my things. There's no point in looking.'

The policemen, who had examined every piece of furniture in the room, now wanted to go into the little cubby-hole where Muche slept. The child had been woken up by the noise, and had been crying, as though he imagined that someone had come to cut his throat.

'This is my little boy's room,' said La Normande, opening the door.

Muche, naked, ran and threw his arms round her neck. She comforted him and put him in her own bed. The policemen came out of the room again almost immediately, and the *commissaire* was about to leave when the child, still very tearful, whispered in his mother's ear: 'They're going to take my exercise books… Don't let them have my exercise books.'

'Yes, that's true,' exclaimed La Normande. 'There are some exercise books. Wait a minute, I'll let you have them. I'm not hiding anything, you see. He wrote things in them. You can hang him as far as I'm concerned.'

She handed Muche's books to the *commissaire*. But the boy jumped out of bed in a fury and began to scratch and bite his mother, who gave him a clout and pushed him back into the bed. He began to howl. In the midst of the uproar, Mademoiselle Saget appeared at the door, craning her neck. Finding all the doors open, she had come in to offer her services to Mère Méhudin. She watched and listened, and said how sorry she was for these poor ladies, who had no one to protect them. Meanwhile, the *commissaire* had begun to read the handwriting specimens in the exercise books, and was looking very serious. The words 'tyranically', 'liberticide', 'anticon-stitutional', and 'revolutionary' made him frown; and when he read the sentence 'When the moment comes, the blow will fall', he tapped the paper and said: 'This is very serious, very serious indeed.'

He passed the books to one of his men and left. Claire, who had not ventured to show her face, opened her door and watched the men go downstairs. Then she came into her sister's room, which she had not entered for over a year. Mademoiselle Saget seemed to be on the friendliest terms with La Normande, fussing round her, adjusting her shawl to keep her well covered, and listening to her indignant comments with the utmost sympathy.

'You're an absolute coward,' said Claire, standing in front of her sister.

La Normande, trembling with rage, sprang up, making the shawl fall to the floor.

'You spying bitch!' she cried. 'Say that again, if you dare.'

'You're an absolute coward,' her sister repeated, in even more insulting tones.

La Normande swung her arm at Claire and hit her so hard in the face that the colour drained out of it, and she leapt on top of her and dug her nails into her neck. They struggled for a moment or two, pulling each other's hair and trying to choke each other. Claire, frail though she was, pushed La Normande back with such tremendous force that they both fell against the wardrobe, smashing the mirror. Muche was sobbing and the old woman was shouting to Mademoiselle Saget to come and help her to separate the sisters. Claire managed to break free.

'Coward! Coward!' she shouted. 'I'm going to go and tell that poor man that you've betrayed him.'

Her mother stood blocking the doorway. La Normande sprang at her from behind and, with Mademoiselle Saget helping, all three of them pushed her back into her room and locked the door. She kicked at the door and smashed everything in the room. Then they could hear nothing but a furious scratching, the sound of metal scraping at the plaster. She was trying to loosen the hinges with her scissors.

'She would have killed me if she'd had a knife,' said La Normande, looking around for her clothes. 'She'll do something dreadful one of these days, with that jealousy of hers. We must keep her in there. If she gets out, she'll bring the whole neighbourhood down on us.'

Mademoiselle Saget hurried downstairs. She arrived at the corner of the Rue Pirouette just as the *commissaire* was turning into the alley next to the Quenu-Gradelles'. She saw immediately what was happening and went into the *charcuterie*, her eyes so bright that Lisa made a sign to her not to say anything while Quenu was there, hanging up strips of *petit salé*. As soon as he returned to the kitchen, the old maid related in a whisper the dramatic scene she had just witnessed at the Méhudins'. Lisa, leaning across the counter, listened with a look of triumph, her hand resting on the dish that contained the pickled veal. A customer entered the shop and asked for a couple of pigs' trotters. Lisa wrapped them up and handed them over, looking very thoughtful.

'I don't bear La Normande any ill will,' she said to Mademoiselle Saget, when they were alone again. 'I used to be very fond of her and I've always been sorry that people caused trouble between us. Look—the proof that I don't bear her a grudge is this photograph, which I saved from falling into the hands of the police, and which I'm quite ready to give back if she comes and asks for it herself.'

She took the photograph out of her pocket. Mademoiselle Saget sniffed at it and sniggered as she read: 'From Louise to her friend Florent.' Then, in her most cutting voice, she said:

'I'm not sure that would be right. You'd be better off keeping it.'

'No, no,' replied Lisa. 'I want all this nonsense to come to an end. Today's the day for making friends again. We've had enough trouble, it's time the neighbourhood got back to normal.'

'Well, shall I go and tell La Normande you're waiting for her?' asked the old woman.

'Yes, that would be very kind.'

Mademoiselle Saget returned to the Rue Pirouette, where she frightened the fishwife out of her wits by telling her that she had just seen her photograph in Lisa's pocket. She was unable, however, to get her to accept her rival's terms. La Normande made certain conditions: she would only go if Lisa came to receive her at the shop-door. The old woman thus had to make two more trips from one to the other before their meeting could be arranged. But at last she had the pleasure of negotiating the reconciliation that was bound to create immense interest and excitement in the neighbourhood. As she passed Claire's door for the last time, she could still hear the sound of scissors scraping at the plaster.

As soon as she had conveyed a definite reply to Lisa, she hurried off to look for Madame Lecœur and La Sarriette. The three of them took up their position at the corner of the fish market, on the footpath opposite the *charcuterie*. Here they would be certain to have a good view. Growing impatient, they pretended to chat among themselves, while keeping an anxious lookout on the Rue Pirouette, from which La Normande was bound to appear. The news of the reconciliation was already travelling through the markets, and while some stallholders stood up to see what was happening, others, even more inquisitive, actually left their posts and took up a position in the covered avenue. All eyes in Les Halles were fixed on the *charcuterie*. The whole neighbourhoood was alive with expectation.

It was a very solemn occasion. When La Normande at last turned the corner of the Rue Pirouette, the excitement was so great that everyone held their breath.

'She's wearing her sparklers,' murmured La Sarriette.

'Look at the way she's walking,' added Madame Lecœur. 'She's so brazen!'

It was true. La Belle Normande was strutting along like a queen who has deigned to accept an offer of peace. She had dressed with the utmost care, her hair was up in curls and she had turned back a corner of her apron to show the cashmere skirt beneath. She was even sporting a new lace bow of unprecedented extravagance. Aware that the entire market was staring at her, she assumed an even haughtier air as she approached the *charcuterie*. She drew to a halt in front of it.

'Now it's La Belle Lisa's turn,' remarked Mademoiselle Saget. 'Watch closely.'

La Belle Lisa left her counter with a smile. She slowly crossed the shop and offered her hand to La Belle Normande. She too had prepared most carefully for the occasion, her linen dazzling white, her appearance immaculate. A murmur ran through the women in the fish market; their heads drew closer together and chattered excitedly. The two women had gone inside the shop, and the paper trimmings in the window prevented them from being seen properly. They seemed to be talking quite cordially, offering each other little gestures of greeting and no doubt paying each other compliments.

'Look!' said Mademoiselle Saget. 'La Belle Normande is buying something. What can it be? I think it's lard. Goodness gracious, did you see that? La Belle Lisa just gave her the photograph; she slipped it into her hand with the lard.'

Fresh salutations were exchanged, and La Belle Lisa, passing beyond the courtesies she had determined upon in advance, accompanied La Belle Normande to the footpath. They stood laughing, showing the neighbourhood what good friends they were. This was a supremely happy moment for Les Halles; the women went back to their stalls, declaring that everything had gone off extremely well.

But Mademoiselle Saget made Madame Lecœur and La Sarriette stay behind for a moment. The drama was not over yet. All three of them stared at the house opposite with an air of such keen curiosity that they seemed to be trying to see through the walls. To pass the time, they began once more to talk about La Belle Normande.

'Now she's without a man,' said Madame Lecœur.

'She's got Monsieur Lebigre,' pointed out La Sarriette, with a laugh.

'But surely Monsieur Lebigre won't be interested any more.'

Mademoiselle Saget shrugged her shoulders.

'You don't know him,' she murmured. 'He won't be bothered by all this. He knows what he's about, and La Normande is well off. They'll get together in a couple of months, you'll see. Mère Méhudin has been working on it for ages.'

'That may well be,' retorted the butter dealer. 'The fact remains that the *commissaire* found her in bed with that Florent.'

'Ah, I forgot to tell you... The beanpole had just left. I was there when they looked in her bed. The *commissaire* felt the sheets. There were two places still warm...'

The old woman paused for breath, then carried on indignantly:

'What really upset me was to hear about all the terrible things that man taught little Muche. You'd never believe it. There was a whole bundle of papers.'

'What sort of terrible things?' asked La Sarriette, her interest aroused.

'All kinds of filthy stuff. The *commissaire* said it was enough to get him hanged... The man is a monster! Interfering with a child like that! Little Muche isn't up to much, but that's no reason for getting him mixed up with the Reds, is it?'

'Of course not,' replied the other two.

'Anyway, they're busy clearing up the mess. I told you, you remember, that there were some funny goings-on at the Quenus'. I was right, wasn't I? Thank God the neighbourhood will be able to breathe easily now. It needed a really good spring-clean. I wasn't the only one getting worried about being murdered in broad daylight. That's no way to live. All the stories and quarrels... And all because of one man, that dreadful Florent. Now here are La Belle Lisa and La Belle Normande making it up. That's very good of them, because they owed it to everyone's peace of mind. Things will go back to normal now, you'll see. Look, there's poor Monsieur Quenu laughing over there.'

Quenu was indeed once more out on the footpath, looking enormous in his white apron, joking with Madame Taboureau's little maid. He seemed extremely jovial. He was squeezing the little maid's hands so tightly that she cried out, and Lisa had a great deal of trouble getting him back into the kitchen. She was pacing impatiently about the shop, afraid that Florent would suddenly appear; she called to her husband to prevent him from bumping into his brother.

'She's very worried,' said Mademoiselle Saget. 'Poor Monsieur Quenu has no idea what's happening. Just look at him, laughing like a child! Did you know that Madame Taboureau said she would have nothing more to do with the Quenus if they continued to get themselves a bad name by letting Florent live with them?'

'Now, I suppose, they'll keep the whole of the inheritance,' commented Madame Lecœur.

'Oh no, my dear. He got his share.'

'Really? How do you know that?'

'Isn't it obvious?' replied the old maid after a momentary hesitation and without offering any reasons for her assertion. 'He's had even more than his share. The Quenus are several thousand francs down over it. When a man has vices, you know, money just vanishes. I don't know whether you heard, but he was involved with another woman…'

'That doesn't surprise me,' interrupted La Sarriette. 'Thin men really fancy themselves.'

'Yes, and she wasn't all that young either. When a man wants it, you know, he wants a lot of it—he'd pick them up out of the gutter. Madame Verlaque, the wife of the previous inspector; you know the one, that sallow-faced woman.'

The other two uttered exclamations of disbelief. Madame Verlaque was hideous!

'It's a fact!' cried Mademoiselle Saget. 'Do you want to call me a liar? There's plenty of proof. Letters have been found from this woman, a whole bundle of them, in which she asks him for money, ten or twenty francs at a time. It's only too obvious. Between the two of them they killed her husband.'

La Sarriette and Madame Lecœur were convinced. But they were beginning to get very impatient. They had been waiting on the footpath for more than an hour and were afraid that somebody might be robbing their stalls. Mademoiselle Saget held them back, however, with yet another story. Florent could not possibly have escaped, she said; he was sure to return, and it would be very interesting to see him arrested. Then she described in the smallest detail the trap that had been set for him, while the butter dealer and the fruiterer continued to scrutinize the house from top to bottom, staring at every opening as if expecting to see the caps of the *sergents de ville* through the cracks. The house, calm and silent, was bathed in the sweet light of the morning sun.

'You'd never think it was full of police,' murmured Madame Lecœur.

'They're in the attics,' said the old woman. 'They've left the window open, just as they found it. Look! Isn't that one of them hiding behind the pomegranate on the balcony?'

They craned their necks, but could see nothing.

'No, it's just a shadow,' said La Sarriette. 'The curtains aren't moving at all. They must be sitting there, waiting.'

At that moment they caught sight of Gavard coming out of the fish market looking worried. They glanced at each other, their eyes shining; not a word passed between them. They had drawn closer together and stood there, rigid in their drooping skirts. The poulterer came over to them.

'Have you seen Florent?' he asked.

They did not reply.

'I need to talk to him,' Gavard went on. 'He isn't in the fish market. He must have gone home. But you would have seen him if he had.'

The three women had turned pale. They were still gazing at one another knowingly, their lips twitching slightly every now and then. As her brother-in-law was still looking at them quizzically, Madame Lecœur said crisply,

'We've only been here about five minutes. He probably came by before we arrived.'

'Well, then, I'll go upstairs and see. I'll risk the five flights,' said Gavard with a laugh.

La Sarriette stepped forward as if she wanted to stop him, but her aunt took her by the arm and held her back.

'Let him go,' she whispered. 'It will serve him right. It will teach him to treat us with more respect in future.'

'He'll stop going about telling people I eat bad meat,' Mademoiselle Saget murmured softly.

They said no more. La Sarriette was very red; the other two still had quite a yellow look about them. They had stopped looking at each other, embarrassed by each other's glances, not knowing what to do with their hands, which they hid beneath their aprons. At last, instinctively, they looked up at the house, and followed, through the very stones of the walls, Gavard's progress up the stairs. When they imagined that he had entered Florent's room, they again exchanged furtive glances. La Sarriette giggled nervously. For a moment they thought that they had seen the curtains move, and imagined that a struggle was taking place. But the front of the house remained as tranquil as ever in the sunshine; a quarter of an hour went by in absolute silence, during which the tension became intense. They were almost overcome by it when at last a man emerged from the alley at the side and ran off to get a cab. Five minutes later Gavard appeared, followed by two policemen. Lisa, who had come out on to the footpath on seeing the cab, hurried back into the shop.

Gavard was very pale. The police had searched him upstairs, and had found his revolver and the box of cartridges. Seeing the *commissaire*'s stern manner, and his expression on hearing his name, Gavard thought that all was lost. This was a terrible ending to all his plotting, and which he had never imagined. The Tuileries* would never forgive him! His legs turned to jelly, as though the firing squad was already waiting. But when he reached the street, he had enough swagger left to walk straight. He even managed to force a smile, believing that Les Halles were watching and were about to see him go bravely to his death.

Meanwhile La Sarriette and Madame Lecœur had run across to him. They asked what was going on, and Madame Lecœur began to cry, while La Sarriette, much moved by the occasion, embraced her uncle. As Gavard held her tightly in his arms, he slipped a key into her hand and whispered in her ear:

'Take everything and burn the papers.'

Then he got into the cab as if he were mounting the scaffold. When the vehicle had disappeared round the corner of the Rue Pierre-Lescot, Madame Lecœur saw La Sarriette trying to hide the key in her pocket.

'There's no point in trying to hide it, my dear,' she said between clenched teeth. 'I saw him give it to you. As sure as there's a God in heaven, I'll go to the prison and tell him everything if you don't treat me right.'

'Of course I'll treat you right, auntie,' replied La Sarriette with an embarrassed smile.

'Let's go to his place straight away, then. There's no point in giving the police time to poke about in his cupboards.'

Mademoiselle Saget, who had been listening intently, followed them, running along as fast as her little legs would carry her. She had lost interest in waiting for Florent now. All the way from the Rue Rambuteau to the Rue de la Cossonnerie she was very humble and full of helpful suggestions, offering to explain things to the doorkeeper, Madame Léonce.

'We'll see, we'll see,' Madame Lecœur curtly replied.

It was necessary, as it turned out, to hold a parley with her. Madame Léonce refused to let them go up to her tenant's apartment.

She looked down her nose at them and seemed shocked at the sight of La Sarriette's badly fastened shawl. But when the old spinster had whispered a few words in her ear, and she had been shown the key, she gave way. Upstairs, she only let them into the rooms one at a time, as upset as if she had been forced to show a party of burglars the place where her own money was hidden.

'Go on, take it all,' she cried at last, throwing herself down in a chair.

La Sarriette was already trying the key in all the cupboards. Madame Lecœur, all suspicion, followed her movements so closely that she exclaimed:

'You're in my way, auntie. At least give me enough room to move my arms.'

At last, opposite the window, between the fireplace and the bed, a cupboard was opened. The four women uttered a sigh. On the middle shelf lay about ten thousand francs in gold pieces, in neat little piles. Gavard, who had prudently placed the bulk of his fortune in the hands of a solicitor, had kept this sum in reserve for the 'great day'. As he solemnly said, his personal contribution to the revolution was ready at a moment's notice. He had sold a few securities and took a special delight in inspecting his ten thousand francs every evening, gloating over them and finding something quite roisterous and insurrectional in their appearance. At night he would dream that battles were being fought in his cupboard; he could hear gunshots, cobblestones being torn up and rolled along, and voices shouting in confusion and triumph; it was his money that provided support for the insurrection.

La Sarriette had stretched out her hands with a cry of delight.

'Keep your paws off!' said Madame Lecœur in a rasping tone.

She looked even more sallow than ever in the reflection of the gold, her face covered in blotches and her eyes glowing feverishly from the liver complaint that was eating away at her. Behind her, Mademoiselle Saget on tiptoe was gazing ecstatically into the cupboard, while Madame Léonce had risen to her feet and was muttering darkly.

'My uncle told me to take everything,' said the young woman.

'What about me? I looked after him!' cried the doorkeeper.

Madame Lecœur was almost choking. She pushed them aside and clung hold of the cupboard, stammering: 'It's mine! I'm his closest relative. You're just thieves. I'd rather throw it all out of the window than let you have it.'

A silence fell. They stood glowering at each other. La Sarriette's shawl had come completely undone; she was showing her heaving breasts, her damp mouth, her pink nostrils. Madame Lecœur became even more ill-tempered as she saw how lovely the girl looked in her excitement.

'Well,' she said in a calmer tone, 'let's not fight about it. You're his niece and I'm prepared to share... We'll each take a pile in turn.'

They brushed the other two aside. The butter dealer took the first pile, which disappeared into her skirts. Then La Sarriette took a pile. They kept a strict eye on each other, ready to fight at the slightest sign of cheating. Their fingers stretched out at regular intervals, first the hideous, gnarled fingers of the aunt, then the white fingers of the niece, as soft and supple as silk. Slowly they filled their pockets. When there was only one pile left, La Sarriette objected to her aunt having it, for it was she who had started. She hastily divided it between Mademoiselle Saget and Madame Léonce, who had not taken their eyes off them as they pocketed the gold.

'Thanks a lot,' grumbled the doorkeeper. 'Fifty francs for cosseting him all these years with my broths and soups! And he told me he had no family!'

Before closing the cupboard, Madame Lecœur searched it thoroughly from top to bottom. It contained political works forbidden by the Customs, pamphlets from Brussels, scandalous stories about the Bonapartes, foreign cartoons ridiculing the Emperor. One of Gavard's favourite indulgences was to shut himself up with a friend and show him all these compromising items.

'He made a point of asking me to burn his papers,' said La Sarriette.

'Well, there's no fire, so that's that—it would take too long. Anyway, the police will soon be here. We'd better get out.'

All four began to descend the stairs; but they had no sooner reached the bottom than the police appeared. Madame Léonce had to go up again and show them round. The other three, hunching their shoulders, hurried out into the street. They walked away quickly, one behind the other, the aunt and the niece hampered somewhat by their bulging pockets. La Sarriette, who was in front, turned round as she stepped onto the footpath of the Rue Rambuteau and said with a laugh:

'It's banging against my thighs.'

This provoked Madame Lecœur to make a crude remark which made them all laugh. They took particular pleasure in the feel of the weight dragging at their skirts like hands caressing them. Mademoiselle Saget had kept her fifty francs in her clenched fist, and looked very serious as she thought of a plan to squeeze some more money out of the full pockets she was following.

'Ah!' she exclaimed, as they reached the corner of the fish market, 'we've arrived just at the right moment. There's Florent about to be nabbed.'

Florent was just returning from his long walk. He went into the office to change his jacket and then began his daily duties, superintending the washing down of the slabs and strolling through the long avenues. It struck him that the women were looking at him rather oddly; they were whispering to each other as he went past, their heads lowered, their eyes full of mischief. They had dreamt up some new pretext to annoy him, he thought. For some time now these huge, terrible women had not given him a day's peace. But when he came to the Méhudins' stall he was very surprised to hear the mother say in a honeyed tone:

'Monsieur Florent, someone asked for you a little while ago. A middle-aged gentleman. He's waiting for you in your room.'

The old fishwife, heaped on her chair, was enjoying revenge at its most refined as she spoke these words, and it caused her huge body to quiver and shake. Florent, still doubtful, glanced at La Belle Normande. She, now completely at one with her mother, turned on her tap and slapped her fish under it, giving no sign that she had heard.

'Are you quite sure?' he asked.

'Yes, absolutely. Isn't that right, Louise?' the old woman continued in an even shriller voice.

Florent concluded that it must be someone who wanted to see him about the big affair, so he decided to return to his room. He was on the point of leaving the market, when, happening to turn round, he saw La Belle Normande watching him with a very serious expression on her face. He passed by the three gossips.

'There's no one in the *charcuterie*, is there?' murmured Mademoiselle Saget. 'La Belle Lisa is not one to compromise herself.'

The shop was, indeed, empty. The front of the building was still bright with sunshine; it had the contented air of a decent, respectable house warming its belly in the first rays of the sun. On the balcony upstairs, the pomegranate was in full flower. As Florent crossed the street, he nodded amiably to Logre and Monsieur Lebigre, who were apparently taking the air on the doorstep of the latter's establishment. They smiled back at him. He was about to dive down the alley when he imagined he saw the pale face of Auguste suddenly disappear at the end of the dark passage. He turned back and glanced into the shop to make sure that no middle-aged gentleman was waiting for him there. But all he saw was Mouton, sitting on a chopping block, displaying his double chin and bristling whiskers, and gazing at him defiantly with his big yellow eyes. When at last he decided to go in by the alley, Lisa's face came into view at the end of it, behind the small curtain of a glass-panelled door.

A hush had fallen over the entire fish market. The huge bellies and enormous breasts held their breath, waiting until he had disappeared. Then, suddenly, there was an explosion; the breasts heaved wildly and the bellies nearly burst with malicious delight. The trick had worked. Nothing could have been funnier. Mère Méhudin shook with silent laughter, like a gourd being emptied. Her story about a middle-aged gentleman had gone all round the market and had struck all the fishwives as extremely amusing. At last the beanpole was to be packed off; they would no longer have his miserable face and convict's eyes to look at. They all wished him a pleasant journey, and hoped that they would get a handsome new inspector. They ran about from stall to stall and would willingly have danced round their slabs like girls escaped from a convent. La Belle Normande stood stiffly watching this outbreak of joy, not daring to move for fear of crying, her hands resting on a large skate to cool her fever.

'You see how the Méhudins just turn their backs on him now that he's got no more money,' said Madame Lecœur.

'Well, they're right,' replied Mademoiselle Saget. 'Anyway, my dear, this is the end, isn't it? You've every reason to be pleased. Let the others do as they please.'

'It's only the other one who's laughing,' remarked La Sarriette. 'La Normande doesn't look very happy.'

Meanwhile, upstairs in his room, Florent let himself be taken like a lamb. The gendarmes, assuming that he would put up a desperate fight, leapt on him roughly, but he gently asked them to let him go. Then he sat down while they packed up his papers, the red sashes, armbands, and banners. This turn of events did not seem to surprise him, indeed it came more as a relief, though he did not fully realize it. But he was deeply unhappy at the thought of all the hatred down below which had driven him to his room. He saw again Auguste's pale face and the lowered eyes of the fishwives; he remembered the words of Mère Méhudin, La Normande's silence, the empty *charcuterie*; and he thought to himself that Les Halles had collaborated in his downfall, that it was the entire neighbourhood that was turning him in. The mud in the streets had risen up and submerged him.

Amid all the faces that flashed through his mind he suddenly saw that of Quenu, and a spasm of agony gripped his heart.

'Come on, downstairs!' barked one of the gendarmes.

Florent rose and began to go down. On the third floor landing he asked if he could go back, saying that he had forgotten something. The men did not want to let him go and hustled him forward. He begged to be allowed back and even offered them the small amount of money he had in his pocket. At length two of them agreed to go back with him, threatening to give him a crack on the head if he tried any tricks. They drew their revolvers out of their pockets. On reaching his room, Florent went straight to the chaffinch's cage, took out the bird, kissed it between its wings, and released it from the window. He watched it fly away and perch on the sunlit roof of the fish market, as though dazed. Then it took wing again and disappeared over Les Halles in the direction of the Square des Innocents. For a few moments he stood there gazing at the sky, the free and open sky; he thought of the pigeons cooing in the Tuileries, and the pigeons in the storage cellars with their throats slit by Marjolin. Then, feeling quite broken, he turned and followed the gendarmes, who, shrugging their shoulders, had put their revolvers back in their pockets.

At the foot of the stairs, Florent stopped in front of the door that led into the kitchen. The *commissaire*, who was waiting for him there, seemed almost touched by his submissiveness, and asked him:

'Would you like to say goodbye to your brother?'

For a moment he hesitated. He looked at the door. A tremendous noise of cleavers and saucepans came from the kitchen. To keep her husband busy, Lisa had hit on the idea of making him start work now on the black pudding which he normally only prepared in the evening. The onions were sizzling on the fire. Florent heard Quenu's cheerful voice above the uproar, saying:

'Yes, this pudding will be really good! Auguste, give me the fat!'

Florent thanked the *commissaire*, but declined his offer, afraid to enter the hot kitchen so full of the smell of frying onions. He walked on, happy in the knowledge that his brother knew nothing of what had happened, quickening his pace as if to spare the *charcuterie* any further trouble. But as the bright sunshine in the street struck him full in the face, he felt a touch of shame, and climbed into the cab with a bent back and an ashen face. He knew that the fish market was gazing at him in triumph; it seemed to him, indeed, that the whole neighbourhood had gathered to celebrate its victory.

'Looked terrible, didn't he?' said Mademoiselle Saget.

'Just like a thief caught red-handed,' said Madame Lecœur.

'I saw a man guillotined once. He looked just like that,' added La Sarriette, showing her white teeth.

They stepped forward, craning their necks in an attempt to see into the cab. Just as it began to move off, the old woman tugged at the others' skirts to draw their attention to Claire, who was coming round the corner of the Rue Pirouette, looking like a mad creature, her hair loose and her fingernails bleeding. She had escaped from her room, and on realizing that she had arrived too late and Florent was being taken away, she ran after the cab, but stopped almost at once with a gesture of impotent rage, shaking her fist at the fast-receding vehicle. Then, quite red in the fine plaster dust covering her, she ran back home to the Rue Pirouette.

'You'd think he'd promised to marry her,' laughed La Sarriette. 'She's totally mad, that one.'

Calm gradually returned to the neighbourhood. Until the markets closed down for the day, little groups of people formed to discuss the events of the morning. They peered constantly at the *charcuterie*. Lisa avoided making any appearance, leaving Augustine in charge of the counter. At last, in the afternoon, she thought it was her duty to tell Quenu everything, for fear that some chatterbox would give him a terrible shock. She waited until she was alone with him in the kitchen, knowing that it was in that part of the house that he was most at ease and would weep less. Moreover, she communicated the news with much maternal solicitude for his feelings. But when he had heard it all, he fell across the chopping block and burst into tears like a child.

'Now, now, you poor thing, don't take on so, you'll make yourself ill,' said Lisa, taking him in her arms.

The tears flowed down his white apron, and his massive frame heaved with sobs. He seemed to be sinking, melting away. When at last he was able to speak, he stammered:

'You don't know how good he was to me when we lived in the Rue Royer-Collard. He kept the place clean and did all the cooking. He treated me like a son. He came back at night covered in mud and so tired he could hardly stand, while I was well fed and kept warm at home. Now they're going to shoot him!'

Lisa told him that Florent would not be shot, but Quenu only shook his head.

'I haven't loved him as much as I should have done,' he continued. 'It's too late now. I've been wicked. I wasn't even sure I should let him have his share of the inheritance.'

'But I offered it to him at least a dozen times,' she cried. 'We've got nothing to reproach ourselves with over that.'

'Oh yes, I realize how kind you are. You would have given him everything. But it wasn't the same for me, I didn't like to part with it; and now it'll weigh on me for the rest of my life. I'll always think that if only I'd shared the money with him, he wouldn't have gone back to his old ways… I drove him to this.'

She became even more gentle with him, telling him to stop tormenting himself. She was sorry for Florent too, though he was as guilty as he possibly could be. If he had had more money, there might have been no limit to his folly. Gradually she contrived to make him realize that the matter could scarcely have ended differently, and that in the end it would be for the better. Quenu was still crying, wiping his cheeks with his apron, trying to suppress his sobs while he listened, and then dissolving into fresh floods of tears. Automatically he had sunk his hands into a heap of sausage meat lying on the block, and was digging holes in it and roughly kneading it.

'Do you remember how unwell you were feeling?' Lisa continued. 'It was because our normal life had been disturbed. I was very worried, although I didn't say so. I could see you were getting very low.'

'I was, wasn't I?' he murmured, containing his sobs for a moment.

'And the shop hasn't been doing very well this year either. It was as if a spell had been put on it. Come on, don't cry. Everything will get better now, you'll see. You must look after yourself, you know, for my sake and Pauline's. You have responsibilities towards us as well.'

He was kneading the sausage meat more gently now. Again he was shaken by emotion, but of a more tender kind, which brought a faint smile to his grief-stricken face. Lisa felt that she had convinced him. She turned and called to Pauline, who was playing in the shop, and sat her on Quenu's knee.

'Pauline, isn't it true that your father should be reasonable? Ask him nicely not to make us sad any more.'

The child did as she was told. They looked at each other, and their fat, sleek forms united in a single, enormous embrace, already feeling cured of the year-long sickness from which they were just emerging. Their big, round faces smiled as Lisa said:

'After all, my dear, there's just the three of us, just the three.'

Two months later Florent was again sentenced to deportation. The affair caused a great stir. The newspapers reported every detail and printed drawings of the accused, as well as of the banners and sashes, and plans of the places where the conspirators had held their meetings. For two weeks the Les Halles conspiracy was the talk of Paris. The police issued statements which became more and more disturbing, and in the end announced that the whole of the Montmartre area was mined. In the Corps Législatif the agitation was so great that the centre and the right forgot their differences over the law on senatorial annuities and made it up by voting, by an overwhelming majority, an unpopular taxation bill. In the wave of panic that swept over the city, even the working-class districts went along without protest. The trial lasted a week. Florent was amazed at the large number of accomplices with which he was credited. He knew only six or seven of the twenty faces he saw in the dock. After the sentence was read out, he fancied that he caught sight of Robine's innocent-looking hat and back disappearing in the crowd. Logre was acquitted, as was Lacaille. Alexandre was given two years' imprisonment for his childlike involvement. As for Gavard, he, like Florent, was condemned to deportation. This was a great blow, and quite spoilt the huge pleasure he derived from the lengthy proceedings, in which he had managed to play a prominent part. He was paying dearly for the way he had vented the spirit of opposition that is typical of the Parisian shopkeeper. Two big tears ran down the gaunt face of this little white-haired boy.

One morning in August, when Les Halles were just waking up, Claude Lantier, who was sauntering about in the midst of the deliveries of vegetables, his red sash drawn tightly round his waist, came to greet Madame François at the Pointe Saint-Eustache. She was sitting among her carrots and turnips, looking very sad. The painter, too, was gloomy, in spite of the bright sunshine which was already softening the deep green velvet of the mountains of cabbages.

'Well,' she said, 'that's that. They're sending him back… I think he's already on his way to Brest.'

She made a sorrowful gesture. Then she gently waved her hands and murmured:

'It's Paris, it's this wretched, terrible Paris.'

'No, no, I know whose fault it is, it's those vile people!' exclaimed Claude, clenching his fists. 'You can't imagine what it was like. The trial was farcical. They even ferreted in a child's exercise books! That stupid public prosecutor made a great fuss about them, going on about respect for children, demagogic education, and so on. It makes me sick just to think about it.'

He shuddered, and hunching his shoulders inside his green coat, he went on:

'A man as gentle as a child. I saw him nearly faint when he saw a pigeon being killed! It looked almost comical to see him between two gendarmes. We'll never see him again. He won't come back this time.'

'He should have listened to me,' said Madame François, after a while. 'He could have come to live in Nanterre with my chickens and rabbits. I was very fond of him. I could tell he was a very decent sort. We could have been happy. It's very sad. You'll get over it, won't you, Monsieur Claude? You must come and see me; I'll make you an omelette.'

There were tears in her eyes. She rose to her feet. She was clearly a strong and spirited woman.

'Well,' she went on, 'here comes Mère Chantemesse to buy some turnips. She's as sprightly as ever, the fat old thing.'

Claude went off and for a while prowled about the streets. The day had risen like a white fountain at the end of the Rue Rambuteau.

The sun, edging above the rooftops, was spreading its rosy light, already falling in warm patches on the footpaths. Claude sensed a gay mood awakening in the vast, echoing markets, piled high with food. It was like the pleasure that comes with recovery from an illness, the high spirits of people relieved of a heavy burden. He saw La Sarriette wearing a gold chain, singing amid her plums and strawberries, tweaking the moustaches of Monsieur Jules, who was wearing a velvet jacket. He caught sight of Madame Lecœur and Mademoiselle Saget walking down one of the covered avenues, their faces less sallow than usual—indeed, almost pink, as they laughed together over some amusing incident. In the fish market, Mère Méhudin, who had gone back to her stall, was slapping her fish, shouting at customers, and getting stuck into the new inspector, a young man whose life she had sworn to make a misery. Claire, seeming more lazy and listless than ever, her hands blue from the cold waters of the tank, was scooping up an enormous heap of snails, glittering with the silver thread of their slime. At the tripe stalls Auguste and Augustine had just bought some pigs' trotters, and were about to set off in a trap for their *charcuterie* in Montrouge. Then, as it was now eight o'clock and already warm, Claude, on returning to the Rue Rambuteau, found Muche and Pauline playing together. Muche was on all fours, while Pauline sat on his back and held on to his hair to prevent herself from falling. And on the roofs of Les Halles, along the gutter, a moving shadow made him look up; it was Cadine and Marjolin, laughing and kissing, warming themselves in the sun, displaying their happy animal love before the whole neighbourhood.

Claude shook his fist at them. He was exasperated by all this joyousness in the streets and on the rooftops. He cursed the Fat people, for they had won. All around he could see nothing but Fat people, increasing in size, bursting with health, greeting another day of eating and digesting. As he halted opposite the Rue Pirouette, the sight that met his eyes was the last straw.

On his right, La Belle Normande, or La Belle Madame Lebigre as she now was, stood at the door of her shop. Her husband had at last been granted permission to combine his wine business with a tobacco agency, a long-cherished dream which he had finally been able to realize through the services he had rendered to the authorities. To Claude, La Belle Madame Lebigre looked superb in her silk dress and curled hair, ready to sit behind her counter, to which all the gentlemen in the neighbourhood flocked to buy their cigars and tobacco. She had become quite distinguished, quite the lady. Behind her, the bar-room had been freshly painted, with sprays of vine leaves against a soft background; the zinc-plated counter shone brightly, and the bottles of liqueur cast even more dazzling reflections in the tall mirror. The mistress of all these things stood smiling in the bright sunshine.

On his left, La Belle Lisa, looking out from the *charcuterie*, occupied the entire width of the doorway. Her linen had never been as white as it was now; never had her pink, refreshed complexion been so neatly framed in smooth waves of hair. She exhibited the deep calm of repletion, a massive tranquillity unruffled even by a smile. She was a picture of absolute quietude, of perfect bliss, not only untroubled but lifeless, as she bathed in the warm air. She seemed, in her tightly stretched bodice, to be still digesting the happiness of the day before; her plump hands, lost in the folds of her apron, were not even outstretched to grasp the happiness of the day, for it was sure to fall into them. And the shop window beside her seemed to display the same bliss. It too had recovered; the stuffed tongues lay red and healthy, the hams were once more showing their handsome yellow faces, and the strings of sausages no longer had the sad look that had so upset Quenu. Hearty laughter rang out from the kitchen at the back, accompanied by the joyful rattle of saucepans. Once again the *charcuterie* exuded health, a kind of greasy health. The great strips of bacon and the sides of pork that hung against the marble brought to the picture the rounded contours of the belly, the belly triumphant, while Lisa, standing there, motionless and imposing, greeted Les Halles with her large, well-fed face.

Then both ladies turned to each other. La Belle Madame Lebigre and La Belle Madame Quenu exchanged a friendly greeting.

Claude, who had no doubt forgotten to have any supper the night before, felt angry at seeing them both looking so well and so respectable, with their great breasts thrust out before them; tightening his belt, he muttered bitterly:

'Respectable people… What bastards!'

EXPLANATORY NOTES

5 *Cayenne*: Cayenne was known as 'Devil's Island'. Captain Alfred Dreyfus was deported there in 1895.

coup d'état: the *coup d'état* of 2 December 1851, planned by Louis-Napoleon Bonaparte, president of the short-lived Second Republic (1848–51), provoked the erection of barricades in Paris (and shooting on the boulevards on 4 December) and Republican uprisings in the provinces (in Provence, for example, as described in Zola's *The Fortune of the Rougons* (*La Fortune des Rougon*, 1871)). More than 25,000 people (including Victor Hugo) went into exile or were arrested and deported to Guiana or Algeria. After the plebiscite of 20 September 1852, Louis-Napoleon was proclaimed Emperor Napoleon III on 2 December 1852 (the date was chosen because it was that of Napoleon Bonaparte's famous victory at the Battle of Austerlitz).

7 *barrier*: a toll barrier, at the gates of Paris, allowing goods entering the city to be checked and taxed.

badge: to indicate that the man is a clerk in charge of the letting of market pitches.

Compas d'or: an old inn, dating from the sixteenth century, which Zola visited while doing research for his novel. See note to p. 185, below.

8 *September*: the action of the novel is thus supposed to begin in September 1858 and to take place over about a year.

shimmers of light: these are Les Halles, the food markets, featuring iron-work and vast expanses of glass, built by the architect Victor Baltard (1805–74) from 1851 onwards. Les Halles were demolished between 1969 and 1972, following the transfer of the markets to Rungis, south-west of Paris; a single pavilion was classified as a historical monument and moved to Nogent-sur-Marne in 1971, where it is now known as the Pavillon Baltard. They were replaced by landscaped gardens and a large underground shopping and leisure complex, known as the Forum des Halles. The complex is now widely acknowledged as an architectural disaster, and it is planned to redevelop the area once more. Adam Gopnik, in his best-selling book *Paris to the Moon* (New York: Random House, 2000), describes the reactions of a friend, Antoine Jacobson, to the disappearance of Les Halles:

> For Antoine, Les Halles was not just the belly of Paris but its heart, and for him the replacement of Les Halles by Rungis is the primordial sin of modern France . . .
>
> 'When the market moved out of Les Halles,' Antoine [said] . . .,

'it effectively changed the relationship between pleasure and play and work in all of Paris. For centuries, because the market was at once a center for restaurants and for ordinary people, a whole culture grew up around it. Shopping and eating, the restaurant and the market, the stroller and the shopper, the artisan and the bourgeois—all were kept in an organic arrangement. And because many of the goods couldn't be kept overnight, it meant that what was left at the end of every day was given to the poor. But for trivial reasons—traffic and hygiene—they made the decision to move the market to Rungis, and left a hole in the heart of Paris. There was no place allotted here for the small artisan, for the small grower, or for the organic market.' (pp. 240–1)

A little of the flavour of the old market atmosphere can still be caught by walking along the Rue Montorgueil and its continuation, the Rue des Petits Carreaux, to the north of the Forum (see note to p. 185, below).

9 *Pointe Saint-Eustache*: the intersection, near the church of Saint-Eustache, of the Rue Montmartre, the Rue Montorgueil, the Rue Rambuteau, and the Rue de Turbigo.

game: it should be noted that Zola takes considerable poetic licence with the chronology of the markets' construction and the development of the neighbouring streets. Generally, he leads the reader to believe that the markets were built and were in operation earlier than was the case. For a detailed examination of Zola's deliberate anachronisms, see Geoff Woollen, 'Zola's Halles: A *Grande Surface* before their Time', *Romance Studies*, 18/1 (2000), 21–30.

corn market: built in 1811, the corn market (the *Halle au blé*) was situated between the Rue du Louvre and the Rue Vauvilliers.

4 *December*: 4 December 1851. An allusion to the disturbances that followed the *coup d'état* of 2 December (see note to p. 5, above).

Élysée: in 1848, the National Assembly decreed that the Élysée Palace, known at the time as the 'Élysée National', should be the official residence of the President of the new Republic—the 'Prince-President', Louis-Napoleon.

11 *Bicêtre*: it was in this hospital (which also served as a prison) that convicted prisoners waited to be sent to penal colonies.

deportation: most of the details here are derived from the *Histoire illustrée du Second Empire* by Taxile Delord. The narrative details that follow are taken from Charles Delescluze, *De Paris à Cayenne, journal d'un transporté*. Both books were published in 1869. Readers of Zola's novel in 1873 would certainly have related the story of Florent not only to the aftermath of Louis-Napoleon's *coup d'état* in 1851 (see note to p. 5, above) but also to much more recent events: the deportations that followed the collapse of the Commune of Paris in 1871. (The 'Commune' refers to the socialist government that briefly ruled Paris in the spring of 1871, following an uprising within Paris after the Franco-Prussian War ended in French defeat. Karl Marx wrote a short book on the Commune during and immediately after the events, entitled *The Civil War in France*.) Having supported the Commune in any way was a political crime, of which thousands were accused. Some of the Communards were shot against what became known as the Communards' Wall in the Père Lachaise cemetery, while thousands of others were tried by summary courts martial of doubtful legality, and thousands shot. Notorious sites of slaughter were the Luxembourg Gardens and the Lobau Barracks, behind the Hôtel de Ville. Nearly 40,000 others were marched to Versailles for trial. The number of those killed during *La Semaine sanglante* (the final, bloody week of street fighting, at the end of May 1871, between working-class Communards and regular troops) can never be established for certain, though it exceeded the number of Parisians killed during the Franco-Prussian War, Robespierre's 'Terror' of 1793–4, and the Second World War. According to Alfred Cobban, in his *A History of Modern France*, iii. *1871–1962* (London: Penguin Books, 1965), 23, 30,000 were killed, perhaps as many as 50,000 later executed or imprisoned, and 7000 exiled to New Caledonia.

hulks: old unseaworthy ships used as prisons in a number of French ports (cf. Charles Dickens, *Great Expectations*, chapter 2).

12 *here and there*: these vendors occupied spots on the pavements around Les Halles, and paid a much lower tax for their pitch than was paid by stall-holders within the markets.

13 *bell*: the sounding of the bell, in the various markets of Les Halles, signalled the beginning and end of the different activities of the day's business.

16 *socks*: the character of Claude Lantier resembles Paul Cézanne in various aspects of his appearance: his large head, his beard, his fine nose, his felt hat, his old overcoat, his red sash, his blue socks. Cézanne and Zola were boyhood friends in Aix, and remained in close contact for years, until the publication of *The Masterpiece* (*L'Œuvre*, 1886) (see note to p. 75, below). Claude must not, however, be identified completely with Cézanne. His ideas about art and some of his interests as a painter reflect those of Zola himself rather than Cézanne. Claude's enthusiasm for early morning scenes in the markets reflect Zola's; Zola had used the pseudonym Claude for his Salon art criticism of 1866; and he had used the same name for his semi-autobiographical novel *La Confession de Claude* (1865).

17 *flâneur*: the French word *flâneur* means stroller, particularly someone who strolls around urban areas. The idea of the *flâneur* was particularly developed by Walter Benjamin in his book *Charles Baudelaire: A Lyric Poet in the Era of High Capitalism*. In Baudelaire's work it was originally applied to nineteenth-century Paris, but is now used more generally.

A key figure in the literature of modernity, the *flâneur* is ambiguous. He observes the metropolitan scene, seeking to evoke the essence of the street, but at the same time is part of the spectacle of the city; he is always inside the mass, yet alienated in relation to the crowd; he can be seen as a detective and philosopher who interprets the meaning of street life or as a melancholic figure who can only feel fulfilled through being part of the transitory and shallow spectacle of urban life.

17 *Rue Pirouette*: the Rue Pirouette, close to Les Halles, was an old street, medieval in aspect, that had escaped Haussmann's urban redevelopment programme. It has now almost completely disappeared.

18 *Murillo*: a Spanish painter (1617–82) who specialized in religious subjects. He had a strong influence on Manet, whom Zola championed. The point here is that Claude, while rejecting classical painting, sees and describes reality in exclusively painterly terms.

19 *jacket*: the jacket and the hat mark the man out as one of the superior types of market porter (known as 'les forts des Halles'), who were better paid than ordinary ones. They were easily identified by their wide-brimmed hats, which makes them stand out in contemporary photographs.

20 *open air*: a reference to the tendency of the Impressionist painters, wishing to represent reality in as direct a manner as possible, to work as often as they could in the open air, in natural light, rather than in a studio.

forest: the image of a forest has close literary associations with that of a cathedral. Les Halles, Zola suggests, are the cathedrals of modern life. He aimed explicitly to play on Victor Hugo's famous novel *Notre-Dame de Paris* (1831). See Auguste Dezalay, ' "Ceci dira cela": remarques sur les antécédents du *Ventre de Paris*', *Les Cahiers naturalistes*, 58 (1984), 33–42; and Ilinca Zarifopol-Johnston, *To Kill a Text: The Dialogic Function of Hugo, Dickens, and Zola* (Newark: University of Delaware Press, 1995), 176–91.

22 *slippers*: it was not unusual in fashionable society to end a party with an early-morning visit to Les Halles.

Baratte's: a well-known restaurant near Les Halles. It was fashionable during the Second Empire.

Marché des Innocents: a herb and vegetable market was established in 1785 on the site of the Cimetière des Innocents. It disappeared with the building of Les Halles, and was replaced by the Square des Innocents.

romanticism: Claude is strongly committed to 'modern' art, to the realism of Courbet, Manet, and Zola—in opposition to more conventional forms of painting (and writing), which still owed much to romanticism.

24 *squirrel*: Zola had planned to make Marjolin the Quasimodo of Les Halles, after the character of that name in Hugo's *Notre-Dame de Paris* (see note to p. 20, above).

Rubens: the famous Flemish painter (1577–1640)—a proponent of an exuberant Baroque style that emphasized movement, colour, and sensuality.

28 *Rue des Halles*: an anachronism: the Rue des Halles was built between 1860 and 1867, while the Rue de Turbigo was opened in 1867—much later than 1858, when the action of *The Belly of Paris* takes place.

34 *still lifes*: a type of painting representing objects, usually inanimate, of which Zola's novel itself offers numerous examples. See Kate Tunstall, '"Crânement beau tout de même": Still Life and *Le Ventre de Paris*', *French Studies*, 58/2 (2004), 177–87.

rillettes: potted meat, made from pork or goose.

andouilles: sausage made of chitterlings.

37 *Le Gard*: a *département* in Provence.

Yvetot: a small town near Rouen in Normandy.

42 *feet*: Zola knew these neighbourhoods well, for he lived there (frequently changing his abode) between 1858 and 1865.

redemption: the revolution of 1848 installed the Second Republic (1848–51) in a climate of extreme political idealism. Numerous political clubs were formed, in which radical ideas were given free rein (they are described ironically by Gustave Flaubert in *A Sentimental Education* (*L'Éducation sentimentale*, 1869), which undoubtedly influenced Zola's often comic descriptions of the political discussions in Lebigre's back room).

44 *Plassans*: Zola's Rougon-Macquart family originated in this imaginary town in the south of France, based on the real town of Aix-en-Provence (Zola's birthplace).

45 *still alive*: Lisa is the daughter of Antoine Macquart and Fine Gavaudan. According to the genealogical tree of the Rougon-Macquart family, established in 1878, she was born in 1827. Her sister is Gervaise, the protagonist of *L'Assommoir* (1877) and the mother of Claude Lantier; her brother is Jean Macquart, the protagonist of *Earth* (*La Terre*, 1887).

46 *petit salé*: a piece of salted bacon.

lardons: strips of bacon.

47 *bouillies*: gruel or mash.

galantine: a dish of poultry, fish, game, or other meat boned, stuffed with forcemeat, cooked, pressed, covered with aspic, and served cold.

50 *saveloys*: cooked dry sausages.

51 *crazy projects*: Aristide Rougon, who assumes the name of Saccard, is one of the protagonists, a property speculator, of *The Kill* (*La Curée*, 1871), and the protagonist, a financier, of *Money* (*L'Argent*, 1891).

marriage: Pauline Quenu will be the heroine of Zola's novel *Zest for Life* (*La Joie de vivre*, 1884).

52 *Devil's Island*: similar details were reported in the English press in 1855–6 by Louis Blanc (1811–82; a French politician and historian with socialist sympathies). Captain Alfred Dreyfus was to be deported to Devil's Island in 1895.

55 *Surinam*: the official name of Dutch Guiana, on the north-eastern coast of South America.

58 *Charles X*: Charles X was king of France from 1820 to 1830. His power depended on the aristocracy and the Church. He was overthrown in the revolution of 1830, which installed Louis-Philippe, the 'citizen-king', on the throne. Louis-Philippe was strongly supported by the bourgeoisie: his reign is known as the 'bourgeois monarchy'. Louis-Philippe was overthrown by the revolution of 1848, but the Second Republic was hijacked by the Prince-President, the future Napoleon III, whose election to the presidency was owed to his success in gaining extensive support among the working class.

citizen-king: at the time of the 1848 revolution, cartoons portrayed Louis-Philippe fleeing with his privy purse.

de Morny: half-brother of Louis-Napoleon, whom he helped to gain power. President of the Corps Législatif until his death in 1865. Represented in the character de Marsy in *His Excellency Eugène Rougon* (*Son Excellence Eugène Rougon*, 1876).

Corps Législatif: the Chamber of Deputies.

59 *expeditionary corps*: an allusion to the Crimean War, which lasted from March 1854 until March 1856. This war opposed a coalition of countries—France, England, Prussia, and the Kingdom of Piedmont-Sardinia—to Russia. Russia was finally defeated at Sebastopol.

75 *disappointment*: Claude is the protagonist of Zola's later novel, *The Masterpiece* (*L'Œuvre*, 1886), which presents a well-documented account of the turbulent Bohemian world in which the Impressionists came to prominence despite the conservatism of the Academy and the ridicule of the general public. It is, however, a story of disappointment and failure. Claude fails to gain admission to the Salon because he refuses to compromise an unattainable artistic ideal in the interests of popular taste. Nothing he produces satisfies him and he progresses from one half-finished canvas to another until his frustration drives him to suicide. Cézanne, seeing himself represented in Claude, ended his long friendship with Zola. See note to p. 16, above.

76 *mother*: a reference to Gervaise Macquart. See note to p. 45, above.

77 *salting*: as Zola noted in his planning notes, winter was the season when such things as dry sausage and cured ham were prepared.

94 *palatines*: a fur cape for the neck and shoulders. The name was derived from the Princess Palatine, sister-in-law of Louis XIV, who popularized this item of dress in 1676.

99 *'48*: the revolution of February 1848. See note to p. 42, above.

101 *throne*: the speech from the throne was in fact delivered every January.

 Hébert: a follower of Jacques Hébert (1757–94), the chief spokesman for the extremist *sans-culottes* faction during the French Revolution. He pressured the Jacobin regime to institute the Reign of Terror. His followers were called Hébertists. He was guillotined on the orders of Robespierre in 1794. Clémence is reminiscent of Louise Michel (1830–1905), a militant Republican (and former schoolmistress) known as the 'Red Virgin of Montmartre', who played a prominent part in the Commune and was exiled to New Caledonia. See note to p. 11, above.

102 *National Convention*: during the insurrection of 10 August 1792, when the populace of Paris stormed the Tuileries and demanded the abolition of the monarchy, the Legislative Assembly decreed the provisional suspension of King Louis XVI and the convocation of a 'national assembly' which should draw up a constitution. The National Assembly was the first French assembly elected by universal male suffrage, without distinctions of class. It lasted from 20 September 1792 to 26 October 1795.

105 *La Clef des songes*: a type of manual, very popular during the nineteenth century, that offered its readers suggestions, in semi-dictionary form, for interpreting dreams.

114 *little*: a popular old ditty dating from the Regency period (1715–23; the Duke of Orléans was Regent during the childhood of Louis XV). It was made fashionable by a Boulevard play in 1855.

115 *muche!*: in working-class slang, this meant: 'Great!' or 'Fantastic!'

123 *shelters*: an authentic detail. The Préfecture de la Seine had taken this decision on these grounds in 1842.

128 *The Social Contract*: an influential work of political philosophy, published in 1762, by the writer Jean-Jacques Rousseau (1712–78). In this treatise, Rousseau expounded the belief that the ideal society is one in which a man's contract is between himself and his fellow men, not between him and a government. Moreover, Rousseau believed that a government can only be legitimate if it has been sanctioned by the people, in the role of the sovereign; *The Social Contract* finally expelled the myth that the King was appointed by God to legislate.

137 *Tuileries*: the Imperial palace, destroyed by the Communards after the fall of the Empire in 1871.

138 *socialist*: the International Working People's Association (*Association internationale des travailleurs*) was founded in London in 1864 with the aim of uniting the workers of all countries. A prime mover in the foundation of the Association was Karl Marx, whose influence on the French working-class movement became significant only after 1868. Until then, the most influential socialist thinker in France was Pierre-Joseph Proudhon (1809–65).

140 *them*: Clémence's insistence on emancipation aligns her with Saint-Simonism and the revolutionary clubs of 1848, which discussed at length the question of the equality of men and women.

149 *Saccards*: see note to p. 51, above.

everybody: in *The Kill*, Saccard makes his fortune in the real-estate speculation generated by Haussmann's redevelopment of Paris.

165 *robes*: Claude distinguishes his own choice of subjects, taken from everyday 'reality', from classicism (which took its subjects from antiquity) and romanticism (which favoured historical, especially medieval, subjects).

positivism: a trend in philosophy (dominant in France in the third quarter of the nineteenth century) which declared natural (empirical) sciences to be the sole source of true knowledge. The founder of positivism and the author of the term 'positivism' was Auguste Comte (1798–1857). Later (p. 187), Claude declares that his artistic masterpiece is not a painting at all, but the still life he created directly out of reality: his arrangement of the Quenus' window display on Christmas Eve.

166 *drawn*: a reference to a brothel observed by Zola during one of his note-taking excursions.

168 *Aux Fabriques de France*: a draper's shop in the Rue du Pont-Neuf whose name Zola had noted.

169 *shrine*: the theme of the department store as a temple to womanhood will be developed by Zola in *The Ladies' Paradise* (*Au Bonheur des Dames*, 1883).

170 *flying buttresses*: since the demolition of Les Halles, these descriptions have acquired almost archaeological value, as indeed have the preceding descriptions of 'old Paris'. They are a kind of novelistic equivalent of the photographs of Charles Marville (who was commissioned in the late 1850s to document the ancient neighbourhoods of the city before encroaching urban modernization changed them for ever) and Eugène Atget (a later, very influential photographer (1857–1927) who, following the tradition of Marville, used his camera to create images that preserved the city's historical past; during the first quarter of the twentieth century, he produced a systematic and highly expressive visual catalogue of Paris, photographing the city's streets, buildings, shopfronts, parks, and people).

180 *day*: there was a serious fire in Les Halles in 1866.

181 *Leda*: in Greek mythology, Leda was the Queen of Sparta, daughter of Thestius and wife of Tyndareus. Seduced by Zeus, who came to her in the form of a swan, she gave birth to an egg. From it hatched the Dioscuri, the twins Castor and Pollux. With Zeus she also had Helen, and with Tyndareus she had Clytemnestra. The themes of sex and (possible) seduction are linked in Zola's text to imagery of fowl.

183 *Gaîté*: a theatre built in 1760 and specializing since 1800 in popular shows and melodrama. It was situated, along with various other theatres, on the

Boulevard du Temple (known as the 'boulevard du crime' because of the melodramas that were often produced there).

185 *Restaurant Philippe*: one of the most famous restaurants in Paris in the second half of the nineteenth century. Specialities included matelote and sole. The restaurant was part of the 'Compas d'or' inn, on the Rue Montorgueil (see notes to pp. 7 and 8, above). The whole inn complex was demolished in 1927. A restaurant-brasserie called 'Le Compas d'or' now exists on this site, at 62 Rue Montorgueil. Other restaurants in the Rue Montorgueil which were celebrated in the nineteenth century, and still exist, are 'L'Escargot' (formerly called 'L'Escargot d'or') at number 38, and 'Au Rocher de Cancale' at number 78 (successor to its more celebrated predecessor opposite, at number 59).

186 *The one will destroy the other*: this phrase echoes a similar one in Victor Hugo's *Notre-Dame de Paris*, in which the priest Claude Frollo reflects on Gutenberg's discovery of the printing press and predicts that the printed book will supersede the stone 'texts' of cathedrals. We read in Chapter 2 that on the mantelpiece in the Quenus' bedroom is a gilt clock 'on which a figure of Gutenberg stood in an attitude of deep thought with his hand resting on a book' (p. 53).

188 *done*: see note to p. 165, above.

190 *prints*: the traditional theme of the fight between Carnival and Lent, or the Fat and the Thin, has inspired innumerable painters and artists. The reference here is probably to Pieter Brueghel the Elder's series of engravings, *The Fight between Carnival and Lent* (1559), of which the central image depicts Carnival as a fat man on a beer barrel jousting with a meat-filled roasting-spit against Lent depicted as a thin man on a prayer-stool jousting with a baker's pole and two herrings. The theme figures as a vehicle for religious, political, and philosophical comment in the writings of the French Renaissance writer François Rabelais (*c.*1494–1553), whose comic heroes are the giants Gargantua and Pantagruel, and in the fables of Jean de La Fontaine (1621–95): 'The Limbs and the Stomach' ('Les Membres et l'estomac'). Mikhail Bakhtin, in his important critical work *Rabelais and His World* (completed 1940, published 1965), sees Rabelais's work as influenced by the popular practices of 'carnival'. The crucial celebration of 'carnival' was Mardi Gras, Shrove Tuesday, on the eve of Lent—a time for feasting and transgression preceding a time for fasting and seriousness.

192 *thyme*: the action of the last two chapters, except the section devoted to a retrospective account of the childhood of Marjolin and Cadine, takes place in the spring following Florent's arrival in Les Halles—that is, in April or May 1859, according to the novel's chronology. Zola may have played on the fact that in January 1858 there occurred the 'Orsini Affair'—an attempt on the Emperor's life by an Italian patriot named Felice Orsini. Orsini threw three bombs at the Emperor and his wife,

Empress Eugénie, as they were on their way to the opera. Eight people were killed and 142 wounded, but the Emperor and his wife were unharmed. Orsini was guillotined on 13 March 1858.

193 *'93*: 1793. A reference to the Revolutionary Terror and the persecution of the clergy at that time.

196 *Code*: the Napoleonic Code, or *Code Napoléon* (originally called the *Code civil des Français*), was established at the behest of Napoleon I. It entered into force in March 1804. It is considered the first successful codification of law in modern Europe, and strongly influenced the law of many other countries. The Code, with its stress on clearly written and accessible law, was a major step in establishing the rule of law.

198 *arrondissement*: in fact, it was only in 1861 that Paris was divided into twenty *arrondissements*—those we know today.

199 *galleys*: the galleys were abolished in 1748, but prisoners condemned to forced labour continued to be referred to as having been 'sent to the galleys'.

209 *annatto*: a red or yellowish red dyestuff containing bixin prepared from the pulp surrounding the seeds of the annatto tree and used especially for colouring oils, butter, and cheese.

223 *themselves*: perhaps an ironic allusion to the famous painting by Édouard Manet, *Le Déjeuner sur l'herbe* (1863), which had created a scandal as much by its technique as by its subject matter. Zola, as a young art critic, had leapt to the defence of Manet in 1867.

227 *Juillet*: the winged figure at the top of the Bastille column, erected to celebrate the revolution of July 1830.

poets: an allusion to the poet Alphonse de Lamartine, who took part in the events of 1848 and was opposed to the choice of a red flag as an emblem of the revolution.

231 *smocks*: in 1869 and 1870, men wearing white smocks mingled with working-class demonstrators against the social policies of the Second Empire regime, and engaged in all sorts of vandalism. It was believed in republican circles that they were agents provocateurs, paid by the authorities for information as well as providing the police with a pretext for brutal repression of the crowds.

232 *Morny*: see note to p. 58, above.

245 *Bois de Boulogne*: recently developed, the Bois de Boulogne had quickly become a favourite playground for upper- and middle-class Parisians. The first and last chapters of *The Kill* take place there.

La Grâce de Dieu: a five-act melodrama by Lemoine and Hemery, produced in 1841.

250 *annuities*: an allusion to the refusal by the Chamber of Deputies to grant the Emperor's request in 1862 to grant an annuity to General Cousin-Montauban,

Count of Palikao. This was the first manifestation of official opposition to the Emperor.

quais: the Haussmannization of Paris was, at one level, official state planning on a monumental and highly symbolic scale, glorifying the Napoleonic Empire as if it were a new Augustan Rome. Another view of the spectacular modernization of the city is to see it as intimately linked to rationalization and to forms of social and political control. From this perspective, the real aim of Haussmann's works was the securing of the city against civil war. He wished to make the erection of barricades in Paris impossible for all time. In the revolutions of 1789, 1830, and 1848, the barricade was a potent weapon of resistance in the dense rabbit-warren streets of the working-class districts in the centre of the city (around Les Halles, for example). Haussmann's straight boulevards and avenues linked the new barracks in each *arrondissement*, thus allowing the rapid deployment of troops in case of insurrection.

264 *Tuileries*: in other words, the government.